D0406915

Issues and Methods
in Rorschach Research

The LEA Series in
Personality and Clinical Psychology
Irving B. Weiner, Editor

Issues and Methods
in Rorschach Research

Edited by

John E. Exner, Jr.
Rorschach Workshops

LAWRENCE ERLBAUM ASSOCIATES, PUBLISHERS
1995   Mahwah, New Jersey

Lawrence Erlbaum Associates, Inc., Publishers
10 Industrial Avenue
Mahwah, New Jersey 07430

Cover design by Kevin Kall

"Dancing Ladies" inkblot on cover, © M R Harrower, 1966.
Reproduced with permission.

Library of Congress Cataloging-in-Publication Data

Issues and methods in Rorschach research / edited by John E. Exner,
Jr. ; with contributions by Marvin W. Acklin . . . [et al.].
p.   cm.
Includes bibliographical references and index.
ISBN 0-8058-1902-9 (alk. paper)
1. Rorschach Test.   I. Exner, John E.   II. Acklin, Marvin W.
(Marvin Wilson), 1949–
BF698.8.R5I495 1995
155.2′842—dc20   95-8835
                                                        CIP

Printed in the United States of America
10 9 8 7 6 5 4 3 2 1

*To Marguerite R. Hertz—A Rorschach pioneer who,
over six decades, weathered the disdain of others
and persisted as a staunch advocate for
credible research about the test to which
she devoted much of her professional life.*

Contents

About the Contributors

Marvin W. Acklin Clinical Studies Program, University of Hawaii at Manoa and Department of Psychiatry, John A. Burns School of Medicine, Honolulu, Hawaii

Glenn Curtiss Jay Haley Veterans Administration Medical Center, Tampa, Florida

Robert R. Dies Department of Psychology, University of Maryland, College Park, Maryland

John E. Exner, Jr. Rorschach Workshops, Asheville, North Carolina

Bill N. Kinder Department of Psychology, University of South Florida, Tampa, Florida

Claude J. McDowell II American School of Professional Psychology, Honolulu, Hawaii

Howard Mcguire Department of Psychology, Long Island University, Brooklyn, New York

Barry A. Ritzler Department of Psychology, Long Island University, Brooklyn, New York

Donald J. Viglione Department of Psychology, California Professional School of Psychology, San Diego, California

Jacqueline K. Vuz Drexel University, Philadelphia, Pennsylvania

Irving B. Weiner Department of Psychiatry and Behavioral Medicine, University of South Florida College of Medicine, Tampa, Florida

Eric A. Zillmer Department of Psychology, Drexel University, Philadelphia, Pennsylvania

Preface

The impetus for this work has been generated by many sources, not the least of which is the fact that most texts concerning research design or data analysis do not deal very directly with many of the issues that confront investigators who use the Rorschach in their research. This is not to suggest that the basic precepts of research design and/or analyses are different for Rorschach research than for other kinds of research. That is not true! Any research that involves the use of the Rorschach or focuses on the nature of the Rorschach should be framed using the same principles that mark any scientific investigation. It is true, however, that Rorschach research is marked by complexity more often than is the case in many other forms of research.

The nature of the test and the test procedures are somewhat different than for most psychological tests. Often, these special characteristics can become critical when research designs involving its use are formulated. Similarly, some of the data of the test are quite different than the customary distributions yielded by other psychological tests and thus, special care must be excercised when considering the variety of tactics that might be used in analyzing test data.

Those who have researched with or about the Rorschach will be quick to offer testimony concerning the difficult challenges that are often encountered. In part, many of these challenges exist because information concerning the test itself, that is, how it works, continues to be incomplete. Many who are sincerely interested in Rorschach research are impeded by this lack of information. Some are also handicapped by a lack of awareness concerning the many special issues that must be considered when the Rorschach is included in a research design.

During the nearly 30 years since the Rorschach Research Foundation (Rorschach Workshops) was established, a very large number of researchers and research assistants has been thrown into confrontations with the array of questions concerning the nature of the test and its appropriate applications. This group completed many successful forays into the arena of Rorschach research, but has also suffered markedly at times because of design blunders or inappropriate decisions concerning data analyses. One of the basic purposes of this work is to share the accumulated wisdom concerning Rorschach research to help investigators of the present and future avoid rediscovering many of those errors.

Most of the authors invited to contribute to this work have not been directly involved in research at the Foundation, but all are noted for their own research with the Rorschach. They have learned, often the hard way, what to do and what not to do in Rorschach research. The reader should not be surprised by some cautions and/or recommendations that appear redundantly across chapters; they illustrate some of the more common knotty issues with which the authors have been confronted in their work. The fact that several authors identify these issues tends to magnify their special importance in Rorschach research efforts.

During the span of more than seven decades since the Rorschach was published, it has proved to be a method that affords valuable information concerning personality structure and psychological functioning. It is also an important source of information through which many issues regarding psychopathology and/or maladjustment can be understood more fully. Unfortunately, many well qualified investigators have avoided research with the test because of the complex issues that are often posed by it. It is true that Rorschach research is not easy, but it is also true that Rorschach research can be extremely rewarding because of the vast array of questions that beg for answers and the large number of studies that are ripe for replication.

There are many issues concerning the Rorschach and its applications that are yet to be addressed. It seems quite likely that the test can be refined much further than is now the case, but to accomplish the task of dealing with the numerous issues that have not yet been addressed and the host of others that require clarification, well thought through designs are required and appropriate methods of data analysis must be selected. Sadly, there is a lengthy history of misinformation concerning the Rorschach that has been created by work that has not been well designed or data that have not been analyzed appropriately, or by conclusions that go well beyond the empirical findings.

If this work is useful, it will add to the information already available to the accomplished researcher or it will provide some enlightenment for the

Rorschach research novice. It should dispel the notion that rote methodology or analyses can be applied routinely to studies involving the Rorschach. Ideally, it will help to improve the quality of investigations in which the test is included, and contribute in some way to an improvement of the overall research yield in the Rorschach community.

CHAPTER ONE

Introduction

John E. Exner, Jr.

Rorschach research can be exciting and rewarding, or it can be frustrating and disappointing. Sadly, it is easy to do bad Rorschach research, but that need not be the case. Good Rorschach research is not that difficult, but it does require care. The main problems that confront most Rorschach investigators are created by two elements. First, the test is very complex and much of the data do not fall neatly into so-called normal distributions of scores common to most other psychological tests. Second, Rorschach research is really personality related research and personality is a very intricate psychological phenomenon. Because of this, investigators must be prepared to contend with the difficult issue of individual differences.

Unfortunately, many who are interested in undertaking Rorschach research often are less well equipped, by reason of training or experience, to form the most appropriate design to address an issue, or select the best method of data analysis to test an issue in a meaningful way. Historically, as psychology has grown and diversified, the relation between those committed to its applications and those committed to research has grown more distant. As a result, many ideas for Rorschach research, devised by those using the test routinely in the clinical setting, are not implemented because of a sense of ineptness concerning experimentation. This is due, at least in part, to the many changes that have occurred since the mid-1960s regarding the level of research expertise that should be required of the clinical student. Before the mid-1960s most all clinical students were required to develop expertise in the methods of research and data analysis. For many, this was an unreasonable requirement, yet it did reflect the scientist-practitioner model strongly advocated by a series of conferences on clinical training

(APA, 1947; Raimy [Boulder Conference], 1950; Strother [Stanford Conference], 1956; Roe [Miami Conference], 1959).

In 1965, the Chicago conference on clinical training reaffirmed the importance of the scientist–practitioner model, but the criteria for the model was redefined in a manner that clearly broadened its parameters and reduced specific requirements (Hoch, Ross, & Winder, 1966). At about the same time, a new degree (Psy.D.) began to be offered, which afforded quality training in the applications of psychology, but with a considerably reduced emphasis on research requirements. During the next decade, many of the more traditional Ph.D. programs in clinical psychology also altered requirements regarding skill development in research; so ultimately, models for training the clinician have been changed to require less expertise in areas of research and more time devoted to the development of clinical skills. An unfortunate byproduct of these changes has been the development of an animosity between those who identify themselves as committed to the clinical applications of psychology and the more traditional models of experimental psychology.

In many ways, the revolution that began in the 1960s against stringent training in experimental methodology has been profitable as clinical students entering the field today are better prepared to address the practical issues with which they are confronted daily. The trade-off, however, has been less positive if research skills are used as a basis for judgment. Clinical students and their postdoctoral counterparts are far less well prepared to conduct scientific inquiry than was once the case. Psychology is supposedly a science, but the output of adequately trained scientists among those graduating from a multitude of doctoral programs in psychology that have a commitment to practice, is woefully lacking. Even when the motive exists, the expertise often does not. This is especially true when Rorschach research is at issue.

Even reasonably well-trained experimental psychologists will probably have trouble researching this awesome and sometimes confusing test unless they are acutely aware of the problems that it poses. Those committing themselves to some research with the Rorschach must begin with the basic notions concerning research and then attempt to expand those notions to the investigation they hope to devise.

Clearly, the overall objective of research is to uncover new knowledge but, within that general framework, specific research targets vary considerably. Some studies are designed to test theoretical propositions, but many are structured to expand information gleaned from previous investigations. Others are designed to replicate findings, and numerous investigations are of a hunt-and-peck variety, which search through available data sets seeking new information or a clarification of previously developed information.

Regardless of whether the objective is specific or broad, the goals of any research are not always easily achieved. Usually, this is not for a lack of ideas. Ideas for research evolve easily from many sources. Some derive from elaborate theoretical positions, others generate from impressions or hunches that accumulate over time, and some are fomented by experiences in which limited information and/or understanding concerning an issue or task breeds questions that, for one frustrating reason or another, do not have answers readily available. Good research is rarely uncomplicated and, no matter how well thought through the propositions or design may be, a risk of failure always exists. Thus, the results can be rewarding and even exciting, or they may breed frustration and disappointment.

Typically, those who become vested in scientific inquiry formulate questions to be addressed through a careful, critical study of relevant literature in order to profit from the findings and experiences of others. Ultimately, a general idea is reduced to a more sharply defined question and then the challenge becomes one of phrasing the question so that it can be investigated empirically, in a systematic and controlled manner. This is the way of research, and Rorschach-related research is no different.

Almost all Rorschach research seeks to test or investigate presumed relationships between phenomena of the test and phenomena of the person. The test, as it is commonly used, seeks to explain the manifestations of psychological organization and functioning, both of which contribute to a better understanding of the individual as a unique entity. But, any understanding of an individual also implies an understanding of groups of individuals, so that the ultimate goal of any research, including Rorschach research, is the development of a set of propositions and interrelated constructs that presents a systematic view of the phenomena of people.

Unfortunately, contemporary textbooks on experimental methodology, measurement, or statistics seem to sidestep many of the confrontations encountered by the Rorschach researcher. This has contributed to the fact that Rorschach history is marked by a huge number of published investigations, which, to the critical reader, are clearly marked by errors in design, implementation, and/or analysis. It sometimes appears as if those most interested in studying the test, or its use as a dependent measure, were least well equipped to understand the intricacies of scientific inquiry or naive to many research issues that are peculiar to the Rorschach. No one should become overly cautious about using the Rorschach in research for which it is appropriate because of its complexity, but, at the same time, no one should be naive in expectations that Rorschach research is simple and straightforward.

In general, errors in Rorschach-related research can be placed into at least one of several categories: hypotheses developed from conclusions reported in flawed studies, poor subject selection, insufficient number of subjects, examiner (experimenter) bias, faulty methodology, failure to account for response styles, failure to understand the nature of the test, inappropriate data analysis, and overgeneralization of results. These errors are not always independent of each other. Often, investigations that focus on the test or its applications are marked by several of these blemishes and yet, for reasons that are not very clear, they find their way into the literature and become cited routinely as Rorschach gospel.

HYPOTHESES BASED ON CONCLUSIONS REPORTED IN FLAWED STUDIES

One of the most common errors is the assumption that anything appearing in the literature is truth. This error probably is most common among studies done by graduate students to meet dissertation requirements, but it is by no means limited to that group of investigators. Every researcher is burdened by the task of a literature review, which, when done thoroughly, illuminates the accumulated findings regarding a question or issue. Exhaustive literature reviews are very time consuming, and during the past two or three decades, a tendency has evolved for investigators to rely more and more on shortcuts that reduce the amount of time required for developing an adequate literature review and/or pinpointing those studies from which a seemingly sound hypothesis is formulated.

The forerunner of the shortcut tactic was *Psychological Abstracts*, a historically important publication of the *American Psychological Association*, which began in 1920s. It contains the titles of published articles together with a very brief summary of the topic investigated. Subsequently, *Dissertation Abstracts* was designed to be like *Psychological Abstracts*, but with a focus on dissertations that might not be published for a considerable period of time, or that might not be published at all. During the past decade or two, the wonders of the computer have permitted the development of new brief forms of collating relevant studies and these have evolved into hard copy publications. They include a variety of *PsyScan* programs, each of which is designed to offer brief reports concerning published and/or unpublished works by using a computer lexicon. Thus, each author is encouraged to note key words—such as *Rorschach, introversive, schizotypal,* and so on—and up to 10 critical key words will be computer entered.

If prospective researchers are interested in a literature review, they merely have to enter a search for key words related to a topic and a computer will spew forth a summary, abstract, or titles of all works related to those topics. It is a marvelous process, but it does not constitute an adequate literature review for several reasons. First, the printout summaries are relatively brief and usually focus on results that may or may not be interpreted correctly. Second, the methodology employed is not described in detail. And, third, the critical words seemingly relevant to a topic may not have been included by the author(s) when the article was written. But, even if an important study is included in the printout, the output falls far short of providing a critical review of the literature. Nonetheless, it appears that this computer-generated output has become a mainstay for researchers who are interested in formulating investigations that include the Rorschach.

Unfortunately, many literature reviews neglect seemingly relevant articles, or fail to provide a critical evaluation of relevant articles and simply proceed with the naive conjecture that all in print is worthy. In effect, these tactics of literature review involve the use of secondary sources and, as every competent researcher is aware, such tactics are fraught with problems. There is no substitute for a careful and critical reading of primary sources. For example, theories concerning object relations have become a major research focus in recent years and, usually, each new study in this area cites the results of previous studies somewhat casually, without concern for whether the scales used to measure object relations have been carefully validated, whether they are reliable, or whether the findings derived from one study have been cross-validated in another study. This is not to demean the importance of research in the area of object relations, but simply to highlight the negligence that seems to have marked many of the studies on the issue.

NUMBER OF SUBJECTS, SUBJECT SELECTION, DATA ANALYSIS

In the ideal circumstance, research questions involving the Rorschach will be cast in the basic framework of science, which is theory. Then, they will be molded directly into traditional experimental models in which all issues are reduced to hypothesis-testing designs. These are the prospective studies that are directed to test well-formulated hypotheses and, historically, they tend to be regarded most favorably by the research community. Usually, they are neat because of their conceptual framework and their meticulous design, but these models can be abused in Rorschach research. If abuses occur, they usually will involve a less than adequate number of subjects, faulty subject selection, or inappropriate data analysis.

For instance, if the number of subjects is relatively small, the traditional approach may not be appropriate because of the intricacies created when humans are involved as subjects. Almost any group of humans will display a substantial variance for many features. People vary for cognitive ability, education, socioeconomic level, and a variety of other variables that can have an indirect relationship to personality structure as measured by Rorschach. That variance may have only a limited impact on Rorschach data at times, but in other instances, it can create a higher risk of both Type I (falsely rejecting the Null hypothesis) and Type II errors (failure to reject the Null hypothesis when it is false) unless the investigator is painstakingly fastidious in subject selection.

For example, consider a hypothetical Rorschach study that involves a traditional hypothesis-testing design in which either Type I or Type II errors are likely to occur. Suppose the operational hypothesis is that the proportion of blends in a record will be greater under a distraction/frustration situation. This is not an unreasonable hypothesis because data related to blends suggest that they have to do with psychological complexity, and it is logical to assume that situational stress increases complexity. In this hypothetical study, two groups of randomly selected nonpatient adults, 20 in each group, are to be used. All will be high school graduates.

Data will be collected from one subject at a time. All subjects will be seated in a small room and required to add columns of seven 5-digit numbers, with a time limit for each column. The subjects in the experimental group will be exposed to a situational frustration experience. During the time that they are adding the columns, loud, seemingly irritating noises will be broadcast at random intervals. The control subjects will perform the same task, but the noise level will be minimal and reasonably constant. When a subject has completed two thirds of the columns, the Rorschach will be administered in the same small room, by one of five examiners (four subjects each, randomly selected from each group), naive to the purpose of the study. Subjects will be of the impression that they will be required to complete the addition of the remaining columns, under the same conditions, after the test is completed.

The design seems to fit a basic multidimensional model. The noise is the independent variable. The number of columns completed and the number of errors become classification measures to confirm the effect of the distraction, and the dependent measure is the number of blends. However, the classification variables may present either of two potential confounds. First, in theory, the randomization process presumes that variations in intelligence will be essentially similar for both groups. It has been established, however, that less intelligent subjects give significantly fewer blends than brighter people. Thus, if the differences in intelligence are substantial for the two groups, then a Type I error may occur.

If one group includes as few as three subjects with IQ's of less than 90, and the other group does not, a significant difference for the number or proportion of blends between the groups might be discovered. If the randomization had involved two groups of 50 subjects each, drawn from a college-level population, this issue could be of less concern. But, in that the criterion for selection is simply graduation from high school and the N is limited to only 40 subjects, the possibility of considerable variation in intelligence and/or math skills increases substantially. In other words, the small sample sizes increase the possibility of group differences in simple math skills and thus, increases the likelihood of either a Type I or Type II error. This possibility could easily be offset by the baseline administration of some arithmetic test, either standardized or designed, and the results used to stratify the randomization of subjects.

Second, even if the two groups have reasonably equal capabilities for addition, another potentially serious confound exists. The randomization process affords no way of knowing beforehand how many in each group might be *introversive*, *extratensive*, or *ambitent* according the the data for the Erlebnistypus (EB). This is critical because each of those three groups differ significantly concerning the proportion of blends they are expected to give. Introversive subjects tend to give fewer blends than extratensives, and ambitents tend to give more blends than extratensives. In addition, introversive subjects are less susceptible to distraction under affective interference.

Assuming that the investigator might plan to address the data using an analysis of variance (ANOVA) model because the number or proportion of blends is a normally distributed variable, either Type I or Type II errors are likely because of the failure to address the issue of the number of subjects in each cell who differ for response style (introversive, extratensive, ambitent). In other words, the relatively small number of subjects in each group (20 in each) may inadvertently load the data in favor of, or against, the hypothesis. If the samples were larger, 50 subjects or more in each group, these potentially confounding variables could be co-varied, but with small samples that is not practical.

Obviously, the astute investigator would be alert to this problem and all subjects would be administered the Rorschach at least 2 weeks before the experimental design is employed to establish baseline data. This would permit a second level of stratification when the randomization of the subjects occurred, so that the experimental and control groups would contain relatively equal numbers of introversive, ambitent, and extratensive subjects. By doing so, however, the statistical manipulations of the data must be approached with great care. Although it is technically true that the N's for the two groups are 20 each, it is also true that each group would contain three cells in which the N's are considerably less than 20. Thus, although a 2 × 3 ANOVA could be computed for the two groups of 20 each, the sizes of the each of the three cells within each group, when subdivided by response style, will be too small to study in a parametric design. Actually, using the normative data concerning nonpatient adults as a point of reference, the expected N's for each cell would be 8 introversives, 8 extratensives, and 4 ambitents.

If a baseline test is not done to stratify the randomization for response style, the possibility of loading the experimental group with an excessive number of extratensive and ambitent subjects is considerable, which could lead to a Type I error. On the other hand, if the control group contains a disproportionally greater number of ambitents and extratensive subjects, a Type II error is likely. In fact, as with the issue of intelligence or math skill, if one group contains as few as two more ambitents or extratensives than the second group, a spurious significant difference is almost inevitable unless extremely conservative *p* values are set.

ISSUES OF PERSONALITY/RESPONSE STYLE DIFFERENCES

As noted earlier, a major issue that has been neglected almost uniformly in Rorschach research concerns the presence, or absence, of basic response styles among the subjects for an investigation. The importance of these styles, sometimes called traits or habits, should never be underestimated when planning research. In many instances, they can create bimodal or even trimodal distributions for some variables. Every group, large or small, will include a considerable variation for basic response styles, and unless those styles happen to be classification and/or independent variables in a traditional hypothesis-testing study, the variance may cancel out results in ways that create errors.

The High Lambda Style

Subjects with a high Lambda style tend to give Rorschach's that are structurally different in several ways when compared to records given by those who do not have a high Lambda style. High Lambda subjects are more likely to be positive on the Coping Deficit Index (CDI), have fewer blends, give proportionally fewer pure *H* answers, and have a greater proportion of *T-less* records than subjects who do not have a Lambda value greater than .99.

This is not to suggest that high Lambda subjects should be excluded from studies that follow a traditional experimental model. It is necessary, however, for the researcher who selects that model to be hyperalert to the multitude of issues that must be considered in selecting subjects and creating cells appropriate for data analyses. Otherwise, the accumulated data are likely to be very misleading if analyzed simply, following the assumption that randomization of a group of subjects will resolve all issues concerning data analysis. That is a naive assumption. It probably has validity if the group exceeds 200 subjects, but that is unlikely for most designs.

It is also naive to assume that people have only one response style that dominates all decision making and behavior. Personality structure is much more complex than that and, typically, personality or psychological organization is marked by many stylistic or traitlike features. One of the major strengths of the Rorschach is that it usually provides data that indicate the presence of various response styles, but these revelations can also create enormous headaches for the researcher.

Introversive and Extratensive Styles

One of Rorschach's (1921) most important contributions was the practical and conceptual formulation of the Erlebnistypus (EB), in which he differentiated introversive and extratensive subjects. He noted that when the EB is distinctly weighed in the *M* direction, it identifies persons who are more prone to use their inner life for basic gratifications. He called this *introversiveness*, carefully emphasizing that it is not the same as the Jungian concept of introversion. Rorschach's notion of introversiveness focuses on the manner in which the resources of the person are used in decision-making and/or problem-solving activities, but does not necessarily imply direct overt behavioral correlates.

Thus, introversive persons may be regarded by others as socially outgoing, but internally, they are prone to use their inner life for the satisfaction of their important needs. Ordinarily, introversives prefer to delay formulating decisions or initiating behaviors until all apparent alternative possibilities have been considered. They usually like to keep feelings at a more peripheral level during problem solving and/or decision making and tend to rely heavily on internal evaluation in forming judgments. They generally are prone to accept systems of logic that are precise and uncomplicated. They usually avoid engaging in trial-and-error explorations and are less tolerant when problem-solving errors occur.

At the opposite pole is the *extratensive* person, whose EB is markedly weighed on the color side of the ratio. Extratensives are prone to use the interactions between themselves and their world for gratification of their more basic needs. It is the depth of affective exchange that often marks the extratensive person; that is, they manifest affect to their world more routinely than do introversives. The extratensive usually merges feelings with thinking during problem-solving activity. This does not mean that thinking is less consistent or more illogical than in an introversive subject, however, the affective impact on ideation tends to cause the extratensive to be more accepting of logic systems that are not precise or marked by greater ambiguity. Their judgments are influenced by the external feedback yielded by trial-and-error activity and, in fact, they usually engage in trial-and-error activity and are far more tolerant than the introversive subject when errors occur.

Rorschach also defined the *ambitent*, that is, one whose EB contains equal, or nearly equal values on each side of the ratio. He postulated (erroneously, as it turns out) that the ambitent may be the most flexible of the three types or styles with regard to the use of resources for obtaining gratification. In reality, ambitents are far less consistent than either introversive or extratensive subjects and, because of their lack of consistency, they are usually less efficient. The ambitent appears to be much more vulnerable to intra- or interpersonal problems. Findings from numerous studies support this position, suggesting that their vulnerability to difficulty in coping situations apparently stems from their failure to develop a consistent preference or style. The result is less efficiency and more vacillation. They usually require more time to complete tasks and appear to invest more energy in the process.

The importance of carefully weighing the potential impact of differences in the EB style when formulating hypotheses or planning research designs cannot be overestimated. Among nonpatient adults, at least two of the three groups differ significantly not only for the means of *M* and *WSumC*, but also for The Experience Actual (*EA*), ambitents lower; Experienced Stimulation (*es*), ambitents higher; the Sum of Shading, ambitents higher; blends, introversives less; Affective Ratio (*AFR*), extratensives higher; human content, introversives higher; Coopeative Movement (*COP*), introversives higher; and abstraction responses, extratensives higher. In addition, the groups differ for several contents, such as blood, explosion, fire, and food (Exner, 1991, 1993). Similar differences are found among the data for outpatients (Exner, 1993). In fact, patients tend to be more extreme for some variables than nonpatients. Some of the differences, by EB style, between patients and nonpatients are illustrated in Tables 1.1 and 1.2.

Obviously, both patient groups have distributions for the Adjusted D Score that are different than the nonpatients groups. Similarly, both patient groups give significantly fewer cooperative movement answers, offer significantly fewer pure *H* responses, tend to exhibit more evidence of irritating internal affective stimulation, and tend to show more evidence of passivity

TABLE 1.1
Frequency Comparisons for 9 Structural Variables
Between 240 Introversive Nonpatient Adults and 128 Introversive
Outpatient Adults with Protocols in Which Lambda < 1.0

	Introversive Nonpatients		Introversive Outpatients	
Variable	N	%	N	%
EBPER > 2.4	61	25	109	85*
Adj. *D* Score > 0	110	46	26	20*
Adj. *D* Score = 0	124	52	89	70*
Adj. *D* Score < 0	6	3	13	10
COP > 2	131	55	20	16*
Pure *H* < 2	2	1	14	11*
(*FM* + *m*) < Sum Shad	15	6	27	21*
Mp > *Ma*	9	4	48	38*
p > *a* + 1	2	1	73	57*

*Chi-square shows proportional frequency difference (*p* < .001).

TABLE 1.2
Frequency Comparisons for 9 Structural Variables
Between 295 Extratensive Nonpatient Adults and 85 Extratensive
Outpatient Adults with Protocols in Which Lambda < 1.0

	Extratensive Nonpatients		Extratensive Outpatients	
Variable	N	%	N	%
EBPER > 2.4	84	28	55	65*
Adj. *D* Score > 0	70	24	32	38*
Adj. *D* Score = 0	205	69	29	34*
Adj. *D* Score < 0	21	7	24	28*
COP > 2	98	33	1	1*
Pure *H* < 2	33	11	56	66*
(*FM* + *m*) < Sum Shad	46	16	20	24
Mp > *Ma*	53	18	22	26
p > *a* + 1	2	1	6	7

*Chi-square shows proportional frequency difference ($p < .001$).

than the nonpatients. The latter is also stylistic. Although it is impossible to conclude without question that the pervasive style has led to the other differences, the issue is quite compelling and should provoke much more research than has been published on this important issue.

The Pervasive Style

It is impossible to overestimate the importance of correctly identifying the presence of a high Lambda style in any research population. The cutoff for such an identification of > .99 is empirically derived, but good judgment should be exercised by the researcher. Unfortunately, the history of the Rorschach has been marked by the flawed assumption that any number of answers, large or small, should be accepted and the record be judged as interpretable. As illustrated by test–retest data (Exner, 1988, 1991, 1993), the composite of a low number of responses plus a high Lambda can represent the performance of a highly resistive subject who is simply attempting to avoid the many demands of the test situation. In effect, these performances depict subtle refusals to take the test. Unfortunately, there is no easy way to distinguish between the low *R*, high Lambda record that illustrates resistance from the low *R*, high Lambda record that reflects a valid indicator of a coping style. This finding contributed significantly to the decision to discard records of less than 14 answers. But this may not resolve the issue of style versus resistence completely.

Obviously, the larger the number of responses, the sturdier the cutoff for the high Lambda style. But, if the record is brief but within acceptable limits, such as 14, 15, or 16 answers, the researcher might consider the possibility of extending the critical cutoff value upward, to as much as 1.1 in the instance of adults or even to 1.2 for the record of a younger subject. This is not a "hard-fast" rule and the ultimate judgment should be made in light of whether or not the remainder of the protocol, that is, those answers that are not simply Pure F answers, is marked by considerable richness and/or complexity. If it is, the extended limits are probably applicable. Conversely, if it is not, the .99 cutoff probably is best retained to define the style.

This is a very important interpretive decision because, if the high Lambda style does exist within the personality organization of a subject, especially an adolescent or adult, it tends to supercede or overlay other stylistic features. It is a very pervasive characteristic. This does not mean that it will always dominate in decision making. More likely, it will be dominant in more complex or threatening situations that are perceived by the subject as challenges to the integrity of the self-concept, or obstacles to the gratification of experienced needs. In either it will probably take precedence over any existing EB style. It is also important to note that whereas either of the EB styles might be altered under unusual circumstances, the high Lambda style typically is not. In fact, it will usually become more pervasive in directing decisions and behaviors.

Although Rorschach conceptualized the EB as possibly illustrating a constitutionally predisposed response tendency that will be a relatively stable psychological feature, he also noted that various conditions might alter the response preference, either temporarily or permanently. For instance, unusual or prolonged stress conditions might elicit a transient alteration in the style, whereas some treatment effects might create a more permanent change. It does seem clear that, whereas an introversive or extratensive style is far more preferential to an ambient status, a pervasive style does pose a potential liability because of the lack of problem-solving flexibility (Exner, 1991, 1993). Among inpatients, pervasive style subjects have been found to have been hospitalized for longer periods. Among outpatients, significantly fewer pervasive style subjects terminate care within 1 year and proportionally more are evaluated negatively for progress by their therapists after both 2 and 4 months. Thus, the issue of stylistic pervasiveness can become quite important in some designs, requiring larger N's to fill each of the five cells concerning style that might be required (pervasive introversive, nonpervasive introversive, ambient, nonpervasive extratensive, pervasive extratensive).

When nonpatient adults are used as subjects, approximately 80% will be either introversive or extratensive with the proportions of each about the same. This distribution is somewhat different than found among patient groups. For instance, most schizophrenic samples include 60% who are introversive, only 10% who are extratensive, and about 30% who are ambitent. Among other patient groups, 40% to 60% are usually ambitents.

Although a few differences do exist between nonpatients and outpatients within each style, and for ambitents, the overall configuration of data for each group is highly consistent. In other words, introversives, whether patients and nonpatients, are highly similar to each other and very different from the groups of extratensive patients and nonpatients. Likewise, both groups of introversive and extratensive subjects are quite different than ambitents.

These stylistic differences are critically important if physiological measures are to be used as dependent variables. Blatt and Feirstein (1977) found that introversive subjects show greater cardiac variability during problem solving. Exner, Thomas, and Martin (1980) recorded cardiac activity, respiratory rates, and galvanic skin response (GSR) for two groups, consisting of 15 introversives and 15 extratensives all having D Scores of 0 or +1 during a 30-minute series of problem-solving tasks. When compared to baseline data, the findings for the cardiac activity are similar to those of Blatt and Feirstein; that is, subjects in the introversive group showed more variability, with a general tendency for the rates to reduce. During a rest period between problems there was significantly less variability, and the rates tended to increase. In other words, the cardiac and respiratory rates of the respiratory introversives tend to go down, but reverse during the rest interval, and the GSR values also tended to become lower throughout the entire 30-minute session.

The extratensive groups showed significantly less cardiac and respiratory variability during the activity phase, with both tending to increase shortly after beginning the task and remaining at a significantly higher level than baseline. During the rest interval the cardiac rate showed more variability than for the introversive group and tended to become lower, as did the respiratory rate. The GSR values for the extratensives tended to increase gradually during the first 10 minutes of the task, and remained significantly higher than the baseline throughout the 30-minute interval.

As indicated earlier, there is also evidence to suggest that extratensives are more susceptible to distraction than introversives. Chu and Exner (1981) studied introversive and extratensive subjects, all with D Scores of 0, for speed and accuracy in addition under two conditions. In one condition subjects worked in a quiet room, whereas in the second they worked in a room with interference conditions created by random noises and flashing strobe lights. The groups did not differ for the number of columns completed or for number of calculation errors under the quiet condition; however, the introversive group completed significantly more columns and made significantly fewer calculation errors than the extratensive group under the interference condition.

Obviously, many Rorschach studies can be designed in which the issues of stylistic differences will be of little importance. On the other hand, many of the variables often used as classification or dependent measures in Rorschach research are related very directly to stylistic features such as reflected in Lambda and the EB. Fortunately, there are ways to address problematic issues such as these, but unfortunately, these issues are often neglected in Rorschach research. When that occurs, there is a substantial risk that the results become nothing more than a simplistic exercise from which no one profits.

THE NATURE OF THE RESPONSE PROCESS

The nature of the test itself poses many challenges that go well beyond some of the more routine issues encountered in psychological research. Obviously, no one should undertake Rorschach research without being fully familiar with the test. This does not simply mean how to administer the Rorschach, or score responses, or how to interpret Rorschach data. It means that the investigator must be acutely aware of how the test works. The nature of the test or response process has been a curiosity for decades and, to some extent remains so. Yet, enough information has been generated during past decades to offer some insights concerning the test process, and those insights create an important cornerstone for those pursuing Rorschach-related investigations. A thorough awareness about the test process will often aid the investigator in avoiding unwanted errors in logic that may relate to the formulation of hypotheses, or more importantly, errors in methodology that can lead to the accumulation of data that, in effect, cannot be subject to analysis or only subjected to the types of analyses that will yield misleading findings.

One of the most common problems that evolves from a misunderstanding of the test process concerns the issue of data analysis that seem to be created by an unequal R. Certainly, the fact that R is not equal for all records poses a challenge. Perry and Kinder (1990) argued that most Rorschach findings should be analyzed in a way that controls for R to the maximum extent. Exner (1992) challenged that recommendation. He presented data concerning nonpatients that suggest that R has little influence for most variables. Nonetheless, he also cautioned that R may be an influencing element for some variables and should be considered when data analyses are planned. Blends are among those variables that do increase with R. Thus, if the range for the number of responses in the hypothetical study described previously is considerable, some method of accounting for R must be included in the planned analyses. If a parametric analysis is used, then a co-variance tactic can be employed; but, because the number of subjects in each cell is very small out of concern for basic response style, a proportional nonparametric will be required.

SHOTGUN STUDIES

A model of investigation that may be prospective or retrospective is one with the general purpose of identifying features that are common within a single group. Unfortunately, these sorts of studies are quite commonplace and, although many never appear in the Rorschach literature because they are easily picked apart by editors and consulting editors, would-be researchers seem to be attracted to them because of their apparent simplicity. In effect, most are predicated on the notion that some wonderous homogeneity exists among subjects who present similar symptoms or who have had similar experiences. It is the assumption of homogeneity that, in theory, constitutes a classification variable, however, such an assumption usually defies the fact that, within any seemingly homogeneous group, the variance for individual members of the group can be considerable because each person is a unique entity.

In some instances, hypotheses will be stated only in vague terms, namely, that the group will manifest common characteristics, or, somewhat more grandiosely, that the group will differ from other groups for some features. When the latter occurs, it is usually the contemporary notions regarding a specific group that provoke a host of hypotheses about specific Rorschach variables, usually far too many to be tested legitimately unless a huge number of subjects is available. For the most part, however, conceptualizations about findings or differences are reserved for an interpretation of findings.

These kinds of investigations are fraught with problems. As already implied, most who undertake these shotgun studies find themselves caught between the need to create some respectable research and an even more pressing desire to learn or demonstrate something about the target population. When the investigator becomes trapped in a quest for "research," the issue of the number of subjects becomes critical because, as a rule, at least 15 subjects should be included in the target (experimental) group for every dependent variable to be considered in a statistical analysis, and even that is a low number if the analyses are nonparametric. Conversely, if investigators offer no specific hypotheses, they can easily be victimized by the issue of variance among subjects within and across the groups studied.

On some occasions, studies such as these can be exquisitely revealing of new information, but only if issues of intragroup and intergroup variance is properly identified and studied very carefully. For instance, it is logical to assume that all battered women will manifest some psychological evidence of their trauma. It is, however, quite unrealistic to assume that all battered women will have the same psychological features or deficits unless it can also be assumed that all had similar psychological organizations prior to the battering. The trauma of chronic battering may impact quite differently on one woman as contrasted to another, simply because they were different prior to the trauma. Some might attempt to contend with the trauma introspectively, as if it were their fault, and indications of depression could become prevalent. The effects of the trauma for others could be reflected in the development of a great anger, which might or might not become manifest in behavior. Another group may have been more helpless and dependent prior to the battering, and the trauma may have increased their sense of helplessness. But, these are simplistic hypotheses that assume any group of battered women can be neatly categorized into as few as three groups—which is highly unlikely.

Unfortunately, most investigators dealing with the issue of battered women or some group with similar traumatic experiences seem to disregard the possibility of multiple subgroups, but rather, one nicely compacted psychological entity in which all, or most all, of the target subjects manifest similar features. Such a finding would be marvelous if true, but the world of people is not that simple. The same problem exists when diagnostic entities are studied. Naive investigators have been led to believe that all subjects falling into one diagnostic category will manifest similar personality characteristics when administered the Rorschach.

The culprits to such fantasy are twofold. One is theory. In theory, a homogeneous element does, indeed, exist within all who are afflicted with this or that diagnosis, or who have experienced a similar trauma. The second culprit is faulty education. Textbooks in psychiatry and abnormal psychology are filled with descriptive lists of features common to all who fall within some designation, whether it be an adjustment disorder or a major depressive episode. Such an assumption flies into the face of the reality of data. All identified as being depressed are not alike! Certainly, all identified as having been exposed to unwanted trauma are not alike. Even schizophrenics, who do have many features in common, are not alike!

Researchers who seek common denominators among groups of subjects who have common experiences or shared diagnoses do pose a major challenge for themselves. They are, at best, naive when they search for some mythical profile of data that might permit them to explain causes or consequences. The Rorschach does have a nomothetic base—that is, data are available from which marked deviations can be detected—but the Rorschach is not simply a nomothetic instrument. Fortunately, the test goes well beyond the nomothetic issue and yields a much more idiographic picture. Thus, those who seek out group descriptions of those who have experienced common trauma or who have shared diagnoses might do better to avoid the Rorschach as the instrument of choice because it will yield more idiographic pictures of subjects than may be desired.

On the other hand, as noted earlier, some shotgun studies can be very revealing if they are well conducted, and there are probably two ways to do so. The first involves a simple descriptive study. It does not really require one or more control groups. It is the investigation designed to describe the features found to be common among a target population of subjects. For instance, it may be that 80% of the subjects have one feature, 70% have another, 65% have a third, and so on. It is not a hypothesis-testing design, but simply one of reporting findings concerning a group of subjects for which some homogeneity does exist, whether it be a diagnosis or some experiential feature. The importance of the report is not to demonstrate that these subjects differ from other subjects, but simply to offer some information concerning their relatively homogeneous features. Such descriptive studies often strengthen conceptual issues and can become a basis for which other prospective studies are designed to test out specific hypotheses.

The second approach to the shotgun study is more conceptual. It begins with a narrow proposition, based on previously generated data or on a theoretical postulate, and it does involve some comparison testing. For instance, one might hypothesize that battered women will have lower self-value than nonpatient women, as illustrated by significantly lower egocentricity indices, tested either parametrically using means and standard deviations for the target and control groups, or nonparametrically (probably preferable) by setting a cutoff score of .33 and studying the frequencies in the target group and control group who fall below the cutoff. Once the prospective comparison is completed, the investigator is free from the burdens of the research design to elaborate, retrospectively, on other findings concerning the target group in a descriptive manner that may ignore the control group or may involve some unplanned comparisons with the control group.

Misusing Normative Data

Studies such as those already described are often confounded because they draw attention to the differences between a target group and published normative data. This tactic is naive at best, and inevitably leads to faulty and misleading conclusions. Almost any group that is homogenous for some features should differ from the published normative data. The normative samples for both adults and children reflect a conglomerate of subjects from eight socioeconomic levels and three major geographic distributions. The only common element to all nonpatient subjects is the absence of a psychiatric history. They represent a vast array of individual differences, with dimensions ranging from well controlled to poorly controlled, introversive to extratensive, high Lambda styles, from the gregarious to the isolated, strange to sturdy, and so on.

The nonpatient data provide some references, and in some instances, they can be used descriptively to highlight deviations. But, they do not provide a control group and any attempts to use them, or extrapolations from them, in a statistical comparison model are, at least, unworthy. Unfortunately, young or new researchers are often misled by those seemingly skilled in the clinical trade to also assume that they are skilled in research. A depressing byproduct of this tragic assumption is the use of normative data in some statistical model that makes no sense, yet often leaves researchers with the ingenuous conclusion that they have made a great discovery. Sadly, the teacher or supervisor of the research may agree with this incredulous conclusion.

OTHER RETROSPECTIVE STUDIES

A model that is often a key source of new information is that involving a retrospective pebble picking through accumulated data sets. Quite often, the yield from this approach presents findings that are very important and usually will lead to the design of a more sophisticated prospective hypothesis-testing study. The hazard, however, concerns the issues of subject variance, or method variance, either of which become critically important in distinguishing the new study from that of a pedestrian report about filed cases to one of involving a careful search through available material.

Although some retrospective studies can be extremely important, the yield will be questionable unless the investigator has been thorough and conservative concerning the data to be analyzed or issued forth in the form of descriptive data. For instance, assume that a hospital or clinic, during a several year period, has routinely administered the Rorschach to newly accepted patients and has maintained reasonably good records concerning the length of hospitalization and/or treatment, plus information about the treatment model(s) employed. A potential gold mine of information seems to exist, but it must be mined carefully.

The first issue to be considered concerns the collection of the data. Were all tests administered prior to treatment? Were the tests administered by the therapists-to-be or by others? To what extent did the test data contribute to the eventual diagnosis of the patient? Were patients randomly assigned to therapists? What criteria were employed to effect discharge and/or termination? And, most importantly, what kind of follow-up information is available regarding the subject? If the answers to all of these questions fall in the "right" direction, the data can provide an extremely useful base from which to plan further studies that will be designed in the conceptual framework of the results.

No one should ignore the possibilities that are inherent in an already existing, but unused database. In many instances, the revelations will not only be useful in clarifying other published findings, but often they will provide a basis for new studies concerning issues that have been discovered.

REPLICATION STUDIES

One of the most important, but least conducted, research models involves replication. A huge number of Rorschach studies have never been replicated and accumulated findings are often accepted as Rorschach gospel. Replications that yield findings similar to those previously reported serve to strengthen interpretative postulates and add to our understanding of the psychology of people. On the other hand, replications of designs that fail to yield similar findings call prior conceptualizations into question.

Possibly, there are two reasons for the failure of more replication works to appear in the literature. First, an unspoken tradition seems to exist in many schools or departments responsible for the training of those who will ultimately enter the Rorschach community. It is the once sternly enforced rule that dissertation research must be innovative, that is, each new study should be creative and contribute significantly to the literature. It is a premise that has plagued doctoral candidates for decades, even though it is somewhat unrealistic. Carefully designed replications often are the grist for understanding. They may seem pedestrian because of their apparent lack of innovation, but when considered in the broader objectives of science, they are like a breath of fresh air. They serve to confirm or challenge prior conclusions.

If the replication confirms previous findings, the new results strengthen the usefulness or understanding of a variable or group of variables. They increase the probability of correct translations of data. On the other hand, if previous findings are not replicated, the new results shed reasonable doubt on some interpretive routines or conclusions regarding groups of people, and point to the need for further research concerning an issue, variable, or group of variables.

SINGLE CASE STUDIES

Occasionally, good research will involve only a single case in which all of the *t*'s are crossed and all of the *i*'s are dotted. The results of such studies may, at times, warrant a hypothetical generalization to populations similar to that of the subject. These are very special kinds of research reports that often create the foundations for future investigations. They add considerably to the literature and to the understanding of people, but they are not done easily. In fact, an extensive single case study may involve more time by an investigator than would be involved in a more massive study concerning many subjects. Nonetheless, they often provide new grist for the arena of research and can easily lead to a better understanding of people as unique entities.

Consider, for instance, the hypothetical case of a sex offender who has pleaded guilty to child molestation and who has been placed on a 5-year probationary sentence with the proviso that psychological treatment be included until such a time as the treating psychologist or psychiatrist certifies that the subject poses no further risk to children. The case presents a fertile field for investigation, assuming that some baseline testing is administered prior to treatment but after sentencing.

The critical data in such a case are fourfold. First, are there features in the baseline test data that might relate to the molestation behavior? Second, as Weiner (1994) pointed out, what data of the test indirectly reflect targets for treatment? Third, how do the data from subsequent tests, possibly taken at 6- to 9-month intervals, and at discharge from treatment, compare to the data of the pretreatment test? In other words, what appears to have changed during each interval of the treatment? Finally, how do the data from each of the tests compare to other information concerning the postsentencing behaviors of the subject?

In a sense, it is a treatment effects study, and although it has only an *N* of one, if the data are thorough, they may offer a basis from which some better understanding of people may occur, some hypotheses concerning treatment effects might be generated, and larger scale studies concerning a specific treatment might be developed. It is important, however, to insure that all four of these issues described are addressed. In some instances, a single case study may follow a developmental model—that is, what happens to the seemingly troubled child when the mixture of treatment and chronological development unfolds. A longitudinal case study concerning a child by Viglione (1990) is an excellent illustration of how such information can contribute much to the literature.

Researchers should never shy away from individual case studies if the accumulated data are in order. On the other hand, researchers should avoid attempting to use data from single cases in a biased fashion. Unfortunately, most published single case studies tend to focus on the dramatic aspects of a subject, such as presenting data concerning a serial killer, a Nazi war criminal, or a well-known scientist or political figure. Although these works may have some historical interest, they contribute little to new knowledge, and in fact, can be misleading at times.

For instance, Meloy (1992) used the data from an ineptly administered Rorschach to demonstrate that in the assassin of Robert Kennedy, Sirhan Sirhan, is (or was) a borderline personality disorder. Meloy, however, was not very conservative about scoring the nearly one third of the responses taken that were not inquired at all. Although attempting to score the noninquired responses for form quality according to criteria, it seems obvious that some bias entered into some of the scoring decisions. As presented, using Meloy's scoring decisions, the record does not have a positive Schizophrenia Index, however, if those noninquired answers were scored more conservatively, the Schizophrenia Index for the record is positive, which would raise a serious question about Meloy's conclusions.

EXPERIMENTER BIAS

The problem of experimenter bias should never be ignored when planning Rorschach research. In effect, the priniciple of experimenter/examiner bias in Rorschach research is always an important issue. It raises a question about the extent to which an awareness of the purpose of a study, or even more importantly, an awareness of hypotheses, effect the interaction between the examiner and the subject.

There are a host of studies in experimental psychology demonstrating that experimenters who are aware of a design and/or hypthesis may, inadvertently, influence the data of the experiment. Obviously, this is not necessarily a critical element in all designs, but it is an element that must be given careful consideration in Rorschach studies. There is indirect evidence to suggest that experimenter/examiner bias may effect some results, and in some instances the impact of the bias may be considerable. For instance, Masling (1965) demonstrated that one group of newly trained examiners set to expect more animal than human content actually obtained such results, whereas a second group trained to expect for more human than animal content also did so. Exner, Leura, and George (1976) used four groups of newly trained examiners to study the Masling findings. They used a videotape of the testings, with two groups administering the test in a face-to-face situation and two groups testing in a side-by-side situation. They found that, consistent with Masling's postulates, nonverbal reinforcements seemed to provoke the desired results, especially if examiners were seated in a face-to-face situation with the subject. The side-by-side seating used in the comprehensive system appears to have rectified some, but not all, of that problem. Strauss (1968) and Strauss and Marwit (1970) presented findings to suggest that the ratios that are critically important in interpretation are not affected if seating is side by side.

Nonetheless, there is no way that an investigator can insure that prior knowledge about the study will not have an impact. Obviously, well-designed studies will involve multiple examiners, blind to the purpose of the study, who will be randomized across groups in the study. It is not just the process of administering the test that might be impacted by prior knowledge of the purpose of a study. It seems logical to suspect that it may also effect some scoring decisions when issues such as is the movement active or passive, whether a shading response should be scored as texture, diffuse shading, or vista, or whether a color response is to be scored as *FC* versus *CF*. Ordinarily, scoring should always be done in the blind.

OVERGENERALIZING OR OVEREMPHASIZING RESULTS

There is nothing more frustrating than to find that the results from a well-planned investigation offer only limited support, or sometimes no support at all, for the original hypotheses. Most investigators, when confronted with such findings, will cull through their findings very meticulously in an attempt to make their results meaningful and important. The motives for doing so are not always pure. Issues of self-esteem, well-being, and professional credibility sometimes play a role in determining how findings will be discussed and especially how limited findings will be made to seem quite important.

Consider, for example, a correlational study involving 100 subjects in which 20 Rorschach variables are correlated with self-report data concerning five interpersonal behaviors. Assume that the correlations for 16 Rorschach variables and the five reported behaviors fall between +.10 and −.10, that is, there is no meaningful relation. Also assume that, for the remaining four Rorschach variables, correlations with the three of the five self-report variables range from +.30 to +.36. Considered in relation to the sample size of 100 subjects, all four Rorschach variables correlate at "statistically significant" levels (ranging from $p < .05$ to $p < .02$) in a two-tailed application. Some investigators, caught up in their enthusiasm, may attempt to reach for astounding conclusions based on these findings while neglecting two important considerations.

First, it is important to remember that 100 correlations have been calculated and, by chance, 8 to 12 of those are expected to reach a p value of .05 if a two-tailed test is applied. Probably, correlations reaching a "significance" level of .05 should be disregarded when interpreting the findings because of the possibility of chance findings. At best, the findings should be addressed very conservatively.

Second, and possibly more important, is the fact that none of the "significant" correlations are greater than .36, which is significant at .02 for a group of this size. The question now focuses on the importance of the finding. Certainly, a p value of .02 is important, but is the correlation itself very revealing? A .36 correlation accounts for only 13% of the variance, which is not a very strong relationship. Some researchers will go to great lengths to proclaim that the results support some theoretical postulate, however, the wise investigator will be very cautious about interpreting the finding.

Sometimes, investigators are prone to manipulate data in unrealistic ways to support a hypothesis or a theoretical issue. This probably occurs more frequently in Rorschach-related studies than should be the case. For instance, a small sample design, involving as few as 20 subjects, might be created to study situational stress effects. Both groups perform the same task, but one of the two groups of 10 subjects perform the task under some stressful circumstance. At some critical point, the Rorschach will be administered. Assume that the dependent variables are m and Y, which, in almost all circumstances, are not normally distributed, and the hypothesis is that subjects in the experimental group will give significantly more m and/or Y than control subjects.

At the onset, the experimenter should be aware that some form of parametric test is inappropriate because of the small sample sizes and because of the nature of the distribution of the two dependent measures. On the other hand, the required frequency of elevations for either m or Y, using a critical cutoff score of more than two m or Y or a combination score of $m + Y$ of more than three, have to be considerable to obtain any support for the basic premise. Assume that only one control subject has more than two m or Y, or more than three $m + Y$. Also assume that six experimental subjects have more than two m, or two Y, or more than three $m + Y$.

The results are interesting, and clearly in the direction of the hypothesis, but if a nonparametric is employed, the result will not be significant because of the small N's. Unfortunately, some investigators will be tempted to use a parametric test to address the data, and if as few as two experimental subjects give many m or Y answers, for instance four or five of either or the combination of the two, the means for the two groups can be demonstrated to be significantly different well beyond the .05 level.

The question is whether the results are really significant and do they afford support for the hypothesis? The answer is "maybe." Some directionality does exist. Elevations in the dependent measures for six experimental subjects versus only one control subject seems impressive, but, are the data unequivocal? Clearly, they are not. Probably, they should be reported, giving major emphasis to the descriptive statistics, that is, the frequency data and some mention of the inappropriate parametric test of the means can be included, noting that it is not a statistic of choice and is mentioned only to give some indirect emphasis to the directional findings. Under no circumstances, however, should the author attempt to argue that the study offers "strong" support for the premise that m and/or Y will increase under situational stress, or extrapolate from the findings to develop a new or expanded conceptual model of Rorschach data and situational stress. In other words, the results may have some merit but they must be presented with exquisite caution. Authors who overgeneralize or overemphasize results only serve their own grandiose needs, and they provide a disservice to others, especially those who will read only an abstract or summary of their work.

The chapters that follow discus in more detail many of the problems and issues addressed here. Hopefully, the substance of this book will encourage the novice researcher to design better studies, and also will encourage experienced researchers to review their own approaches to the study of this intriguing test.

REFERENCES

American Psychological Association (1947). Committee on training in psychology. Recommended graduate training program in clinical psychology. *American Psychologist, 2,* 539–558.

Blatt, S. J., & Feirstein, A. (1977). Cardiac response and personality organization. *Journal of Consulting and Clinical Psychology, 45,* 111–123.

Chu, A. Y., & Exner, J. E. (1981). EB style as related to distractibility in a calculation task. Workshops Study No. 280 (unpublished), Rorschach Workshops.

Exner, J. E. (1988). Problems with brief Rorschach protocols. *Journal of Personality Assessment, 52,* 640–647.

Exner, J. E. (1991). *The Rorschach: A comprehensive system: Vol. 2. Interpretation* (2nd ed.). New York: Wiley.

Exner, J. E. (1992). R in Rorschach research: A ghost revisited. *Journal of Personality Assessment, 58,* 245–251.

Exner, J. E. (1993). *The Rorschach: A comprehensive system: Vol. 1. Basic foundations* (3rd ed.). New York: Wiley.

Exner, J. E., Leura, A. V., & George, L. M. (1976). *A replication of the Masling study using four groups of new examiners with two seating arrangements and video evaluation.* Workshops Study No. 256 (unpublished), Rorschach Workshops.

Exner, J. E., Thomas, E. A., & Martin, L. S. (1980). *Alterations in GSR and cardiac and respiratory rate in Introversives and Extratensives during problem solving.* Workshops Study No. 272 (unpublished), Rorschach Workshops.

Hoch, E. L., Ross, A. O., & Winder, C. L. (Eds.). (1966). *Professional preparation of clinical psychologists.* Washington, DC: American Psychological Association.

Masling, J. (1965). Differential indoctrination of examiners and Rorschach responses. *Journal of Consulting Psychology, 29,* 198–201.

Meloy, J. R. (1992). Revisiting the Rorschach of Sirhan Sirhan. *Journal of Personality Assessment, 58,* 548–570.

Perry, G. G., & Kinder, B. N. (1990). The susceptibility of the Rorschach to malingering: A critical review. *Journal of Personality Assessment, 54,* 45–57.

Raimy, V. (Ed.). (1950). *Training in clinical psychology.* New York: Prentice-Hall.

Roe, A. (Ed.). (1959). *Graduate education in psychology.* Washington, DC: American Psychological Association.

Strauss, M. E. (1968). Examiner expectancy: Effects on Rorschach Experience Balance. *Journal of Consulting Psychology, 32,* 125–129.

Strauss, M. E., & Marwit, S. J. (1970). Expectancy effects in Rorschach testing. *Journal of Consulting and Clinical Psychology, 34,* 448.

Strother, C. (Ed.). (1956). *Psychology and mental health.* Washington, DC: American Psychological Association.

Viglione, D. J. (1990). Severe disturbance or trauma induced adaptive reaction: A Rorschach child case study. *Journal of Personality Assessment, 55,* 280–295.

Weiner, I. B. (1994). Rorschach assessment. In M. E. Maruish (Ed.), *The use of psychological testing for treatment planning and outcome assessment* (pp. 249–278). Hillsdale, NJ: Lawrence Erlbaum Associates.

CHAPTER TWO

Conceptual Issues in Rorschach Research

Robert R. Dies

The majority of recent studies of the Rorschach have been group comparisons or correlational investigations, with only slightly more than 10% of the projects conducted since 1985 introducing some form of experimental intervention. This suggests that most investigators have been much more concerned with clinical relevance than scientific rigor in their explorations of the Rorschach. Most of these projects have been conducted within a broad spectrum of mental health settings in the search for meaningful diagnostic patterns, but there have been relatively few attempts to experimentally monitor important variables that might affect the internal validity of the investigation. Consequently, a variety of potentially confounding factors relating to subject selection, group composition, missing or inappropriate control groups, variations in administration and/or scoring, and situational influences have often made results difficult to understand.

Ideally, any comparative or correlational study will isolate the critical dimensions that account for group differences, and researchers will be able to rule out alternative explanations of their findings. However, as Gelso and Fretz (1992) noted, nearly every study of this type is highly imperfect and contains inevitable flaws. They proposed the "bubble hypothesis" to illustrate how investigators must struggle with the inherent trade-offs in conducting psychological research: "This concept likens the research process to a sticker on a car windshield. Once a bubble appears in the sticker, it is impossible to eliminate it. Pressing the bubble simply causes it to pop up in another place. Each attempted solution causes a problem to appear elsewhere" (p. 110).

Many such bubbles appear in Rorschach research. Although some of these problems reflect methodological shortcomings, a substantial proportion relate to difficulties in interpreting the meaning of results once the data have been collected. Most of these bubbles fall into at least one of four major categories: identifying the clinical significance of group differences, applying strictly empirical rather than conceptually anchored research models, failing to understand criterion problems in the relationships between Rorschach variables and independent measures, and exploring new indices or special scales.

ISSUES OF GROUP DIFFERENCES

The basic strategy in group comparison studies is to contrast two or more clinical groups (or normal controls) in order to identify reliable differences in Rorschach performance (e.g., schizophrenic vs. borderline patients, sexually abused youngsters vs. a group of normal schoolchildren, or short-term vs. long-time heroine users). Once the statistically significant contrasts are obtained, many investigators attribute these differences to the central "clinical reality" that prompted their investigation. Thus, if schizophrenics show more cognitive mismanagement than borderline patients, it is presumably because they are schizophrenic. If sexually traumatized children manifest more morbid content than normal subjects, it is assumed to be due to their having been abused. This search for diagnostic signs has been the most popular focus of Rorschach research for many decades.

Although many such studies are worthwhile, there are several fundamental errors that often occur in this group contrast approach. Obviously, the lack of adequate controls allows for too many alternative interpretations of the obtained differences (e.g., confounds in subject recruitment, the lack of diagnostic homogeneity in the samples being compared, and variations in contextual factors influencing the groups). Moreover, as argued by Vincent and Harman (1991), statistical significance for group data does not equate with clinical validity in the ideographic application of the test.

Perhaps the most fundamental problem with regard to interpreting group differences is that distinction does not represent essence. First, it is impractical to guarantee that differences actually relate to the principal clinical characteristic that defines the group being investigated and, second, it is difficult to assure that the key ingredients are unique to the target group.

Suppose, for example, one is interested in testing the idea that there are discrete Rorschach indicators of organic brain dysfunction. Assume that a group of patients with known cerebral deficits is available, plus a comparison sample comprised of patients who are hospitalized for various medical complications. In contrasting the organic and medical controls, highly significant differences on Piotrowski's (1937) neurological signs are obtained (e.g., below average number of responses, sparse human movement, evidence of color naming, and expressions of perplexity and impotence). Obviously, it would be naive to assume that the pathognomic Rorschach signs for neurological impairment have been established without extensive cross-validation with a range of alternative clinical groups. In fact, such replications have generally failed to support the efficacy of these indices for diagnosing organicity (Frank, 1991).

Nonetheless, the Rorschach literature is replete with investigations of this nature. For example, Leifer, Shapiro, Martone, and Kassem (1991) attempted to establish clinical indicators of sexual abuse in children by comparing their victimized youngsters with an age-matched group of girls who were medical patients in a local hospital. The study was well conceptualized in terms of hypothesized differences along such critical dimensions as ego functioning, adaptive coping, affective integration, and interpersonal engagement, with several Rorschach structural and/or content scores anchoring each of the hypotheses. Furthermore, the authors also were sensitive to other factors that might affect the generalizability of their findings, and they made an effort to carefully define their clinical sample. Despite these precautions, however, the distinctions between the two groups were attributed to their status as sexually abused, rather than to other possible differences between subjects. Thus, the sexually abused girls were described as showing more disturbances in thinking, more negative affect, and greater sexual preoccupation. An unresolved question is whether these differences would remain consistent if the comparison group had been matched for overall levels of psychopathology? Nonetheless, the efforts of these authors to form an adequate control group reflects a critical issue in group comparison research.

Wald, Archer, and Winstead (1990), for example, seriously erred concerning control group problems in their investigation of Rorschach patterns of mothers of incest victims. They compared the scores of their target group with those of control subjects drawn from the adult normative sample published for the Comprehensive System, equated for age, education, socioeconomic standing, marital status, and the presence of children in the home. Statistically significant contrasts were described in terms of the features characterizing the mothers of the sexually abused youngers; that is, they were depicted as psychologically immature, prone to psychotic episodes, and generally interpersonally unavailable and aloof. But how do we know that these differences are not a function of unknown confounds, such as using normative subjects whose motivations and circumstances surrounding testing were enormously different, or that the contrasts truly represent qualities that are unique to this special class of mothers? Thus, these distinctive features may not document the "essence" of the particular group.

This issue of clinical essence can be explored more meaningfully by examining either the amount of overlap between comparison groups or by evaluating the proportion of subjects in the target group who actually manifest the presumed cardinal features. Weisburg, Norman, and Herzog (1987), for example, examined the personality organization and functioning of normal weight bulimic women using control groups of nonpatients and depressed outpatients. They found statistically significant differences among the groups, and characterized their normal weight bulimics as having a limited capacity to modulate affect ($CF + C$ greater than FC), manifesting high levels of anger and negativity (AG and Space responses), lacking a consistent coping style (Ambitent), withdrawing from affective stimulation (*Afr*), and displaying an egocentric or grandiose orientation to the world (Egocentricity Index and Reflection responses). Ironically, whereas their bulimic subjects were indeed higher on these criteria than the comparison groups, a greater percentage of their target group failed to demonstrate the presumed problems!

In an effort to extend these findings by differentiating between *DSM–III–R* diagnosed purging and nonpurging bulimics, Smith, Hillard, Walsh, Kubacki, and Morgan (1991) did not confirm many of the findings. When they did obtain differences between their patient groups and controls, a majority of their subjects did not manifest the clinical features predicted by the Weisberg et al. study. For example, the eating disorder patients were expected to have a much higher frequency of ambitents than the normal subjects, but only 37% of the eating disorder patients in the Smith et al. study met that criterion. Thus, it is unrealistic to conclude that Weisberg and her colleagues really established uniquely distinguishing characteristics of bulimic patients.

The early work leading to the development of the original Schizophrenia Index used in the Comprehensive System illustrates similar problems (Exner, 1986a). At that time, four dimensions characterizing the schizophrenic syndrome—namely, evidence of thought disorder, impaired perceptual accuracy, poor emotional controls, and limited or ineffective interpersonal life—were explored. All four criteria were found in the schizophrenic samples, but only the first two served to differentiate the schizophrenics from most other diagnostic groups. Although evidence of both malfunction in affective control and interpersonal ineptitude were present in the schizophrenic patients, neither of those features could be regarded as a hallmark of that particular syndrome, as measured by Rorschach data.

An ideal predictive test would produce high sensitivity (i.e., the proportion of correctly identified positive cases) and high specificity (i.e., the percentage of accurately designated negative instances), and low false-positive and false-negative rates (Maris, 1992). Although the original Schizophrenic Index was quite sensitive, it was not sufficiently specific because too many nonschizophrenics were misdiagnosed by the index as displaying forms of perceptual distortion and cognitive slippage presumably characteristic only of schizophrenics.

Elwood (1993) showed that the conclusions of test validation studies must be interpreted cautiously because these investigations typically compare samples of equal or similar size, which maximizes the probability of accurate group classification. Elwood illustrated how the predictive power of test scores may be dramatically affected by local base rates. Thus, a test that accurately classifies 90% of the subjects as schizophrenic in a study with a base rate of 50% (e.g., 100 schizophrenic patients compared to 100 nonpatient control subjects) may only identify half the clinical sample when an outpatient facility's base rate for schizophrenia is only 10%. In this case, "a positive test score adds no more validity than the toss of a coin" (Elwood, 1993, p. 412).

Goldfried, Stricker, and Weiner (1971) warned that investigators must inevitably decide what tolerance for error is acceptable within their own settings. Thus, if an index to identify thought disorders improves upon base-rate predictions and leads to more effective treatment planning for accurately classified patients, it might be useful to apply the index more broadly, even though interventions for incorrectly labeled patients are not improved substantially. The assessment of suicide potential provides an obvious example. Given the low base rate for suicide, the most accurate prediction is that patients will not take their own life. Nonetheless, most clinicians would prefer to tolerate error on the side of overestimating the risk (false positives) when there are apparent signs, despite the extra effort required by unnecessary suicide precautions (Goldfried et al., 1971; Maris, 1992).

Many Rorschach investigators have been far too cavalier in interpreting statistically significant group differences as diagnostic signs of the disorder they are examining, without considering alternative explanations, replicating their results with other samples and proper controls, or carefully examining false-positive/false-negative rates within their target group.

Although the studies cited earlier apply a group contrast design, similar criticisms can be leveled against investigations that overinterpret the clinical value of positive findings when Rorschach variables correlate significantly with self-report or behavioral criteria. In short, distinctiveness should not be interpreted to reflect essence, and this is true even when the ostensible sign has been cross-validated and is buttressed by substantial empirical verification. Perhaps the best illustration is the current Schizophrenic Index (Exner, 1991), which evolved only after more than 30 discriminant function analyses, each involving a variety of patient samples. The new SCZI correctly identifies more than 80% of schizophrenics for whom the diagnosis is formulated independent of the Rorschach. The SCZI has modest false-positive (0% to 15%) and false-negative rates (12% to 22%). Still, some schizophrenic patients are not positive on the index, and other patients may demonstrate some of the characteristics defined by the criteria, even though they are not schizophrenic (e.g., Singer & Brabender, 1993). In other words, even with carefully defined variables, caution must be exercised in the conceptual process. This is especially true when the investigator approaches research from a strictly empirical point of view without a coherent theoretical framework linking Rorschach variables and dimensions of personality.

EMPIRICAL VERSUS CONCEPTUAL APPROACHES TO RESEARCH

Although a metanalytic review of the Rorschach literature has documented the reliability and validity of the test (Parker, Hanson, & Hunsley, 1988), the impression lingers that the Rorschach is, at best, a more subjective instrument that relies heavily on the intuitive skills of the clinician. A principal source of this prejudice is the failure of investigators to provide a meaningful conceptual scheme for their research. Too often researchers employ a "hit-or-miss" empirical approach to Rorschach validation with little forethought about the selection of variables to explore, and minimal effort to furnish a systematic rationale to account for potential results. Consequently, correlations between Rorschach variables and independent criteria are often not detected, or when they are, the clinical significance of the associations are often difficult to decipher.

It has been shown that conceptual approaches to Rorschach research are much more likely to support the value of the test. For instance, Atkinson, Quarrington, Alp, and Cyr (1986) analyzed a sample of 120 validation studies published between 1930 and 1980, by classifying them either as empirical or conceptual, depending on whether or not the investigators had provided an a priori rationale as to why the Rorschach indices were pertinent to the discrimination attempted between two groups. They also differentiated between studies applying only signs or single variables versus those using clusters or the combination of signs into sets. These authors found that conceptual studies, both sign and cluster, were much more successful than either form of empirical study in documenting the validity of the Rorschach.

Weiner (1986) underscored many advantages of the conceptual approach to Rorschach research. He noted that studies identifying personality processes or dimensions that predict and explain the connections between Rorschach variables and independent criteria are much more likely than empirical models to offer an understanding of why the test works as it does, facilitate interpretation of the test protocol in a more efficient and focused manner, foster clear communication of results to clinicians who are less familiar with the Rorschach, and encourage speculation about unexplored associations between test and nontest behaviors.

The literature is replete with studies attempting to link Rorschach variables with scores on other tests, or to contrast two or more groups on the Rorschach, without offering a set of hypotheses about expected results. These investigations vary in the range of Rorschach variables selected for examination. In more limited domain studies, one or two Rorschach variables are highlighted, but a wide net is cast to find statistically significant correlations with other variables. For example, Duricko, Norcross, and Buskirk (1989) sought Rorschach and Minnesota Multiphasic Personality Inventory (MMPI) correlates of the Egocentricity Index, $3r + (2)/R$, and then offered post hoc speculations about the few reliable results that were extracted. In other cases, investigators are less selective about the target variables in the Rorschach, and simply conduct a broad sweep through the quantitative findings. For example, Exner (1986b) examined 49 basic Rorschach scores to ascertain differences among schizophrenic, schizotypal, and borderline patients. Perhaps the only justification for that approach was that the differences among the three groups were very substantial for many of the variables. In other instances, comparing three groups for so many variables would probably produce some differences, but not enough to cast neatly into a coherent framework.

When studies are conducted with the objective of detecting differences between diagnostic groups, or to uncover relationships among Rorschach variables and other dimensions, the lack of a conceptual model makes it difficult to discriminate between clinically meaningful and fortuitous results. The heuristic value of such exploratory research is often obvious, but the vast majority of such studies are rarely replicated, and even when they are, differences among findings often pose serious questions about the validity of the conclusions.

When investigators have not offered theoretical formulations to account for potential results, they are forced to engage in post hoc reasoning, an exercise that is often fraught with difficulties given the lack of solid theory or previous empirical work on which to base these interpretations. The typical ploy is for the investigator to qualify the results by introducing some other Rorschach variables or personality dynamics that might account for the findings.

For instance, Belter, Lipovsky, and Finch (1989) failed to establish statistically reliable associations between the Egocentricity Index and self-report measures of self-concept and depression. They offered three speculations to account for the nonsignificant results: that it might be inappropriate to draw conclusions about self-concept solely on the basis of the one Rorschach variable, the self-report measures might be invalid, and/or the meaning of the Egocentricity Index might be unique for different individuals. To illustrate, for one individual a low score on the Egocentricity Index might accurately represent self-devaluation, and this would also be confirmed by a self-report measure, whereas for another person the objective inventory may not correspond with the Rorschach Index because of the person's defensive efforts on more transparent measures to deny negative aspects of the self.

Similarly, Harder, Greenwald, Ritzler, Strauss, and Kokes (1988) proposed that the presence of multiple Space responses for a normal individual may reflect independence strivings, self-assertion, or even oppositional tendencies, used in the service of constructive coping. In contrast, the same finding of negativism and self-expression may represent a counterproductive rejection of reality-based adjustment in a more disturbed person.

The bottom line is that single variables, or even constellations comprised of multiple criteria, may take on different meanings as a function of other Rorschach structural or qualitative findings. As Exner (1987, p. 3) noted, "Single variables have little or no meaning, and if studied independently can often be very misleading in the interpretive process." Exner noted that the variables must be reviewed in clusters that relate to various psychological operations or characteristics, such as capacities for control, tolerance for stress, coping preference, organizing and processing information, emotional responsiveness and control, self-concept, and the like. Recently, Exner (1991) presented a case of brief reactive psychosis, in which the patient showed major perceptual distortion and cognitive slippage of the type often found in schizophrenic records. Indeed, this woman met five of the six criteria on the Schizophrenic Index, which ordinarily provides considerable confidence that a schizophrenic diagnosis is warranted. Yet, a careful evaluation of the patterns of scores led to the conclusion that the psychotic material represented psychological sequelae stemming from a recent traumatic episode (e.g., all of the perceptual distortions, and most of the serious cognitive mismanagement, were associated with morbid content). Even within standard Comprehensive System interpretation, one goes beyond formal scores to examine sequence, behavior, and responses with projective content (Viglione, Brager, & Haller, 1991).

Researchers who engage in simplistic forms of empirical research often seem to ignore the contextual embeddedness of Rorschach variables, particularly when they focus on isolated factors and fail to articulate a well-reasoned conceptual framework for interpreting the complex nature of their results. To expect one-to-one correspondence between Rorschach variables and nontest criteria is a gross oversimplification that ignores the complexity of personality. Fortunately, there are growing indications that researchers are becoming much more sophisticated in their efforts to get beyond non-conceptual and trial-and-error approaches to Rorschach investigation. Recent studies are more likely to apply complex statistical integration of Rorschach data (e.g., factor analysis, multiple discriminant function analysis), and/or to offer guidelines for how variables may coalesce into more broadly defined dimensions of personality or psychopathology (e.g., multiple criteria to evaluate self-perception or interpersonal style, indices to assess levels of depression or likelihood of a schizophrenic disorder). The principal advantages of these efforts to integrate individual indicators or signs into empirically derived clusters and to offer conceptual links between Rorschach variables and independent criteria should be obvious.

Two studies linking Rorschach data to psychotherapeutic process illustrate the empirical integration of individual signs into an appropriate conceptual framework. Alpher, Perfetto, Henry, and Strupp (1990) rationally selected 15 Structural Summary variables relating to cognitive style, affective expression, and the capacity to form meaningful object relationships, and then entered these scores into a series of stepwise regressions to reduce the pool of predictors. They were able to demonstrate a reasonably strong association between personality attributes as measured by the Rorschach and judgments of the clients' potential for engaging in the process of dynamic psychotherapy. Similarly, Colson, Pickar, and Coyne (1989) extracted (via factor analysis) six major dimensions from a set of 19 Rorschach variables and established a number of interesting connections with the extent and type of treatment difficulty.

Factor analytic studies with the Rorschach have consistently shown that a relatively limited set of dimensions summarize much of the common variance in the interpretive process (Anderson & Dixon, 1993). Meyer (1992b) indicated that these dimensions exist across 40 years of research, despite the use of different variables, scoring systems, subject populations, and factor analytic methods. The point, however, is not to extol a particular method for empirical integration of Rorschach findings, but rather to encourage investigators to move beyond relatively simple empirically based sign approaches to research. Efforts to interpret statistically significant effects in shotgun studies are less likely to yield meaningful generalizations than similar efforts based on carefully defined constellations or coherent sets of Rorschach variables proposed in advance of the actual implementation of the study.

In the conceptual approach to Rorschach interpretation, and research, there is an effort to identify personality processes or dimensions (usually based on multiple Rorschach criteria) that can account for both features of test behavior and some aspect of the individual known empirically to be associated with this Rorschach variable (Weiner, 1986). For example, in designing a research project on changes following psychotherapy, it would be more appropriate to specify in advance what shifts in Rorschach performance would be expected, than it would be to simply examine any statistical effects that emerged from a long list of Rorschach variables. Thus, Weiner and Exner (1991) selected 27 indices of adjustment difficulty from the Rorschach that might relate to insufficient treatment progress. These variables were organized into six principal dimensions: adequate stress management; capacity to handle experiences attentively, openly, consistently, and conventionally; problems in moderating affective displays appropriately; difficulties in using ideation effectively; problems relating to self-examination; and, difficulty in feeling comfortable in relationships. These conceptual clusters greatly facilitated the interpretation of the changes promoted by psychotherapy.

When the first edition of volume 1 describing the Comprehensive System was published in 1974, guidelines for how to work through the Structural Summary data were not sufficiently developed, and the major constellations (e.g., Depression Index, DEPI; Hypervigilance Index, HVI; SCZI; Suicide Constellation, S-Con) were not yet available (Exner, 1974). As a consequence, interpretation was more often guided by the skills or whims of the clinician than by empirically derived dimensions. Subjectivity often characterized the integration of data. Single signs were weighed too heavily and the absence of a coherent framework for integrating the complexity of results of the typical Rorschach record was obvious. Unfortunately, these same limitations are inherent in much of the research in this field.

As the Comprehensive System has evolved, the empirical foundation has grown substantially, and it has been possible to fine-tune the understanding of the Rorschach. The latest refinements in the Comprehensive System (Exner, 1991, 1993) demonstrate the cluster approach to interpretation of basic Rorschach data. The empirical and conceptual foundations of the Rorschach have been strengthened substantially over the years, so that it is no longer necessary, in either clinical work or in research, to rely on hit-or-miss or shotgun approaches. Rorschach interpretation is no longer an arbitrary scan of the findings in pursuit of what looks interesting to the clinician, but an empirically grounded, and conceptually driven, process. Researchers can apply the same strategies in their empirical efforts as well, instead of approaches that explore a collection of variables that appear to have accumulated somewhat haphazardly without a meaningful framework to underpin the data compilation.

Although the constellations and clusters that now guide the interpretive process are based on considerable empirical work, the publication of these refinements is often recent. As a consequence, there is limited but growing evidence of their impact in the literature, and more investigators have turned to these clusters in an effort to conceptualize their empirical efforts.

CRITERION PROBLEMS
(RORSCHACH VERSUS INDEPENDENT CRITERIA)

In many Rorschach validation studies, variables are correlated with various independent criteria, such as scores on self-report measures, performance on other types of psychological tests, interpersonal ratings, or behavioral measures. It is not unusual to find that the correlations obtained in these projects are either statistically nonsignificant or of only moderate clinical utility. This is true for investigations with children and adolescents (e.g., Archer & Gordon, 1988; Belter et al., 1989; Duricko et al., 1989; Shapiro, Leifer, Martone, & Kassem, 1990), as well as those with adults (e.g., Boswell, 1989; Greenwald, 1990, 1991; Simon, 1989).

When faced with disappointing associations between Rorschach data and scores on other tests, some investigators question the validity of the Rorschach variables or clusters, but it is equally plausible to assume that the difficulty relates more to criterion problems than to limitations in the Rorschach.

For instance, Ball, Archer, Gordon, and French (1991) explored the relationship between the original Depression Index and clinical elevations on the depression scale of the Personality Inventory for Children, plus diagnostic evaluations provided by the treatment teams in both outpatient and inpatient settings. Significant correlations between the Rorschach findings and the other measures of depression were not detected. Other researchers using the Rorschach have obtained similar findings (e.g., Leifer et al., 1991; Lipovsky, Finch, & Belter, 1989; Shapiro et al., 1990). Ball et al. proposed that their negative findings were most likely a result of using different informants and modes of measurement to assess depression. Thus, both the depression scores on the inventory and the clinicians' diagnostic judgments represent external perceptions of the child, whereas the Rorschach is based on the child's own responses to the test. Ball and his co-workers (1991) noted that markedly divergent ratings occur when different informants are used to identify childhood depression.

In a study related to that postulate, Crowley, Worchel, and Ash (1992) found that self-report, peer-report, and teacher assessments of depression were unrelated. Results such as these are generally interpreted in terms of *method variance*, that is, correlations across similar types of measures (e.g., two self-report scales) are almost invariably higher than correlations across divergent sources of information (e.g., self-report tests and the Rorschach). According to Crowley et al. (1992), multitrait–multimethod analyses frequently reveal a method effect nearly twice as large as the trait effect. Such differences across data sources are quite common in the literature, whether the construct being assessed is anxiety (where physiological recordings, self-reports, and behavioral ratings often show very little correspondence); empathy as perceived by clients, therapists, or independent raters; or evaluations of therapeutic outcome (e.g., Dijkman-Caes, Kraan, & DeVries, 1993; Meyer, 1992b; Strupp & Hadley, 1977). No one method is uniformly superior, but all contribute to the understanding of the variable under review. It would be a tactical error to infer that one instrument is invalid based on low correlations with other measures of the same construct. Like the proverbial blind men and the elephant, the measures may be focusing on different aspects of the variable being evaluated. For instance, "self-report measures may focus on internal states (e.g., guilt and low self-esteem), whereas other-report measures address external behaviors (e.g., lack of friends and suicide attempts)" (Crowley et al., 1992, pp. 190–191).

Based on factor analytic work, Meyer (1992b) argued that self-report data should not be applied as validational criteria for the Rorschach, because they often sample distinct domains of personality "with the primary data pool of the Rorschach being tacit, less consciously mediated processes, and that of self-report inventories being cognitive schemata about the self" (p. 120). There is considerable evidence to show that similar types of measures may be subject to comparable situational influences. Thus, self-report inventories are generally more transparent as to their focus, so individuals who hope to manage the impression they leave with their clinicians are much more able to do so (e.g., Schretlen, 1988). In contrast, the Rorschach as a complex perceptual-cognitive task is less obvious as an assessment tool. Although subjects can shift the content of their responses fairly easily, it is much more difficult to control the vast majority of the variables that comprise the Structural Summary. A common finding in the assessment literature is that clients who appear to be relatively "normal" on self-report measures of psychopathology may on the Rorschach appear to be much more disturbed, or vice versa (e.g., Acklin, 1993b).

Ros Plana (1990) found that nonpatients asked to simulate depression on the Rorschach generally were not able to do so, but their performance on a self-report measure (MMPI) consistently produced classical 2-7 depressed MMPI profiles. Conversely, another group of nonpatients, who were provided information about the characteristics of clinical depression and asked to appear depressed on the Rorschach and MMPI, were usually able to produce a depressed looking Rorschach and gave MMPI profiles that were uniformly 2-7's; however, the MMPI T-Scores were elevated unrealistically and the F–K data uniformly indicated that the records were faked.

Often, clinicians confront an apparent quandary when a discrepancy seems to exist between Rorschach findings and other test data; that is, which test is providing the truth about their client when there is no reason to suspect attempts at simulation? The most reasonable answer is that both methods furnish a meaningful glimpse at the individual. The self-report measures, and ratings based on behaviors in social settings, reflect the individual's capacity to create certain impressions when the cues are clear as to what behaviors are expected by others. The less familiar stimulus features in the Rorschach, however, make it more difficult for psychologically troubled individuals to inhibit the expression of their underlying liabilities or faulty means of conceptualizing or processing information.

Edell (1987), for example, demonstrated that persons with borderline psychopathology often exhibit more thought disorder on less structured tests, such as the Rorschach, yet manifest relatively intact performance on more structured instruments. Similarly, Blatt, Tuber, and Auerbach (1990) argued that in more obvious social contexts (e.g., self-report measures and behavioral rating contexts) individuals appear to express more adaptive responses, whereas on other types of psychological tests, especially the Rorschach, subjects seem to present their more deviant potential. This method variance must be understood in attempting to predict behavior. If the effort is to understand how the individual will behave in highly structured and familiar situations, perhaps the self-report inventories will prove to be more effective. But the more basic operations of the personality structure as detected on the Rorschach may more accurately characterize a broader range of behaviors by the subject, especially those that may be emitted in more ambiguous and less predictable environmental contexts.

Recent reviews of the literature on interrelationships between Rorschach and MMPI variables indicate rather limited associations within both adolescent and adult samples (e.g., Archer & Krishnamurthy, 1993a, 1993b). Nevertheless, most clinicians suggest that their joint use in an assessment battery will contribute to *incremental validity* (e.g., Acklin, 1993a; Weiner, 1993). Thus, Weiner (1993, p. 149) argued that "apparent contradictions between Rorschach and MMPI results are generative and not invalidating." Although most examiners may feel more confident when the two tests convey similar impressions, seemingly incompatible findings may contribute even more to differential diagnosis and treatment planning.

On the other hand, inconsistencies between Rorschach findings and information gleaned from other measures, may also be related to Rorschach failures. Some of these failures are methodological. For instance, if the findings are interpreted as a sign of some underlying dynamic, the Rorschach may not yield the desired result. The original Depression Index (DEPI) is a good illustration of this and, in spite of the fact that many investigators were willing to interpret their negative results as a function of method variance, the truth of the matter is that the original DEPI did not work well, especially for children and adolescents. Rorschach findings should never be regarded as sacred, and this may account for the fact that the literature is replete with failed validity studies in which investigators were attempting to identify diagnostic signs or content symbolism to infer latent personality dynamics. In most instances, Rorschach findings do seem to provide an accurate picture of psychological operations. For instance, when cognitive slippage is noted as a result of a substantial elevation in the six Special Scores (DV, INC, DR, FAB, ALOG, CONTAM), it is very likely that the individual will show the same ideational mismanagement in other settings. Similarly, an individual who is prone to perceptual distortion or idiosyncratic responding on the Rorschach (e.g., $X+\%$, $Xu\%$, $X-\%$) will most likely display comparable misinterpretations in other situations. Finally, individuals who make considerable effort to organize the stimulus features of the Rorschach (e.g., Lambda, Zf, W:D:Dd) will be similarly motivated elsewhere in their transactions with the environment. These are empirically derived findings that are conceptually sensible. Even when investigators approach the Rorschach as a direct sample of behavior, however, the correlations between Rorschach data and validational criteria may be less than optimal. Yet, the problem may not be with the Rorschach, but rather with either the nature of the sample under review or the construct being considered.

The issue of the construct itself may be most important. For example, what is depression, and does this concept have the same meaning for different individuals? From their study of method variance, Crowley et al. (1992) concluded that "the implication of these results to the conceptualization of depression suggests that children may experience depressive symptomatology in several different ways. For instance, one child may experience depression internally, whereas another child may exhibit signs of depression externally or interpersonally" (pp. 200–201). It was these very problems that caused Exner (1991) to attempt some discrimination concerning those diagnosed as depressed, subdividing them into those who are emotionally distraught; those who are cognitively discouraged, sluggish, and self-defeating; and, those who manifest learned helplessness. That effort led to the new Depression Index by incorporating a broader range of empirically derived criteria, tapping affective, behavioral and cognitive variables. The new DEPI has led to substantially greater success in identifying depression in both adults and children with Rorschach data, and this success is largely because the revised DEPI evolved from improved conceptualizations of the constructs.

Finally, it should be noted that many validation studies concerning the Rorschach focus on specific diagnostic issues. A major problem in these works is the adequacy of the criteria used to define the target group. Failures in reliable discrimination between those who "do" and those who "do not" display the particular diagnostic credentials are as much the responsibility of the diagnostic system (if not more so) than they are the presumed limitations of the clinical instrument. Thus, clinicians may use different sources of data to render diagnostic judgments (information variance) or differ in how they interpret or integrate such information (criterion variance) (Kirk & Kutchins, 1992). The diagnostic categories are far from homogeneous. A good example is depression. As Wiener (1989) noted, "Depression is used indiscriminantly as a label for a state, trait, sign, syndrome, disease, as a category name and, at the same time, as an explanatory concept" (p. 297). He observed that 286 possible combinations of signs or symptoms can result in a diagnosis of Dysthymic Disorder, given the presence of dysphoric mood. In the face of such diagnostic unreliability, the failure to document ideal discrimination between groups should not be construed as a problem inherent in the Rorschach technique. Regrettably, too many investigators have questioned that Rorschach for just such failures.

NEW INDICES OR CONTENT SCALES

It has been quite common for researchers to develop new indices or to explore special content scales in their efforts to understand personality or psychopathology. Thus, in slightly less than half of the studies conducted since 1985, investigators have incorporated variables that are not formally part of the Comprehensive System. A brief overview of these efforts may highlight several of the conceptual issues that bias Rorschach research as based on these approaches.

A simple tally of the traditional variables that have been the focus of Rorschach investigation in recent years reveals that the total number of responses (R), perceptual accuracy ($X+\%$, $Xu\%$, $X-\%$), Human Movement (M), Sum Shading, and Weighted Sum Color have been the most frequently examined variables. That R should be so popular is undoubtedly related to concerns about needing to control for the total number of responses in Rorschach research (e.g., Exner, 1992; Lipgar, 1992; Meyer, 1992a, 1993), and based on its centrality in defining basic some Rorschach dimensions.

The popularity of the other variables is related to the relative priority given to three central issues in the literature—*affective features* (Sum Shading and Weighted Sum Color), *ideation* (M), and *cognitive mediation* ($X+\%$, $Xu\%$, $X-\%$). Unfortunately, as noted earlier, these variables have not been investigated within the framework of more inclusive clusters (Exner, 1991), but mainly as single scores to be correlated with other independent criteria. Such simplistic approaches to research give a hit-or-miss impression to the field, and contribute to the inconsistencies, confusion, and even disarray that is evident in the Rorschach literature.

A number of Rorschach variables have received very little or no attention in the professional journals: *EBPervasive*, Level 2 Special Scores, the Obsessional Style and Hypervigilance Indices (OBS and HVI), $S-\%$, Location Sequencing, Confabulation Scores (CONFAB), Color Projection (CP), Shading-Shading Blends, the Coping Deficit Index (CDI), and Cooperative Movement (COP), among others. Three basic reasons account for this lack of research emphasis, namely, the newness of the variables (*EBPer*, COP, Lv2 Sp Sc, OBS, HVI, CDI, $S-\%$), the rarity of occurrence of the variables in Rorschach protocols (CP, Shading-Shading Blends, CONFAB), and the difficulty in researching the variable, such as Location Sequencing (Yama, Call, & Entezari, 1993).

Several texts have summarized special Rorschach clinical and research scales to assess personality and psychopathology (e.g., Aronow & Reznikoff, 1976; Goldfried et al., 1971; P. M. Lerner, 1975). The publication dates reveal that such approaches have been available for decades. An examination of recent literature, however, shows that some methods have proven to be more popular than others. These include measures of interpersonal/object relations, defensive operations, negative content, thought disorder, and several specialized indices. The once common emphasis on homosexual and organic signs (e.g., Goldfried et al., 1971) has waned for obvious reasons, and so has the focus on therapy prognosis, although it seems reasonable to predict that this latter area will receive renewed attention given the growing emphasis on the application of research measures in therapeutic practice

(R. R. Dies, 1991; R. R. Dies & K. R. Dies, 1993), and the incorporation of the Rorschach into psychotherapy research in more systematic ways (e.g., Exner & Andronikof-Sanglade, 1992; Weiner & Exner, 1991).

An area of considerable interest in the recent Rorschach literature is that of *interpersonal/object relations*, as documented by a number of major reviews (e.g., Fishler, Sperling, & Carr, 1990; Stricker & Healey, 1990; Tuber, 1989, 1992). Within this area, the Mutuality of Autonomy (MOA) Scale has received the most attention (Urist, 1977). The MOA is popular in empirical work with children (e.g., Donahue & Tuber, 1993; Leifer et al., 1991; Tuber, 1989; Tuber & Coates, 1989) and with adults (e.g., Berg, Packer, & Nunno, 1993; Blatt, Ford, Berman, Cook, & Meyer, 1988; Blatt, Tuber, & Auerbach, 1990; Strauss & Ryan, 1987). The MOA focuses on developmental movement toward separation–individuation by assigning scores to both animate and inanimate movement responses on the Rorschach. It is a 7-point continuum ranging from reciprocity–mutuality on one end to envelopment–incorporation on the other.

The Concept of the Object Scale (Blatt, Brenneis, Schimek, & Glick, 1976) has also attracted a fair amount of recent focus in the empirical literature (e.g., Blatt et al., 1988, 1990; Fritsch & Holmstrom, 1990; Stuart et al., 1990). In this approach, human figures on the Rorschach are assessed according to developmental principles of differentiation, articulation, motivational nature of the action, and the degree of integration of object and action, content of action, and nature of the interaction. Other measures of interpersonal/object relations include the Rorschach Interaction Scale (Graves, Phil, Mead, & Pearson, 1986), the Separation–Individuation Theme Scale (Coonerty, 1986), the Empathy Object Relationship Scale (Rydin, Asberg, Edman, & Schalling, 1990), the Symbiotic Phenomena Content Scale (Hirshberg, 1989), and the Poor/Good Human Experience Scale (Perry & Viglione, 1991).

Stricker and Healey (1990) concluded that "although the quality of research is improving, it remains plagued by the limitations of small numbers of subjects, few correlations with nontest data, such as clinicians' ratings or behavior checklists, and the large problem of accurately and reliably diagnosing the patient populations" (p. 227). The proliferation of such approaches is undoubtedly related to the current popularity of object-relations theory, borderline phenomena, and the ongoing quest to develop scales to quantify Rorschach content (Acklin, 1993b).

Two problems mentioned earlier are quite prevalent with these object relations rating systems. First, the idea that distinction means essence, and second the difficulties associated with criterion problems. The typical approach in using object relations coding schemes is to contrast two diagnostic groups, such as sexually abused girls (Leifer et al., 1991) or gender disturbed boys (Tuber & Coates, 1989), eating disordered patients (Strauss & Ryan, 1987), or borderline and depressive subjects (Stuart et al., 1990). Unfortunately, many investigators who detect significant differences between such groups conclude that they have identified a unique characteristic of their target sample, when in fact they have not attempted to replicate their contrasts with other comparison groups. Any obtained differences could just as readily be a function of different levels of pathology across diagnostic and normal groups, contextual differences in Rorschach administration, or a host of other influences. These studies have often taken single-sign approaches to research, without anchoring their variables in more broadly defined clusters.

Many of the content approaches to interpersonal assessment or object relationships base their ratings on Rorschach Movement scores or Human Content, which represent a very small portion of the information generated in the typical Rorschach. Thus, a handful of responses are used to offer broad generalizations about the quality of their subjects' interpersonal relationships. Most of these procedures are heavily influenced by psychoanalytic theory, so responses are generally interpreted as symbolic expressions of underlying personality dynamics. To assume that a few Rorschach answers, such as "something being consumed by fire" or "a giant impaled by a tree" directly reflect the person's sense of malevolence, overwhelming engulfment, and destruction in social relationships is a rather substantial conceptual leap for which empirical data are, essentially, nonexistent.

The mediating role of the person's defenses, the presence of other more constructive responses in the same record, and other structural variables will serve to qualify the manifestation of these more pathological imprints in the individual's actual interpersonal exchanges. For instance, Rorschach Form Quality will serve to moderate the impact of such deviant content in the persons' symptomatic expression (e.g., Blatt, Tuber, & Auerbach, 1990; Fritsch & Holmstrom, 1990).

Content-oriented approaches generally have been criticized as requiring too many chains of inference to specify the links between content symbolism and behavior in social contexts. Thus, according to Goldfried et al. (1971),

> the more closely a Rorschach index parallels the actual behavior it will be used to understand, discriminate, or predict, the greater the likelihood that it will be capable of the task. On the other hand, the more the Rorschach index is symbolic of the behavior being studied, the wider is the latitude for the kinds of unknown or uncontrolled sources of error variance that generally complicate symbolic interpretations of behavior. (p. 392)

A major limitation in these content-based methods is the failure to examine test–retest reliability, in spite of evidence that Rorschach content is quite susceptible to conscious manipulation. Thus, individuals who are instructed to provide different answers in a second Rorschach administration are quite able to do so; shifts in content are quite dramatic even though the Structural

Summary variables appear to be relatively unchanged (Exner, 1993). Obviously, content is not unimportant, as documented empirically by the role of special content scores in the Comprehensive System (e.g., AG, COP, MOR), but content is less reliable and clearly secondary to structural variables.

Research findings concerning the role of projection in Rorschach interpretation, which serves as the cornerstone for content approaches, suggest that it probably has been overemphasized. Stimulus classification appears to play a much more substantial role in forming most Rorschach responses (Exner, 1989). Most instructors who teach the Rorschach caution graduate students not to test family members and/or loved ones, due to the frequent appearance of unusual and seemingly disturbed responses, given by people who otherwise appear to be quite well adjusted. It has been argued (Exner, Armbruster, & Mittman 1978; Exner, 1991, 1993) that these kinds of answers tend to result from the failure of the subject to censor them after they are formed. Thus, situational factors, such as familiarity with the examiner, volunteering for psychological research (R. R. Dies & K. R. Dies, 1992), and malingering (Perry & Kinder, 1990), can often produce answers that otherwise might be discarded. Thus, approaches that rely on Rorschach content are potentially unreliable, and are somewhat precarious when issues of the validity of content scales are raised. This is especially problematic in efforts to use the Rorschach to identify enduring features of personality and/or to predict future behaviors that ignore the situational embeddedness of many aspects of personality (Ross & Nisbett, 1991). Goldfried and his colleagues (1971) labeled this the *problem of unmeasured variables*, which highlights both present and future extratest factors, as well as other variables relating to the criterion, that have not been sampled in the assessment process but influence the expression of subsequent actions.

The conceptual problems found with measures of interpersonal/object relations are also present with the other areas of content evaluation, particularly those that regard content as symbolic signs of underlying personality dynamics. In the area of *defensive operations*, for example, two approaches have dominated the scene, namely the Lerner and Lerner Scale for assessing primitive defenses (P. M. Lerner, 1990) and the Rorschach Defense Scales developed by Cooper and Arnow (e.g., Cooper, Perry, & Arnow, 1988; Cooper, Perry, & O'Connell, 1991). In the former, human figure responses are reviewed to judge the expression of the specific borderline defenses of splitting, devaluation, projective identification, and denial, whereas the latter scale employs a broader sampling of content to assess a more extensive listing of defensive operations. Although both procedures demonstrate some success in discriminating between pathological groups, they suffer from the same types of conceptual problems noted for the measures of interpersonal/object relationships.

H. Lerner, Albert, and Walsh (1987), for instance, conducted a concurrent validity study of the two rating systems to examine their effectiveness in discriminating among neurotic, inpatient and outpatient borderline, and schizophrenic patients. Although the authors argued that their findings "lend convincing support to the contention that borderline patients exhibit a specific and discernible defensive constellation" (p. 343), there were several problems with their investigation that raise serious doubts about the merits of their conclusions. First, they noted that most of their subjects, regardless of diagnostic label, displayed Rorschach content indicative of borderline defenses (i.e., the distinction is not essence problem) and, second, patients with schizotypal personality disorders were assigned to the borderline group on the basis of symptomatic overlap (i.e., the criterion problem). Finally, the results demonstrated that inpatient and outpatient borderline subjects differed from each other on the defense of Omnipotence, and did not jointly differ from the neurotics on any of the other defenses, and both only differed from the schizophrenic patients on the defense of Devaluation. Clearly, it would be difficult to agree with the authors' interpretation that "borderline" patients manifest a "specific and discernible" defensive structure.

H. Lerner et al. (1987) showed that rating systems may differ in the criteria they employ to define the same defense, reflecting their divergent theoretical foundations—that is, developmental structural deficit (Cooper et al., 1988) versus structural conflict (P. M. Lerner & H. Lerner, 1980)—and use different content to arrive at their judgments, but there is still appreciable commonality in their conceptualizations. Nevertheless, content symbolism is given priority in the interpretive process. Cooper et al. (1988) summarized that problems remain even when formal scores are incorporated (i.e., location, shape, color, and shading); the structural parameters often provide more information about cognitive style than defensive functioning per se.

The fact that content is important for understanding underlying personality dynamics and psychopathology cannot be eschewed. And, there is also agreement that those Rorschach responses containing Human Content (and Movement) may be especially revealing about interpersonal relationships and defensive functioning. No approach to the Rorschach disregards the qualitative aspects of such responses, after examination of the formal properties of Rorschach data within the clusters relating to Self (e.g., Pure H:Nonpure H, MOR, $3r+(2)/R$) and Interpersonal Perception (e.g., HVI, PER, COP, AG, Isol/R). On the other hand, it is somewhat impractical, especially in research, to attempt to squeeze so much meaning out of these types of projective material.

The research in the third area of content mentioned earlier (i.e., the focus on *negative content*) lends additional credence to this position. In this category, the most popular scales have been Elizur's (1949; Goldfried et al., 1971) scoring for Anxiety and Hostility. Studies using this approach to scoring have been popular for both children (e.g., Leifer et al., 1991; Singh, 1986; A. Spigelman & G. Spigelman, 1991a) and adults (e.g., Carlsson, 1987; Martin, Blair, & Hatzel, 1987; Rydin et al., 1990). Holt's (1977) measure of Primary Process Thinking (e.g., Caprara, Holt, Pazielli, & Giannotti, 1986; Hilsenroth, Hibbard, Nash, & Handler, 1993) and the Body-Image Boundary scoring system (e.g., Fisher & Cleveland, 1958; Jupp, 1989; Lumpkin, Pasternak, Cooper, & Pasnak, 1986; A. Spigelman & G. Spigelman, 1991b) have also been widely used. Findings concerning these various measures suggest that ratings of content that more directly portray affect will be more successful than judgments based on indirect material. In other words, a response of "two people fighting" will contribute more to behavioral prediction than will a response of a "knife," which may imply aggressive thoughts, or one of "the red represents anger," which reflects hostility more symbolically.

The problem with many of the projects involving negative content (and this is true in general for studies of content) is that authors often invent their own measures, and then publish their findings with little effort to cross-validate their rating systems or to build on prior research. The measures often have similar names, but use different criteria to anchor their variables. To illustrate, scales have been published recently to assess derepressed content (Viglione et al., 1991), primitive content (Perry & Viglione, 1991), traumatic content (Armstrong & Loewenstein, 1990), and projected apprehension and danger (Lipgar & Waehler, 1991). Most of these measures use traditional content categories (e.g., An, Bl, Ex, Fi, Sx), but there are glaring inconsistencies in how these codes are used across the various research initiatives. Thus, problems with external validity abound and contribute significantly to conceptual problems.

The final category of content scale relates to measures of thought disorder. Here too, a variety of scales exist, but these approaches are based primarily on the premise that Rorschach content represents a sample of a type of thought distortion or preoccupation rather than an indirect sign of an underlying conflict or defense. Thus, there is the Thought Disorder Index (e.g., Carpenter et al., 1993; Edell, 1987; Harris, 1993; Holzman, Shenton, & Solovay, 1986; Shenton, Solovay, & Holzman, 1987), Blatt's measure of impaired thinking (e.g., Blatt et al., 1988), an index of primitive thought (Rydin et al., 1990), and Wilson's (1985) measure of thought disorder (Saunders, 1991), among others. For the most part, the goal is to evaluate the types of cognitive dysfunction included in the six Critical Special Scores in the Comprehensive System (i.e., DV, DR, INC, FAB, ALOG, and CONTAM), but there is considerable variation in the criteria and complexity used to define the variables in the rating schemes.

Other types of derived measures or new scores also appear in the literature to assess a variety of constructs, including: alexithymia (Acklin & Bernat, 1987), dissociation (Saunders, 1991), energy level (Insua & Loza, 1986), and grandiosity (Berg, 1990; Hilsenroth et al., 1993). But, there is very little replication and most of these investigations fail to provide a solid conceptual framework to interpret their results. When significant group contrasts are obtained with such measures, it is generally difficult to disentangle meaningful from serendipitous results, to eliminate competing explanations of the findings (due to problems with internal validity), or to place much confidence in generalizations that may be offered (due to difficulties relating to external validity).

CONCLUSIONS

Investigators often overlook a number of central problems that may seriously jeopardize the merits of their conclusions. Some studies lack appropriate control groups, and researchers have not devoted sufficient attention to adequate definition of their clinical samples or to unknown confounds that might compromise the integrity of their results. This chapter highlights four major problems that relate to the conceptual aspects of Rorschach research. These problems relate to the meaning of group differences, empirical versus conceptual approaches to research, criterion problems or the relationship between Rorschach variables and independent measures, and the exploration of special content scales or indices derived from structural data.

In each of these four areas, investigators have often failed to establish a conceptual foundation for their research. They have focused on a relatively narrow band of Rorschach variables and have not anchored these scores in clusters or data sets that integrate potential findings into a more coherent framework for interpretation. As a consequence, many studies give a hit-or-miss impression, and generalizations across investigations are difficult due to inconsistent or often confusing results. Some researchers have questioned the validity of the Rorschach because they have failed to fully understand the pervasive influence of criterion problems in their empirical investigations. Thus, faced with nonsignificant or limited results, researchers have dismissed particular Rorschach scores or constellations as unproductive, instead of recognizing that the criterion measures may have been inappropriate, or that the nature of the correlations should have been expected given the differing perspectives on personality or psychopathology furnished by the Rorschach and other assessment instruments.

In examining group differences, researchers have tended to misinterpret their own findings as Rorschach signs that define the essence of their clinical samples. Although group differences are often obtained, the resulting clinical signs do not prove to be unique or even characteristic of a majority of the patients manifesting particular diagnostic credentials. Investigators often fail to explore base rates or false-positive/false-negative rates to truly evaluate the discriminatory potential of their Rorschach indices, or often fail to cross-validate their Rorschach signs in relationship to alternative comparison groups. These failures make it impossible to conclude that a distinguishing feature is indeed a hallmark of a particular disorder. The lack of planned comparisons and a sound conceptual structure frequently makes it difficult to account for unanticipated differences and, unfortunately, many investigators do not adequately consider alternative explanations of their findings.

Efforts to evaluate Rorschach content in the areas of object relations, defensive functioning, and negative affect have relied too heavily on content symbolism, despite substantial evidence that the Rorschach is more effectively viewed as a complex cognitive-behavioral task. Although content approaches certainly cannot be discounted as purely intuitive and without empirical grounding, the findings suggest that the integration of structural variables and content within empirically derived clusters would produce better results.

REFERENCES

Acklin, M. W. (1993a). Integrating the Rorschach and the MMPI in clinical assessment: Conceptual and methodological issues. *Journal of Personality Assessment, 60,* 125–131.

Acklin, M. W. (1993b). Psychodiagnosis of personality structure: II. Borderline personality organization. *Journal of Personality Assessment, 61,* 329–341.

Acklin, M. W., & Bernat, E. (1987). Depression, alexithymia, and pain prone disorder: A Rorschach study. *Journal of Personality Assessment, 51,* 462–479.

Alpher, V. S., Perfetto, G. A., Henry, W. P., & Strupp, H. H. (1990). The relationship between the Rorschach and assessment of the capacity to engage in short-term dynamic psychotherapy. *Psychotherapy, 27,* 224–229.

Anderson, T., & Dixon, W. E. (1993). The factor structure of the Rorschach for adolescent inpatients. *Journal of Personality Assessment, 60,* 319–332.

Archer, R. P., & Gordon, R. A. (1988). MMPI and Rorschach indices of schizophrenic and depressive diagnoses among adolescent inpatients. *Journal of Personality Assessment, 52,* 276–287.

Archer, R. P., & Krishnamurthy, R. (1993a). Combining the Rorschach and the MMPI in the assessment of adolescents. *Journal of Personality Assessment, 60,* 132–140.

Archer, R. P., & Krishnamurthy, R. (1993b). A review of MMPI and Rorschach interrelationships in adult samples. *Journal of Personality Assessment, 61,* 277–293.

Armstrong, J. G., & Loewenstein, R. J. (1990). Characteristics of patients with multiple personality and dissociative disorders on psychological testing. *Journal of Nervous and Mental Disease, 178,* 448–454.

Aronow, E., & Reznikoff, M. (1976). *Rorschach content interpretation.* New York: Grune & Stratton.

Atkinson, L., Quarrington, B., Alp, I. E., & Cyr, J. J. (1986). Rorschach validity: An empirical approach to the literature. *Journal of Clinical Psychology, 42,* 360–362.

Ball, J. D., Archer, R. P., Gordon, R. A., & French, J. (1991). Rorschach depression indices with children and adolescents: Concurrent validity findings. *Journal of Personality Assessment, 57,* 465–476.

Belter, R. W., Lipovsky, J. A., & Finch, A. J. (1989). Rorschach Egocentricity Index and self-concept in children and adolescents. *Journal of Personality Assessment, 53,* 783–789.

Berg, J. (1990). Differentiating ego functions of borderline and narcissistic personalities. *Journal of Personality Assessment, 55,* 537–548.

Berg, J. L., Packer, A., & Nunno, V. J. (1993). A Rorschach analysis: Parallel disturbance in thought and in self/object representation. *Journal of Personality Assessment, 61,* 311–323.

Blatt, S. J., Brenneis, C. B., Schimek, J. G., & Glick, M. (1976). *A developmental analysis of the concept of the object on the Rorschach.* Unpublished manual, Yale University School of Medicine, Department of Psychiatry, New Haven, CT.

Blatt, S. J., Ford, R. Q., Berman, W., Cook, B., & Meyer, R. (1988). The assessment of change during the intensive treatment of borderline and schizophrenic young adults. *Psychoanalytic Psychology, 5,* 127–158.

Blatt, S. J., Tuber, S. B., & Auerbach, J. S. (1990). Representation of interpersonal interactions on the Rorschach and level of psychopathology. *Journal of Personality Assessment, 54,* 711–728.

Boswell, D. L. (1989). Rorschach EB as a predictor of imaging style. *Perceptual and Motor Skills, 68,* 1001–1002.

Caprara, G. V., Holt, R. R., Pazielli, M. F., & Giannotti, A. (1986). The development of primary process in children's Rorschachs. *Journal of Personality Assessment, 50,* 149–170.

Carlsson, A. M. (1987). Personality analysis using the Rorschach test in patients with chronic, non-malignant pain. *British Journal of Projective Psychology, 32,* 34–52.

Carpenter, J. T., Coleman, M. J., Waternaux, C. M., Perry, J., Wong, H., O'Brian, C., & Holzman, P. S. (1993). The Thought Disorder Index: Short-form assessments. *Psychological Assessment, 5,* 75–80.

Colson, D. B., Pickar, D. B., & Coyne, L. (1989). Rorschach correlates of treatment difficulty in a long-term psychiatric hospital. *Bulletin of the Menniger Clinic, 53,* 52–57.

Coonerty, S. (1986). An exploration of separation–individuation themes in the borderline personality disorder. *Journal of Personality Assessment, 50,* 501–511.

Cooper, S. H., Perry, J. C., & Arnow, D. (1988). An empirical approach to the study of defense mechanisms: I. Reliability and preliminary validity of the Rorschach Defense Scales. *Journal of Personality Assessment, 52,* 187–203.

Cooper, S. H., Perry, J. C., & O'Connell, M. (1991). The Rorschach Defense Scales. II. Longitudinal perspectives. *Journal of Personality Assessment, 56,* 191–201.

Crowley, S. L., Worchel, F. F., & Ash, M. J. (1992). Self-report, peer-report, and teacher-report measures of childhood depression: An analysis by item. *Journal of Personality Assessment, 59,* 189–203.

Dies, R. R. (1991). Clinician and researcher: Mutual growth through dialogue. In S. Tuttman (Ed.), *Psychoanalytic group theory and therapy.* Madison, CT: International Universities Press.

Dies, R. R., & Dies, K. R. (1992). *Malingering PTSD in the Rorschach: An experimental exploration.* Unpublished manuscript, University of Maryland, College Park, MD.

Dies, R. R., & Dies, K. R. (1993). The role of evaluation in clinical practice: Overview and group treatment illustration. *International Journal of Group Psychotherapy, 43,* 77–105.

Dijkman-Caes, C. I. M., Kraan, H. F., & DeVries, M. W. (1993). Research on panic disorder and agoraphobia in daily life: A review of current studies. *Journal of Anxiety Disorders, 7,* 235–247.

Donahue, P. J., & Tuber, S. B. (1993). Rorschach adaptive fantasy images and coping in children under severe environmental stress. *Journal of Personality Assessment, 60,* 421–434.

Duricko, A. J., Norcross, J. C., & Buskirk, R. D. (1989). Correlates of the Egocentricity Index in child and adolescent outpatients. *Journal of Personality Assessment, 53,* 184–187.

Edell, W. S. (1987). Role of structure in disordered thinking in borderline and schizophrenic disorders. *Journal of Personality Assessment, 51,* 23–41.

Elizur, A. (1949). Content analysis of the Rorschach with regard to anxiety and hostility. *Rorschach Research Exchange and Journal of Projective Techniques, 13,* 247–284.

Elwood, R. W. (1993). Psychological tests and clinical discriminations: Beginning to address the base rate problem. *Clinical Psychology Review, 13,* 409–419.

Exner, J. E. (1974). *The Rorschach: A comprehensive system* (Vol. 1). New York: Wiley.

Exner, J. E. (1986a). *The Rorschach: A comprehensive system: Vol. 1. Basic foundations* (2nd ed.). New York: Wiley.

Exner, J. E. (1986b). Some Rorschach data comparing schizophrenics with borderline and schizotypal personality disorders. *Journal of Personality Assessment, 50,* 455–471.

Exner, J. E. (1987). Computer assistance in Rorschach interpretation. *British Journal of Projective Psychology, 32,* 2–19.

Exner, J. E. (1989). Searching for projection in the Rorschach. *Journal of Personality Assessment, 53,* 520–536.

Exner, J. E. (1991). *The Rorschach: A comprehensive system: Vol. 2. Interpretation* (2nd ed.). New York: Wiley.

Exner, J. E. (1992). *R* in Rorschach research: A ghost revisited. *Journal of Personality Assessment, 58,* 245–251.

Exner, J. E. (1993). *The Rorschach: A comprehensive system: Vol. 1. Basic foundations* (3rd ed.). New York: Wiley.

Exner, J. E., & Andronikof-Sanglade, A. (1992). Rorschach changes following brief and short-term therapy. *Journal of Personality Assessment, 59,* 59–71.

Exner, J. E., Armbruster, G., & Mittman, B. (1978). The Rorschach response process. *Journal of Personality Assessment, 42,* 27–38.

Fisher, S., & Cleveland, S. E. (1958). *Body image and personality.* New York: Van Nostrand Reinhold.

Fishler, P. H., Sperling, M. B., & Carr, A. C. (1990). Assessment of adult relatedness: A review of empirical findings from object relations and attachment theories. *Journal of Personality Assessment, 55,* 499–520.

Frank, G. (1991). Research on the clinical usefulness of the Rorschach: 2. The assessment of cerebral dysfunction. *Perceptual and Motor Skills, 72,* 103–111.

Fritsch, R. C., & Holmstrom, R. W. (1990). Assessing object representations as a continuous variable: A modification of the concept of the object on the Rorschach scale. *Journal of Personality Assessment, 55,* 319–334.

Gelso, C. J., & Fretz, B. R. (1992). *Counseling psychology.* Orlando, FL: Harcourt Brace Jovanovich.

Goldfreid, M. R., Stricker, G., & Weiner, I. B. (1971). *Rorschach handbook of clinical and research applications.* Engelwood Cliffs, NJ: Prentice-Hall.

Graves, P. L., Phil, M., Mead, L. A., & Pearson, T. A. (1986). The Rorschach Interaction Scale as a potential predictor of cancer. *Psychosomatic Medicine, 48,* 549–563.

Greenwald, D. F. (1990). An external construct validity study of Rorschach personality variables. *Journal of Personality Assessment, 55,* 768–780.

Greenwald, D. F. (1991). Personality dimensions reflected by the Rorschach and the 16PF. *Journal of Clinical Psychology, 47,* 708–715.

Harder, D. W., Greenwald, D. F., Ritzler, B. A., Strauss, J. S., & Kokes, R. F. (1988). The Last–Weiss Rorschach Ego-Strength Scale as a prognostic measure for psychiatric inpatients. *Journal of Personality Assessment, 52,* 106–115.

Harris, D. (1993). The prevalence of thought disorder in personality-disordered outpatients. *Journal of Personality Assessment, 61,* 112–120

Hilsenroth, M. J., Hibbard, S. R., Nash, M. R., & Handler, L. (1993). A Rorschach study of narcissism, defense, and aggression in borderline, narcissistic, and cluster C personality disorders. *Journal of Personality Assessment, 60,* 346–361.

Hirshberg, L. M. (1989). Rorschach images of symbiosis and separation in eating-disordered and in borderline and nonborderline subjects. *Psychoanalytic Psychology, 6,* 475–493.

Holt, R. R. (1977). A method for assessing primary process manifestations and their control in Rorschach responses. In M. Rickers-Ovsiankina (Ed.), *Rorschach psychology* (pp. 375–420). New York: Kreiger.

Holzman, P. S., Shenton, M. E., & Solovay, M. R. (1986). Quality of thought disorder in differential diagnosis. *Schizophrenia Bulletin, 12*, 360–372.

Insua, A. M., & Loza, S. M. (1986). Psychometric patterns on the Rorschach of healthy elderly persons and patients with suspected dementia. *Perceptual and Motor Skills, 63*, 931–936.

Jupp, J. J. (1989). Fisher and Cleveland barrier and penetration scores: Correlations with Rorschach category scores. *Perceptual and Motor Skills, 69*, 1011–1018.

Kirk, S. A., & Kutchins, H. (1992). *The selling of DSM: The rhetoric of science in psychiatry.* New York: Aldine DeGruyter.

Leifer, M., Shapiro, J. P., Martone, M. W., & Kassem, L. (1991). Rorschach assessment of psychological functioning in sexually abused girls. *Journal of Personality Assessment, 56*, 14–28.

Lerner, H., Albert, C., & Walsh, M. (1987). The Rorschach assessment of borderline defenses. *Journal of Personality Assessment, 51*, 344–354.

Lerner, P. M. (Ed.). (1975). *Handbook of Rorschach scales.* New York: International Universities Press.

Lerner, P. M. (1990). Rorschach assessment of primitive defenses: A review. *Journal of Personality Assessment, 54*, 30–46.

Lerner, P. M., & Lerner, H. (1980). Rorschach assessment of primitive defenses in borderline personality structure. In J. Kwawer, H. Lerner, P. Lerner, & A. Sugarman (Eds.), *Borderline phenomena and the Rorschach* (pp. 257–274). Madison, CT: International Universities Press.

Lipgar, R. M. (1992). The problem of R in the Rorschach: The value of varying responses. *Journal of Personality Assessment, 58*, 223–230.

Lipgar, R. M., & Waehler, C. A. (1991). A Rorschach investigation of mothers of behaviorally disturbed infants. *Journal of Personality Assessment, 56*, 106–117.

Lipovsky, J. A., Finch, A. J., & Belter, R. W. (1989). Assessment of depression in adolescents: Objective and projective measures. *Journal of Personality Assessment, 53*, 449–458.

Lumpkin, V. G., Pasternak, R. J., Cooper, G. D., & Pasnak, R. (1986). Prediction of differences in Rorschach protocols from the Personality Assessment System. *Perceptual and Motor Skills, 63*, 175–184.

Maris, R. W. (1992). Overview of the study of suicide assessment and prediction. In R. W. Maris, A. L. Berman, J. T. Maltsberger, & R. I. Yufit (Eds.), *Assessment and prediction of suicide* (pp.). New York: Guilford.

Martin, J. D., Blair, G. E., & Hatzel, D. J. (1987). Rorschach correlates of state and trait anxiety in college students. *Perceptual and Motor Skills, 64*, 539–543.

Meyer, G. J. (1992a). Response frequency problems in the Rorschach: Clinical and research implications with suggestions for the future. *Journal of Personality Assessment, 58*, 231–244.

Meyer, G. J. (1992b). The Rorschach's factor structure: A contemporary investigation and historical review. *Journal of Personality Assessment, 59*, 117–136.

Meyer, G. J. (1993). The impact of response frequency on the Rorschach constellation indices and on their validity with diagnostic and MMPI-2 criteria. *Journal of Personality Assessment, 60*, 153–180.

Parker, K. C. H., Hanson, R. K., & Hunsley, J. (1988). MMPI, Rorschach, and WAIS: A meta-analytic comparison of reliability, stability, and validity. *Psychological Bulletin, 103*, 367–373.

Perry, G. G., & Kinder, B. N. (1990). The susceptibility of the Rorschach to malingering: A critical review. *Journal of Personality Assessment, 54*, 47–57.

Perry, W., & Viglione, D. J. (1991). The Ego Impairment Index as a predictor of outcome in melancholic depressed patients treated with tricyclic antidepressants. *Journal of Personality Assessment, 56*, 487–501.

Piotrowski, Z. (1937). The Rorschach inkblot method in organic disturbances of the central nervous system. *Journal of Nervous and Mental Disease, 86*, 525–537.

Ros Plana, M. (1990). *An investigation concerning the malingering of features of depression on the Rorschach and MMPI.* Unpublished doctoral dissertation, University of Barcelona.

Ross, L., & Nisbett, R. E. (1991). *The person and the situation: Perspectives of social psychology.* New York: McGraw-Hill.

Rydin, E., Asberg, M., Edman, G., & Schalling, D. (1990). Violent and nonviolent suicide attempts—a controlled Rorschach study. *Acta Psychiatrica Scandinavica, 82,* 30–38.

Saunders, E. A. (1991). Rorschach indicators of chronic childhood sexual abuse in female borderline inpatients. *Bulletin of the Menninger Clinic, 55,* 48–71.

Schretlen, D. J. (1988). The use of psychological tests to identify malingered symptoms of mental disorder. *Clinical Psychology Review, 8,* 451–476.

Shapiro, J. P., Leifer, M., Martone, M. W., & Kassem, L. (1990). Multimethod assessment of depression in sexually abused girls. *Journal of Personality Assessment, 55,* 234–248.

Shenton, M. E., Solovay, M. R., & Holzman, P. (1987). Comparative studies of thought disorders: II. Schizoaffective disorder. *Archives of General Psychiatry, 44,* 21–30.

Singer, H. K., & Brabender, V. (1993). The use of the Rorschach to differentiate unipolar and bipolar disorders. *Journal of Personality Assessment, 60,* 333–345.

Singh, S. (1986). Correlates of Rorschach measure of hostility. *Psychological Studies, 31,* 98–102.

Simon, M. J. (1989). Comparison of the Rorschach Comprehensive System's Isolation Index and MMPI Social Introversion score. *Psychological Reports, 65,* 499–502.

Smith, J. E., Hillard, M. C., Walsh, R. A., Kubacki, S. R., & Morgan, C. D. (1991). Rorschach assessment of purging and nonpurging. *Journal of Personality Assessment, 56,* 277–288.

Spigelman, A., & Spigelman, G. (1991a). Indications of depression and distress in divorce and nondivorce children reflected by the Rorschach test. *Journal of Personality Assessment, 57,* 120–129.

Spigelman, A., & Spigelman, G. (1991b). The relationship between parental divorce and the child's body boundary definiteness. *Journal of Personality Assessment, 56,* 96–105.

Strauss, J., & Ryan, R. M. (1987). Autonomy disturbances in subtypes of anorexia nervosa. *Journal of Abnormal Psychology, 96,* 254–258.

Stricker, G., & Healey, B. J. (1990). Projective assessment of object relations: A review of the empirical literature. *Psychological Assessment, 2,* 219–230.

Strupp, H. H., & Hadley, S. W. (1977). A tripartite model of mental health and therapy outcomes. *American Psychologist, 32,* 187–196.

Stuart, J., Westen, D., Lohr, N., Benjamin, J., Becker, S., Vorus, N., & Silk, K. (1990). Object relations in borderlines, depressives, and normals: An examination of human responses on the Rorschach. *Journal of Personality Assessment, 55,* 296–318.

Tuber, S. (1989). Assessment of children's object-representations with the Rorschach. *Bulletin of the Menninger Clinic, 53,* 432–441.

Tuber, S. (1992). Empirical and clinical assessments of children's object relations and object representations. *Journal of Personality Assessment, 58,* 179–197.

Tuber, S., & Coates, S. (1989). Indices of psychopathology in the Rorschachs of boys with severe gender identity disorder: A comparison with normal control subjects. *Journal of Personality Assessment, 53,* 100–112.

Urist, J. (1977). The Rorschach test and the assessment of object relations. *Journal of Personality Assessment, 41,* 3–9.

Viglione, D. J., Brager, R., & Haller, N. (1991). Psychoanalytic interpretation of the Rorschach: Do we have better hieroglyphics? *Journal of Personality Assessment, 57,* 1–9.

Vincent, K. R., & Harman, M. J. (1991). The Exner Rorschach: An analysis of its clinical validity. *Journal of Clinical Psychology, 47,* 596–599.

Wald, B. K., Archer, R. P., & Winstead, B. A. (1990). Rorschach characteristics of mothers of incest victims. *Journal of Personality Assessment, 55,* 417–425.

Weiner, I. B. (1986). Conceptual and empirical perspectives on the Rorschach assessment of psychopathology. *Journal of Personality Assessment, 50,* 472–479.

Weiner, I. B. (1993). Clinical considerations in the conjoint use of the Rorschach and the MMPI. *Journal of Personality Assessment, 60*, 148–152.

Weiner, I. B., & Exner, J. E. (1991). Rorschach changes in long-term and short-term psychotherapy. *Journal of Personality Assessment, 56*, 453–465.

Weisberg, L. J., Norman, D. K., & Herzog, D. B. (1987). Personality functioning in normal weight bulimia. *International Journal of Eating Disorders, 6*, 615–631.

Wiener, M. (1989). Psychopathology reconsidered: Depressions interpreted as psychosocial transactions. *Clinical Psychology Review, 9*, 295–321.

Wilson, A. (1985). Boundary disturbance in borderline and psychotic states. *Journal of Personality Assessment, 49*, 346–355.

Yama, M. F., Call, S. E., & Entezari, P. (1993). A new test of an old hypothesis: A quantification of sequence in the Rorschach. *Journal of Personality Assessment, 60*, 60–73.

CHAPTER THREE

Formulating Issues in Rorschach Research

Donald J. Viglione and John E. Exner, Jr.

Rorschach research can be grossly and imperfectly differentiated between investigations aimed to validate the test and investigations that assume the test is valid for specific purposes. Within that differentiation, several general research models can be identified. For instance, classic experimental methodology is sometimes used in research that seeks to validate the aspects of the test. In these designs, subjects are randomly assigned to groups, exposed to experimental manipulations, and Rorschach variables are dependent measures. Although these type of studies occur rather infrequently in Rorschach literature, they often have yielded very important findings about the test and its applications.

Some examples of this type of research are Colligan and Exner (1985), who studied brief exposure times with schizophrenics, medical patients, and nonpatients; Exner (1989), who investigated response sets and projection; Exner, Armbruster, and Mittman (1978), who studied several issues of response set on the response process; Haller and Exner (1985), who investigated temporal consistency of structural data; and Viglione and Exner (1983), who studied social-evaluative stress. Knowledge about the Rorschach would be greatly enhanced by more experimental and response process investigations.

A second type of design also focuses on issues of test validity. It is the test–retest form of investigation oriented to learn more about the temporal consistency of variables. Numerous such studies have been published (Exner, 1986; Exner, Armbruster, & Viglione, 1978; Haller & Exner, 1985). The results of these studies offer important information about test variables, and some correlational and factor analytic studies address interrelationships among variables. Although these types of studies provide information about test variables, and sometimes about the test process (Exner, 1988), they also are subject to overinterpretation when readers do not fully appreciate the fact that such intra-Rorschach studies lack independent validity criteria (Exner, Viglione, & Gillespie, 1984; Mason, Cohen, & Exner, 1986). Unfortunately, it appears that these and other intercorrelational and factor analytic studies have induced researchers to attribute undue importance to findings without independent validity criteria.

Another type of correlational study is reported more often in meetings than in print. These are the studies that report numerous, often insignificant, correlations between self-report measures and the Rorschach. They tend to highlight the potential amount of method variance, possibly peculiar to self-report, when contrasted to studies with stronger results between Rorschach variables and variables other than derived from self-report (Shapiro, Leifer, Martone, & Kassem, 1990).

A fourth type of research constitutes the majority of published studies. These are investigations in which the Rorschach is accepted as valid for specific purposes. These designs aim to explore differences between some target group relative to comparison groups, or to search out homogeneity with a target group. Typically, they involve purportedly homogeneous diagnostic groups or groups who have shared a common experience. These are essentially cross-sectional studies and, sometimes, have contributed much to the knowledge and understanding of Rorschach scores. In most of these investigations, Rorschach variables generally are used as dependent variables in parametric analysis. Unfortunately, many of these studies suffer a lack of adequate control groups or from data analysis problems.

A fifth type of research focuses more directly on issues of construct validation. Much of this research comes from psychoanalytic traditions and aims to validate psychoanalytic constructs: Blatt, Brenneis, Schimek, and Glick (1976) studied the representation of psychoanalytic objects in the Rorschach; Cooper, Perry, and Arnow (1988) addressed the issue of defense mechanisms; Coonerty (1986) investigated separation–individuation; Hirshberg (1989) identified images in symbiosis in separation among eating disordered subjects; P. Lerner and H. Lerner (1980) studied primitive defenses in borderline patients; Russ (1987) investigated creativity and adaptive regression; and Urist (1977) studied mutuality of autonomy.

At times, these studies focus more on the validation of a scale being used or developed than on the underlying construct. In these works, psychoanalytic notions are translated into Rorschach scores and compared among groups who theoretically differ on some underlying trait. The designs are most often cross-sectional or correlational, but some authors have been more ambitious in utilizing predictive and longitudinal factors. For instance, Blatt et al. (1976) used a logitudinal design with multiple testings over 20 years, whereas Cooper, Perry, and O'Connell, (1991) used a format involving multiple structured interviews and self-report instruments over a 3-year period after the initial Rorschach. Others, such as Blatt, Tuber, and Auerbach (1990) and Urist (1977), have gone beyond mere diagnostic contrasts and utilized more compelling criterion variables. These authors constructed behavioral rating scales to address social interactions and relationships. Being behaviorally based, these measures do not share measurement variance with the Rorschach and also permit much easier generalization to real work correlates.

THE LITERATURE AS A BASIS FOR RESEARCH

Investigators who become intrigued with an issue usually turn to the literature with the expectation that, when culled through carefully, it will reveal information regarding the accumulated wisdoms that focus on the issue at hand. Supposedly, the literature that provides a summation of theory and findings to date, calls attention to questions and hypotheses, and findings concerning variables are specified. In theory this is true, but in practice the literature can be like a pit into which the naive researcher may fall if exquisite caution is not exercised. Although thousands of Rorschach-related studies have been published, a substantial proportion have been marked by flaws of one sort or another.

CRITICALLY EVALUATING THE LITERATURE

It is impossible to overestimate the importance of a careful and critical evaluation of literature when formulating a research plan. Unfortunately, all literature cannot be afforded equal weight. Some journals do not use blind peer review in evaluating submitted manuscripts, and a few exist in which almost any article can be published provided the author(s) pays the cost for the publication. Fortunately, most Rorschach-related publications do not appear in those journals, but occasionally, some articles concerning the Rorschach do appear in them, and obviously, they should be evaluated very cautiously.

This does not necessarily mean that all publications in well-regarded journals can be assumed to have equal quality because, in spite of conscientiousness, investigators often become negligent, possibly because their commitment sometimes clouds over potential flaws in their concepts or designs. Then too, published studies vary greatly for clarity concerning important parameters. This variability poses a substantial challenge to readers, especially those who are reviewing the literature with an eye to formulating research. When research goals, variables, operational definitions, or hypotheses are vague, little can be extracted, and some of what is extracted may be misleading; or, when conclusions extend well beyond the realistic limits of the data, the naive reader is easily misled.

Although it is easy to be critical of authors because of their errors, the main criticism probably should be leveled at those who perpetuate those errors in subsequent research. In other words, investigators who accept conclusions naively, or who fail to address previously published works critically, do little more than sustain those errors in the future. Even seemingly solid studies that, as a group, illustrate the great variety in Rorschach research, can be and should be addressed critically by anyone vested in research. Despite good designs, careful analyses, and reasonable interpretations, many studies also incorporate the same weaknesses that should be detected by the serious investigator.

Many studies are flawed because of issues involving methodology or data analysis, but a seemingly larger number fall into one of three categories of problems regarding the basic formulations that underpin the study. The first of these include studies that do not have specified hypotheses. Instead, the study is conceptualized only in very vague terms. This can lead to many problems in sorting through data and/or interpreting findings. A second category consists of studies in which there is a failure to delineate hypotheses in a conceptual framework. This also poses some serious stumbling blocks to data analyses and to the interpretation of findings. A third group involves studies in which hypotheses have been generated from an inadequate understanding of the issue, or without a critical evaluation of the literature related to an issue.

Failing to Specify Hypotheses

Sometimes, Rorschach researchers are enticed to conduct studies in which the objectives are not very precise. Rorschach's are routinely administered to subjects under many different conditions and a naive assumption seems to be that Rorschach variables will produce an ideal, homogeneous picture of personality features within a group. Historically, many investigators have addressed questions about Rorschach findings without grounding those questions in a framework concerning personality, and have calculated hundreds of significant tests in hopes of uncovering truths about the test and/or truths about people (Cronbach, 1949; Weiner, 1977). In most of these studies, it has been common to try to develop checklists of scores that appear to have some discriminating potential. For instance, a checklist might discriminate between successful accountants and successful pilots. Unfortunately, such findings usually contibute little and have only a remote possibility of being replicated.

Typically, investigators who do this sort of research do not frame research questions in a theoretical context, or even with regard for the results of previous empirical work. Instead they develop investigations that are predicated on questions such as "What if . . . ?" or "Let's see . . ." The resulting designs are variously described as "shotgun," "pebble picking," or "hunt-and-peck" approaches. At times, the results of such approaches can be very important, mainly because they raise new questions to be addressed in future research. Major problems exist within most such studies, however, because investigators usually do not specify the basic building blocks found in most research, that is, reasonably well-developed hypotheses and specification of independent variables, dependent variables, and controls. Even when a hypothesis is offered, it is very general and not well grounded. More often than not, there is no solid underpinning for one hypothesis versus other possibilities, and often, there is no systematic identification of variables expected to effect the phenomenon under study. In addition, there is no attempt to categorize potential influences into independent, classification, or dependent variables, or to account properly for controls or randomized (error) variables (Meehl, 1978).

Fortunately, such extreme flaws are less common in contemporary Rorschach research than was once the case. It is likely that progress in research design, and specific cautions about Rorschach research, such as offered by Cronbach (1949) and Weiner (1977), have improved the quality of Rorschach investigations, prompting more studies that test specific hypotheses based on concepts derived from an understanding of personality and/or psychopathology. Nonetheless, many Rorschach studies are still diffuse and more closely resemble random pebble-picking rather than enlightened hypothesis testing.

For instance, Lipgar and Wahler (1991) attempted to identify characteristics of 30 mothers of behaviorally disturbed infant boys and selected Beck Rorschach variables associated with intellectual, affective, and interpersonal domains. This study would have been improved considerably if they had identifed the specific mechanisms that might explain the difficulties these women might have as mothers. In addition, it would be better to have been more precise about state effects, such as accounting for changes on the Rorschach resulting from the experience with difficult infants. In addition, Lipgar and Wahler did not offer explicit hypotheses, and the reader is left with the task of vaguely reconstructing one—namely, the supposition that mothers of behaviorally disturbed children should look worse on the Rorschach. In fact, the research aims are stated in an open-ended fashion and too closely resemble a curiosity rather than a scientific question, that is, "Let's see if these groups differ so that we can learn something that they may be helpful therapeutically." The many ways that one can falter as a mother, the even more numerous personality issues that might be associated with these interactional behavioral patterns, and the effects of the child and the perceived failure on the personality of the mother make the target group extremely heterogeneous, and the results difficult to evaluate.

These criticisms are not offered to discourage exploratory research, for at times, it can yield very important findings. For instance, the original validation data concerning m was derived from a classic study by Shalit (1965) in which Rorschachs were collected under very adverse and seemingly stressful circumstances. On the other hand, most pebble-picking works do not approximate the Shalit study. Instead, most are grounded in a rather simplistic assumption of homogeneity within a group, that is, all sex abusers will have similiar features, or all sexually abused individuals will have common characteristics. Studies such as these may be worth conducting, but only if there is a clear reason to expect that the findings will provide the level of discimination that is implicit in the general hypothesis.

Failing to Form Meaningful Hypotheses

Well-designed studies try to address reality. They employ methods that convey a reasonable understanding of the Rorschach, in terms of its construction, interpretation, or ability to discriminate. Studies are sometimes designed in accordance with these understandings and hypotheses may be offered, but they are overly diffuse. These are the investigations that include many independent and dependent variables. Usually the results do not yield much, and the studies themselves have many pitfalls. For instance, a study involving 3 independent variables and as many as 10 dependent variables can be designed, but at least 150 subjects would be required to assure statistical confidence in testing the several hypotheses that would be involved. Ordinarily, dependent variables should be selected in a conceptually meaningful framework, and the number selected should be reasonable in light of the number of available subjects. If the dependent variables are selected in the context of some theoretical or empirical position, the probability of positive results is increased. Similarly, unconfounded and pertinent independent variables allow unambiguous and accurate attribution of results. Associated variables that are controlled in the research design strengthen the likelihood of a true test of a hypothesis, and confidence in ruling out rival hypotheses.

In the optimal situation, researchers will clearly specify their aims by translating the research questions into general, descriptive hypotheses, couched in nonstatistical language. These assertions usually are called *substantive* or *logical hypotheses* and are translated into *statistical hypotheses*. The statistical hypotheses refer to the actual expectations of the numerical data, that is, statements about means, interactions, beta weights, and so on. Taken together, these characteristics are the basic parameters of scientific investigation. When they are carefully developed and well articulated, they allow a test of ideas thoughtfully, and research becomes an efficient learning tool.

Stated more succinctly, the building blocks of a study should be carefully thought through before a study begins. Unfortunately, many published studies do not provide a detailed description of independent variables, dependent variables, control groups, and/or the substantive and statistical hypotheses. And, in many instances, statistical hypotheses are left to the discussion of the analysis. These works are often difficult to understand and/or evaluate. Ideally, published works should be explicit and easily understood, and above all, the design should be clear, including a statement that clearly outlines the aim of the study and the substantive hypotheses. Optimally, that description establishes a conceptual link that grounds the substantive hypotheses in personality theory and/or earlier research findings (Weiner, 1977).

Good research is like a finely crafted tool that allows others to learn from the hard-won data, and when the Rorschach is involved, hypotheses should both have a perceptual and empirical rationale. The perceptual rationale connects the Rorschach variable, as a perceptual experience, with the related personality feature or behavior it purports to measure. For example, one perceptual rationale for *M* and ideation is that the blots are actually not moving and that the subject has attributed the response with a fragment of fantasy. If a perceptual rationale is not firmly established in the literature, it should be articulated in formulating the research design. In some instances, the study is basically conceptual, whereas in other instances, it may be more pragmatic, that is, based on some empirical rationale in which the hypotheses are grounded in previous findings that support or conflict with an argument.

Unfortunately, it is not uncommon for prospective researchers to neglect literature outside their own interest area. For instance, those researchers who use the Comprehensive System usually cite the work of Exner and his coworkers exclusively. Similarly, researchers oriented toward a psychoanalytic framework often confine their support for designs to studies sharing the same point of view. No one really profits from studies that are provincially based. The key to a well-developed research formulation is the literature. If used wisely, the literature becomes the cornerstone for a study, but if alluded to only casually, the literature becomes a basis for deception. There are several issues that a reader should consider when evaluating revelant literature.

Failure to Evaluate Previous Findings Carefully

One of the most serious lapses that can be found in published works concerns the casual acceptance of the conclusions in published works as some sort of truth. This often creates a domino effect in the literature. In other words, a first flawed study is erroneously interpreted to have demonstrated "something." A second investigator accepts the flawed conclusion as truth, and proceeds to build another investigation based on that false truth, and although obtaining equivocal findings, interprets the data as if those of the first study remain "carved in stone." Subsequent investigators continue in perpetuating the error from the first study, partly because the results of the second study are cast within the framework of the first, and they proceed to continue in a replication of designs, data analyses, or conclusions that are in line with the first finding.

For instance, A. Spigelman and G. Spigelman (1991) studied barrier and penetration responses and divorce. They used a nonclinical sample of 90 schoolchildren, 46 from divorced families, and 44 from nondivorced families. They formulated clear, substantive hypotheses. The conceptual basis for selection of barrier and penetration responses on body image issues is convincing. They postulated that parental divorce is related to weakened boundary definiteness among children. Unfortunately, they failed to address the issue of minimal empirical support for the validity of barrier and penetration scores as a measure of body boundaries. Accordingly, it is difficult to rule out rival hypotheses (e.g., depression) as an alternative explanation for their findings that children from divorced families produced relatively fewer barrier responses and more penetration responses.

Similarly, Belter, Lipovsky, and Finch (1989), in their study concerning the Egocentricity Index, stated their research aim and the substantive hypotheses, and the statistical hypotheses are easily inferred. They studied 65 children and generated correlations between the index and self-report measures of self-concept. Although the goals and design of their study are clear and well articulated, they may have missed out on a chance for more sturdy findings by not asking themselves about rival hypotheses. For instance, they could have controlled variables such as the age of their child and adolescent subjects, thus reducing error variance and increasing effect size. Thus, readers might question the lack of controlled variables and exclude it from their literature review.

Failure to Challenge Methodology

The design of a study usually is the most crucial to any evaluation of findings or conclusions. Investigators formulating a new study must always evaluate the methodology of others who have published on the same topic. When design flaws are noted, some will be minor and judged as relatively unimportant, but in other instances, the design will contain major flaws that cast serious doubt on the data reported as well as the conclusions drawn. Unfortunately, some articles do not include a clear description of the method, which tends to obscure the results. For instance, Revere, Rodeffer, and Dawson (1989) addressed long-term changes in 13 schizophrenic inpatients treated with psychodynamic group psychotherapy. They asserted that their study is preliminary with the goal to study treatment effects rather than the Rorschach, so that it may be unfair to criticize it. However, the Rorschach advocate may be intrigued by an apparently large effect of psychodynamic treatment for these severely disturbed patients. Unfortunately, the authors only defined the Rorschach variable as "standard determinants" and "subscales" of reality perception and relationships without identifying the actual quantities (p. 210). This vagueness makes it impossible to learn from or about the Rorschach variables and reduces confidence in their findings.

Failure to Consider Alternative Analyses or Conclusions

Sometimes, those reviewing relevant literature are prone to naively accept, as appropriate, the method(s) by which the data have been analyzed. For instance, a study by Rosensky, Tovian, Stiles, Fridkin, and Holland (1987) on learned helplessness is an example of an acceptable selection of dependent variables consistent with explicit hypotheses. They used 50 undergraduate subjects randomly assigned to either of two groups, and selected 19 of the 89 variables for which normative data were available that were related in the literature to depression. Nonetheless, a critical reader might take serious issue with these authors for the specification of individual scores (e.g., T, TF, and FT) rather than summaries of these variables (the total number of T responses on the record). In other words, from a theoretical perspective, the various subtypes all measure the same underlying construct so that the best dependent variable available would be the total number of texture responses, the one that captures the most individual differences.

Hirshberg (1989) investigated symbiotic and separation images in the Rorschachs of 62 eating disordered women. The original design aimed to differentiate eating disorder subtypes: anorexic, anorexic with concurrent bulimia, postanorexic bulimic, and bulimic. Hirshberg presented a literature review indicating that these four subtypes corresponded to meaningful psychological patterns. He attempted to refine his static groups in a way that captures important differences in personality. It is impractical to initiate a static group design unless one is sure that each group is adequately represented in the potential sample. Unfortunately, small sample sizes in this study induced Hirshberg to combine two of the subgroups into a psychologically heterogeneous group. Any comparisons of combined groups is confounded as there is no easy way to attribute differences. In other words, after taking care to justify hypotheses by differences among groups, it does not make sense to combine groups for expediency. Logically, collecting data for more subjects is a better choice so as to purify groups and allow sturdier, more meaningful statistical comparisons.

Naively Accepting Conclusions

As noted earlier, investigators are often hasty in their acceptance of published conclusions. In many instances, this may be because studies have been frequently cited in earlier research or because studies have become regarded as especially notable by their recurrent inclusion in review articles. Five such studies are used as illustrations here. All are respectable works and have gained distinction. Nonetheless, they do illustrate how a casual acceptance of findings or conclusions may mislead potential investigators who do not critique literature relevant to their research interests cautiously and thoroughly.

The first is a clever, well-thought-out, and clearly presented study by Ryan, Avery, and Grolnick (1985). They used the Mutuality of Autonomy (MOA) scale to predict social and academic adaptation of children. Sixty subjects were randomly selected from the fourth to sixth grades of a grammar school. Subsequently, scales from the MAO were correlated with self-reports and teacher reports that were collected 1 month later. This study is a good example of an investigation that not only validates the main substantive hypothesis that object relations effect child behavior, but also the auxiliary hypothesis that the MOA is an acceptable measure of object relations. Substantive hypotheses are clearly asserted, statistical hypotheses are implied and obvious, and interscorer reliability issues are handled adequately. To their credit is the attempt of the authors to establish the precision of the MOA by demonstrating discriminative validity. An especially notable design feature is their use of a scale that appears to measure perception of control in self, powerful others, and unknown sources along three dimensions. As the authors noted, general psychology measures, or those reflecting more behavioral understandings of personality, are seldom coupled with psychoanalytic measures. Certainly, Rorschach research could benefit from integrating the two in well-designed studies.

This work, however, does have some problems. Meaningful descriptive data were not presented. Because of this omission, the reader cannot rule out assumption violations and distorted correlations. Experimentwise, the issue of a Type I error is not addressed, even though 36 correlations are calculated and $p < .10$ is used in addition to more appropriate levels. Information about the raw number of responses scored for MOA is not provided. Its inclusion would clearly help the reader place the findings in the context of one's Rorschach knowledge. Like many Rorschach investigators, Ryan and his colleagues could not resist the temptation of overinterpreting weak results, that is, correlations in the .20's.

Although the strength of effects would be classified as small (Cohen, 1977), the choice of some criterion variables, such as grades and single-item summary judgments by teachers, make the results practically significant. Grades and judgments (about social adjustment, working well with others, self-esteem) are meaningful and easily understood, but they are also influenced by many factors so that there is not much room for the object relations effect. Delaying the teacher's report for one month does reduce confounding by contemporaneous factors. In addition, the variables share little method variance. One psychometric principle that is clearly supported in this study is that considering more responses (referring to the MOA score) generally is more reliable than using single responses (highest or lowest MOA). In effect, it supports the notion that the longer the Rorschach, the more reliable will be the data (longer is better).

A second study by Armstrong and Lowenstein (1990) represents the flawed, but common practice of comparing a target group to the norms for the Comprehensive System (Exner, 1986). They attempted to discover psychological correlates of multiple personality and dissociative disorder. When large enough, new samples can be considered to be representative data for the group of interest. In this case, however, the number of subjects is very small ($N = 14$). The authors readily admitted that theirs is a preliminary study and, to their credit, it is important to note that dissociative and multiple personality disorders are not numerous. Nonetheless, for purposes of illustrating questionable research practices, the method of comparing a small sample of data to the normative data must be highlighted.

Normative data are deliberately heterogeneous. They are collected to reflect the broad variance that exists for many variables among nonpatients. Thus, almost any homogenous group will be different for some variables when compared to this deliberately heterogeneous population. Exner (1991) called attention to this phenomena and has also cautioned about basic differences that exist among nonpatients who differ for basic personality styles (introversives vs. extratensives). In the Armstrong and Lowenstein study, some statistically significant differences were bound to occur because of the supposed homogeneity of their group, almost regardless of their sample size. But the large sample size of the normative data increased the likehood of this Type I error.

The possibility of false-positive results might have been reduced if these authors had formulated more specific substantive hypotheses. Unfortunately, the authors only hypothesized that the target sample would show a distinctive test pattern and offer more traumatic content. The authors did identify general categories of Rorschach responses that were of interest (such as reality testing, coping style, affect) but did not offer specific hypotheses that could be subjected to statistical evaluation and thus, did not select variables based on conceptual issues. As a result, the threat of experimentwise, Type I error cannot be calculated. To keep the nominal alpha level at .01, the investigators calculated a 99% confidence interval around the means of their sample and considered results significant only when the means for nomative data for the Comprehensive System were not contained in this range. Although this method is conservative, it does not fully take into consideration that outliers can greatly distort Rorschach indicators of pathology in such small samples. Often nonparametric statistics are more appropriate in this context. Some of these concerns would be cleared up if descriptive data were presented. In addition, such data would allow one to determine whether the reported differences are interpretively meaningful.

A third example is drawn from some of the work by Russ. Russ' (1987) work on children's play is an excellent example of using the Rorschach in theoretically based research. In much of her work Rorschach parameters are used to measure hypothetical constructs and establish the relations among these constructs, so by most definitions, her endeavors would be classified as involved with construct validation. Nonetheless, a recent study (Russ & Grossman-Mckee, 1990) is worth critical examination. It focused on primary process and adaptive regression, as measured in Rorschach responses, and its relationship to children's play and fantasy. As is typical of Russ and her coworkers, the literature review was well written and informative. The authors documented their methods better than most, allowing others to replicate their design easily. This comprehensiveness is especially notable in their detailed description of the calculations underlying their measures of primary process and adaptive regression and is followed by the presentation of descriptive statistics. Ranges, however, would be helpful, or at least a reference to management of the skew issue. There is some ambiguity around subject selection in that the reasons for administering the Rorschach to only 46 of the original 60 subjects, apparently drawn from a presumably larger sample, are not clear.

Accordingly, one must question the generalizability of the findings. The examiners were not blind to the purpose of the study, but they did not have critical information about other scores, so that bias may not be an issue. Another methodological issue is that the affect-in-play scale was modeled after Holt's (1977) Rorschach primary process scoring, so that there may be some redundancy between the independent and dependent variables. If this is true, conclusions drawn from the results may be suspect.

Furthermore, the odd pattern of correlations between the various components of the Adaptive Regression (AR) score with the criterion variables highlights a common question in the use of Rorschach, namely, the use of multivariable composite scores. In other words, how does one establish and test the validity of weightings and algorithms? Other data (Kleinman & Russ, 1988) also suggest that more careful scrutiny is warranted in this regard for AR. Also, the correlation with nonprimary process play is not fully appreciated as a threat to discriminant validity. To the authors' defense, it is very difficult to analyze such large correlational matrices with incumbent distortions of Type I and Type II errors, and the possible effects of skew. Furthermore, the correlations are greater in magnitude than is often the case in such research, so that Russ and Grossman-McKee probably do not exaggerate trivial effects. Nonetheless, the authors suggested that the findings are clearer than they appear to be. It may be that there are one or two underlying factors for these various scales, so that factor analytic approaches may be useful in identifying latent variables.

Another study worth considering is that of Coonerty (1986), which was selected for the Beck Award by the Society of Personality Assessment. It is a well-designed investigation from the construct validation point of view, with the aim of validating Mahler's theory of separation–individuation. It contrasted borderlines and schizophrenics on a Rorschach scale of separation–individuation responses, created by Coonerty. Although the study has many strengths, it raises some issues about the use of archival data and the development of new scales. Records were drawn from case files, and more information about how the author addressed the implications of archival research would be helpful. For example, groups were formed by one of two judges by applying *DSM–III* criteria in chart review. The judges demonstrated 88% agreement, but some reviewers might argue that this retrospective procedure may be subject to some error, especially by the fact that many of the records were collected prior to the publication of *DSM–III*. Other researchers might adopt a more conservative technique to ensure accurate group assignment by requiring that two independent judges agree on diagnosis and eliminating subjects for which the judges disagree.

In addition to group assignment, issues of reliability and replicability would be enhanced by having two judges agree on scoring of the Rorschach. Moreover, an evaluation of generalizability would be improved by citing how many subject files had to be reviewed to accumulate the 100 subjects used in the study. This study also highlights issues concerning the development of a multivariable, composite Rorschach scale. To minimize shrinkage and increase power, initial studies should adopt more conservative judging techniques, as noted earlier. On the other hand, the author took care to have 20 protocols rescored by a second judge and found 96% agreement. As in many reports of Rorschach reliability, readers are impressed with the high reliability rating but are not sure of what is agreed. Does it mean that the raters agreed for 96% of the responses? If only 4% of the responses are scored on the scale, the 96% is not that impressive. Or does it mean that of the responses selected by the one judge, that the second rater agreed 96% of the time with the first rater? On the other hand, would the second rater have selected the same responses to rate? Fortunately for this study, the 96% rating is so high that in almost all scenarios it is more than adequate. Coonerty reported an alpha coefficient of .85, which is quite impressive as an estimate of internal consistency, but she hypothesized a differential performance by schizophrenics and borderlines. The meaning of this impressive internal consistency is paradoxical in that the hypothesis and finding would suggest limited internal consistency among these items across scales.

The Coonerty findings are generally positive, but her conclusions assume that the various assumptions for the test are met. For instance, her decision to covary R does present potential problems, because of the lack of a linear relationship and of other assumption violations. Not withstanding these problems, the Coonerty study applied the results to the theory as a confirmation. Viewed from a different perspective, it can easily be argued that the discussion suggests that the author made an error common in psychoanalytic research or clinical practice by attributing adult Rorschach differences to specific childhood events (P. Tyson & R. L. Tyson, 1990). The results are consistent with the theory, but Rorschach results can never be used to establish specific etiologies in the distant past. To do so is very speculative and probably could only be validated through a complex, longitudinal design.

Coonerty also hypothesized a differential performance of schizophrenic and borderline subjects across subscales that corresponds to different developmental levels. Such differential expectations are typical of studies that utilize scales with multiple subscales, each of which measure different levels of severity of disturbance or immaturity (e.g., Berg, 1990; Cooper et al., 1988; Hirshberg, 1989; P. Lerner & H. Lerner, 1980; H. Lerner, Sugarman, & Barbour, 1985). In some of these studies one must question subject selection practices or the appropriateness of assignment of individual scores to supposed levels of psychopathology (Berg, 1990). Like most of these studies, Coonerty made differential predictions for her groups on the various subscales and finds different base rates across subscales. In her study it may be no accident that the only nonsignificant finding occurred in the group with the lowest mean scores. In other words, for that comparison, the fact that relatively few responses qualified for that category may have decreased reliability, decreased strength of effect, decreased power, and ultimately led to nonsignificant results. Cluster analysis may be adaptable as a statistical technique to address the question of different patterns across subscales.

As far as the Coonerty study itself is concerned, it may be that limitations of the test rather than limitations regarding the validity of the theory accounts for the results. Basically, in conducting such research, it is best to recognize that the test measures some differences much better than others and that confounding influences must be ruled out to the extent possible. This problem of ruling out inadvertent third factors is the fundamental problem in cross-sectional, essentially correlational, research (Meehl, 1978, 1990). In this case, can we be sure that Coonerty's results are not due to form quality differences, thinking disturbances, or anatomy content responses? All appear to be interrelated with her scale.

Even studies that appear methodologically clean, and far less complex than the Coonerty investigation, usually can be subject to critical evaluation. For instance, Viglione and Exner (1983) is an example of a classical experimental design with random assignment. Designs such as this supposedly eliminate the confounding problem of subject selection that are so common to cross-sectional or correlational designs (Meehl, 1990). The researchers task is to design an intervention that is powerful enough to induce changes in the Rorschach dependent variables. Viglione and Exner assigned subjects to either an ego-involving stress group and a control group, each with 30 subjects. They did check the effectiveness of the stress intervention with a self-report, anxiety scale. This intervention check helped to interpret the negative results. The statistical hypothesis in this simple study was clearly asserted, namely, that experimental subjects would report more shading responses than control subjects. The results revealed no significant difference between groups and were interpreted to indicate that the test is "not affected by limited social-evaluative stress," and has been interpreted (Exner, 1991) as supporting the notion that stress must be of sufficient strength and induce a sense of loss of control to effect diffuse shading (Y). Technically, this is clearly an incorrect assumption.

As Cohen (1990) pointed out, with a large enough sample, a miniscule difference between any two groups can be made statistically significant. The question of interest becomes whether one has enough power to detect the smallest difference that is practically significant. The conventions for a medium size difference effect would translate to a mean difference of .6 on m. If one could score a .6 on this variable, it would seem to be of some interpretive significance. With only one planned comparison, the danger of Type I error was minimized in the Viglione and Exner study, however, with only 60 subjects the conditional probability of uncovering a medium-size effect is only about 50% (Cohen, 1990). Accordingly, this study lacks enough subjects to establish definitively the Null hypothesis that limited social-evaluative does not affect Y. In that sense it brings up the issue of "proving" the Null hypothesis (Cohen, 1990). In other words, this experiment has limited power.

If one were to replicate the Viglione and Exner study, the ideal number of subjects might not be a great many more than 60. Indeed, the probability of missing a medium-size effect in two independent studies with 60 subjects each is (approximately because .5 is approximate, independence between studies calls for multiplication) is .5 × .5, or .25. Furthermore, if in both studies the means for the cells were approximately equal, it would be highly unlikely that systematic Type II error was occurring. In that case, one could more assuredly agree with the Viglione's and Exner's conclusion. Including descriptive data also would allow one to address this Type II error problem more directly, as well as the issues of "proving" the null and practical significance.

McCown, Fink, Galina, and Johnson (1992) improved on and extended the Viglione and Exner study. Taking a lead from that study, they attempted to incite experimental stresses that were powerful enough to make a difference and over which subjects experienced little control. They took into consideration a central finding in stress research that subjects' experience of control over the stress is a critical determinant of one's reaction. From rather larger differences between cells (from .5 to .75 SD) in this experiment with random assignment of 25 subjects per group, they concluded that m was associated with stress, whereas Y was more specifically related to perceived, uncontrollable stress.

Although this is essentially a well-thought-through study, it does have critical weaknesses. For example, this study suffers from the many statistical uncertainties that plague Rorschach studies. Specifically, the question of the appropriateness of the ANOVA in this study is questionable, and the reader does not have sufficient information about the distributions of m and Y to judge the worthiness of the findings. The authors did note the controversy about the application of parametric statistics to some Rorschach variables and cited a source (Kirk, 1982) that does not reflect the more current concern about the distorting effects of the violations of ANOVA statistical assumptions. In addition, they noted that few published Rorschach studies have employed nonparametric statistics, something they probably should have criticized rather than imitated. In their discussion, it appears that the authors confused issues of homogeneity of variance and normal distribution. It is true that an examination of the standard deviations of the cells suggests, as the authors indicated, that variances are homogenous. On the other hand, without more detailed descriptive data, one cannot assuredly interpret the results. Without ranges and frequencies, as presented in Exner (1986, 1991), one cannot determine whether the findings result from general trends among all the subjects, or from the effect of individual extreme scores or floor or ceiling effects. For example, one or two extreme scores (4, 5) in some of the experimental groups may account for the significant differences.

Statistical procedures should always be a source of concern for the critical eye. If complete descriptive data are available, one can make a much better determination about the appropriateness of parametric or nonparametric statistics. In addition, if an ANOVA is used, one must conclude that elevations in the target variables are associated with the independent variables. Thus, in the McCowan et al. study, one might interpret the findings to suggest that relative elevations in m and Y are associated with stress and uncontrollable stress respectively. On the other hand, if one wants to make a statement about the interpretation of the particular *values* of these variables, for example, ascribing a certain interpretation to Y (such as > 2), one must categorize the data and using that value as a cutoff, employ nonparametric tests such as Chi-square or logistic regression. To their credit, McCown et al. interpreted their results rather conservatively in this regard once they accept the ANOVA as a valid statistical tool.

A SUMMARY OF CAUTIONS

The formulation of a research issue is often as difficult, or possibly even moreso, as creating the methodology and deciding how to handle the data collected. When reviewing the literature, the prospective researcher must always be alert to many issues such as:

1. Failure to base research on personality concepts with measurable behavioral referents.

2. Failure to utilize modern theories, methods, and measures from empirical and academic clinical psychology.
3. Failure to articulate specific research hypotheses.
4. Implicit hypotheses tests that are not specified.
5. Inappropriate selection of variables.
6. Inappropriate control groups in diagnostic studies.
7. Experimenter bias.
8. Poor interscorer reliability.
9. Abuse of normative data.
10. Overreliance on ambiguous, confounded results.
11. Failure to recognize limitations of the test.
12. Insufficient concern with discriminant validity.
13. Failure to address assumptions of parametric statistics.
14. Failure to institute controls to decrease error variance.
15. Unacceptable, experimentwise Type 1 error.
16. Confusion of statistical significance, practical significance, and strength of effect.
17. Working with inadequate power.
18. Omitting descriptive data.
19. Failure to recognize that interpretive significance is not linearly related to Rorschach variables.
20. Using the Rorschach to validate itself.
21. Failure to recognize skew and outliers.
22. Poor management of response productivity.
23. Failure to recognize findings based on too few responses.
24. Excessive generalization of findings.
25. Treating nonsignificant or trivial results as important.
26. Failure to consider alternative explanations.

ACKNOWLEDGMENTS

Thanks to Mark Sherman, Julian Meltzoff, Mark Bortz, Connie Carlton, Mike Downing, and Avid Khorram for their help in preparing this chapter.

REFERENCES

Armstrong J. G., & Lowenstein, R. J. (1990). Characteristics of patients with multiple personality and dissociative disorders on psychological testing. *Journal of Nervous and Mental Disease, 178*, 448–454.

Belter, R., Lipovsky, J., & Finch, A. (1989). Rorschach egocentricity index and self-report in children and adolescents. *Journal of Personality Assessment, 53,* 783–789.

Berg, J. L. (1990). Differentiating ego functions of borderline and narcissistic personalities. *Journal of Personality Assessment, 55,* 537–547.

Blatt, S. J., Brenneis, C. B., Schimek, J. G., & Glick, M. (1976). Normal development and psychopathological impairment of the concept of the object on the Rorschach. *Journal of Abnormal Psychology, 85,* 364–373.

Blatt, S. J., Tuber, S. B., & Auerbach, J. S. (1990). Representation of interpersonal interactions on the Rorschach and level of psychopathology. *Journal of Personality Assessment, 54,* 711–728.

Cohen, J. (1977). *Statistical power analysis for the behavioral sciences.* New York: Academic Press.

Cohen, J. (1990). Things I have learned so far. *American Psychologist, 45,* 1304–1312.

Colligan, S., & Exner, J. E., Jr. (1985). Responses of schizophrenics and nonpatients to a tachistoscopic presentation of the Rorschach. *Journal of Personality Assessment, 49,* 129–136.

Coonerty, S. (1986). An exploration of separation–individuation themes in the borderline personality. *Journal of Personality Assessment, 50,* 501–511.

Cooper, S. H., Perry, J. C., & Arnow, D. (1988). An empirical approach to the study of defense mechanisms: Reliability and preliminary validity of the Rorschach Defense Scales. *Journal of Personality Assessment, 52,* 187–203.

Cooper, S. H., Perry, C., & O'Connell, M. (1991). The Rorschach Defense Scales: II. Longitudinal perspectives. *Journal of Personality Assessment, 56,* 191–201.

Cronbach, L. J. (1949). Statistical methods applied to Rorschach scores: A review. *Psychological Bulletin, 46,* 393–429.

Exner, J. E., Jr. (1986). *The Rorschach: A comprehensive system: Vol 1. Interpretation* (2nd ed.). New York: Wiley.

Exner, J. E., Jr. (1988). Problems with brief Rorschach records. *Journal of Personality Assessment, 52,* 640–647.

Exner, J. E., Jr. (1989). Searching for projection in the Rorschach. *Journal of Personality Assessment, 53,* 520–536.

Exner, J. E., Jr. (1991). *The Rorschach: A comprehensive system: Vol. 2. Interpretation* (2nd ed.). New York: Wiley.

Exner, J. E., Jr., Armbruster, G. L., & Mittman, B. (1978). The Rorschach response process. *Journal of Personality Assessment, 42,* 27–38.

Exner, J. E., Jr., Armbruster, G. L., & Viglione, D. (1978). The temporal stability of some Rorschach features. *Journal of Personality Assessment, 42,* 474–482.

Exner, J. E., Jr., Viglione, D. J., & Gillespie, R. (1984). Relationships between Rorschach variables as relevant to the interpretation of structural data. *Journal of Personality Assessment, 48,* 65–69.

Haller, N., & Exner, J. E., Jr. (1985). The reliability of Rorschach variables for inpatients presenting symptoms of depression and/or helplessness. *Journal of Personality Assessment, 49,* 516–521.

Hirshberg, L. (1989). Rorschach images of symbiosis and separation in eating disordered and in borderline and non-borderline subjects. *Psychoanalytic Psychology, 6,* 475–493.

Holt, R. R. (1977). A method for assessing primary process manifestation and their control in Rorschach responses. In M. Ricker-Ovsiankina (Ed.), *Rorschach psychology* (2nd ed., pp. 421–454). Huntington, NY: Krieger.

Kirk, R. (1982). *Experimental design: Procedures for the behavioral sciences* (2nd ed.). Belmont, CA: Brooks/Cole.

Kleinman, M. J. K., & Russ, S. W. (1988). Primary process thinking and anxiety in children. *Journal of Personality Assessment, 52,* 254–262.

Lerner, P., & Lerner, H. (1980). Rorschach assessment of primitive defenses in borderline personality structure. In J. Kwawer, H. Lerner, P. Lerner, & A. Sugerman (Eds.), *Borderline phenomena and the Rorschach test* (pp. 257–274). New York: International Universities Press.

Lerner, H., Sugarman, A., & Barbour, C. G. (1985). Patterns of ego boundary disturbance in neurotic, borderline and schizophrenic patients. *Psychoanalytic Psychology, 2,* 47–66.

Lipgar, R. M., & Wahler, C. A. (1991). A Rorschach investigation of mothers of behaviorally disturbed boys. *Journal of Personality Assessment, 56,* 106–117.

Mason, B. J., Cohen, J. B., & Exner, J. E. (1985). Schizophrenic, depressive, and nonpatient personality organizations described by Rorschach factor structures. *Journal of Personality Assessment, 49,* 295–305.

McCown, W., Fink, A. D., Galina, H., & Johnson, J. (1992). Effects of laboratory-induced controllable and uncontrollable stress on Rorschach variables *m* and *Y. Journal of Personality Assessment, 59,* 564–573.

Meehl, P. E. (1978). Theoretical risks and tabular asterisks: Sir Karl, Sir Ronald, and the slow progress of soft psychology. *Journal of Consulting and Clinical Psychology, 46,* 806–834.

Meehl, P. E. (1990). Why summaries of research on psychological theories are often uninterpretable. *Psychological Reports, 66,* 195–244.

Revere, V., Rodeffer, C., & Dawson, S. (1989). Changes in long-term institutionalized schizophrenics with psychotherapy. *Journal of Contemporary Psychotherapy, 29,* 203–219.

Rosensky, R. H., Tovian, S. H., Stiles, P. G., Fridkin, K., & Holland, M. (1987). Effects of learned helplessness on Rorschach responses. *Psychological Reports, 60,* 1011–1016.

Russ, S. W. (1987). Assessment of cognitive–affective interaction in children: Creativity, fantasy and play research. In J. Butcher & C. Spielberger (Eds.), *Advances in personality assessment* (Vol. 6, pp. 141–155). Hillsdale, NJ: Lawrence Erlbaum Associates.

Russ, S. W. (1987). Assessment of cognitive-affective interaction in children: Creativity, fantasy and play research. In J. Butcher & C. Spielberger (Eds.), *Advances in personality assessment* (Vol. 6, pp. 141–155). Hillsdale, NJ: Lawrence Erlbaum Associates.

Russ, S. W., & Grossman-McKee, A. (1990). Affective expression in children's fantasy play, primary process thinking on the Rorschach, and divergent thinking. *Journal of Personality Assessment, 54,* 756–771

Ryan, R. M., Avery, R. R., & Grolnick, W. S. (1985). A Rorschach assessment of children's Mutuality of Autonomy. *Journal of Personality Assessment, 49,* 6–12.

Shalit, B. (1965). Effects of environmental stimulation on *M, FM,* and *m* responses in the Rorschach. *Journal of Projective Techniques and Personality Assessment, 29,* 228–231.

Shapiro, J. P., Leifer, M., Martone, M. W., & Kassem, L. (1990). Multimethod assessment of depression is sexually abused girls. *Journal of Personality Assessment, 55,* 234–238.

Spigelman A., & Spigelman G. (1991). Relationship between parental divorce and the child's body boundary definiteness. *Journal of Personality Assessment, 56,* 96–105.

Tyson P., & Tyson R. L. (1990). *Psychoanalytic theories of development.* New Haven, CT: Yale University Press.

Urist, J. (1977). The Rorschach test and the assessment of object relations. *Journal of Personality Assessment, 57,* 120–129.

Viglione, D. J., & Exner, J. E. (1983). The effects of state-anxiety and limited social-evaluative stress on the Rorschach. *Journal of Personality Assessment, 47,* 150–154.

Weiner, I. B. (1977). Approaches to Rorschach validation. In M. A. Rickers-Ovsiankina (Ed.), *Rorschach psychology* (2nd ed., pp. 575–608). Huntington, NY: Krieger.

CHAPTER FOUR

Variable Selection
in Rorschach Research

Irving B. Weiner

Rorschach's *Psychodiagnostics* was published in 1921. And, for the next 50 years, clinical scholars who regarded his test as a useful assessment instrument had their hands full defending it against harsh criticism. Rorschach loyalists typically defended the test by enumerating the inadequacies of the research studies that criticized it (see Blatt, 1975; Hertz, 1934; Holt, 1967; Piotrowski, 1937; Weiner, 1972, 1977). There was a time when so much energy was being expended on defense that one wondered if a Rorschach offense would ever take the field, and there was reason to worry whether the tide would turn before defections to more favored fields of study had fatally thinned the ranks of Rorschach researchers.

Fortunately for the field of clinical psychology and those whom it serves, this gloomy picture has brightened considerably during the last 20 years. Well-designed Rorschach studies have appeared with increasing frequency, and a growing body of robust data has cast the test in an increasingly positive light. The results of a metanalysis reported in the *Psychological Bulletin* indicate that the Rorschach has demonstrated adequate reliability, stability, and validity by usual psychometric standards, and is comparable to the Minnesota Multiphasic Personality Inventory (MMPI) and the Wechsler Adult Intelligence Scale (WAIS) in these respects (Parker, Hanson, & Hunsley, 1988). The defense of the test, which at times has seemed fragile, is now quite sturdy. Those who currently believe the Rorschach is an unscientific or unsound test with limited utility have not read the relevant literature of the last 20 years; or, having read it, they have not grasped its meaning.

Accordingly, it seems appropriate to depart from practices common in the past that focus on how Rorschach research has gone wrong, with illustrations of ill-advised procedures and unjustified conclusions, and focus instead on how Rorschach research can be designed to go right, with illustrations of sound methodology and appropriate inferences that have illuminated the merits of the instrument. One of the more important aspects of doing so includes consideration of important guidelines for selecting variables to study in Rorschach research. Those who design research in accord with these guidelines will enhance their prospects for obtaining meaningful results that demonstrate wide generalizability and help to resolve critical practical and theoretical issues.

The selection of variables in Rorschach studies begins with the recognition that these studies can proceed in either of two ways, depending on whether investigators are interested primarily in doing research *on* the Rorschach or *with* the Rorschach. Research on the Rorschach seeks to learn about how the test works and what it measures, such as how aspects of chromatic color use correlate with manifest emotionality, or whether the Comprehensive System Depression Index (DEPI) distinguishes depressed from nondepressed patients as effectively among children as among adults. Research with the Rorschach seeks to use the test as a measure of some phenomenon being studied, such as whether there are age or sex differences in patterns of manifest emotionality as measured in part by Rorschach color use, or whether people who are depressed, as measured in part by DEPI, display more interpersonal dependency than nondepressed people. As these examples indicate, both ways of approaching Rorschach research require the selection of Rorschach variables and also of *predictor* or *predicted* variables, which are those measured phenomena to be examined for their relationship to the selected Rorschach variables.

Predictor variables are *independent* variables such as characteristics of people, their actions, or their experiences that are expected to predict particular kinds of Rorschach responses. In studies of predictor variables, the Rorschach becomes a set of dependent variables in relation to these predictors, and hypotheses are advanced concerning such matters as how schizophrenics, depressives, violent criminals, or abuse victims perform on the Rorschach and how their performance differs from that of other groups of subjects.

Predicted variables are *dependent* variables such as past, present, or future events or aspects of a person's status that are expected to be predictable from Rorschach responses. In studies of predicted variables, the Rorschach provides independent variables in relation to these predicted phenomena, and hypotheses are advanced concerning such matters as whether and how the Rorschach can identify who among a group of people has been sexually abused, who has a schizophrenic disorder or depressive disorder, or who will terminate prematurely from psychotherapy. Many of the same considerations apply in effective selection of Rorschach and predictor/predicted variables in research studies, but both raise some unique issues that should be discussed separately.

SELECTING RORSCHACH VARIABLES

Two decisions need to be made in selecting Rorschach variables for a research study: which ones and how many? Generally speaking, the likelihood of obtaining reliable and useful findings in Rorschach research is increased by choosing variables that are precisely defined, that are easy to identify and understand, that reflect how the test is used in actual practice, and that are not too numerous. In specific terms, then, the Rorschach variables studied or used in research should be refined, interactive, conceptually based, selective, and reliably scorable.

Refined Variables

Refined variables are Rorschach codes that go beyond gross categorizations of location, determinant, and other structural or thematic features of a protocol to include ways in which most of these features can be meaningfully subcategorized. The location score W is a good example of an *unrefined* variable. Rorschach (1921/1942, p. 42) originally related use of the whole blot in formulating a response to intellectual level. Specifically, he concluded from his data that people who give seven or more W's can be expected to have above-average intelligence. The fact is, however, that an investigator who attempts to predict a high IQ from the presence of more than six W's, or to correlate W with IQ, or to use W as an index of intelligence in a study concerned with intellectual functioning is very likely to get negative results and to create a misleading impression that the Rorschach has failed to live up to a realistic expectation.

W fails as a research variable because it is a gross score. There are well-established differences between Whole responses that involve some perceptual integration or synthesis of blot details ($W+$) and those that are simplistic (Wo) or imprecise (Wv), particularly with respect to their implications for cognitive maturation and the ability to form complex concepts. Accordingly, whereas W responses yield little information about intellectual ability, the number and percentage of $W+$ responses in a record have been found to correlate significantly with Wechsler IQ and with problem-solving ability (Acklin & Fechner-Bates, 1989; Blatt & Allison, 1963).

Moreover, refined Developmental Quality scoring for location choice has shown some potential as a non-IQ index of intellectual capacity. Gerstein, Brodzinsky, and Reiskind (1976), studying Black and White 7- to 14-year-old schoolchildren with similarly low IQs, found a significantly higher frequency of integrated location choices in the records of the Black children. Hence it may be that refined location choice variables can help to identify intellectual abilities in subjects who for one reason or another are unable to put their best foot forward on a standard measure of intelligence.

The significance of human movement (*M*) in Rorschach responses provides another ready example of the benefits that accrue from using refined as opposed to unrefined variables in research. Delivering *M* responses has long been taken as an index of ego strength, and underproduction of *M* has often been used to help identify adjustment difficulties (see Goldfried, Stricker, & Weiner, 1971, chap. 9). However, although the absence of *M* is a fairly reliable indicator that something important is missing from a subject's repertoire of resources for coping with the demands of daily living, merely having *M*, even in abundance, by no means guarantees good adjustment. Even more than *W* responses, *M* responses differ enormously from each other. Some are perceptually accurate and some contain perceptual distortions; some involve real figures seen in their entirety and some consist of figures that are mythical or seen only in part; some are seen in commonly used locations and some in unusual or arbitrarily demarcated parts of the blots; some are engaged in active movement and some in passive movement. An accumulation of passive, poor form human movement responses (*Mp–*) seen in *Dd* locations and with (*H*), *Hd*, or (*Hd*) content points to adjustment difficulties of various kinds, not to good ego strength.

Such refinements in examining human movement variables are captured not only in the scoring subcategories of the Comprehensive System but also in coding schemes developed from an object relations perspective to facilitate sophisticated interpretation of human content responses. For example, Blatt, Brenneis, Schimek, and Glick (1976) were able to demonstrate a significant relationship between severity of psychopathology and the frequency with which human figures on the Rorschach are inaccurately or only partially perceived or are seen as engaged in unmotivated, incongruent, nonspecific, or malevolent activity. More recently, Perry and Viglione (1991) found a close relationship between indices of ego strength and a measure of object relations called "Poor:Good Human Experience." The Poor:Good Human Experience variable is based on a multifaceted coding of human responses that takes into account their form quality, whether they are partial or fictionalized, whether they involve cooperative or aggressive interactions, and whether they are elaborated in a dissociated or illogical manner.

In selecting Rorschach variables in research, then, the first step is to ensure that they fully reflect current knowledge and contemporary practice with respect to scoring specificity. Number of *W* will work satisfactorily as an index of a global approach in attending to experience, but not as a measure of intelligence; number of *M* will work well in an index of coping style such as Erlebnistypus (EB), but not as a measure of ego strength. In Rorschach research, as elsewhere, you get what you pay for.

Gross or unrefined variables may suffice if they are used as such in practice and if there is no basis in previous research for subcategorizing them. The number of Popular (*P*) responses in a record exemplifies a gross score for which no reliable subcategories have been demonstrated. On the other hand, when much is known and applied with respect to the corollaries of refined subtypes of variables, researchers who work with gross categories of these variables that fail to incorporate what has been learned are unlikely to obtain gratifying results or earn the respect of informed colleagues.

Interactive Variables

Rorschach variables selected for research should reflect the fact that the basic scores or contents of the test, taken individually, rarely have any specific or consistent implications for personality functioning. For the most part, meaningful inferences from Rorschach data derive from conjoint examination of several features of the structural summary or of thematic imagery in their relationship to each other. Because experienced and knowledgeable practitioners use Rorschach variables interactively, for good reason, researchers are well advised to do likewise.

For example, $X+\%$ provides substantial information concerning the extent to which people are perceiving themselves and their experiences in the way that most people would. In good clinical practice, however, the adequacy of a subject's reality testing is determined not solely from $X+\%$, but also from the frequency of highly conventional responses (*P*), idiosyncratic but accurate perceptions ($Xu\%$), and distorted and inaccurate perceptions ($X-\%$). Researchers working with form level as a general variable will accordingly do well to include all four scores in their design. Similarly, a Food response in a record suggests the presence of dependency needs, but a content index of dependency powerful enough to fare well as a variable in practice or in research studies should include not only scored food responses but also interactive imagery involving such themes as people eating, being fed or nurtured in some way, leaning on each other, and so on.

Interactive variables enhance the validity and utility of Rorschach inferences not only by mirroring clinical wisdom, but also because they constitute a broader measure than variables used separately, by enhancing reliability. One important example in this regard is the Comprehensive System *D* score, which is based on the relationship between the number of human movement and chromatic color responses in a record to the number of animal movement, inanimate movement, achromatic color, and shading responses. As a broadly based, interactive measure of the extent to which subjects have sufficient personality resources at their disposal to cope with the demands they are experiencing, the *D* score has consistently shown significant correlations with measures of stress tolerance, self-control, and subjectively felt distress (Exner, 1986a, chap. 14; 1991, chap. 6).

A second noteworthy example of fruitful use of interactive variables, drawn from thematic analysis of Rorschach content, is Urist's (1977) Mutuality of Autonomy (MOA) scale. The MOA scale rates all human, animal, and inanimate object relationships described in Rorschach responses on a 7-point scale ranging from "mutual empathic relatedness" at the most adaptive end of the scale to "malevolent engulfment and destruction" at the least adaptive end of the scale. Although the scores on this broad-based scale do not necessarily identify the quality of subjects' actual interpersonal relationships, they have been found to provide a useful measure of severity of psychological disorder (Blatt, Tuber, & Auerbach, 1990).

Rather than relying on individual scores or contents as variables, then, researchers should employ clusters or configurations that combine to provide multifaceted measures of the variables under study. Two other thematic indices that serve well as further examples are Fisher and Cleveland's (1958) *Penetration* score and its present-day descendent, the Comprehensive System *Morbid* score (Exner, 1986a, chap. 16), both of which are multiple-criteria content scores that have regularly demonstrated meaningful correlations with negative attitudes toward one's body.

Certain exceptions to the need for interactive Rorschach variables may arise, depending on the predictor or predicted variables with which the Rorschach is expected to relate. For example, the absence of any Texture response, the presence of Reflection responses, and the use of Color Projection appear to have valid behavioral correlates independently of other characteristics of a Rorschach protocol (Exner, 1991, chaps. 7 & 8). Such exceptions aside, combinations of basic variables into broadly based indices of personality functioning will substantially enhance a researcher's likelihood of obtaining significant and useful findings.

Successful application of cluster and configuration methodology in Rorschach research has a long history. Using categories developed by Rapaport, Gill, and Schafer (1946) for discriminating among types of deviant verbalizations on the Rorschach, Watkins and Stauffacher (1952) developed the Delta Index, a set of 15 weighted scores for various types of illogical or dissociated responses that proved moderately successful in distinguishing between schizophrenic and nonpatient subjects (see Goldfried et al., 1971, chap. 10). The Delta Index was subsequently refined and expanded by Johnson and Holzman (1979) into the Thought Disorder Index (TDI), which weighs verbal responses on both the Rorschach and the Wechsler Adult Intelligence Scale according to their pathological quality. The TDI yields useful information concerning the nature and severity of thinking disorders, and it is making important contributions in research on the characteristics and course of schizophrenia.

As another important illustration from the past, Klopfer, Kirkner, Wisham, and Baker (1951) developed a Prognostic Rating Scale (PRS) for the Rorschach that assigns positive or negative weights to several features of the movement, color, shading, and form-level elements of each response. Although the PRS configuration never became widely used clinically and rarely appears in contemporary research, earlier studies demonstrated respectable validity for its predictions of overt behavior change in clinical and hospital patient populations (see Goldfried et al., 1971, chap. 12).

Over the years, numerous researchers have regularly demonstrated the utility of clusters and configurations of Rorschach variables in generating gratifying results. Two recent examples of this strategy have introduced Rorschach scales that may receive considerable use in the future. Cooper, Perry, and O'Connell (1991) developed the Rorschach Defense Scales, which combine aspects of response structure, verbal content, and the examiner–subject relationship to assess reliance on each of 15 defense mechanisms—such as projection, intellectualization, and denial. Findings to date indicate that defense preference, as measured by these scales, can predict in part the future course of affective disturbance and social relatedness.

Perry and Viglione (1991) combined their Good:Poor Human Experience variable with the frequency of depressed contents and scores for poor form-level and cognitive slippage to form an Ego Impairment Index (EII). In their initial work with this index, Perry and Viglione were able to demonstrate significant relationships between EII and response to treatment among depressed outpatients.

Conceptually Based Variables

To promote the possibility of obtaining significant and substantively meaningful results, researchers should focus on Rorschach variables that bear some conceptual relationship to the predictor or predicted variables to which their empirical relationship will be examined. The first step in establishing such a conceptual relationship consists of articulating some personality characteristics associated with the Rorschach variables that are to be used or studied. For example, to say that people who give a preponderance of *FC* over *CF* responses are relatively reserved and restrained in how they experience and express emotions, whereas people who give a preponderance of *CF* over *FC* responses are relatively intense and spontaneous in their emotionality, provides a good reason for including the *FC:CF+C* ratio in a study concerned with predicting to or from aspects of affective style. Rorschach variables that cannot readily be conceptualized in terms of personality characteristics are best excluded from efforts to design definitive research until they are better understood.

A second companion step in conceptualizing an anticipated relationship in Rorschach research involves articulating some implications that the personality characteristics being measured by a Rorschach variable have for the phenomena with which the Rorschach is expected to relate. Continuing with the example of color use, the personality characteristics of having a relatively forthcoming affective style, as measured by Rorschach color use favoring *CF* and *C* over *FC* responses, could well have a lot to do with the phenomenon of being the kind of person whom other people find easy to get to know.

When Rorschach research includes test variables that are neither well understood nor conceptually related to predictor or predicted variables in the study, grief will often attend the outcome. Insignificant findings will emerge with dismaying regularity and, in those rare instances in which positive findings occur fortuitously, scant basis will be available for explaining why the data have turned out well.

It is an inescapable fact that insufficient conceptualization of Rorschach variables used in research will usually diminish the impact of any results that are obtained. A relationship between Rorschach variables and personality or behavioral characteristics that cannot be explained in terms of generally understood features of the human condition remains shrouded in mystery. Mysterious, seemingly inexplicable findings are of little use in generating new hypotheses for study and are of little use in relating Rorschach findings to other information concerning how and why people think, feel, and act as they do. When Rorschach researchers say that a relationship exists but cannot say why it exists, personality researchers are less likely to envision possibilities for the Rorschach to inform them about psychological processes, and they are accordingly unlikely to allow Rorschach findings to influence their work. Well-thought-through conceptualizations concerning the selection of variables in Rorschach research contributes to the advancement of knowledge and enhances the status of the instrument among personality researchers.

It is regrettable to note that far too many pieces of Rorschach research have been conducted with inadequate attention to selecting conceptually based Rorschach variables. These are "shotgun" or "fishing expedition" types of research in which a random conglomeration of variables is thrown into a statistical hopper and the researcher hunts or fishes around to see if any of them relates to any others, or to variables independent of the Rorschach. Occasionally, such an approach does yield useful findings, but for each study that has a positive yield, there are dozens of this type that yield nothing of substance. Moreover, it is not uncommon for this nonconceptual approach to include more variables than can be managed effectively in the data analysis, resulting in a chaotic and uninterpretable matrix of findings. The number of variables in a study can be as important to a meaningful piece of research as choosing conceptually based variables.

Selective Variables

After researchers have narrowed their choice to refined, interactive, and conceptually based Rorschach variables to include in a particular study, they still need to be selective in determining how many variables to include. The jeopardy in this regard is including a large number of variables, many of which bear only a distant relationship to the topic under study, just "to see what happens." This jeopardy has been nourished into monstrous proportions by computer technology, which has enhanced large-scale data analysis enormously, but has also created temptation to throw all available information into the search for relationships. "Why not add these scores in?", the researcher may ask. "It won't do any harm, and maybe we'll learn something."

Failure to be selective does do harm, however. Whatever is learned from looking at everything is usually not worth the risk of being unable to document anything. All-inclusive curiosity in the absence of an informed focus generates data analyses in which performing a very large number of statistical tests increases the possibility of statistically significant differences appearing by chance. Consider the outcome, for example, if 50 correlations, t tests, or one-way ANOVA's are calculated and only four yield a value significant at the .05 level of confidence. Nothing useful can be inferred from the results: Four significant findings at .05 among 50 findings is a chance result by usual standards, and both the investigator who formulated the predictions of the study and the Rorschach as a measure of the variables in the study appear to have been inadequate to their task.

But suppose that the four statistically significant relationships that emerged in this hypothetical study are in fact reliable and meaningful, and suppose further that most of the other 46 statistical tests should not have been run at all, because there was little reason to expect them to demonstrate relationships among variables. Then the excess baggage of irrelevant variables and superfluous statistical tests will have obscured the soundness and potential utility of the four significant relationships obtained. As a general principle, then, the more researchers can limit their Rorschach variables to those that have a clearly specifiable relationship to predictor or predicted variables being examined, the more likely they are to obtain positive results and the less likely they are to have the significance of good data impugned by the insignificance of bad data that should not have been analyzed. Cohen (1990, p. 1304) captured the point being made here with a simple principle for selecting variables in research studies: "Less is more."

On the other hand, the benefits of conceptually formulated studies limited to a relatively small number of carefully selected Rorschach variables do not preclude a respectable place in Rorschach research for exploratory investigations. Preliminary large-scale examinations of Rorschach variables under certain circumstances or with certain groups of subjects can generate fruitful hypotheses for subsequent, more focused research. Moreover, an exploratory study in which a broad range of Rorschach variables is examined under circumstances or with people having some well-established or frequently hypothesized characteristics can lend construct validity both to the characterization of these subjects and to the Rorschach as a means of measuring these characteristics.

Exner (1986b) achieved such an end in an exploratory study of whether patients with *DSM–III* diagnoses of schizotypal or borderline personality disorder could be differentiated from each other and from schizophrenic patients on the Rorschach. Among several significant differences that emerged from his data, 68.5% of the schizotypal patients but only 17.9% of the borderline patients were found to have an introversive EB style, whereas 48.8% of the borderlines but only 2.6% of the schizotypals were extratensive. This difference in preferred coping style fits well with prevailing notions about these two conditions, namely, that schizotypal disorder has a primary cognitive element involving ideational peculiarities, whereas borderline disorder has a primary affective element involving emotional instability.

Because 60% of the schizophrenics in Exner's study were introversive and only 10% extratensive, moreover, the Rorschach EB data are consistent with the widely endorsed formulation of schizotypal, but not borderline disorder, as a schizophrenia spectrum condition. By contrast with the important implication of these results for psychopathology theory and differential psychodiagnosis, an exploratory study examining numerous Rorschach variables in relation to conditions or events that cannot be or have not been formulated in terms of personality processes is unlikely to generate any results, whether positive or negative, that can be explained meaningfully.

In addition, being selective in choosing Rorschach variables for research does not mean the number of variables must always be small. The prospects of getting meaningful results is jeopardized not by numerous variables per se, but by a surplus of variables that do not relate to any other variables in the study and could not have been expected to do so. In an examination of personality change during long- and short-term psychotherapy, for example, Weiner and Exner (1991) used 27 different Rorschach variables. However, each of these variables was selected on the basis of specific reasons for regarding it as an index of adjustment difficulty and as a potential measure of progress in psychotherapy.

For example, one of the variables examined was a low Egocentricity Index, which signifies low regard for oneself in comparison to others and should become less frequent over time among patients receiving psychotherapy, if psychotherapy is effective. Presumably because of the conceptual basis on which they were selected, 24 of the 27 Rorschach indices of adjustment difficulty became significantly ($p < .05$) less frequent among these patients over time, which served to demonstrate both that psychotherapy can promote positive personality change and the Rorschach can provide a valid measure of such change.

RELIABLY SCORABLE VARIABLES

Basic psychometric principles indicate that the correlation between two variables is limited by the extent to which each is reliable. Reliability, which is an index of how closely an obtained score for a variable approximates its true score, can be estimated in several ways, such as by examining temporal stability (retest correlations) and interitem consistency (Cronbach's alpha). Obviously, researchers will enhance their prospects of finding substantial correlations between variables by working only with variables of established reliability. Before even beginning to apply any reliability estimate to a set of obtained scores, however, investigators need to have good reason to believe that these obtained scores can be and have been reliably determined in the first place, that is, that there is substantial interscorer agreement concerning what these scores should be.

Accordingly with the Rorschach, any variables selected for study in hopes of being able to relate them significantly with some other variables should previously have demonstrated adequate rater reliability. As the standard for adequate rater reliability, trained scorers should be able to achieve a minimum of 80% agreement for variables included in the research, and for some variables, such as location choice, the percentage of agreement should be considerably higher. The scores used in the Comprehensive System satisfy this requirement; substantial interrater agreement was required for inclusion in the system, and most of the codes used in it have subsequently shown better than 90% agreement among trained examiners (Exner, 1986a, pp. 134, 168). A great many other specialized scales and configurations developed by Rorschach researchers have likewise proved capable of being reliably scored.

However, investigators need to recognize that whether a variable can be reliably scored does not ensure that it has been reliably scored in their particular study. For Comprehensive System variables, as well as for other scales and configurations, investigators should restrict their study to those that can be reliably scored by their scorers among their subjects. The *Journal of Personality Assessment* has set a formal policy in this regard for Rorschach studies to be considered for publication (Weiner, 1991). At least 20 protocols from the research sample, or a substantial percentage of the protocols in a small-sample study, should be scored independently by two of the people involved in scoring the total sample of records. The percentage of agreement between these scorers should then be determined for broad categories of scoring, such as Location and Developmental Quality, Determinants, Form Quality, and Content. With respect to Form Quality, for example, if the 20 records average 20 responses, there will be 400 Form Quality scores, and of these at least 80%, or 320, should have been coded the same way by both scorers.

Should a study using the Rorschach be concerned solely with Location Choice or Popular responses, the acceptability criterion should probably be increased to at least 90% agreement to demonstrate sufficient scoring reliability to warrant including the Rorschach in the study. Locations and Populars are simple scores, and scoring disagreements about them rarely occur except by negligence. Failure to achieve an 80% or higher agreement level on a variable being used in the particular study leaves two choices: Either drop that variable from the data analysis or, especially if the variable has previously demonstrated adequate scorer reliability, have the records re-scored by Rorschach examiners who are sufficiently trained and experienced to achieve the level of agreement that is known to be obtainable.

Investigators also need to appreciate that there may be times when intuitively appealing and richly explanatory ways of coding the Rorschach will defy efforts to achieve adequate scoring agreement. Creative researchers who have a good grasp of the Rorschach and a keen understanding of personality dynamics are easily capable of generating new ways of coding Rorschach responses, particularly with respect to content, that seem conceptually sound and potentially informative. However, to serve the best interests of researchers concerned with sustaining the credibility of the Rorschach and the confidence of research consumers interested in being informed by the literature, investi-gators should refrain from collecting or seeking to publish Rorschach scales for which adequate interscorer agreement cannot be achieved.

On the other hand, there is no reason to anticipate that creative concep-tualization and sound psychometrics will prove incompatible. What can be learned, for example, from images of human figures who are alternately leaning toward and pulling back from each other, or who are explicitly described as trying to decide whether to hit or caress each other? From an object relations perspective, there is good reason to believe that such re-sponses reflect ambivalence in interpersonal relatedness, perhaps as a con-sequence of defensive use of splitting, and may therefore provide a clue to borderline personality disorder.

Exactly this line of reasoning was followed by Coonerty (1986), who formulated a Separation–Individuation Theme Scale for the Rorschach that included a score for figures separating and coming together and was exam-ined in samples of schizophrenic and borderline subjects. Before proceeding, however, Coonerty developed a rater's manual for her scale and demon-strated that independent scorers trained in its use could achieve 96% agree-ment in rating its various categories. Not surprisingly, then, her sophisticated conceptualization of variables and her attention to reliable scoring of these variables resulted in her being able to demonstrate significantly more nu-merous themes of separation–individuation in the Rorschach records of bor-derline than schizophrenic subjects. The broader implications of this example speak to a central theme of this chapter: Whatever their preferred ways of viewing the Rorschach, investigators who design good research with the test usually will get good results.

SELECTING PREDICTOR AND PREDICTED VARIABLES

To promote significant and useful findings in Rorschach research, the pre-dictor and predicted variables with which Rorschach variables are to be correlated should, like these Rorschach variables, be *refined* and *conceptu-*

ally based. In addition, every effort should be made to include behavioral as well as inferential variables and to guarantee the independence of these variables from the Rorschach data.

Refined Variables

There are many easy ways of achieving negative results in research with the Rorschach and other assessment instruments. The easiest of these involves correlating Rorschach variables with global or heterogeneous characterizations of people or their behavior. To take demographics as a ready example, knowledgeable clinicians recognize that groups of males and females, Blacks and Whites, adolescents and adults, and rural and urban dwellers are as likely to differ among themselves as from each other with respect to personality style. Unless some previously demonstrated or clearly formulated reasons can be advanced for anticipating personality differences between broad groups of subjects, the likelihood of differentiating between them even with carefully selected Rorschach variables is minimal. Hence, hypotheses concerning Rorschach differences among grossly defined subject groups rarely generate confirmatory findings.

On the other hand, accumulated wisdom and new ideas can be used to refine research variables in ways that will guarantee meaningful results in Rorschach studies. Consider, for example, an investigation regarding aspects of schizophrenic disorder. Schizophrenia is a global category of psychopathology that embraces a considerable range of possible personality functioning. The schizophrenia of acutely disturbed first admission patients is markedly different from the schizophrenia of chronically disturbed and multiply hospitalized patients, and substantial differences also exist between paranoid and nonparanoid schizophrenics, incipiently disturbed and remitting schizophrenics, and medicated and nonmedicated schizophrenics. Accordingly, in selecting subjects for research on schizophrenia, such subgroupings ought to be as carefully specified as subcategories of Rorschach scores.

If a piece of Rorschach research is designed in this way—that is, if carefully defined subgroups of schizophrenic patients are compared with each other or with other equally well-defined nonschizophrenic subject groups along Rorschach dimensions on which there is good reason to expect them to resemble or differ from each other—the data will be useful and informative no matter how they turn out. Results consistent with expectation will confirm theory and solidify existing knowledge. Unexpected results will indicate that there is more to be learned about certain aspects of schizophrenic disorder and/or their manifestations on the Rorschach, and they will point in new research directions for doing so. The results of Rorschach research that is properly designed around refined variables, whatever these results may be, cannot be brushed aside as unreliable or artifactual.

The literature provides numerous other examples of why and how global characterizations of people and their actions must be refined and subcategorized to support incisive research. If a research question concerns personality disorder, the selection of variables to predict or be predicted by Rorschach variables must take account of what is known or can be hypothesized about different varieties of personality disorder (e.g., see Millon, 1981; Widiger, Frances, Spitzer, & Williams, 1988). Studies of psychotherapy effects should distinguish among different forms of psychotherapy extending over different intervals of time (see Lambert, Shapiro, & Bergin, 1986). An examination of the origins or consequences of substance abuse must recognize that drugs differ in the factors that lead to their use and in the effects they cause (see Kandel, Davies, Karus, & Yamaguchi, 1986). Research on the psychological consequences of having been sexually abused should consider the differential impact of such factors as the age at which the abuse occurred, whether the abuser was a stranger or a familiar person, and whether the abuse was physical as well as sexual (see Finkelhor, 1990).

Conceptually Based Variables

Because the Rorschach measures personality processes, it can be expected to relate meaningfully only to variables that are determined by personality processes. Like the Rorschach variables with which they will be correlated, then, predictor and predicted variables in Rorschach research should lend themselves to conceptualization in terms of personality functioning. When predictor and predicted variables lack relevance for personality functioning, they are unlikely to correlate with any Rorschach variables, and their failure to do so provides no useful information.

This consideration in attempting to design fruitful personality assessment research has traditionally been discussed in terms of the amount of *nonpersonality variance* that inheres in a predictor or predicted variable (see Goldfried et al., 1971, chap. 13; Weiner, 1977). The more nonpersonality variance that is inherent in a variable, the more its occurrence or extent is determined by factors unrelated to personality processes and the less effectively it can be measured by a personality assessment instrument. Accordingly, Rorschach researchers who want to maximize their likelihood of obtaining significant relationships and of being able to explain these relationships in meaningful ways should select predictor and predicted variables having as much personality variance as possible.

As an example of what can happen when predictor or predicted variables only partially embrace personality variance, consider the very important matter of posthospital adjustment in psychiatric patients. The adequacy of their course following discharge from inpatient treatment will certainly depend in part on personality characteristics of these patients, such as how capable they are of perceiving their experiences accurately and how well they can tolerate frustration. However, their posthospital adjustment will also be influenced substantially by such potent environmental factors as where and with whom they live; what kinds of family, school, or work responsibilities they have to shoulder; and the kinds of outpatient treatment facilities and interpersonal support networks that are available to them. Because some part of the variance in posthospital adjustment derives from personality characteristics, Rorschach variables may contribute to successful prediction as one component of a discriminant function that includes adequate attention to these other factors. On the other hand, given the amount of nonpersonality variance in posthospital adjustment, the researcher who sets out to predict it from Rorschach variables alone is courting negative results that will have little meaning.

Meaninglessness is especially likely to result when Rorschach research is attempted with variables that embrace hardly any personality variance. Illustrative in this regard are efforts to use the Rorschach for diagnosing of conditions that arise independently of personality determinants. People can become brain damaged, for example, whatever their personality style, and becoming brain damaged, although it affects personality functioning in various ways in individual cases, does not bring with it any distinctive "brain-damaged personality." The psychological hallmarks of brain damage are cognitive, linguistic, and/or perceptual-motor impairments that may sometimes be reflected on the Rorschach (as, for example, by perseverative concept formation), but are not directly measured by the Rorschach. The psychological assessment of brain damage calls for measures of cognitive, linguistic, and perceptual-motor capacities, not measures of personality.

Another noteworthy blind alley for diagnosis by personality assessment involves substance abuse. Although psychological factors figure prominently in the disposition to excessive drug use, there is no such thing as an "alcoholic personality" or a "heroin addict personality," any more than there is a brain-damaged personality. The best way to find out if someone has a drinking problem is to put away the personality tests and ask the person. Considerable time has been wasted looking for alcoholism in the Rorschach. It has not been found because it is not there, and it is not there because being an alcoholic does not embrace any distinctive personality characteristics. The lesson taught by such realization is that Rorschach research should exclude predictor or predicted variables that cannot be distinctively conceptualized in terms of personality processes.

Behavioral Variables

Behavioral variables are observable features of what people are likely to be, to do, or to have experienced. In terms of actual events, for example, a person may be female or divorced; may become violent when provoked or submissive when challenged; or may have experienced hospitalization, school failure, or death of a parent in childhood. Because observable events can for the most part be identified objectively, they provide highly reliable variables for inclusion in research studies.

Observable events vary in this regard, however, depending on how complex they happen to be. Whether a person is married is a highly objective phenomenon concerning which there can be little disagreement if the necessary facts are available. Deciding whether a married person is an adolescent or an adult is a bit more complicated, however; the identification can be made reliably, but only after agreement is reached concerning whether some particular age should be the criterion for establishing the boundary between adolescence and adulthood, or whether being married makes a difference, or whether other factors, such as being a parent, should be used to categorize people as adolescents or adults. Even more complicated would be determining whether a mother or father is providing good parenting, because some subjective judgments are necessary concerning what kinds of behaviors in what proportion constitute good parenting. Nevertheless, data consisting of observable events generally tend to be highly reliable, because they involve relatively little inference between what is recorded (e.g., this person is 17 years old) and what is concluded (e.g., this person is an adolescent).

By contrast, personality tests provide inferential, not behavioral, variables. Even a response to a face valid self-report item on a structured, presumably "objective" personality assessment instrument contains sufficient subjectivity to require inferential interpretation. Suppose, for example, that a subject checks "Yes" to a personality inventory item "I am a neat and tidy person." The behavioral variable in this instance is checking "Yes" to the item, "I am a neat and tidy person," and neither clinicians nor researchers are much interested in whether this person goes around all day checking "Yes" to the item, "I am a neat and tidy person." What is of interest instead is whether this the individual is in fact a neat and tidy person. The individual's saying so certainly points in this direction, without requiring much of an inferential leap, and this inference is more likely to be reliable than concluding from the person's saying, "I am a neat and tidy person," that the individual had a strict mother, an authoritarian father, or trouble with toilet training. This does not mean that these latter hypotheses are unreasonable, just that they are more highly inferential and thus less certainly reliable than merely concluding that the subject is in fact a neat and tidy person.

Nevertheless, even this conclusion will be less than perfectly objective. If our subject is age 17, can we be as positive that the subject is a neat and tidy person as we are that the subject is an adolescent? Perhaps this person's standards of what it means to be neat and tidy differ from those of most people, in which case we are dealing with misperceptions. Perhaps this person sees being neat and tidy as a good thing or a bad thing to be and is approaching the self-report test situation with fake-good or fake-bad motivation, in which case we could be dealing with exaggeration or defensiveness. In all such instances, there are subjective processes that intervene between what people are really like and how they choose to respond to self-report items.

Similarly on the Rorschach, the obtained data are inferential to a greater or lesser extent. Some patterns of responding provide relatively objective data, because they are closely representative of the conclusions usually inferred from them. Subjects who give very few Whole responses and an abundance of Detail responses, for example, are probably people who in their daily lives often fail to see the forest for the trees. By contrast, thematic analysis of Rorschach responses is relatively subjective, because multiple levels of inference are required to construct a bridge between such percepts as, "Two people tugging on something they both want to have," and inferences such as unresolved sibling rivalry. Experienced Rorschach clinicians are well aware of the importance of distinguishing among their interpretations with respect to just how much inference they involve, in order to give greatest emphasis in their reports to those that are fairly close to the data, and hence relatively reliable, and to be more tentative and speculative in commenting on those that are more highly inferential and need to be taken as hypotheses rather than certainties.

Hopefully these introductory comments on the nature of behavioral and inferential variables demonstrate that, to some degree or another, all personality tests are inferential measures. Even the so-called objective tests, let alone projective tests, have a large subjective element, because subjects decide what to report and what not to report and because they judge themselves ("Am I neat and tidy?") by their own personal standards. With respect to research, this observation signifies that Rorschach studies using other personality test findings as predictor or predicted variables are doing little more than correlating one inferential measure with another. Correlating inferential measures with each other compounds whatever unreliability may be inherent in each of them and fails to ground whatever relationships they may demonstrate in real-life behavior. Only by including behavioral as well as inferential variables in their research designs can investigators use Rorschach data effectively to expand knowledge about what people are likely to be, to do, or to have experienced.

To elaborate on this important consideration, research without behavioral variables lacks utility because, like research without conceptualization, its negative findings are difficult to explain and its positive findings have limited explanatory power. Taking the negative case first, suppose that an investigator seeks to correlate the Comprehensive System D score, which provides an index of experienced distress, with state or trait anxiety as measured by the State–Trait Anxiety Inventory (STAI). Some preliminary efforts of this kind indicate that correlations between these two inferential measures are likely to prove minimal (Exner, personal communication, 1991). The question is, what do low correlations between Rorschach D and STAI mean? Is D an unreliable (i.e., inaccurate) measure of experienced distress and therefore unlikely to show a high correlation with STAI? Or is STAI an unreliable measure of anxiety and therefore unlikely to show a high correlation with D? Or are both unreliable measures and therefore unlikely to show high correlations with anything? Or are both reliable measures that accurately sample somewhat different and only slightly correlated components of stress/anxiety?

These questions are difficult to answer in the absence of operational definitions of experienced distress and state and trait anxiety that involve observable events. To what extent are the subjects experiencing palpitations or other physiological indications of distress/anxiety, for example; or are they having recurrent nightmares; or are they described by others as being tense and irritable; or have they been given a formal diagnosis of some anxiety disorder? If no such behavioral data have been included in a study in which the Rorschach is being compared with other tests, then virtually nothing can be learned from insignificant findings.

Even when significant correlations are found between Rorschach variables and other inferential measures, the intrinsic interest of the data and their implications for further research do not prevent them from being essentially weak data. Consider the relationship between Rorschach Popular (P) responses and Scale 4 (Psychopathic Deviate) on the MMPI. In terms of inattention to or disregard for conventional ways of thinking and behaving, there is good conceptual basis for expecting a substantial correlation between infrequent P and an elevated 4. But what does it mean if a large correlation is in fact found between these two inferential variables? Such a finding constitutes weak data, because it cannot answer the crucial question, "So what?"

To gain some explanatory power and provide an answer to "So what?", let us beef up this hypothetical study by adding some good behavioral indices of social conformity, such as frequency of getting into difficulty with authority. Now if positive results emerge, with P and 4 correlating negatively with each other and correlating significantly in opposite directions with frequency of difficulties with authority, the investigator has hold of something important. Both P and 4 have been found associated with behaviors they would theoretically be expected to predict, which helps to demonstrate their construct validity; a predictive capacity has been demonstrated that has practical as well as psychometric implications; and, in addition, a possibility has been created for improving on this predictability with a discriminant function combining the two test variables of infrequent P and elevated 4.

Despite the generally minimal import of research correlating tests with one another, there is one circumstance in which such studies may serve an important purpose. This circumstance involves construct validity research in which the nature and meaning of a test are examined in a nomological net comprising numerous other tests presumed to measure the same personality characteristics. In a useful study of this kind, Belter, Lipovsky, and Finch (1989) examined the relationship of the Comprehensive System Egocentricity Index to several self-report measures of self-concept in a sample of children and adolescents, including the Piers–Harris Children's Self-Concept Scale, the Children's Depression Inventory, and the Nowicki–Strickland Locus of Control Scale for Children. Their findings indicated that this Rorschach variable differs from these self-report measures in which aspects of self-concept are being tapped.

Investigators who commit themselves to identifying objective events and behavioral variables for inclusion in their Rorschach studies will find that even a little ingenuity can yield substantial returns. Easily attainable facts and fairly simple subject manipulations, conceptualized in terms of Rorschach variables, can lend considerable external validity to obtained relationships and provide a powerful demonstration both of personality processes and of the capacity of the Rorschach to measure these processes.

With respect to objective events, some noteworthy findings have emerged from comparisons by A. Spigelman and G. Spigelman (1991) of children from divorced and nondivorced families. Consistently with the literature on the impact of family breakup, they found significantly higher scores on the Rorschach Depression Index (DEPI) among divorce than nondivorce children. Similarly, in accord with general expectation, Acklin (1990) found Rorschach evidence of poorer perceptual accuracy and less efficient visual scanning in learning disabled compared to normally functioning children. As a third example of impressive external construct validation, Shapiro, Leifer, Martone, and Kassem (1990) demonstrated significantly more depression on the Rorschach among sexually abused girls, as measured by DEPI and two of its components evaluated separately (*Morbid* content and achromatic color), than among a comparison group of nonabused girls.

As for subject manipulations, some studies of Texture (*T*) use provide good examples of how research can be designed to demonstrate solid external validity. The frequency with which subjects use *T* in formulating their responses has long been thought to provide information about their orientation toward physically close, psychologically intimate, and mutually supportive relationships with other people. The mode for *T* is one, which characterizes the records of approximately 80% of nonpatient subjects beginning at age 7. Approximately 10% of nonpatients give zero *T*, which has been taken to indicate discomfort with closeness, aversion to intimacy, and lack of anticipation of supportive relationships, even though support from others may be viewed from afar as desirable. The remaining approximately 10% of nonpatient subjects give more than one *T*, which has traditionally been interpreted to signify some affective hunger or experience of emotional deprivation manifest in more than the usual amount of needing, wanting, and seeking close, intimate, and supportive relationships.

In one piece of research, the "waiting-room study," subjects were job-seekers coming to a personnel office for an interview. They were directed to a waiting room in which there was a couch, a matching easy chair next to the couch at a right angle, and a third easy chair separate and at some distance from the other two pieces of furniture. One other "job applicant" (one of the experimenters) was in the room, seated at the far end of the couch away from the adjacent easy chair. The dependent variable of the study consisted simply of where the subject chose to sit: on the couch, in the easy chair next to the couch, or in the easy chair across the room. The main independent variable was zero *T* on the Rorschach, which was found to be significantly associated with choosing the most interpersonally distant place to sit. By contrast, subjects with more than one *T* tended to sit as close as possible to the collaborator (Exner, 1986a, chap. 14).

In the other study, the "marriage-license study," couples applying for a marriage license were solicited as subjects and given the Rorschach. One year later they were contacted and asked about the course of their marriage. With respect to *T*, those couples in which both partners had *T* in their records, and also those in which neither husband nor wife had used *T*, were relatively likely to report getting along well or at least planning to remain together. By contrast, those couples who had differed in *T*, with one spouse using *T* and the other not using *T*, were likely to have reported more marital disputes or difficulties, and some had even separated or were anticipating separation (Exner, personal communication, 1991).

Consistent with basic theory about marital compatibility, those couples who shared a similar orientation toward closeness and intimacy had managed well together by keeping a degree of distance comfortable to both. The disputing couples, on the other hand, had apparently made each other uncomfortable by one spouse seeking a closer or more distant relationship than the other spouse would have preferred. By employing a simple but highly relevant dimension of objective variability, this modest study yielded powerful evidence of the construct validity of *T* responses and the role of a shared orientation toward intimacy in sustaining a workable marriage.

VARIABLE INDEPENDENCE

To have powerful implications, hypothesis-testing research must employ variables that are either independent of each other or have some known preexisting relationship that can be measured and taken into account. In the absence of independence or controllable dependence, variables become hopelessly confounded or *contaminated*, and contamination of variables precludes drawing any meaningful inference from obtained results. Suppose, for example, a hypothesis is advanced that the students in school A are brighter than the students in school B. Suppose further, however, that shool A has admission requirements that include a demonstrated level of attainment on a standard test of intelligence, whereas school B has no such requirement. An empirical comparison will then be destined to demonstrate that school A's students are brighter than school B's students, because that is in part how they got into school A in the first place. Being in school A or B and being more or less intelligent are not independent events, and any relationship between them will thus be confounded and meaningless for any purpose except to confirm in circular fashion what is already known.

As simplistic as this example appears, and despite widespread familiarity with the importance of avoiding contamination of variables in hypothesis-testing research, failure to avoid such confounding all too often shows up in Rorschach and other personality assessment research. The invalidating impact of working with nonindependent variables is especially likely to intrude on clinical research concerned with differential diagnosis.

Suppose, for example, that an investigator interested in the diagnostic efficiency of the Comprehensive System Schizophrenia Index (SCZI) compares patients in a clinical facility who have been diagnosed as having a schizophrenic disorder with patients who have been assigned some other diagnosis. But suppose also that the psychologists who conducted the Rorschach examinations used the SCZI score in part as a basis for commenting on whether the patients in the study were schizophrenic, and suppose further that the comments of these psychologists influenced the final diagnosis that was assigned. Then the SCZI scores of the patients in the study and whether they were diagnosed schizophrenic are hopelessly confounded. Whenever Rorschach findings are likely to have influenced how subjects are subsequently viewed, described, or labeled, then the diagnostic validity and utility of the Rorschach cannot be adequately assessed by examining the views, descriptions, or labels subsequently attached to these subjects.

Although the problem of contamination of variables poses a challenge to Rorschach investigators, especially in clinical settings in which Rorschach testing is an integral part of mental health service delivery, there are effective ways of keeping Rorschach variables independent of the diagnostic or descriptive variables with which they are to be correlated. A simple but usually impracticable solution is to withhold any utilization of the Rorschach data until the subjects in a research study have already been identified as having some particular condition or disorder. The Rorschachs can even be administered by persons other than the psychologist conducting the diagnostic evaluation for clinical purposes, who then would base a report on other test findings.

Although sound in theory, such withholding of the fullest possible diagnostic evaluation borders in clinical practice on unethical conduct and is unlikely to satisfy the requirements of a human subjects review committee. Unless Rorschach researchers are conducting their study in a facility that customarily omits the Rorschach from its diagnostic test batteries, withholding the Rorschach data rarely proves appropriate as a means of minimizing contamination of variables.

A second possibility consists of establishing independence of variables by demonstrating that the Rorschach variables being studied were in fact not used by the examiners in formulating their clinical inferences about the subjects in the study. For the most part, however, this possibility will be limited to studies of novel configurations that examiners are unlikely to have used in drawing conclusions about the predictor or predicted variables in the study. For example, Weiner (1961), in a study of some potential but previously unidentified Rorschach indices of schizophrenia, demonstrated that the psychologists who had examined the patient sample did not consider these indices to be associated with schizophrenia.

A similar situation would obtain presently if an examiner were interested in whether SCZI helps to identify depression, because neither available data nor recommended clinical practice point to SCZI as helpful for this purpose. By and large, however, the extensive accumulation and broad dissemination of information on Rorschach indices of clinical phenomena severely limit the possibilities for investigators to explore test variables that Rorschach examiners are not already utilizing in determining whether these phenomena are present.

Accordingly, the better prospects for achieving independence of variables lie not in how the Rorschach is used, but in how non-Rorschach variables are identified. In clinical settings, for example, independence of variables can be achieved by assessing such non-Rorschach phenomena as whether patients are depressed, thought disordered, paranoid, or ready for hospital discharge separately from the actual clinical evaluation process in which the Rorschach has participated. Independent assessment with such structured interview methods as the Schedule for Affective Disorders and Schizophrenia (SADS) or the Structured Interview for *DSM–III–R* (SCID), for example, administered by research personnel not involved in patient care, can be used for diagnostic classification. Behavioral ratings by hospital or clinic personnel unacquainted with the Rorschach findings, using any of a variety of available patient rating scales, can provide independent measures of many other features of what these patients are like as people and how they may be expected to behave in the future.

CONCLUSIONS

This chapter began with reference to a time when Rorschach advocates had assumed a primarily defensive posture in the face of heavy attack on the psychometric soundness of the test. In these olden days most psychologists who found the test useful in their clinical work chose not to do psychometric battle. Instead, many Rorschachers countered their critics by arguing that Rorschach interpretation is art, not science, and should be judged accordingly, or that the Rorschach is not a test at all, but merely a stimulus to fantasy or a semi-structured interview. Some practitioners may still prefer to view and use the Rorschach in such ways, and they are of course free to do so—although presenting Rorschach interpretation as an entirely subjective process is unlikely to help psychologists make a favorable impression in sophisticated clinical case conferences or courtroom proceedings of the 1990s.

More to the present point, there is nothing about creative clinical interpretation or intuitive speculation based on the Rorschach that necessarily precludes empirical examination of reliability and validity. If such examinations are poorly designed, they will yield disappointing findings. However, the point of this chapter is that, for the Rorschach just as for any other apparently useful measuring instrument, good research will yield good data. With particular respect to selection of variables for study in Rorschach research, this chapter has indicated the importance of using Rorschach variables that are refined, interactive, conceptually based, selective, and reliably scorable; discussed the advantages of using non-Rorschach variables that are refined, conceptually based, behavioral, and independent; and illustrated how such considerations in the selection of variables increases prospects for obtaining statistically significant, conceptually meaningful, and practically useful findings.

REFERENCES

Acklin, M. W. (1990). Personality dimensions in two types of learning-disabled children: A Rorschach study. *Journal of Personality Assessment, 54*, 149–159.

Acklin, M. W., & Fechner-Bates, S. (1989). Rorschach Developmental Quality and intelligence factors. *Journal of Personality Assessment, 53*, 537–545.

Belter, R. W., Lipovsky, J. A., & Finch, A. J., Jr. (1989). Rorschach Egocentricity Index and self-concept in children and adolescents. *Journal of Personality Assessment, 53*, 783–789.

Blatt, S. J. (1975). The validity of projective techniques and their clinical and research contributions. *Journal of Personality Assessment, 39*, 327–343.

Blatt, S. J., & Allison, J. (1963). Methodological considerations in Rorschach research: The *W* response as an expression of abstractive and integrative strivings. *Journal of Projective Techniques, 27*, 267–278.

Blatt, S. J., Brenneis, C. B., Schimek, J. G., & Glick, M. (1976). Normal development and psychopathological impairment of the concept of the object on the Rorschach. *Journal of Abnormal Psychology, 85*, 364–373.

Blatt, S. J., Tuber, S. B., & Auerbach, J. S. (1990). Representations of interpersonal interactions on the Rorschach and level of psychopathology. *Journal of Personality Assessment, 54*, 711–728.

Cohen, J. (1990). Things I have learned (so far). *American Psychologist, 45*, 1304–1312.

Coonerty, S. (1986). An exploration of separation–individuation themes in the borderline personality. *Journal of Personality Assessment, 50,* 501–511.

Cooper, S. H., Perry, J. C., & O'Connell, M. (1991). The Rorschach defense scales: II. Longitudinal perspectives. *Journal of Personality Assessment, 56,* 191–201.

Exner, J. E., Jr. (1986a). *The Rorschach: A comprehensive system: Vol. 1. Basic foundations* (2nd ed.). New York: Wiley.

Exner, J. E., Jr. (1986b). Some Rorschach data comparing schizophrenic with borderline and schizotypal personality disorders. *Journal of Personality Assessment, 50,* 455–471.

Exner, J. E., Jr. (1991). *The Rorschach: A comprehensive system: Vol. 2. Interpretation* (2nd ed.). New York: Wiley.

Finkelhor, D. (1990). Early and long-term effects of child sexual abuse: An update. *Professional Psychology, 21,* 325–330.

Fisher, S., & Cleveland, S. E. (1958). *Body image and personality.* New York: Van Nostrand Reinhold.

Gerstein, A. I., Brodzinsky, D. M., & Reiskind, N. (1976). Perceptual integration on the Rorschach as an indicator of cognitive capacity: A developmental study of racial differences in a clinic population. *Journal of Consulting and Clinical Psychology, 44,* 760–765.

Goldfried, M. R., Stricker, G., & Weiner, I. B. (1971). *Rorschach handbook of clinical and research applications.* Englewood Cliffs, NJ: Prentice-Hall.

Hertz, M. R. (1934). The reliability of the Rorschach inkblot test. *Journal of Applied Psychology, 18,* 461–477.

Holt, R. R. (1967). Diagnostic testing: Present status and future prospects. *Journal of Nervous and Mental Disease, 144,* 444–465.

Johnson, M. H., & Holzman, P. S. (1979). *Assessing schizophrenic thinking.* San Francisco: Jossey-Bass.

Kandel, D. B., Davies, M., Karus, D., & Yamaguchi, K. (1986). The consequences in young adulthood of adolescent drug involvement. *Archives of General Psychiatry, 43,* 746–754.

Klopfer, B., Kirkner, F. J., Wisham, W., & Baker, G. (1951). Rorschach prognostic rating scale. *Journal of Projective Techniques, 15,* 425–428.

Lambert, M. J., Shapiro, D. A., & Bergin, A. E. (1986). The effectiveness of psychotherapy. In S. L. Garfield & A. E. Bergin (Eds.), *Handbook of psychotherapy and behavior change* (3rd ed., pp. 157–212). New York: Wiley.

Millon, T. (1981). *Disorders of personality.* New York: Wiley.

Parker, K. C. H., Hanson, R. K., & Hunsley, J. (1988). MMPI, Rorschach and WAIS: A meta-analytic comparison of reliability, stability, and validity. *Psychological Bulletin, 103,* 367–373.

Perry, W., & Viglione, D. J., Jr. (1991). The Ego Impairment Index as a predictor of outcome in melancholic depressed patients treated with tricyclic antidepressants. *Journal of Personality Assessment, 56,* 487–501.

Piotrowski, Z. A. (1937). The reliability of Rorschach's Eerlebnistypis. *Journal of Abnormal and Social Psychology, 32,* 439–445.

Rapaport, D., Gill, M., & Schafer, R. (1946). *Diagnostic psychological testing* (Vol. 2). Chicago: Year Book Publishers.

Rorschach, H. (1921/1942). *Psychodiagnostics.* Bern: Hans Huber.

Shapiro, J. P., Leifer, M., Martone, M. W., & Kassem, L. (1990). Multimethod assessment of depression in sexually abused girls. *Journal of Personality Assessment, 55,* 234–248.

Spigelman, A., & Spigelman, G. (1991). Indications of depression and distress in divorce and nondivorce children reflected by the Rorschach test. *Journal of Personality Assessment, 57,* 120–129.

Urist, J. (1977). The Rorschach test and the assessment of object relations. *Journal of Personality Assessment, 41,* 3–9.

Watkins, J. G., & Stauffacher, J. C. (1952). An index of pathological thinking in the Rorschach. *Journal of Projective Techniques, 16,* 276–286.

Weiner, I. B. (1961). Three Rorschach scores indicative of schizophrenia. *Journal of Consulting Psychology, 25,* 436–439.

Weiner, I. B. (1972). Does psychodiagnosis have a future? *Journal of Personality Assessment, 36,* 534–546.

Weiner, I. B. (1977). Approaches to Rorschach validation. In M. A. Rickers-Ovsiankina (Ed.), *Rorschach psychology* (2nd ed., pp. 575–608). Huntington, NY: Krieger.

Weiner, I. B. (1991). Editor's note: Interscorer agreement in Rorschach research. *Journal of Personality Assessment, 56,* 1.

Weiner, I. B., & Exner, J. E., Jr. (1991). Rorschach changes in long-term and short-term psychotherapy. *Journal of Personality Assessment, 56,* 453–465.

Widiger, T. A., Frances, A., Spitzer, R. L., & Williams, J. (1988). The DSM–III personality disorders: An overview. *American Journal of Psychiatry, 145,* 786–795.

CHAPTER FIVE

Subject Variables in Rorschach Research

Robert R. Dies

Those contemplating research with the Rorschach are faced with a host of problems relating to subject recruitment and selection, identification of appropriate control or comparison groups, and monitoring confounding variables that might subtly influence their subjects' participation in the study. These pragmatic issues often pose more serious threats to adequate research than problems associated with basic experimental design, statistical analysis, or the interpretation of results.

AN OVERVIEW OF RECENT RORSCHACH RESEARCH

In planning Rorschach research, it is essential to become familiar with how previous investigators have addressed these practical problems. This is generally accomplished through a careful literature review. Such a review has provided a framework for this chapter. A comprehensive survey of recent empirical reports was conducted to develop an overview of the current status of Rorschach research. The goal was to identify at least 150 investigations for critical review. An initial examination of *Psychological Abstracts* and *Index Medicus* suggested that it would be necessary to retrieve articles published since 1985 to fulfill this quota. The completed search included 175 empirical investigations published from 1986 through 1993. During this 8-year period, there were also numerous reviews of the Rorschach empirical literature on such specialized topics as research with the elderly (Hayslip & Lowman, 1986), borderline personality disorders (Acklin, 1993; J. Gartner, Hurt, & A. Gartner, 1989), suicidal patients (J. R. Eyman & S. K. Eyman,

1991), malingerers (Perry & Kinder, 1990), children's object relations (Tuber, 1992), and the integration of Rorschach and Minnesota Multiphasic Personality Inventory (MMPI) findings (Archer & Krishnamurthy, 1993).

The articles were published in 38 different journals (research projects included as chapters in books were not included), but only a few professional journals devote much space to Rorschach research. Only five periodicals published at least five Rorschach papers over the 8-year period, and half (49.2%) of these appeared in the *Journal of Personality Assessment*. A majority of the journals (24) included only one study. It may come as a surprise to some that there are less than two dozen empirical articles published each year in the Rorschach literature. This may, in part, be a reflection of the difficulty of conducting meaningful research with the test. The need to generate a reasonably large sample, the requirement for individualized administration, the lack of an adequate team of trained examiners, and the sheer amount of time required to process the data may seem prohibitive to even the seasoned researcher.

In the following sections, an overview of recent empirical work is presented, followed by a number of recommendations for effectively managing the types of practical problems that are commonly encountered in this aspect of Rorschach investigation. Obviously, any consideration of subject selection must be concerned with both *internal validity*, that is, the confidence that conclusions from an individual Rorschach study are the correct ones, and with *external validity*, or the capacity to generalize across related investigations (Campbell & Stanley, 1963).

Demographic Variables and Sample Sizes

Table 5.1 outlines the types of subjects that have been included in recent Rorschach research. Empirical investigations with children and adolescents (51 studies) have been separated from those conducted with adults (124 studies). In several instances, multiple articles have been published using the same subject pool, but these are counted as only one investigation in Table 5.1.

The fact that over two thirds (71%) of the research is focused on adult subjects may accurately reflect the interests of clinicians and researchers in the field; on the other hand, it may also represent the ease of subject recruitment. Thus, it is often more expedient to rely on samples of convenience. This frequently means undergraduates and nonpatient adults (as noted in Table 5.2), allowing investigators to avoid the problem of seeking parental permission to involve youngsters in a research endeavor.

The data in Table 5.1 reveal some interesting findings. For both younger and older populations, the samples often are vaguely defined by age. The category of "mixed" includes approximately 25% of the studies for both

TABLE 5.1
Demographic Variables in Rorschach Research: 1986–1993

Children/Adolescents (51 Studies)		N	(%)	Adults (124 Studies)	N	(%)
Age	Young (4–12)	18	(35.3)	Early (18–45)	66	(53.2)
	Teen (13–18)	21	(41.2)	Mid (46–60)	1	(0.9)
	Mixed (3–18)	12	(23.5)	Older (61–76)	7	(5.6)
				Mixed (18–76)	31	(25.0)
				Unspecified	19	(15.3)
Gender	> 67% Male	18	(35.3)	> 67% Male	26	(21.0)
	Balanced	24	(47.0)	Balanced	33	(26.6)
	> 67% Female	6	(11.8)	> 67% Female	38	(30.6)
	Unspecified	3	(5.9)	Unspecified	27	(21.8)
Race	< 10% Minority	6	(11.8)	< 10% Minority	16	(12.9)
	11%–20%	3	(5.9)	11%–20%	9	(7.3)
	21%–30%	0	(0.0)	21%–30%	3	(2.4)
	> 33%	9	(17.6)	> 33%	9	(7.3)
	Unspecified	33	(64.7)	Unspecified	87	(70.2)
Groups	Only one	15	(29.4)	Only one	54	(42.5)*
	Two compared	25	(49.0)	Two compared	42	(33.1)
	Three	6	(11.8)	Three	16	(12.6)
	Four or more	5	(9.8)	Four or more	15	(11.8)
	Sample Size	(Average)	74.8	Sample Size	(Average)	87.9
	Group Size	(Average)	41.0	Group Size	(Average)	58.0

*One publication reports results from several studies, thus the total number of investigations for this section is 127.

younger and adult samples, and for the latter a significant proportion of the empirical reports fail to provide any information on the age of their subjects (unspecified = 15.3%). For both groups, important developmental patterns have been largely ignored in the literature. Significant Rorschach changes have been documented in normative samples for children and adolescents (Exner, 1993; Wenar & Curtis 1991), and such trends would certainly warrant further investigation in the adult literature.

At present, it is clear that younger adults are overrepresented in the research (53.2%, plus those contained in the mixed and unspecified categories), and that senior citizens are grossly underrepresented. The age span in the mixed age category for adults is 18 to 76 years of age, with several studies including subjects ranging from older teenagers to septuagenarians, without any acknowledgment that such heterogeneity could be a problem in understanding the findings!

Most of the recent studies include samples that are reasonably balanced according to gender, or appropriately gender specific (e.g., male sex offenders, female anorexic patients, gender disturbed boys). However, Table 5.1 also shows that a sizable percentage of studies neglect to report gender

TABLE 5.2
Inpatient (IP) and Outpatient (OP)
Samples in Rorschach Research: 1986–1993

	Children/Adolescents				Adult			
Categories	IP	OP	Total	(%)	IP	OP	Total	(%)
Affective	9	1	10	(19.6)	9	4	13	(10.5)
Anxiety disorders	0	1	1	(2.0)	0	5	5	(4.0)
Borderline	4	0	4	(7.9)	8	10	18	(14.5)
Conduct/antisocial	9	1	10	(19.7)	5	3	8	(6.5)
Eating disorders	0	0	0	(0.0)	0	5	5	(4.0)
Gender identity	0	2	2	(3.9)	0	0	0	(0.0)
Learning disabled	0	3	3	(5.9)	0	0	0	(0.0)
Multiple personality	0	0	0	(0.0)	2	0	2	(1.6)
Narcissistic	0	0	0	(0.0)	0	3	3	(2.4)
Organic	1	0	1	(2.0)	0	1	1	(0.8)
Personality disorder	0	0	0	(0.0)	3	2	5	(4.0)
PTSD	0	0	0	(0.0)	2	1	3	(2.4)
Schizophrenic	2	0	2	(3.9)	18	4	22	(17.7)
Schizotypal	0	0	0	(0.0)	2	2	4	(3.2)
Sex offenders	1	1	2	(3.9)	0	1	1	(0.8)
Sexually abused	0	3	3	(5.9)	0	1	1	(0.8)
Substance abusing	0	0	0	(0.0)	1	1	2	(1.6)
Mixed	8	8	16	(31.4)	10	16	26	(21.0)
Unspecified	2	1	3	(5.9)	1	2	3	(2.4)
Nonpatients								
Normal adults	—	—	—		—	28	28	(22.6)
Medical patients	—	4	4	(7.8)	1	8	9	(8.1)
Students	—	21	21	(41.2)	0	32	32	(25.8)
Normative Data			5	(9.8)			14	(11.3)

Note. The percentage represents the proportion of studies including each type of sample. Because many investigations used more than one type of group, the percentage will exceed 100% within the Children/Adolescent ($n = 51$ studies) and Adult ($n = 124$ studies) categories.

composition of their samples; for adults this figure is over one fifth of the investigations (21.8%). Although gender differences on most Rorschach variables have not been found to be significant for adults (Exner, 1993), the number of female and male subjects within the samples should at least be reported, even if gender contrasts are not systematically explored.

Racial composition of the groups examined in Rorschach investigations has received very little mention in the literature. Most researchers simply do not report figures for their subjects' race or ethnicity. Quantitative comparisons between different racial groups have not been the focus of recent research, with the exception of a few studies making cross-cultural comparisons with very limited samples. Although a number of investigators noted that their experimental groups were comparable in terms of racial composition, it is not feasible, on the basis of current research, to determine whether or not racial differences across comparison groups have contributed to any biases in the vast majority of studies conducted with the Rorschach (Frank, 1992, 1993).

Finally, it is apparent from Table 5.1 that most of the empirical projects using the Rorschach incorporate only one or two groups (sightly more than 75% of the studies), and that the sample sizes are relatively small. Although the figures for adults seem more favorable, with total samples averaging nearly 90 subjects and groups averaging over 50 members, these numbers are inflated by the presence of several "outlier" studies with exceedingly large samples. Graves, Phil, Mead, and Pearson (1986), for example, studied 1,032 medical students, and Wagner and Frye (1990) retrieved 938 records from outpatient files that had accumulated over an extended period of time. The top 10 studies with adult subjects are all larger than investigations with children or adolescents—with one exception, a factor analytic study using inpatient adolescents (Anderson & Dixon, 1993). The average number of participants for these 10 adult studies is 377. Six of these projects employ large undergraduate samples, 1 is a huge community-based project, 2 are collaborative studies orchestrated through Rorschach workshops, and 1 is the archival investigation by Wagner and Frye. Without these investigations, the adult literature is roughly comparable to that for children and adolescents, that is, research designs with only one or two groups, and a total sample of approximately 75 subjects.

Diagnostic Variables in Rorschach Research

Table 5.2 presents a summary of the types of subjects examined in recent Rorschach research. The diagnostic labels are generally those furnished by the investigators. For both the child/adolescent and adult studies, nonpatient samples represent the largest proportion of research volunteers—that is, 41.2% and 48.4% (students and normal adults combined), respectively. In most instances these nonpatient groups were the focus of the investigation and not serving as comparison groups for clinical samples.

Although many studies use diagnostically diverse groups to examine Rorschach variables, the three patient groups that receive the most attention are the Affective Disorders, Personality Disorders, and Schizophrenics. By combining several of the various Axis II disorders listed in Table 1.2 (i.e., Antisocial, Borderline, Narcissistic, and Schizotypal), it becomes apparent that the Personality Disordered groups are the most frequent focus of recent Rorschach investigation. As noted later in this chapter, however, there is considerable diversity in how these patient groups are defined, and how well diagnostic considerations and confounding variables are controlled in many of these investigations.

104

Characteristics of Studies in Rorschach Research

Table 5.3 summarizes the type of investigations that are conducted with the Rorschach. Although correlational studies with only one group are common, group contrasts are much more prevalent in both the child/adolescent (68.6%) and adult (52.4%) literature. As noted earlier, these groups are often small and heterogeneous with regard to age, gender, and diagnostic classification. The purpose of the vast majority of these investigations is to establish Rorschach "signs" that will differentiate diagnostic groups, a goal that may be virtually impossible to accomplish given the ambiguities in the system of diagnostic classification, the multifaceted ways that dimensions of personality may manifest in the Rorschach, and the importance of incorporating life history and other test findings in any personality evaluation.

Intervention studies, the third type of investigation noted in Table 5.3, have not been common in recent years. Altogether, there have been 19 such studies (11%) among the empirical reports published during the 8-year period reviewed. Five of these (one adolescent and four adult) examine changes resulting from treatment interventions, whereas the remainder represent ex-

TABLE 5.3
Characteristics of Rorschach Research: 1986–1993

		Children/ Adolescents (51 Studies)		Adults (124 Studies)	
		N	(%)	N	(%)
Type of study	Correlational	14	(27.5)	42	(33.9)
	Group comparison	35	(68.6)	65	(52.4)
	Intervention used	2	(3.9)	17	(13.7)
Scoring system	Exner	34	(66.7)	64	(51.6)
	Klopfer	5	(9.8)	12	(9.7)
	Rapaport	3	(5.9)	9	(7.3)
	Beck	0	(0.0)	3	(2.4)
	Piotrowski	1	(2.0)	2	(1.6)
	Harrower	1	(2.0)	0	(0.0)
	Holtzman	0	(0.0)	1	(0.8)
	Schafer	1	(2.0)	1	(0.8)
	Unspecified or special content	6	(11.8)	32	(25.8)
Rorschach	Altered blots/instructions	2	(3.9)	27	(21.8)
administration*	Special inquiry	11	(21.6)	13	(10.6)
	Tape recording	0	(0.0)	7	(5.6)

Note. The category of "Altered blots/instructions" includes group administrations, restriction in the number of responses allowed, use of only a subset of Rorschach cards, special administration procedures (e.g., computerized), and actual experimental modification of the cards. Most of the items under the "Special inquiry" section relate to inquiry following each card or content focused inquiry.

perimental interventions exploring the impact of different instructions, duration of blot exposure, effects of motor inhibition on Rorschach movement scores, and similar phenomena.

Table 5.3 also shows that there is considerable variability among studies in the administration and scoring procedures employed in Rorschach research. Although some of this diversity is simply a function of the nature of the investigation (e.g., studies of thought disorder may rely on only a subset of Rorschach cards to gather modest samples of patients' verbalizations), it is also evident that straightforward comparisons across projects using different Rorschach methods will be problematic at best. Overall, 17.6% of the child/adolescent projects and 31.6% of the adult studies incorporate some unique feature in their Rorschach testing. These include group administration (7), use of only a subset of cards (8), restriction of the number of responses given by subjects (6), inquiry after each card (14), specialized questioning to generate content elaboration (9), the tape-recording of sessions (7), and other idiosyncratic variations. The impact of most of these differences on Rorschach findings has not been carefully explored, but these specialized strategies certainly represent potentially confounding factors in the interpretation of results.

RECOMMENDATIONS FOR RESEARCH

The survey of recent research suggests that numerous problems continue to plague empirical studies using the Rorschach. Generally, the samples are small and loosely defined in terms of age, gender, race, and diagnostic composition. Variations across investigations in terms of Rorschach scoring systems and methods of administration create additional problems for clinicians and investigators who hope to gain a clear understanding of the test and its applications from this body of literature. This section reviews the problems relating to subject selection, control groups, and confounding variables, and offer recommendations for how to overcome some of the practical problems that have frequently compromised the value of Rorschach research.

SUBJECT SELECTION

The foundation for most research is the presence of a carefully defined sample of sufficient magnitude to allow for the exploration of potential relationships among Rorschach variables and external criteria, and to offer reasonably confident generalizations about their results. Unfortunately, the number of research volunteers and the composition of the clinical groups have often been sources of major concern.

Sample Size

One fourth (25.1%) of the investigations with the Rorschach in recent years contain groups with 20 or fewer subjects in their research design. Georgoff (1991), for example, compared four terminally ill hospice patients with four cancer survivors to explore Rorschach differences in personality structure. In commenting on one contrast between her two groups, the author noted that nearly all of the responses of a specific type were provided by one patient. This points to a core problem with small samples, namely, the potential for misleading results due to a few deviant or unrepresentative subjects. This is often labeled the "outlier" problem in personality or psychotherapy research. Very few investigators have examined this outlier effect (e.g., Stevens, Edwards, Hunter, & Bridgman, 1993).

Those investigations with more substantial samples are at the opposite extreme. In this situation, researchers may be able to demonstrate reliable results, but the actual group differences or statistical associations may be clinically meaningless. For example, an investigator may report statistically significant correlations between Rorschach variables and self-report measures (e.g., Greenwald, 1990), but the correlations are only in the mid-twenties and account for a negligible amount of the overall variance. Imagine what the situation is like when the samples are unusually large. If a sample includes 100 subjects, a correlation of less than .20 is significant at the 5% confidence interval. The issue of sample size and statistical power is addressed more completely later in this book, and has been addressed frequently in the recent Rorschach literature (e.g., Acklin, McDowell, & Orndoff, 1992; Exner, 1992; Meyer, 1993).

There is no magic number that will serve as a benchmark for the ideal sample size. Too many other considerations play into the equation, such as the patient variables under consideration, the base rates of the variable in the clinical setting (Elwood, 1993), the heterogeneity of samples being compared, and the research design being implemented. Within a carefully controlled experimental design using well-matched clinical groups, the samples do not need to be as large, but with exploratory studies in uncharted areas, larger samples are essential. It is obvious, however, that too many of the investigations in the recent Rorschach literature have employed clinical samples that have not been adequate, due to the presence of numerous confounding variables across comparison groups.

Reducing Potential Confounds

The review of recent research unearthed a broad range of factors that raise serious questions about the findings and conclusions offered by many investigators. The clinical samples in many studies have been poorly defined.

In Table 5.1, the category "unspecified" was applied quite frequently for Age, Gender, and especially Race, and in both Tables 5.1 and 5.2 the heading of "mixed" was also overused for Age and Diagnosis. Indeed, the global description provided by many investigators renders their studies virtually uninterpretable.

Abraham, Mann, Lewis, Coontz, and Lehman (1990), for example, compared borderline, schizophrenic, and organic patients to detect differences in perceptual accuracy and cognitive dysfunction. Regrettably, the authors furnished only limited information on their subjects' age, gender, and average IQ. When it came to interpreting their results, the authors' were quite tentative in accounting for the lack of group differences. Was their sample too small? Were the diagnostic groups different along certain dimensions not mentioned by the investigators (e.g., chronicity, secondary diagnoses, medication)? Did the lack of homogeneity within their groups prevent consistent differences from emerging on the Rorschach? Without a more detailed description of the sample, it is simply not possible to explain the findings.

Whereas some researchers have used such global concepts as schizophrenic to characterize their samples (e.g., Adair & Wagner, 1992; Edell, 1987; S. Kreitler, H. Kreitler, & Wanounou, 1988; Suzuki, Peter, Weisbender, & Gillespie, 1987), there are other studies in the Rorschach literature to indicate that more refined discriminations are essential. For instance, DiNuovo, Laicardi, and Tobino (1988) found important differences between "florid" and "withdrawn" schizophrenics on indicators of disordered thinking, perceptual accuracy, and emotional control. Johnson and Quinlan (1993) established differences between paranoid and nonparanoid schizophrenics. Similarly, Holzman, Shenton, and Solovay (1986) demonstrated that even within the category of schizoaffective disorder there was sufficient evidence of heterogeneity to consider subclassifications.

The failure of researchers to furnish more detailed descriptions of their schizophrenic samples makes it very difficult to draw meaningful conclusions. For some investigators, the schizophrenic group was composed of chronically disabled patients averaging over 3 years of institutional care (e.g., S. Kreitler et al., 1988), whereas for other researchers chronic patients were explicitly excluded from the study (e.g., DiNuovo et al., 1988). Clearly, the schizophrenic samples evaluated in various studies are quite diverse, so that it is not appropriate to conclude that the category of schizophrenia has much homogeneity.

Perhaps this problem is no more apparent than with the "borderline" patient. Zalewski and Archer (1991) found dramatic differences in the standards used to define this diagnostic grouping. These criteria include the use of discharge diagnoses, specialized guidelines developed by specific investigators, retrospective application of *DSM–III* criteria to hospital records, and varying theoretical conceptualizations. In the survey of articles published from 1986 through 1993, 22 investigations of borderline patients were identified, 1 with children, 3 with adolescents, and 18 with adult samples. Those with younger samples studied inpatients, whereas those with adults were more varied in including both inpatient and outpatient groups. The samples differed in terms of age and gender balance, secondary diagnoses, mixture of hospital versus clinic samples, medication, and checklists used to formulate the diagnosis.

One illustration should be sufficient to demonstrate the problem of trying to understand Rorschach findings from this body of literature. Whereas some investigators established a range of meaningful differences on the Rorschach between borderline and schizotypal patients (e.g., Edell, 1987; Exner, 1986), others decided to collapse these two groups into a single diagnostic category called borderline (e.g., Lerner, Albert, & Walsh, 1987). Such major discrepancies in the fundamental definition of diagnostic groups are unlikely to contribute to substantial progress in our understanding of findings based on Rorschach research (Gartner et al., 1989; Zalewski & Archer, 1991). Unfortunately, the confusion over diagnostic issues, and the resulting inability to identify clear patterns in test performance, leads many professionals to sharply question the potential value of the Rorschach, not the vagaries in the prevailing diagnostic practice.

The literature is replete with examples of investigators who express their dismay that perhaps their diagnostic groups were too broadly defined, that is, that it was not appropriate to assume that a label such as schizophrenia (DiNuovo et al., 1988), borderline (J. Gartner et al., 1989), eating disordered (Smith, Hillard, Walsh, Kubacki, & Morgan, 1991), learning disabled (Acklin, 1990), or elderly (Gross, Newton, & Brooks, 1990) adequately delineated their sample. Although certain common elements can be found within a particular diagnostic group (e.g., perceptual impairment and cognitive disruption with schizophrenic patients), there may also be vast differences along other dimensions. Thus, female victims of sexual abuse share an unfortunate history of violation leading to their placement into a common category, but their reaction to the personal tragedy may differ depending on the age at the time of the abuse (Zivney, Nash, & Hulsey, 1988), whether or not they are cognitively and emotionally active versus more constricted (Shapiro, Leifer, Martone, & Kassem, 1990), and their perceived family environment (Nash, Hulsey, Sexton, Harralson, & Lambert, 1993).

Of course, the type of descriptive information that is important to highlight regarding subjects will vary as a function of the nature of the research focus. Certainly, for institutionalized patients such factors as prior hospitalizations, global functioning, medication, alternative treatments (e.g., Electro-Convulsive Therapy, ECT), and so forth are essential to report. For studies with children, educational attainment, intellectual achievement, social class, and type of school environment may be critical. Whereas gender effects may be minimal for many variables, age could be a much more salient consideration (Exner, 1993). Yet, the simple reporting of group averages or even the range may not be sufficient. For example, a group composed of children and adolescents spanning the ages from 7 to 15 may seem adequate, but numerous developmental differences may be "hidden" within this global description. Other investigators might judge that their sample is comparable, when in fact the groups are decidedly different based on the age distributions (e.g., 80% preteens and 20% teenagers in one study versus a 20%–80% split in the other). Finding a difference across the two studies in cognitive functioning may just reflect the differential balance in age in the respective samples (e.g., Wenar & Curtis, 1991).

The presence of such unknown confounds is often overlooked by investigators. Several of these were mentioned earlier, such as the number of prior hospitalizations, social class, and psychopharmacology (including type and dosage). Other important considerations include secondary diagnoses, situational influences, and motivational factors. A few additional illustrations may be useful.

Acklin and Bernat (1987) attempted to evaluate the relationship between depression and chronic low back pain. The authors reported that half of their subjects admitted to varying degrees of substance abuse, and that half were also receiving compensation, or contemplating litigation in an effort to obtain financial remuneration through the legal system. Both of these factors could certainly influence the findings within the study, and patently effect generalizability to other investigations in which such potentially biasing experiences were less evident.

Caprara, Holt, Pazielli, and Giannotti (1986) assessed the development of primary process by comparing test–retest Rorschachs with normal Italian schoolchildren. In discussing their study, the authors noted several artifacts that compromised their results, attributing some of the differences to the situation of testing or modifications in the atmosphere of the school over time. Other studies of change as the result of treatment casually mention, but rarely systematically report, the influence of life events on the subjects' progress through psychotherapy or their performance on the Rorschach. Gerstle, Geary, Himelstein, and Reller-Geary (1988) documented 1-year pretreatment to posttreatment changes for a number of Rorschach variables, but offered little information beyond a few sentences on the nature of the inpatient treatment regime. Other possible influences on follow-up testing were not considered, including expected developmental changes in their 9-year-old subjects, despite evidence that children's Rorschachs show only moderate stability over time (Exner, Thomas, & Mason, 1985; Exner & Weiner, 1994).

It is quite apparent that a multitude of confounding variables may exist in virtually any study using the Rorschach. Thus, it becomes essential that researchers first identify and then evaluate the importance of such variables, and furnish reasonably detailed information (e.g., means, ranges, distributions) about them to facilitate comparisons across studies. The criteria for subject selection should be described in detail, including any efforts to ensure interrater reliability in the diagnostic assignments. The bottom line is that researchers should think more critically about the nature of their clinical sample and generate a list of factors that could influence their results. Although it is certainly not feasible to eliminate all of these potentially biasing factors, due to practical limitations within clinical settings, there are options that can be employed when the data are analyzed; but these adjustments are not always appropriate.

At the very least, the investigator should explore the role of any potential confound in the interpretation of results. The goal is to rule out alternative explanations in understanding the findings. For example, if there are medication differences among patients, it would be useful to cite literature showing that this may not be a critical factor in understanding indices of disordered thinking or perceptual impairment (e.g., Exner, 1993). Similarly, finding brief records with certain children and adolescents seems appropriately viewed as a form of resistance, but only if other factors such as intellectual limitations, severe depression, anxiety, or problems regarding the issue of social desirability can be ruled out (Finch, Imm, & Belter, 1990).

CONTROL GROUPS

A problem that characterizes many investigations is the failure of researchers to provide proper control groups for determining the influence of critical variables in Rorschach performance. In the aforementioned treatment study by Gerstle and his colleagues (1988), and in others by Campo, Dow, and Tuset (1988) and Alterman, Slap-Shelton, and DeCato (1992), it would have been valuable to include a control group of subjects who were administered the Rorschach over the same time period as the subjects in the target group. Any differences between the treated and untreated groups on the second Rorschach can be attributed more definitively to the therapeutic program if the effects of time or other intervening variables can be discounted through the test–retest design.

Issues of Matching and Relative Equivalence of Groups

The selection of appropriate control or comparison groups is a crucial matter. Unfortunately, some investigators have employed the concept of *matching* in a very casual and erroneous manner. Matched groups are essentially identical for certain variables. For example, two groups might be matched groups for age, sex, marital status, and level of education. This means that subjects have been selected in pairs, so that for each 20-year-old single male who has completed 12 years of education that has been selected for the target or experimental group, there will be a 20-year-old single male who has completed 12 years of eduation in the control group. Matching for some variables is rather easy to do, but as the number of variables on which subjects are to be matched increases, or as the nature of the variables becomes more precise, the task can become a nightmare. For instance, Exner (1966) found it necessary to screen the records of more than 4,000 schoolchildren to match 33 pairs for age, sex, Stanford–Binet IQ, and exact grade point average for the preceding school year. It was the inclusion of the last variable, grade point average, that made the matching so difficult.

Sometimes, research objectives call for a design in which matching is used. Suppose, for example, an investigator postulates that changes in physiological measures such as galvanic skin response (GSR), pupillary constriction, and heart rate will be greater during the administration of the Rorschach when subjects take the test in the afternoon rather than in the morning. The same examiners will be used for both groups. Thus, the independent variable is time of day and the three physiological measures are the dependent variables. Should matching for any variables be considered in this design? Generally, the answer depends on the size of the groups. If the study includes a large number of subjects, such as 50 or more in each group who are drawn from the same subject pool, and they are randomly assigned, exact matching is probably not very important. However, if the number in each is modest, such as 25 or fewer, some matching probably should occur, at least for general factors that might affect the dependent measures (e.g., age, sex, and weight). In fact, the more astute investigator will go beyond those three variables and consider matching more precisely for other issues such as visual acuity, and the baselines for GSR, pupil size, and heart rate. Matching does not necessarily require exactness for every variable. In the illustration, matching for age might be by ranges, such as 20 to 25, 26 to 30, and so on. Similarly, baseline heart rates also might incorporate ranges, such as 67 to 70, 71 to 74, and so on. Nonetheless, if matching is applied, any selection of ranges or categories should be logical and conservative.

Most researchers try to avoid the demands of matching whenever possible. Some designs will permit the use of subjects as their own controls, and although this is ideal for some studies, it is not very applicable for most Rorschach research. The more common way to avoid the matching issue is by using either or both of two tactics. The first is simple random assignment, which can be used when a sizable number of subjects is available and they are to be assigned to two or more groups in a manipulation design. The likelihood that groups will be similar for many basic variables is substantial when they are randomly formed. This postulate is then confirmed (or rejected) by using the second tactic, that is, testing the assumption of *relative equivalence*.

The assumption of relative equivalence is also applicable when two or more groups are used but subjects are not randomly assigned, such as in studies comparing schizophrenics with depressives or evaluating the effects of treatment A versus the effects of treatment B. Relative equivalence is tested by simply calculating significance tests, comparing groups for the variables in question. If the results are not significant at a selected level, such as .05, or more conservatively .01, the investigator can assume that the two groups do not differ for the variable(s) in question. This does not mean the groups are matched, or even that they are the same. It merely demonstrates that the groups are not significantly different from each other for the variable(s) in question. Stated differently, the groups can be assumed to have a relative equivalence for certain variables because they do not differ significantly for those variables. In turn, this finding reduces the probability that those variables will have a confounding impact on the data. Obviously, as group sizes become smaller, the alpha level used to designate significance should be quite conservative.

The Purpose of the Control Group

Careful consideration regarding the role of the control group(s) is quite important. Sometimes a control group of nonpatients is deemed most suitable, whereas in other instances the proper comparison sample is one or more other patient groups. The focus of the study, and sometimes the hypotheses that have been formulated, create the framework for this decision. DiNuovo and his co-workers (1988), for example, decided to control for the effect of hospitalization in their investigation of schizophrenics, so they selected a control group of patients in the orthodontic section of the hospital.

The central issue in defining control groups is the variable(s) for which it may be important to "control." In some designs, simple demography such as age, sex, marital status, and completed education may suffice to create the definition for the group. Other designs may require that the control group(s) be defined more precisely and selected on the basis of more complex criteria such as length of hospitalization, socioeconomic level, age at the time of symptom onset, levels of intelligence, medication history, or some other combination of factors. If the target sample in an investigation is a diagnostic group, different clinical groups from the same setting often represent the most effective contrast or control groups. If the focus of the research is on thought disorder, for instance, a comparison between schizophrenic patients and major affective disorders may be most germane (e.g., Shenton, Solovay, & Holzman, 1987). For a study on learning disabled children, a matched group of youngsters (i.e., age, gender, social class, classroom attendance) from the same or similar school, controlling for IQ, might be most appropriate (e.g., Harper & Scott, 1990). On the other hand, two different types of learning disabled children, classified as spatial or language impaired according to their patterns of neuropsychological abilities on the Wechsler Intelligence Scale for Children–Revised (WISC–R), might be more effective (Acklin, 1990).

If an investigator hopes to demonstrate that a certain pattern on the Rorschach is unique to a particular diagnostic group, a sample of nonpatients probably will be quite inappropriate to use as a control group. The hypothesized differences might be evident, but it has not been demonstrated that the patient group differentiates from other patients (with other diagnoses) within the same setting. Thus, schizophrenic patients may manifest considerably more thought disorder than a group of nonpatient controls, but show fewer discernible differences when compared with bipolar patients (Holzman et al., 1986). Before it is possible to argue that a particular constellation of Rorschach variables is characteristic of schizophrenic patients, there must be contrasts made with other diagnostic groups who might also elevate on those features contained in the Rorschach index: inpatient and outpatient nonschizophrenics, affective disorders, characterological disorders (Exner, 1993).

Obviously, besides the careful selection of appropriate controls, investigations should provide reasonably thorough descriptions of the other variables discussed earlier (e.g., age, gender, race, number of admissions). In this fashion, the critical factors that might explain differences on the Rorschach can be addressed more competently. Without this detailed description of the samples it is much more difficult, if not virtually impossible, to interpret any statistical contrasts. Differences that are viewed as related to specific diagnostic issues might in fact be associated with discrepancies in such confounding variables as inequities in global functioning or imbalance in the distribution of secondary diagnoses.

It would be wise for investigators to systematically explore the effects of potentially confounding variables. Gallucci (1989), for example, attempted to ensure comparability of his groups of very bright children by conducting chi-square analyses on demographic variables, and then used multivariate analyses to confirm that groups were relatively equivalent for such factors as number of parents in the home and their ages, family income, number of siblings, and scores on a behavioral checklist. A careful approach to sample description permits greater confidence in interpreting any significant differences in Rorschach variables between groups.

Failure to Examine Unplanned Differences Between Groups

The recent Rorschach literature is replete with studies that have seemingly ignored this critical issue. There are studies with systematic differences between target groups and control groups on demographic variables such as gender, age, and education (e.g., Berg, 1990; Edell, 1987), differential drop-out rates (e.g., Leifer, Shapiro, Martone, & Kassem, 1991), co-morbid diagnosis (e.g., Hilsenroth, Hibbard, Nash, & Handler, 1993), and varying motivation for testing (Morgan & Viglione, 1992). Thus, several investigators have solicited their control subjects through newspaper advertisements and paid them for their participation in the study (e.g., Goddard & Tuber, 1989; Marsh & Viglione, 1992; Stuart et al., 1990), whereas other subjects have been urged by their therapists to participate in research (e.g., Richman & Sokolove, 1992). Still other researchers have overlooked differences between experimental and control groups in terms of their setting, such as inpatient versus outpatient status or contrasts across school or clinic environments (e.g., Acklin & Alexander, 1988; Tuber, Frank, & Santostefano, 1989). If the experimental and control groups are differentially recruited, derived from substantially divergent clinical contexts, or show numerous differences on factors that might affect their Rorschach performance, it would be ill-advised to conclude that the obtained differences are the sole product of the target variable, such as diagnostic classification. The impact of these major differences across groups is seldom fully explored, despite threats to the internal validity of any conclusions that are offered regarding Rorschach differences between the samples.

Inappropriate Use of Published Norms

A special example of the problem of differences across comparison groups is the misuse of normative data for statistical evaluation. It has been noted that almost any group that is homogeneous for some features should differ from the published reference groups (Exner, 1993), which consist of samples that are deliberately diverse on such issues as socioeconomic class and geographic distributions. Nevertheless, at least 19 studies published from 1986 to 1993 have used the normative samples for statistical comparison. These investigations are wide ranging and cover such varying groups as learning disabled children (Acklin, 1990), multiple personality disorders (Armstrong, 1991), agorophobics (de Ruiter & Cohen, 1992), mothers of behaviorally disturbed children (Lipgar & Waehler, 1991), battered women (Kaser-Boyd, 1993), Nazi war criminals (Resnick & Nunno, 1991), and "never-married" men (Waehler, 1991). Invariably, differences between experimental samples and normative controls are discovered.

Although the reference norms may serve as guidelines for noting extreme deviations from expected values, or in some cases when comparing results from other large-scale heterogeneous samples, it is not appropriate to include them in small sample research for formal statistical contrasts (Exner, 1993). The interpretation of any differences will be almost meaningless. This is especially true when one considers that all previous attempts to use normative findings have ignored important differences even within the reference group patterns, and have simply evaluated means and standard deviations. That is, recent research indicates that certain refinements in the normative data are necessary to identify important individual differences, such as those relating to certain coping styles (Exner, 1993). Individuals who choose to delay in formulating decisions, preferring to keep feelings at a more peripheral level during problem solving (i.e., introversives), may appear quite different when evaluating Rorschach variables related to affect or ideation, than another group of individuals who prefer to merge feelings with thinking during problem solving (i.e., extratensive subjects). These important differences in stratified samples have been overlooked until very recently (Exner, 1993), but are obviously critical in appropriate application of the normative data.

MAINTAINING STANDARD PROCEDURES

Table 5.3 summarized Rorschach administration and scoring variations that make comparisons across studies quite problematic. Obviously, violations in standard practice, such as group administration of the test, using only a subset of the cards, and restricting the number of responses provided by a subject, will limit the external validity of the findings. Some of these variations have been evaluated and found to be quite important. For example, inquiry after each card tends to produce more responses (Exner, 1993). But other factors have not been carefully researched; the tape recording of a Rorschach administration may seem like a relatively harmless modification, but that is only speculation and requires empirical evaluation. Certain literature makes it clear that some investigators have been rather insensitive to subtle factors that could jeopardize the comparability of their findings to those obtained by other researchers.

The Problem of Brief Records

Recent research indicates that protocols with fewer than 14 responses are quite likely to be invalid (Exner, 1988). In fact, this finding prompted a complete revision of the normative tables for the Comprehensive System. When the 1982 reference norms for children were evaluated, it was necessary to discard 15% of the records because of the low number of responses. The survey of articles published from 1986 to 1993 indicates that investigators were highly variable in their definitions of invalid records. Thus, some studies have used cutoffs for R as low as 10 (Gacono, 1990; Mattlar, Tarkkanen, Carlsson, Aaltonen, & Helenius, 1993; Simon, 1989), 11 (Gacono & Meloy, 1991; Tuber, 1989), 12 (Gacono & Meloy, 1992), and 13 responses (DiNuovo et al., 1988). Two studies with small samples accepted as few as 6 responses from their subjects (Clerici, Albonetti, Papa, Perati, & Invernizzi, 1992; Meyer & Tuber, 1989), and another with a large sample had group averages for R as low as 13.5 (Shimonaka & Nakazatro, 1991).

When to Administer the Test

This issue is especially critical with patients who are recent admissions to the hospital. There is considerable variability in the literature regarding this point, but many investigators have assessed their patients within the first few days of their admission (e.g., Archer & Gordon, 1988; Belter, Lipovsky, & Finch, 1989; DiNuovo et al., 1988; Edell, 1987). Holzman and his colleagues (1986) argued that it was necessary to evaluate psychotic patients as close to the beginning of their hospital stay as possible in order to minimize the masking effects of drug treatment on thought disorder. However, recent research suggests that it may be advisable to delay the test administration for at least a week. When the Rorschach is given to patients who are in an acutely psychotic condition, the results may be quite misleading. The intensity of the patients' disarray, in part related to the distress of being committed to the hospital, may create a form of temporary cognitive and perceptual disruption that is not characteristic of their basic personality structure. The concern about medication effects may be unwarranted, especially when the patient has been stabilized. Psychopharmacological interventions appear to have minimal influence on most Rorschach variables, and certainly no impact on those variables associated with central dimensions of personality (Exner, 1993).

Other Confounding Situational Factors

As noted earlier, variations in Rorschach administration may influence the obtained results (Table 5.3), and such factors as subject motivation and involvement in litigation may impact on how findings are interpreted. Although there is some debate about the ability of subjects to fake a Rorschach successfully without detection, there is no doubt that performance can be altered (Dies, 1994; Frueh & Kinder, 1994; Netter & Viglione, 1994; Perry & Kinder, 1990; Schretlen, 1988). Concern here is not with the issue of malingering, but focuses more on subtle situational sets that may introduce biases in the interpretation of Rorschach data.

A significant number of investigators report reliability figures on interrater agreement on Rorschach coding, but few provide much information on the circumstances surrounding testing, that is, the subjects' prior experience with psychological evaluations, the number of examiners and their qualifications, placement of the Rorschach in the assessment battery, and so forth. Although most of these issues may seem unimportant, there is very little recent research to evaluate their influence. Can we be certain that a pretest interview has not biased test results? This question is raised, for example, by Armstrong and Loewenstein (1990), who studied patients with multiple personalities and dissociative disorders. Prior to taking the Rorschach, each patient was informed that testing would be useful for people who feel as if they have different parts of themselves or feel very divided; they were encouraged by the examiners to permit their separate personalities to participate in the evaluation process. It would appear on the surface that this instructional set is not significantly different than the types of instructions provided in much of the malingering literature, but the potentially biasing effects of this clinical interview were not discussed by the authors. At the very least, unique pretesting instructions make it difficult to compare such studies with others using different intructional sets. Labott, Leavitt, Braun, and Sachs (1992), for example, reminded their patients diagnosed with multiple personality that the "host" personality should remain present throughout the Rorschach administration.

CONCLUSIONS

This chapter has focused on pragmatic problems relating to subject selection, establishing appropriate control groups, and minimizing the effects of confounding variables that might jeopardize the confidence investigator's can place in their findings. It seems clear that the value of many recent empirical investigations has been compromised by the failure of researchers to address these practical issues very effectively. Their descriptions of clinical samples are overly general and groups often are defined quite inconsistently from study to study. There are critical differences both within and across investigations in how comparison/control groups are managed (e.g., differential recruitment, selection of clinical and control groups from different settings, imbalances in the composition of samples). The potential impact of numerous variables is frequently overlooked. These include features inherent in the samples (e.g., previous hospitalizations, level of global functioning, secondary diagnoses), factors relating to test administration and scoring, and a range of situational variables that could influence the subjects' participation in the research.

Efforts to provide more comprehensive description of samples, to avoid any differential treatment of subjects across comparison groups, to weigh the probable impact of potential confounds, and to adopt more uniform standards, will go a long way toward improving the quality of Rorschach research.

REFERENCES

Abraham, P. P., Mann, T., Lewis, M. G., Coontz, B., & Lehman, M. (1990). The cognitive synthesis test and the Rorschach indicators of internal and external reality in schizophrenic, borderline and organic/psychotic adolescents. *British Journal of Projective Psychology, 34,* 34–44.

Acklin, M. W. (1990). Personality dimensions in two types of learning-disabled children: A Rorschach study. *Journal of Personality Assessment, 54,* 67–77.

Acklin, M. W. (1993). Psychodiagnosis of personality structure: II. Borderline personality organization. *Journal of Personality Assessment, 54,* 67–77.

Acklin, M. W., & Alexander, G. (1988). Alexithymia and somatization: A Rorschach study of four psychosomatic groups. *Journal of Nervous and Mental Disease, 176,* 343–350.

Acklin, M. W., & Bernat, E. (1987). Depression, alexithymia, and pain prone disorder: A Rorschach study. *Journal of Personality Assessment, 51,* 462–479.

Acklin, M. W., McDowell, C. J., & Orndoff, S. (1992). Statistical power and the Rorschach: 1975–1991. *Journal of Personality Assessment, 59,* 366–379.

Adair, H. E., & Wagner, E. E. (1992). Stability of unusual verbalizations on the Rorschach for outpatients with schizophrenia. *Journal of Clinical Psychology, 48,* 250–256.

Alterman, A. I., Slap-Shelton, L., & DeCato, C. M. (1992). Developmental level as a predictor of alcoholism treatment response: An attempted replication. *Addictive Behaviors, 17,* 501–506.

Anderson, T., & Dixon, W. E. (1993). The factor structure of the Rorschach for adolescent inpatients. *Journal of Personality Assessment, 60,* 319–332.

Archer, R. P., & Gordon, R. A. (1988). MMPI and Rorschach indices of schizophrenic and depressive diagnoses among adolescent inpatients. *Journal of Personality Assessment, 52,* 276–287.

Archer, R. P., & Krishnamurthy, R. (1993). A review of MMPI and Rorschach interrelationships in adult samples. *Journal of Personality Assessment, 61,* 277–293.

Armstrong, J. (1991). The psychological organization of multiple personality disordered patients as revealed in psychological testing. *Psychiatric Clinics of North America, 14,* 533–546.

Armstrong, J. G., & Loewenstein, R. J. (1990). Characteristics of patients with multiple personality and dissociative disorders on psychological testing. *Journal of Nervous and Mental Disease, 178,* 448–454.

Belter, R. W., Lipovsky, J. A., & Finch, A. J. (1989). Rorschach egocentricity index and self-concept in children and adolescents. *Journal of Personality Assessment, 53,* 783–789.

Berg, J. L. (1990). Differentiating ego functions of borderline and narcissistic personalities. *Journal of Personality Assessment, 55,* 537–548.

Campbell, D. T., & Stanley, J C. (1963). Experimental and quasi-experimental designs for research. Chicago: Rand McNally & Company, 1963.

Campo, V., Dow, N., & Tuset, A. (1988). Rorschach, O.R.T. and follow-up. *British Journal of Projective Psychology, 33,* 31–53.

Caprara, G. V., Holt, R. R., Pazielli, M. F., & Giannotti, A. (1986). The development of primary process in children's Rorschachs. *Journal of Personality Assessment, 50,* 149–170.

Clerici, M., Albonetti, S., Papa, R., Penati, G., & Invernizzi, G. (1992). Alexithymia and obesity: Study of the impaired symbolic function by the Rorschach test. *Psychotherapy and Psychosomatics, 57,* 88–93.

de Ruiter, C., & Cohen, L. (1992). Personality in panic disorder with agoraphobia: A Rorschach study. *Journal of Personality Assessment, 59,* 304–316.

Dies, R. R. (1994). The Rorschach Comprehensive System: Current status and clinical applications. *Independent Practitioner, 14,* 96–106.

DiNuovo, S., Laicardi, C., & Tobino, C. (1988). Rorschach indices for discriminating between two schizophrenic syndromes. *Perceptual and Motor Skills, 67,* 399–406.

Edell, W. S. (1987). Role of structure in disordered thinking in borderline and schizophrenic disorders. *Journal of Personality Assessment, 51,* 23–41.

Exner, J. E. (1966). Variations in WISC performances as influenced by differences in pre-test rapport. *Journal of General Psychology, 74,* 299–306.

Exner, J. E. (1986). Some Rorschach data comparing schizophrenic with borderline and schizotypal personality disorders. *Journal of Personality Disorders, 50,* 455–471.

Exner, J. E. (1992). R in Rorschach research: A ghost revisited. *Journal of Personality Assessment, 58,* 245–251.

Exner, J. E. (1993). *The Rorschach: A comprehensive system: Vol. 1. Basic foundations* (3rd ed.). New York: Wiley.

Exner, J. E., Thomas, E. A., & Mason, B. (1985). Children's Rorschachs: Description and prediction. *Journal of Personality Assessment, 49,* 13–20.

Exner, J. E., & Weiner, I. B. (1994). *The Rorschach: A comprehensive system: Vol. 3. Assessment of children and adolescents* (2nd ed.). New York: Wiley.

Eyman, J. R., & Eyman, S. K., (1991). Personality assessment in suicide prediction. *Suicide and Life-Threatening Behavior, 21,* 37–55.

Finch, A. J., Imm, P. S., & Belter, R. W. (1990). Brief Rorschach records with children and adolescents. *Journal of Personality Assessment, 55,* 640–646.

Frank, G. (1992). The response of African Americans to the Rorschach: A review of the research. *Journal of Personality Assessment, 59,* 317–325.

Frank, G. (1993). The use of the Rorschach with Hispanic Americans. *Psychological Reports, 72,* 276–278.

Frueh, B. C., & Kinder, B. N. (1994). The susceptibility of the Rorschach Inkblot Test to malingering of combat-related PTSD. *Journal of Personality Assessment, 62,* 280–298.

Gacono, C. B. (1990). An empirical study of object relations and defensive operations in antisocial personality disorder. *Journal of Personality Assessment, 54,* 589–600.

Gacono, C. B., & Meloy, J. R. (1991). A Rorschach investigation of attachment and anxiety in antisocial personality disorder. *Journal of Nervous and Mental Disease, 179,* 546–552.

Gacono, C. B., & Meloy, J. R. (1992). The Rorschach and the DSM–III–R antisocial personality: A tribute to Robert Lindner. *Journal of Clinical Psychology, 48,* 393–406.

Gallucci, N. T. (1989). Personality assessment with children of superior intelligence: Divergence versus psychopathology. *Journal of Personality Assessment, 53,* 749–760.

Gartner, J., Hurt, S. W., & Gartner, A. (1989). Psychological test signs of borderline personality disorder: A review of the empirical literature. *Journal of Personality Assessment, 53,* 423–441.

Georgoff, P. B. (1991). The Rorschach with hospice cancer patients and surviving cancer patients *Journal of Personality Assessment, 56,* 218–226.

Gerstle, R. M., Geary, D. C., Himelstein, P., & Reller-Geary, L. (1988). Rorschach predictors of therapeutic outcome for inpatient treatment of children: A proactive study. *Journal of Clinical Psychology, 44,* 277–280.

Goddard, R., & Tuber, S. (1989). Boyhood separation anxiety disorder: Thought disorder and object relations psychopathology as manifested in Rorschach imagery. *Journal of Personality Assessment, 53,* 239–252.

Graves, P. L., Phil, M., Mead, L. A., & Pearson, T. A. (1986). The Rorschach Interaction Scale as a potential predictor of cancer. *Psychosomatic Medicine, 48,* 549–563.

Greco, C. M., & Cornell, D. G. (1992). Rorschach object relations of adolescents who committed homicide. *Journal of Personality Assessment, 59,* 574–583.

Greenwald, D. F. (1990). An external construct validity study of Rorschach personality variables. *Journal of Personality Assessment, 55,* 768–780.

Gross, A., Newton, R. R., & Brooks, R. B. (1990). Rorschach responses in healthy, community dwelling older adults. *Journal of Personality Assessment, 55,* 335–343.

Harper, G., & Scott, R. (1990). Learning disabilities: An appraisal of Rorschach response patterns. *Psychological Reports, 67,* 691–696.

Hayslip, B., & Lowman, R. L. (1986). The clinical use of projective techniques with the aged: A critical review and synthesis. *Clinical Gerontologist, 5,* 63–94.

Hilsenroth, M. J., Hibbard, S. R., Nash, M. R., & Handler, L. (1993). A Rorschach study of narcissism, defense, and aggression in borderline, narcissistic, and Cluster C personality disorders. *Journal of Personality Assessment, 60,* 346–361.

Hilsenroth, M. J., Hibbard, S. R., Nash, M. R., & Handler, L. (1993). A Rorschach study of narcissism, defense, and aggression in borderline, narcissistic, and Cluster C personality disorders. *Journal of Personality Assessment, 60,* 346–361.

Holzman, P. S., Shenton, M. E., & Solovay, M. R. (1986). Quality of thought disorder in differential diagnosis. *Schizophrenia Bulletin, 12,* 360–372.

Johnson, D. R., & Quinlan, D. M. (1993). Can the mental representations of paranoid schizophrenics be differentiated from those of normals? *Journal of Personality Assessment, 60,* 588–601.

Kaser-Boyd, N. (1993). Rorschachs of women who commit homicide. *Journal of Personality Assessment, 60,* 458–470.

Kreitler, S., Kreitler, H., & Wanounou, V. (1988). Cognitive modification of test performance in schizophrenics and normals. *Imagination, Cognition, and Personality, 7,* 227–249.

Labott, S. M., Leavitt, F., Braun, B. G., & Sachs, R. G. (1992). Rorschach indicators of multiple personality disorder. *Perceptual and Motor Skills, 75,* 147–158.

Leifer, M., Shapiro, J. P., Martone, M. W., & Kassem, L. (1991). Rorschach assessment of psychological functioning in sexually abused girls. *Journal of Personality Assessment, 56,* 14–28.

Lerner, H., Albert, C., & Walsh, M. (1987). The Rorschach assessment of borderline defenses: A concurrent validity study. *Journal of Personality Assessment, 51,* 334–348.

Lipgar, R. M., & Waehler, C. A. (1991). A Rorschach investigation of mothers of behaviorally disturbed infants. *Journal of Personality Assessment, 56,* 106–117.

Marsh, A., & Viglione, D. J. (1992). A conceptual validation study of the texture response on the Rorschach. *Journal of Personality Assessment, 58,* 571–579.

Mattlar, C. E., Tarkkanen, P., Carlsson, A., Aaltonen, T., & Helenius, H. (1993). Personality characteristics for 83 paraplegic patients evaluated by the Rorschach method using the comprehensive system. *British Journal of Projective Psychology, 38,* 20–30.

Meyer, G. J. (1993). The impact of response frequency on the Rorschach constellation indices and on their validity with diagnostic and MMPI-2 criteria. *Journal of Personality Assessment, 60,* 153–180.

Meyer, J. R., & Tuber, S. (1989). Intrapsychic and behavioral correlates of the phenomenon of imaginary companions in young children. *Psychoanalytic Psychology, 6,* 151–168.

Morgan, L., & Viglione, D. J. (1992). Sexual disturbances, Rorschach sexual responses, and mediating factors. *Psychological Assessment, 4,* 530–536.

Nash, M. R., Hulsey, T. L., Sexton, M. C., Harralson, T. L., & Lambert, W. (1993). Long-term sequelae of childhood sexual abuse: Perceived family environment, psychopathology, and dissociation. *Journal of Consulting and Clinical Psychology, 61,* 276–283.

Netter, B. E. C., & Viglione, D. J. (1994). An empirical study of malingering schizophrenia on the Rorschach. *Journal of Personality Assessment, 62,* 45–57.

Perry, G. G., & Kinder, B. N. (1990). The susceptibility of the Rorschach to malingering: A critical review. *Journal of Personality Assessment, 54,* 47–57.

Resnick, M. N., & Nunno, V. J. (1991). The Nuremberg mind redeemed: A comprehensive analysis of the Rorschachs of Nazi war criminals. *Journal of Personality Assessment, 57,* 19–29.

Richman, N. E., & Sokolove, R. L. (1992). The experience of aloneness, object representation, and evocative memory in borderline and neurotic patients. *Psychoanalytic Psychology, 9,* 77–91.

Schretlen, D. J. (1988). The use of psychological tests to identify malingered symptoms of mental disorder. *Clinical Psychology Review, 8,* 451–476.

Shapiro, J. P., Leifer, M., Martone, M. W., & Kassem, L. (1990). Multimethod assessment of depression in sexually abused girls. *Journal of Personality Assessment, 55,* 234–248.

Shenton, M. E., Solovay, M. R., & Holzman, P. (1987). Comparative studies of thought disorders: II. Schizoaffective disorder. *Archives of General Psychiatry, 44,* 21–30.

Smith, J. E., Hillard, M. C., Walsh, R. A., Kubacki, S. R., & Morgan, C. D. (1991). Rorschach assessment of purging and nonpurging bulimics. *Journal of Personality Assessment, 56,* 277–288.

Stevens, D. T., Edwards, K. J., Hunter, W. F., & Bridgman, L. (1993). An investigation of the color-affect hypothesis in Exner's Comprehensive System. *Perceptual and Motor Skills, 77,* 1347–1360.

Stuart, J., Westen, D., Lohr, N., Benjamin, J., Becker, S., Vorus, N., & Silk, K. (1990). Object relations in borderlines, depressives, and normals: An examination of human responses on the Rorschach. *Journal of Personality Assessment, 55,* 296–318.

Suzuki, A., Peters, L., Weisbender, L., & Gillespie, J. (1987). Characteristics of American and Japanese schizophrenic patients elicited by the Rorschach technique and demographic data. *International Journal of Social Psychiatry, 33,* 50–55.

Tuber, S. B. (1989). Children's Rorschach object representations: Findings for a nonclinical sample. *Psychological Assessment, 1,* 146–149.

Tuber, S. (1992). Empirical and clinical assessments of children's object relations and object representations. *Journal of Personality Assessment, 58,* 179–197.

Tuber, S. B., Frank, M. A., & Santostefano, S., (1989). Children's anticipation of impending surgery. *Bulletin of the Menniger Clinic, 53,* 501–511.

Waehler, C. A. (1991). Selected Rorschach variables of never-married men. *Journal of Clinical Psychology, 47,* 123–132.

Wagner, E. E., & Frye, D. (1990). Diagnostic and intellectual implications of the fragmented Rorschach W:D ratio. *Perceptual and Motor Skills, 71,* 887–890.

Wenar, C., & Curtis, K. M. (1991). The validity of the Rorschach for assessing cognitive and affective changes. *Journal of Personality Assessment, 57,* 291–308.

Zalewski, C., & Archer, R. P. (1991). Assessment of borderline personality disorder: A review of MMPI and Rorschach findings. *Journal of Nervous and Mental Disease, 179,* 338–345.

Zivney, O. A., Nash, M. R., & Hulsey, T. L. (1988). Sexual abuse in early versus late childhood: Differing patterns of pathology as revealed on the Rorschach. *Psychotherapy, 25,* 99–106.

CHAPTER SIX

Special Issues in Subject Selection and Design

Barry A. Ritzler & John E. Exner, Jr.

Subject selection is a critical procedure for all psychology research. Except under unusual circumstances, subject characteristics cannot be altered for the purpose of experimental manipulation. Therefore, effective subject selection is essential in assuring at least quasi-experimental status for most of our studies in psychology. Furthermore, the complex and dynamic nature of the human personality carries the potential for confounding effects likely to obscure the meaning of research results. Judicious subject selection is important in reducing experimental error. There is no question that reliability and validity, as well as generalizability, depend to a large extent on appropriate subject selection.

Compared to psychology research in general, Rorschach research places special emphasis on subject selection. The large majority of independent variables in Rorschach studies are immutable subject variables replete with confounding potential. Also, many dependent variables derived from the test protocol are assumed or hypothesized to be estimates of long-standing subject characteristics, which hopefully have been made available for assessment by appropriate subject selection.

Another reason why subject selection is especially important for Rorschach research is that the test procedure is an interaction between subject and examiner typically under circumstances extraneous to the intended experimental conditions (Schachtel, 1966; Schafer, 1954). For instance, in a study of schizophrenic cognitive functioning, patients with a diagnosis of paranoid schizophrenia (a subject variable) may be tested by the psychologist who is a member of the treatment team that makes decisions regarding the patient's hospital status. The impact of the test situation is likely to have a different effect on the Rorschach performance of patients with paranoid inclinations compared to nonparanoid individuals. Such subject–situation artifact-producing interactions often are ignored by investigators. Even if paranoid subjects are tested in a nonclinical setting by technicians, the potential for subject–situation confounds exists because of the intrusive, novel, and even cryptic nature of the Rorschach experience. Consequently, the influence of the test situation should always be considered during subject selection.

Finally, subject selection is important for Rorschach research because cultural influences and personality predispositions have differential effects on results yielded by structural summary data. For instance, the normative data for more than 20 structural variables differs radically for individuals with a basic cognitive (introversive) problem-solving style compared to individuals with a basic intuitive (extratensive) style (Exner, 1991, 1993).

Before proceeding to the main body of this text, a reassurance is in order. The Rorschach test, though susceptible to the many nuances and complexities of human characteristics and experiences, enables us to track the effects of all these factors across individuals because of its comprehensive and empirical nature. That is, if we know who our subjects are, and are clear as to the probable impact of the assessment situation, we can go far in giving clarity, relevance, and ultimately, validity to our test results. However, if we are cavalier about subject selection, we risk bogging our results into the quicksand of human complexity.

SUBJECT AVAILABILITY

A simple, but essential, problem in subject selection is availability. Often, psychologists find themselves in settings with clients representing certain diagnostic categories or demonstrating certain phenomena of clinical interest. Frequently, there is a temptation to "do a study" using the Rorschach. Such ventures should be undertaken with caution, because of the near certainty that several confounding factors are associated with the subjects' availability. Usually, the nature of the clinical setting will seriously restrict the representativeness of the available sample. Whenever possible, the sample should be augmented by including subjects who, although not typical of the institution's clients, are nevertheless representative of the general population being studied. If such augmentation is not possible, particular care should be taken to qualify the generalizability of the results. Such concerns, of course, are not specific to Rorschach research. Any clinical study that attempts to take advantage of subject availability should be reviewed for possible confounding factors. With the advent of more sophisticated methods of Rorschach analysis such as the Comprehensive System (Exner, 1991, 1993), however, more and more Rorschach psychologists are being tempted to do a study. Whereas such motivation can be a boon to the Rorschach and general clinical literature, potential researchers should let theory and deductive reasoning guide their research efforts ahead of subject availability.

An often-researched population, notorious for its availability, is college undergraduates, who usually are used as nonpatient controls. In Rorschach research, college undergraduates have more to offer than simple availability. They typically are cooperative and even eager to participate, primarily out of curiosity regarding the Rorschach and/or a wish to obtain extra credit. They also tend to be achievement oriented and often strive to be creative. Consequently, their Rorschachs tend to be relatively substantial in length and complexity. They qualify as nonpathological subjects in the sense of being motivated to make a good impression by giving a good performance. Also, compared to other nonpatient controls, they tend to be more flexible in their availability for research participation and are more likely to be accessible for follow-up testing and observation.

Unfortunately, the college undergraduate often is not a good nonpatient control, sometimes for the same reasons they are "good" Rorschach subjects. Their motivation, achievement orientation, and concerns with demonstrating their creativeness often lead to records that are quite different than those obtained from the general nonpatient population. Thus, $X+\%$'s are often lower than expected from nonpatients. It is also important to note that, demographically, they are typically younger, better educated, and from higher socioeconomic backgrounds than other controls and many patient groups, especially inpatient groups. Therefore, they tend to yield a more homogeneous sample than most patient groups, often resulting in narrow, truncated frequency distributions on some Rorschach variables, thereby lowering the power of statistical analyses.

In spite of their availability and motivation, college undergraduates are probably useful as control subjects only when the patient samples are roughly equivalent to them in terms of involvement in the task, demographic characteristics, and range of scores. It seems more practical to use this readily available population in manipulation studies, that is, those in which a single group of volunteer students will be randomized into two or more groups for the purposes of evaluating the impact of some independent variable on Rorschach performance.

THE SUBJECT–SITUATION INTERACTION

Ideally, Rorschach research should be conducted in settings where the only situational influences are those of interest to the study. Strictly controlled laboratory conditions usually, but not always, achieve this ideal. Clinical situations, on the other hand, are fraught with potential confounding effects. Of course, laboratory studies create limitations for generalization and more naturalistic studies may do much better in capturing human personality as it "really is," but not without loss of precision and clarity of results. In addition, certain subjects are more likely than others to be sensitive to situational influences.

When subjects are being selected, the researcher should ask the following questions: What elements of the test situation are likely to elicit effects that interfere with those elicited by the experimental conditions? What are those effects and how can they be controlled? And (critically for subject selection) which subjects are likely to show a greater or lesser response to the confounding situational variables? In particular, are these differential subject–situation effects likely to distort between-group differences in the statistical analysis?

Such clinical phenomena as paranoia, high anxiety, a sense of helplessness, inferiority feelings, and oppositional attitudes are examples of subject variables that are very likely to interact with the confounding effects of the research setting. If meaningful research is going to be conducted using the Rorschach to study clinical issues, such problematic confounds will occur. The effectiveness of Rorschach studies will be increased if the researchers are alert to such confounds and take whatever steps possible to identify and control for their interference.

STYLE AS A CONFOUNDING VARIABLE

Recent analysis (Exner, 1991, 1993) of the interactive nature of the Comprehensive System data clusters has revealed pervasive effects of two indicators of basic personality styles that should be taken into consideration when samples are selected for research.

The first critical stylistic indicator is Lambda, the ratio of Pure F responses to all other responses. Previous studies (Exner, 1986) have shown that a high Lambda (> .99) indicates that "the subject is prone to minimize the importance of, and/or ignore, some elements of the stimulus field" (Exner, 1991, p. 125), whereas, a low Lambda (< .31) signifies "that the subject may become more involved than is customary, sometimes because of an over-incorporative style, but more often because of an unusual frequency of psychological demands experienced by the subject" (Exner, 1991).

Currently, the critical level at which Lambda is most likely to become a confounding variable is the upper level (> .99). Personality functioning of individuals with a high Lambda is likely to be dominated by a simplistic orientation marked by insufficient scanning and/or a reluctance to become involved in complicated, stressful situations. The effect of such a style on Rorschach performance is that important distinctions derived from Comprehensive System variables other than Lambda are muted and, in extreme cases, essentially nullified. For example, because high Lambda means fewer responses with determinants other than form, it ordinarily is associated with decreased values of *EA* (the sum of *M+WSumC*), *es* (the sum of *FM+m+Sum Shading*), and the proportion of Blends to *R*. Because of its association with a simplistic approach to organizing experience, it also creates a potential for decreased values of *Zf*. These relationships suggest that the overly simplistic style represented by high Lambda probably limits the expression of some personality characteristics that may exist as underlying potential. Of course, it also could be that high Lambda individuals simply do not possess even the potential for such characteristics. Whatever the case, the presence of high Lambda usually identifies a person whose personality will be more limited in some ways.

Because of the major impact of high Lambda, care should be taken when such protocols appear in a research sample. One sure way of eliminating the confounding of high *L* would be to exclude such records from the sample. This drastic strategy, however, has serious implications for the generalizability of the study. Another solution might be to form separate groups of protocols with Lambda > .99 and < 1.00. This approach, however, creates extra cells for the research design and places an added burden on subject recruitment, which might make the study unfeasible. A third method for controlling the confounding effect of high *L* would be to test groups for relative equivalence on the high–low *L* dichotomy. If Lambda is determined to be an important variable in a design, the objective would be to achieve relatively equal proportions of high *L* subjects in each group included in the study.

In some studies, the likelihood of being able to obtain relatively equal proportions of high *L* subjects may be remote, or at the very least can create other sorts of problems. This occurs if two or more samples are being compared from different populations that have different proportions of high *L*. For instance, if inpatient schizophrenics are being compared with character disorder subjects, the reference group data for the Comprehensive System (Exner, 1993) suggest that the schizophrenic sample will probably include approximately 39% high *L* subjects, whereas the character disorder sample is likely to include about 68% of subjects with a high *L*. If an investigator were to force relatively equal numbers of high *L* subjects in each group, one of the two groups would probably become unrepresentative of the population that it is supposed to represent. In such a circumstance, the only logical recourse to the high *L* problem would be to use analysis of covariance or multiple regression techniques to statistically control for the Lambda effect. Such a solution, however, would not be appropriate if the Lambda effect is essential to the phenomena under investigation. If the effect is important, no effort should be made to equate the samples for high *L* or to remove its effect by statistical manipulation. Whatever the solution, a Rorschach study (regardless of the system used) that does not take into account the possible confounding effect of high Lambda is likely to result in inaccurate, or at least insufficient, findings.

An even more frequently occurring confounding factor—one that probably qualifies as pervasive—is that measured by the *Erlebnistypus* ratio (*M:WSum C*), which is used to identify the problem-solving styles (or coping styles) referred to as introversive or extratensive, or the absence of an identifiable, consistent problem-solving style (ambitent). When the normative data for the Comprehensive System were subdivided to create separate norms for subjects with introversive and extratensive styles, the results show markedly different patterns for many variables, including a substantial number that have no direct relationship to the human movement or color responses. For instance, because introversives give a preponderance of *M* responses and extraversives favor chromatic color responses, it is not surprising to find that extraversives have a significantly higher Affective Ratio and more color-shading blends, whereas introversives show more responses with human content and more cooperative movement responses. Differences that do not seem directly related to *M* and chromatic color scores are more intriguing. For example, introversives show a higher Experience Actual, have a greater frequency of Adjusted D scores that exceed 0, and proportionally fewer subjects for who (*FM+m*) is less than *Sum Shading*. Perhaps the most puzzling difference is that nonpatient introversives almost never give responses with blood content (1% frequency compared to 24% for extratensives), whereas extratensives have a much lower frequency of explosion responses (2% compared to 27% for introversives). These differences combined with the highly stable nature of the EB for adults suggest that introversives and extraversives are probably two distinct types who are likely to show many differences in terms of Rorschach performance and general behavior patterns and tendencies.

Again, if the concepts being tested in the study are logically associated with differences in coping or problem-solving style, the effects of introversive and extratensive orientations probably cannot, or should not, be effectively controlled (e.g., when subjects with affective disorders such as depression are being compared to cognitive disorders such as schizophrenia). In other studies in which the issue of coping style is not obvious, investigators should consider the possibility of using EB data as a classification (independent) variable to differentiate groups. If Rorschach data are selected as dependent variables, the analyses should include some method of controlling for the styles, such as covarying or analyzing the findings by subgroups that are defined by styles. If these cautions are not observed, the potential for the results being confounded by problem-solving style are considerable.

Although no other stylistic indicators are associated with pervasive confounding effects of the sort detected with high Lambda or EB style, there are some salient features of personality that should not be ignored casually when selecting groups or planning analyses. For instance, a positive Coping Deficit Index (CDI) usually occurs in the context of a relatively impoverished record with an overall suppression of critical ratios, percentages, and derivations from the structural summary. A sample that has a disproportionate number of subjects with a positive CDI probably should be avoided unless coping deficit is an essential factor in the sample criteria. Impoverished records are more likely to yield ratios and derived scores that are more deviant from the norm. A definitive study of this hypothesis has not been conducted, but until such evidence is available, it probably is best to err on the conservative side by controlling for a positive CDI when this index is not a defining characteristic of the sample in question.

Other stylistic indicators that logically are candidates as overall confounding variables do not necessarily have such pervasive effects. Evidence of passivity in interpersonal relations, as measured by the $a{:}p$ ratio, or those positive for hypervigilance (HVI), do not appear to manifest consistently homogeneous features. Similarly, the three critical levels of the texture response ($T = 0$, $T = 1$, and $T > 1$), although important for understanding the relationship orientation of subject, do not differentially affect other Comprehensive System variables. Consequently, they probably will not need to be considered as factors that should be controlled in sample selection. Nevertheless, it might be heuristically useful to check for such stylistic difference across samples when they are not involved as independent or dependent variables.

The nature of the research design and/or the circumstances in which the study takes place may turn such stylistic variables into confounding factors even though they are not generally a problem. For example, a study using the Rorschach to investigate marital conflict, the T variable should be either analyzed or controlled because it has been demonstrated that correspondence between marriage partners' T scores is associated with compatibility (Exner, Sternklar, Johnston, Zalis, & Thomas, 1982). That is, marriages were much more likely to show conflict if one partner scored $T = 0$ and the other $T > 0$. Somewhat surprisingly (but not illogically), two individuals with $T = 0$ were about as likely to have a compatible marriage as two individuals with $T > 0$. At any rate, these relationships illustrate why certain Rorschach indicators that usually do not represent a potential confound should be checked if the phenomenon under investigation is associated with a Rorschach indicator that is not being used as an independent or dependent variable.

HOMOGENEITY: A DECISION

Another important issue concerning research subject selection is homogeneity of samples. When experimental and control samples are being compared, within-group homogeneity for the independent variable represented by the group is essential. If the sample sizes are small (as they usually are in Rorschach research) homogeneity across groups on potential confounding variables also is desirable because the samples usually are not large enough to depend on random distribution of the confounding effects. By establishing as much homogeneity as possible on potential confounding variables, the investigator can restrict the range of these variables across groups and thereby limit their interference. Such range restriction, however, restricts the generalizability of the study and may not be desirable in all cases.

The trade-off between homogeneity and representativeness is most critical in correlational studies. Overly homogeneous subject selection (e.g., college undergraduates in a study of depression) are likely to result in truncated samples that do not have enough range to yield significant correlations when a true association exists in the more extended general population (e.g., depression in all humans). For instance, the Morbid Content Rorschach variable (MOR) is not likely to distinguish college students with relatively high and low scores on a self-report measure of depression, but will easily distinguish depressed patients from nondepressed nonpatients.

Sample homogeneity is particularly important in the selection of control groups. For instance, a study attempting to investigate the personality characteristics of ulcer patients might use medical patients with symptoms other than ulcers as a control group. Such a control, however, would likely result in an overly heterogeneous collection of Rorschach protocols, thereby obscuring any real differences attributable to the ulcer condition. A more appropriate control group might be patients with gall bladder disorders to provide a more homogeneous control group, making it likely that the degree of impact of the disorder and its treatment consequences would be similar to that of the ulcer patients resulting in comparison groups of equivalent homogeneity.

RORSCHACH DATA AS INDEPENDENT VARIABLES

Different problems arise for subject selection depending on whether the Rorschach data are used as independent or dependent variables. When the Rorschach is used to define an independent variable, the focus for subject selection is on the actual test performance. Consequently, subject selection must take into account non-Rorschach subject variables and Rorschach subject variables, that is, the actual scores of the subjects. When the Rorschach is used to measure a dependent variable, the focus is on the potential performance of the subject and subject selection can only be based on non-Rorschach subject variables and their potential relationship with Rorschach variables.

When the issue is defining an independent variable, the Rorschach most often is used to classify subjects for assignment to contrasting groups. In this context, control groups are defined as subjects who do not possess the characteristic measured by the independent variable or who show the typical or normative level of the characteristic identified as the independent variable.

In the most straightforward use of the Rorschach to classify subjects, a single measure (e.g., the number of popular responses) is designated as the independent variable. Such simple circumstances afford an opportunity to emphasize an important issue; that is, for the purposes of classification, some Rorschach variables have interpretive meaning that provides discrete categories or levels well suited for group classification. Examples are the texture variable (T), which provides three levels ($T = 0$, $T = 1$, and $T > 1$) corresponding to three distinct attitudes regarding close interpersonal relationship (with $T = 1$ as the normative control group) and Reflection scores, which, when greater than zero, signify a narcissisticlike perception of the self. Apparently, the Reflection variable permits only a dichotomous classification because the absolute number of reflection responses does not seem to matter; one is enough to identify the narcissistic feature, and more than one apparently does not signify more narcissism. Consequently, subjects without reflection responses would constitute the logical control group.

In contrast to the single variables that yield discrete classifications, many Rorschach variables are *continuous* or *dimensional* in nature (Millon, 1990; Trull, Widiger, & Guthrie, 1990), requiring the investigator to select cutoff points for group classification as dictated by the research design. A logical procedure for classifying levels of the independent variable with a continuous measure is to use a normative sample's parameters to determine cutoff points. Caution is recommended, however, for applying normative data to research samples that are likely to be quite different than the more heterogenous normative sample. An alternative procedure for specifying levels of the independent variable would be to use the parameters of the total research sample. This method, however, does not avoid the problem of regression to the mean on the dependent variable when levels of the independent variable are defined by scores that are far from the mean on the independent variable. Consequently, single Rorschach variables with a continuous distribution of interpretive significance do not make good classification variables. When using single measures, investigators are better off limiting themselves to independent variables such as T or reflections that yield discrete classifications with clear interpretive significance. (Such continuous versus discrete properties of Rorschach variables also apply to more complicated types of Rorschach independent variables.)

The use of a single Rorschach variable has the advantage of relative simplicity in the definition of the independent variable; however, such simplicity often does not correspond to the complexity of the researcher's question. Usually, human characteristics that require more than one Rorschach variable for accurate definition are the target of the study. Consequently, combinations of single Rorschach variables may make the best independent variables. The most simple form of such combinations is the derived score that plays a prominent role in the Comprehensive System structural summary. A good example is the Adjusted D Score, the Comprehensive System measure of an individual's characteristic capacity for control and vulnerability to stress. The Adjusted D Score is a composite of 10 single Rorschach variables (M, FC, CF, C, FM, m, C', T, V, and Y). The levels of the Adjusted D Score (e.g., -2, -1, 0, $+1$, $+2$) represent z scores from the normative sample. As such, even though the Adjusted D Score essentially is a continous score, the large number of variables contributing to it give it more stability than the single Rorschach continous variable. Nevertheless, caution should be exercised when subjects are selected on the basis of such a composite score. For instance, a low Adjusted D Score (e.g., -2) can be the result of relatively low levels of M, FC, CF, and C (the Experience Actual composite—an estimate of personality resources), or relatively high levels of FM, m, and Sum Shading (the Experience Stimulation composite—an estimate of stresses acting on the personality). These different circumstances would identify distinctly different types of individuals who probably should not be combined at the same level of an independent variable without appropriate controls.

Another example of a derived score is the Egocentricity Index ($3r+(2)/R$), an estimate of an individual's preoccupation with self. Again, high scores can result from several reflection responses or a high number of pairs without reflections. If no control is exercised over the presence of narcissism at the high levels of the Egocentricity Index, it will have questionable validity as an independent variable. Nevertheless, it is a much better indicator of self-preoccupation than reflections or pairs alone.

Although a derived scored based on a combination of single measures has advantages over a single measure used alone as a classification variable, a basic limitation exists that makes derived scores insufficient as independent variables for many studies using the Rorschach. Namely, most questions addressed in Rorschach research will involve more than the circumscribed characteristic defined by a solitary derived score. For instance, the study may be concerned with depression or suicide potential. No derived score can adequately measure these more global processes. Instead, the investigator may find the more comprehensive indices such as the Comprehensive System Depression Index (DEPI) or the Suicide Constellation (S-CON) to be more appropriate to guide subject selection. Such indices, based on several derived scores and single measures with specific cutoff points, provide more comprehensive and potentially more stable classification variables. For instance, in the Comprehensive System, groups could be classified as Depression (DEPI > 5), Depressive Features (DEPI = 5), and Control (DEPI < 5). The S-CON measure from the Comprensive System provides a dichotomy of Suicide Risk (S-CON > 7) and Control (S-CON < 8).

A basic problem for the index approach to subject selection is the number of false negatives (and, to a lesser extent in most cases, the number of false positives) that occur when cutoff scores are specified. In addition, many global psychological functions such as information processing, mediational activity, and so on, are not measured by a single index. Thus, the researcher interested in using data concerning the global functions as independent or classification variables is forced to make logical classifications based on a combination of derived scores, single scores, and general indices to identify characteristics. Information processing is a good example. The Comprehensive System cluster concerning information processing includes the single scores for *Zf* (Organizational Frequency); *DQ* (Developmental Quality); and PSV (Perseverations); derived scores Lambda, *W:D:Dd*, *W:M*, and Location Sequence; and the indices OBS (Obsessive Style) and HVI (Hypervigilance Index). Used collectively, they provide a general assessment concerning the adequacy and style of information processing. If a scheme is developed to use some or all of these variables in an experimental classification index, the resultant classifications are potentially more valid than any single score or derived combination of two or three scores because more information is contributing to the classification. There is a fly in this ointment, however: The investigators are left to their own devices for selecting points of differentiation.

Most Rorschach investigators have not utilized this tactic of subject selection. Consequently, no examples exist for classification at the cluster level. The following are a few suggestions, with an example, of how such classification might be accomplished for subject selection when complex Rorschach data are used as an independent variable. The example used with each suggestion will be using the Rorschach to classify affective disorder as an independent variable.

1. Likert scale ratings: With the cluster technique, investigators could use Likert scale ratings to classify subjects at specific points along a hypothetical continuum. For instance, the affect cluster of the Comprehensive System provides a sequence of interpretive steps that should enable investigators to classify most individuals in at least five categories from severe affective problems to exceptional affective adjustment. The problems with such a method are the same that plague most attempts to use Likert scale ratings: the points on the scale often are difficult to define; the scale points often do not represent equal intervals; little or no previous validation exists for most Likert scales (this would be particularly true for Rorschach studies attempting to classify subjects at a cluster level); raters tend to favor the midpoints on the scale and avoid the extreme ratings; interrater reliabilities often are difficult to attain at an acceptable level. Nevertheless, if such problems can be resolved, Likert scale ratings based on Rorschach clusters

are likely to be particularly useful because they would be based on more validated and standardized data than most assessment situations permit.

2. Logical and clinically meaningful combinations of cluster variables: Subject classification categories could be defined by meaningful combinations of cluster variables. For instance, affect cluster variables could be used to define two clinically meaningful dimensions of affective adjustment—the salience of affective experience and the degree of affective disturbance—to form critical groups to test the hypothesis that there is a significant interaction between the two dimensions. That is, the variables of Erlebnistypus (as a measure of problem-solving style) and Affective Ratio (as a measure of the degree to which an individual responds to or avoids affective stimulation) could be used to define affective salience. An extratensive style combined with an Affective Ratio greater than .85 would define high affective salience, whereas an introversive style with an Affective Ratio less than .53 could define low affective salience (the cutoff points are defined by one standard deviation above and below the mean from the normative sample). Similarly, the affect cluster variables of Experience Stimulation (es) and color-shading or shading-shading blends could be used to define affective disturbance. Four groups could be formed by selecting subjects with high affect salience–high affective disturbance; high affect salience–low affective disturbance; low affect salience–high affective disturbance; and low affect salience–low affective disturbance to test the hypothesis that affective disturbance is particularly debilitating in the presence of high affect salience and is attenuated when affect is not as crucial to the individual's basic coping style.

The advantage of such use of cluster variables for subject selection is that it maximizes the amount of Rorschach information for identifying groups that differ on composite characteristics of greater complexity than those defined by lower levels of classification. The primary disadvantage is that such variable combinations have not been validated as composites and, consequently, may have less value than the standard indices (e.g., DEPI, SCZI, etc.). Nevertheless, any study using such composites to successfully predict scores on the dependent variable would add to the construct validity of the composite. At any rate, the combining of cluster variables into logical composites has promise for using the Rorschach to identify individuals with contrasting styles in the areas of personality functioning covered by the Comprehensive System clusters.

Another method for using cluster data in subject selection is to use the entire fund of interpretive data to define an independent variable. For instance, if an investigator wants to select subjects who are likely to show gregarious, emotionally expressive, and occasionally outrageous, impulsive behavior (i.e., the "party animal"), the clusters Interpersonal Perception, Affect, and Control could be used in their entirety to identify such individuals.

In the same way, schizo-affective individuals who, in spite of their pathology, are able to maintain reasonably effective levels of social and work functioning (i.e., the old-fashioned "ambulatory schizophrenic") could be reliably identified by a complete cluster interpretation. The advantage to this method of subject selection is that it uses a standardized routine for incorporating the entire fund of cluster data with ample opportunity for cross-confirmation of individual interpretations. The major disadvantage is that such subject classification has not been used in previous research and would have to be clearly addressed and demonstrated each time a personality type is initially defined by the total cluster interpretation method. The essential point is that previous Rorschach studies seldom have used the full range of data yielded by the Structural Summary augmented by selected content interpretation. In other words, it is now possible to go beyond the fragmented, discrete variable method of classifying subjects to a more wholistic, "comprehensive," and potentially more meaningful procedure for subject selection.

RORSCHACH DATA AS DEPENDENT VARIABLES

When the Rorschach data are chosen as dependent variables, the investigator is predicting a specific Rorschach outcome. Consequently, subject selection is not determined by existing Rorschach data. Nevertheless, the nature of the Rorschach technique and the extent and limitations of the data it yields must be considered. For instance, the use of Rorschach findings would be appropriate as dependent variables if subjects are selected and categorized on the basis of general behavioral patterns or personality styles rather than discrete, highly specific behaviors. For example, the Comprehensive System variable Aggressive Movement (AG) would most probably distinguish professional football players from librarians (individuals with different general patterns of aggressive behavior), but would be a poor choice to distinguish football players from serial murderers (both aggressive types who express aggression in different specific behaviors). This is not to say that professional football players would not differ from murderers on the Rorschach, but that when subjects are selected on the basis of different specific expressions of the same general personality style, a broader level of Rorschach measurement (e.g., the cluster level) may be more appropriate as a dependent variable than the lower level discrete measures (such as the AG response).

The general issues of appropriate controls, the degree to which a sample is representative of the target population, and sample homogeneity also are critical when Rorschach data are used as dependent variables. Too often, the Rorschach has been described as invalid or has yielded insignificant results when the research design and procedures have not provided for adequate subject selection. Given an issue relevant to Rorschach assessment, with adequate research design and correct subject selection, the Rorschach offers many data sets that can serve quite well as dependent variables.

ARCHIVAL DATA: TREASURE CHEST
OR PANDORA'S BOX?

Consider the following scenario: Sometime in the early 1950s, psychologists in the department of psychiatry of a large medical center began to administer the Rorschach as part of a routine test battery given to every inpatient admission. Five psychologists did all testing. Two used the Klopfer method of Rorschach administration (Klopfer & Davidson, 1962), two used Beck's method (S. Beck, A. Beck, Levitt, & Molish, 1961), and one administered the test according to Rapaport's system (Rapaport, Gill, & Schafer, 1946). One of the psychologists using the Klopfer method and one using the Beck method did not bother to score the protocols because they relied entirely on a psychoanalytically oriented content analysis method of interpretation.

The practice of testing every patient continued into the early 1960s when an increasing admission rate combined with the decreasing popularity and reputation of the Rorschach resulted in the technique becoming optional for the admission assessment. By the late 1960s, admission assessments were discontinued and patients were tested by referral only. The Rorschach was included sporadically in referral assessments depending on the referral question and the time available for the assessment. By this time, two of the original psychologists had retired. In the mid-1970s, with the advent of the Comprehensive System and the hiring of two new staff psychologists recently graduated from Ph.D. programs where the Comprehensive System was taught, the Rorschach began to reappear more frequently in the assessment battery. The original psychologist who used the Rapport technique continued to do assessments, but the remaining two charter members of the psychology staff assumed administrative roles and stopped testing. As referrals continued to increase, psychology interns and practicum students (from a training program established at the medical center in 1968) began to administer the technique under the supervision of the staff psychologists.

Although all of the interns had been introduced to the Rorschach in their training programs, there was considerable variability in their experience. Some practicum students had not yet taken the Rorschach course in their training programs and simply administered the technique after a brief training exercise with the staff psychologists, but did not participate in scoring or interpretation. The other practicum students either were currently in the Rorschach course or had just finished it and were required to score and interpret with supervision. Although both psychologists supervised the students, they did not have enough time to observe more than a few of the student Rorschach administrations (and most of those were by the most inexperienced students). One of the staff psychologists attended several workshops on the Comprehensive System during the late 1970s and early 1980s. The other who used the system relied on the Exner texts and his colleague's reports to keep him informed of the changes in the scoring method.

All protocols had been kept on file through the years along with other test data and the basic chart information regarding the patient's hospital treatment. The Rorschach responses were filed in their original handwritten, note-taking formats. By 1986, the archives contained approximately 2,700 protocols—2,000 collected before the mid-1960s, 200 from 1965 to 1975, and about 500 since 1976.

In 1986, an intern entered the training program with a dissertation project using the Rorschach to study schizophrenia. She had applied to the internship site because of its Rorschach archives and had obtained permission from her training program faculty and the medical center psychologists to use the Rorschach files. By the end of the year, she had abandoned her original plan and had chosen to do a dissertation on the Minnesota Multiphasic Personality Inventory (MMPI).

How did the student become discouraged? What happened to the 2,700 protocols? Nearly 40% were from patients diagnosed as schizophrenic. In this imaginary (but all too likely) scenario, the treasure chest turned into a Pandora's box of confusing and essentially useless data.

The first problem with archival Rorschach data is simple, but not resolvable. It concerns legibility. Some protocols will be totally unreadable and will have to be excluded from the study. Other protocols will be partially illegible, forcing a decision on the investigator about whether the lost information is too extensive to assure a valid protocol, or whether enough information be gleaned from the legible part of the protocol to justify including it in the study?

A second simple, but serious, problem occurs when response locations are absent or poorly specified. If no location information is available, the protocol probably cannot be used for most Comprehensive System studies because accurate location is essential for the scoring of most critical variables (i.e., Location itself, Developmental Quality, Form Quality, Populars, Organizational Activity, and Special Scores). Sketchy location information may allow such scoring to take place, but may place a serious strain on reliability. Archival records that use a location numbering system such as Beck's (S. Beck et al., 1961) may appear to have adequate specificity, but may be misleading. A significant proportion of responses on most records are given to areas of the blot that do not appear in the Beck tables (the Dd 99 location designated by the Comprehensive System). Such unusually located responses require specific location chart designation for proper scoring. There is no substitute for an accurate and complete location chart. However, even when such charts exist, they may not have (probably have not) been drawn carefully enough to assure highly accurate locations. An important feature of an adequate location is the inclusion of detailed designation of parts of a response that are critical to scoring. Too often, a neatly drawn and carefully designated location will only use the designation "(Response number) = W" for complex whole responses whose specific parts must be known for accurate scoring.

A more subtle problem for archival studies lies in the Rorschach scoring system orientation of the test administration. For older archives, this orientation is almost certainly not that of the Comprehensive System. Of course, when a different system has been used to guide the administration, the Comprehensive System scoring guidelines can be used to score the protocol, but in some instances, the inquiry phase of the administration will not include probes and requests for clarification that are important for Comphrehensive System scoring. A more likely problem, however, is that of overinquiry, which is likely to result when an examiner is using another system of administration. For instance, Klopfer recommended the use of an "analogy period," which he illustrates in the following manner: "Let us assume that the use of color or action in some of the responses needs clarification. Usually, there is one Rorschach response in which the subject has referred to the color of the area or to action. The examiner should point out this response to the subject and say, 'In this case, you said the color made you think of . . . ; how was it here?' Or 'Here you called it a beautiful butterfly because it was colored. Now try to select those responses in which color helped.' " (Klopfer & Davidson, 1962, p. 41). In another example, Beck encouraged the use of the following inquiry routine to probe for the presence of human movement: "The response in figure II may be 'two men' (either lateral half). E asks, 'In what way are they like men?' S replies, 'They look like it.' E asks, 'In any special way?' S says, 'They're shaped like men.' E asks, 'Anything else about them that recalls men?' The reply is still indecisive, and E now tries the question, 'Are they any particular kind of men?' " (S. Beck et al., 1961). Such suggestive maneuvers would be in violation of the Comprehensive System's more conservative inquiry guidelines and would most likely result in an overrepresentation of determinants other than form (Gibby & Stotsky, 1953).

A special case of the administration technique problem occurs when the technician administering the Rorschach has followed the Rapaport method of inquiry (Rapaport et al., 1946) immediately after the response period for each card rather than the more conventional inquiry, which follows the response period for all 10 cards. Although Rapaport reasonably argued that immediate inquiry served to minimize the role of memory, early introduction of increased examiner activity and interest runs the risk of biasing the subsequent responses by making them reactions to the card plus the examiner activity rather than essentially reactions to the card alone. Consequently, considerable caution and qualification should be exercised when using Comprehensive System scoring with Rapaport-style protocols. A most unfortunate problem for archival studies occurs when the assessing psychologist has been interested in content analysis only and has not administered the Rorschach with the intent of scoring the responses. Usually, such protocols have little, if any, inquiry. They simply cannot provide highly reliable scores.

Ritzler and Nalesnik (1990) studied the effect of inquiry on the Comprehensive System structural summary. They found that with adequate location information, inquiry had little effect on Location, Developmental Quality, Reflections, Pairs, Populars, and Organizational Activity. A small, but significant attenuation occurred with movement responses, content, and the special scores Abstract, Aggressive Movement, and Cooperative Movement. A more significant and critical effect was noted concerning Color, Shading, and special scores Incongruous Combination, Fabulized Combination, and Morbid. However, by using a more liberal, modified version of the scoring system they were able to bring the totals in these categories more in line with the inquiry-assisted scores. In contrast, some important system variables lost their reliability when inquiry information was excluded from the scoring process. These lost categories included Vista, and the special scores Deviant Verbalizations, Deviant Responses, Autistic Logic, Confabulation, Personal, and Perseveration. Consequently, protocols with insufficient inquiry probably are not adequate for accurately assessing the Comprehensive System cluster of Ideation and the clinical phenomena of psychosis, particularly schizophrenia. Also, caution should be exercised in using inquiry-poor protocols in the research assessment of the Comprehensive System clusters of Interpersonal Perception and Self Perception. When an attempt is made to study these clusters using inquiry-poor protocols, some attempt should be made to use the sort of scoring modifications recommended in the Ritzler–Nalesnik study. Inquiry seems much less critical, however, for the clusters Affect, Mediation, and Information Processing. Unless the investigation is aimed at assessing precise subtleties of the process associated with these clusters, inquiry-poor protocols probably are adequate for research analysis.

The scenario example illustrates another important problem for many clinical archive Rorschach studies. Subjects tested during the period when all clients were given the Rorschach are likely to provide a sample that is significantly different from one composed of clients tested on referral only. The second group is a far more selective sample and probably could not be considered "random" in any meaningful sense. Furthermore, it should be noted that, in the scenario, there were at least two periods of selective referral assessment—that is, the periods before and after the hiring of the two Comprehensive System psychologists. Any archival investigator should make an effort to specify the conditions under which a protocol was entered into the archive. If the selection criteria (which are not likely to be optimal for the investigator's research purposes) can be accurately specified, then there will be less of a chance that the results of the study will be inappropriately generalized. For most studies, protocols obtained under different archival conditions probably should not be included in the same sample.

The scenario also illustrates the problem of examiner experience and, by assumption, competence. Archives seldom provide definitive information about the examiner. An important safeguard against examiner incompetence is a careful scrutiny of each protocol by the investigator. Protocols with glaring and crucial examiner errors—especially those that inappropriately "lead" the subject—probably should be eliminated from the study unless the scores affected by the errors are not critical to the study or the study is merely exploratory.

A related issue to examiner competence is the adequacy of previous scoring of the archive protocols. For most purposes, the protocols probably should be rescored in their entirety for the current study by carefully trained scorers unless the investigator is certain the original archive scoring was done by experts. Even so, if the Comprehensive System is used, no scoring should be accepted if it was done prior to the publishing of the latest Comprehensive System Workbook. Following this guideline, an archive of Nazi war criminal Rorschachs have been rescored four times in the last 10 years! If practical matters make such scoring updates impossible, the study report should specify which workbook edition was used.

Finally, archive studies will be limited by the amount and precision of background, diagnostic, and other critical information available on the subjects. These data are susceptible to most of the problems already cited for the Rorschach protocols. The quality of chart information varies within an archive as a function of time, individuals involved in providing the information, and format variations (e.g., *DSM–II* vs. *DSM–III–R*).

The preceding discussion is meant to introduce caution, but not discouragement for archival studies. In most instances, archive material goes beyond convenient availability as a reason for investigation. Usually, the archive will be the only way to obtain a sample that has meaning for a particular study. For instance, the Ritzler Nazi Rorschach archive provides a rare opportunity to study a clearly documented sample of totalitarian rank-and-file subjects. Also, longitudinal studies often become feasible with the help of adequate archives. Indeed, the value of an adequate archive has so much potential that it seems worthwhile to recommend that Rorschach rearchers begin to create their own protocol archives. A purposefully created archive could have all of the characteristics considered optimal for such a collection and could be used for multiple purposes in future investigations. The normative and reference group protocols published concerning the Comprehensive System constitute an archive that has enabled the development of the current version of the system.

USES AND ABUSES OF NORMATIVE
AND REFERENCE DATA

Adequate norms are the linchpin of the empirically based Comprehensive System. Specifically, the new guided cluster search routine approach to interpretation uses the normative data collected for the Comprehensive System to identify meaningful deviations in a subject's record (Exner, 1991, 1993) and to establish cutoff scores of interpretive significance.

For any norms to be useful, they must be derived from as large and as representative a sample of nonpathological subjects as possible. Given the nature of Rorschach subject availability, Exner's cohort of 700 is a sample of impressive proportions. As to the adequacy of the sample's characteristics, the reader is left to judge from the following description:

> The sample was randomly selected from an available group of 1332 adult inpatient records. The final selection was stratified to include 350 females and 350 males, 140 subjects from each of five geographic areas: Northeast, South, Midwest, Southwest, and West. Attempts were made to equalize the numbers of males and females from each region, but that was not always possible because the sample for some regions are markedly uneven for sex. . . . The mean age for the group is 32.35 (SD = 11.93, medium = 30, mode = 22) with a range of 19 to 70 years. The subjects average 13.25 years of education with a range of 8–18. (Exner, 1991, pp. 33–34)

Many investigators have succumbed to the temptation to use the Exner norms as a control group, but there is a major difference between using norms for interpretation with an empirically based system and using a normative sample as a control group in research. First, unless the experimental samples are unusually large, there will be an inordinate inequality in the numbers of subjects in the experimental and normative groups. Such inequality will stretch the credibility of statistical reasoning. Even if an unusually large experimental sample is available, the bloated numbers are likely to result in statistically significant findings that have no practical relevance. More critically, few experimental samples are likely to approximate the Exner normative sample for demographic characteristics. Extreme caution should be used in comparing experimental groups with the Exner norms (or any other normative sample) when there is not a good match on demographic characteristics.

In reporting the results of a Comprehensive System analysis of 199 Rorschachs of Nazi war criminals, Ritzler (1985) referred to the Exner norms to give meaning to my interpretations of the results, because no appropriate control groups were available. Ritzler acknowledged, however, that the Exner norms did not constitute an appropriate control group for the Nazi war criminals. Consequently, when a specific cutoff score had been specified by Exner (cf. Exner, 1991, p. 37), Ritzler referred to a difference between the Exner norms and the Nazi sample as "significant" only when the percentage of Nazis exceeding the cutoff was greater than 20%. When cutoff scores were not available, *t* tests were calculated, comparing the two groups and required a level of $p < .001$ for significance. These guidelines enable some tentative conclusions to be drawn about the Nazi data, but with a careful admonishment the reader may accept the conclusions as speculations with, at best, modest empirical support. If such cautions are observed with the use of norms as comparison data, then, the tactic is admissable. Nevertheless, the use of norms that do not adequately match the experimentsl sample(s) is no substitute for well-controlled comparison groups.

Another problem with the use of norms as research comparison groups is that the normative data usually are not gathered by the same research team under similar testing situations. In particular, the test situation of the experimental groups is likely to be much more uniform and specific than the test situations for the nonpatient normative sample. For instance, the nonpatient protocols that constitute the normative data for the Comprehensive System were collected by scores of examiners in dozens of settings—a fact that adds to the general representiveness of the sample at the expense of uniform conditions desirable for most experiments with fewer subjects.

A larger caution is necessary for the samples referred to by Exner as "reference groups." These are relatively large samples representing major diagnostic groups. Exner has emphasized that because "no stratification effort was made . . . the data for these . . . groups *should not be considered normative in any sense*. Rather, they afford a comparative review of these samples with findings from adult nonpatients, which may be help concerning each of the groups, but is by no means diagnostically practical" (Exner, 1991, pp. 54, 95; italics in original). In other words, the reference groups published concerning the Comprehensive System are not as adequately representative as his nonpatient normative sample. Consequently, it probably is correct to avoid using such reference group data as comparison groups under all circumstances, with the possible exception of highly exploratory and preliminary investigations.

A meaningful rule of thumb may be that, as a reference group becomes less representative of the population from which it has been drawn, and particularly as it deviates more from the characteristics of an investigator's experimental samples, the less appropriate it becomes as a comparison group. A stricter and clearly superior rule is "test your own comparison groups!"

CONCLUSIONS

Whereas subject selection in Rorschach research is subject to the same problems generally encountered in psychology research, the Rorschach method presents some unique dilemmas for the investigator when it comes to choosing subjects. This chapter has summarized these Rorschach issues and has offered some cautions and remedies. With appropriate attention to the task of subject selection, investigators will be able to address important Rorschach research questions and effectively exploit the method as a research tool. There is no apparent reason why the problems of subject selection should dampen enthusiasm for Rorschach study.

REFERENCES

Beck, S., Beck, A., Levitt, E., & Molish, H. (1961). *Rorschach's test I: Basic processes* (3rd ed.). New York: Grune & Stratton.

Exner, J. (1991). *The Rorschach: A comprehensive system: Vol. 1. Basic foundations* (3rd ed.). New York: Wiley.

Exner, J. (1993). *The Rorschach: A comprehensive system: Vol. 2. Interpretation* (2nd ed.). New York: Wiley.

Exner, J. E., Sternklar, S., Johnston, M., Zalis, T., & Thomas, E. A. (1982). *The relation of several Rorschach variables to reports of disputes during the first year of marriage.* Unpublished manuscript.

Gibby, R., & Stotsky, B. (1953). The relation of Rorschach free association to inquiry. *Journal of Consulting Psychology, 17,* 425–428.

Klopfer, B., & Davidson, H. (1962). *The Rorschach technique: An introductory manual.* New York: Harcourt Brace Jovanovich.

Millon, T. (1990). Classification in psychopathology: Rationale, alternatives, and standards. *Journal of Abnormal Psychology, 100,* 245–261.

Rapaport, D., Gill, M., & Schafer, R. (1946). *Psychological diagnostic testing* (Vol. 2). Chicago: Yearbook Publishers.

Ritzler, B. (1985, March). *Nazi Rorschachs: Shards of psychohistory.* Paper presented at the meeting of the Society for Personality Assessment, Berkeley, CA.

Ritzler, B., & Nalesnik, D. (1990). The effect of inquiry on the Exner Comprehensive System. *Journal of Personality Assessment, 55,* 647–655.

Schachtel, E. (1966). *Experiential foundations of Rorschach's test.* New York: Basic Books.

Schafer, R. (1954). *Psychoanalytic interpretation in Rorschach testing.* New York: Grune & Stratton.

Trull, T., Widiger, T., & Guthrie, P. (1990). Categorical versus dimensional status of borderline personality disorder. *Journal of Abnormal Psychology, 99,* 40–48.

CHAPTER SEVEN

Reviewing Basic
Design Features

John E. Exner, Jr., Bill N. Kinder, & Glenn Curtiss

The preceding chapters have focused on numerous components that are related to the creation of quality Rorschach research. They include a careful conceptualization of the problem, defining the issue to be addressed, identifying the relevant variables for the study, and selecting the appropriate subjects. None of these components are different from those commonly found in all research in psychology. Under optimal circumstances, any research in psychology will be formulated out of curiosity and reflect the motivation of the investigator to strive for a design that will reflect the best efforts of scientific inquiry. In that context, each of the previously discussed issues are afforded full weight as the research design is formulated and the appropriate approach to analyzing the data is selected.

In reality, however, researchers are prompted by different motives that frequently have a significant influence on the characteristics of a design or the tactics selected for analyzing the data. Some investigators are in situations where research is required, such as the graduate student facing the prospect of a dissertation. The burden created by the requirement can cause the researcher to become preoccupied with the issue of completion and potential flaws in design may be overlooked until it is too late, or methods of analyzing the data may be selected out of convenience instead of using methods that may challenge the data to the utmost. Other investigators may find themselves in situations in which it seems necessary to design projects in accord with a research prospectus that is congruent with models that are rewarded, as in instances when funding possibilities dictate the sort of research that one might undertake. Often, those who follow this path tend to use methods of addressing data that are "literature traditional," that is, it has been done this way previously so it must be appropriate. A third group of researchers are prompted by needs for recognition wherein the publication of research is equated, at least in part, to the achievement of professional status. Their motives are often influenced by the need to "prove a point." Thus, some select methods of data analysis are likely to yield "significance" even though they violate many of the assumptions of the statistic to do so.

None of the varied motives to do Rorschach research preclude quality scientific inquiry, but all hold forth the possibility that researchers will become too ego involved with their investigation and, at times, that involvement can lead to inadvertent errors in design or the manner in which the data have been addressed. Actually, the design itself usually will dictate the most appropriate method of analyzing data and astute researchers will avoid errors if they pause after outlining a study, and review the design systematically by raising a series of challenges concerning it. No matter how carefully a design may have been outlined, it may be flawed by the inclusion of methodology that might bias the findings, or by the failure to include methodology that might yield data that are more precise in light of the underlying purpose of the study.

The purpose of the final review of a design is twofold. First, it represents an active search for potential flaws that may affect the integrity of the data. Second, it insures that preconceived approaches to the analysis of the data will follow naturally from the design itself. This review eliminates potential flaws by altering the design before committing the study to a model that may include confounding features and, in turn, identifies various approaches to the data that will be appropriate or inappropriate.

THE GENERAL ASSUMPTIONS

The first aspect of the review involves the general assumptions underlying the study: Have the assumptions evolved from a careful and critical review of the literature? Do the assumptions rely excessively on ambiguous or confounded results in other research? Are the assumptions consistent with theories that have some demonstrated support?

THE SPECIFIC HYPOTHESES

The review then moves on to the specific hypotheses that have been formulated: Are the hypotheses articulated in a meaningful way that can be tested by any of a variety of statistical applications? Are the hypotheses based on personality concepts that have measurable behavioral referents?

THE USE OF CLASSIFICATION VARIABLES

One of the most important elements of the review should concern the selection of classification variables. A great deal of Rorschach research includes the use of classification variables. Statistically, they become treated as independent variables that differentiate one group from another; but, unlike the traditional independent variable, they do not involve a manipulation. Instead, they are demographic characteristics of subjects that, in theory, permit the division of subjects into discrete groups. The critical question in selecting classification variables focuses on the *discreteness* of the groups in light of the classification.

For instance, numerous investigators have attempted to study the differences between schizophrenics and depressives. It is an important area of research, but findings can easily be confounded by the fact that all schizophrenics are not alike and the various categories of depression are marked by even much greater heterogeneity. These issues can become confounded even more by the fact that about 20% of inpatient schizophrenics also manifest characteristics of marked depression. The matter can be clouded further by the fact that depression, as a symptom, is quite common among almost all types of psychological or psychiatric disturbance. Depression is often concurrent with anxiety, anger, social isolation, tension, impulse control problems, eating disorders, family discord, and so on. Even serial murderers may be depressed.

In some studies, intragroup differences such as are present in most diagnostic groups may be irrelevant and broad definitions of the groups such as typified by the various *DSM* categorizations may suffice. For instance, a design to test the hypothesis that significantly more subjects diagnosed as schizotypal personality disorder will show an ideational (introversive) coping style than will subjects diagnosed as borderline personality disorder could use people differentiated into the two groups by *DSM* criteria. As a consequence, all subjects in each group can be treated equally from a statistical view. However, many research issues require much more precision in defining classification. Quite often, a careful differentiation of subjects into subgroups can be vitally important. For instance, does a schizophrenic sample consist entirely of first admission inpatients, or are some outpatients or prior admission subjects also included? Does a schizophrenic sample include or exclude those with marked paranoid features? Has the duration of the illness been considered, and so on? In studies concerning substance abuse, are subjects subgrouped by socioecomic level or occupations, and are preferred versus available substances a matter that should require further subgrouping? In studies concerning depression, is the issue of antidepressant mediation weighed appropriately?

There are many aspects of demography that go well beyond age, sex, and completed education that should also be a point of concern for the astute researcher when classification variables are involved. Take, for instance, a study of the elderly, defined as persons who are age 65 or older. Assume that an investigator has formulated a basic postulate that some of the processing and mediational cognitive operations of the elderly, as measured by Rorschach variables, will show more impairment in an elderly group than in a control group of adults between the ages of 25 and 50. One might defend a design for such a study by arguing that the researcher is simply studying age effects and it is appropriate to gather as many subjects from each of the two groups as are available. But suppose that the elderly sample is drawn from mostly nursing homes and the adult control group is drawn mainly from a blue-collar workforce. The results could be analyzed, but are they meaningful? Obviously not! It is inappropriate to assume that nursing home elderly reflect all elderly, and it is equally inappropriate to assume that a blue-collar workforce sample represents all younger adults. Thus, although the data could be analyzed, most or all of the conclusions reached would be misleading and generally unrelated to the initial postulate of the study. Thus, although the question or hypothesis is legitimate, the design has abrogated the issue.

THE USE OF INDEPENDENT VARIABLES

The traditional design involving the use of an independent variable almost always requires that subjects be randomly selected from the same population. Doing so provides the basis for the null hypothesis (performance of the groups will not be significantly different) and sets the circumstance from which the impact of the independent variable (manipulation) can be measured. One of the most important issues concerning independent variables is whether they really do provoke the sort of impact that is expected. In most designs involving a manipulation, investigators will offer an operational definition of the independent variable. For instance, an investigator might postulate that distractions that occur while taking the Rorschach will increase the frequency of diffuse shading answers (*SumY*). The experimental group will be subjected to a distracting stimuli while taking the test, such as randomly issued loud noises in the hallway outside of the testing room, or the frequent ringing of a telephone in the next room. Control subjects will take the test in the same room but without any external distracting stimuli.

Usually, some method should be included in a design to test the efficacy of the manipulation, in this instance a method that will provide some information insuring that the subjects were aware of the distractors. This is not always easy to accomplish in Rorschach research. Sometimes, a posttest questionnaire that asks the subject various questions about the test situation may suffice, but in many instances less direct measures may be required.

For instance, assume that an investigator wants to study the effects of a strictly regimented diet on the frequency of animal movement answers (*FM*). Posttest questionnaire data might be interesting, but would serve little use in demonstrating that the dietary routine had a significant impact on the subjects. Obviously, more direct measures such as weight loss would provide better evidence concerning the impact of the manipulation.

As the probable impact of the independent variable becomes more subtle, the importance of including some measure about its effects increases substantially. Thus, any time a manipulation is used as an independent variable, some logical and arguably defensible tactic should be included to demonstrate that the manipulation has had some effect, and in some instances the data concerning the effect probably should be included in the format for the analysis of the data.

THE SELECTION OF DEPENDENT VARIABLES

One of the most important features of the design review concerns the *a priori* selection of dependent variables. Dependent variables should relate directly to the hypotheses formulated. Unfortunately, many pieces of Rorschach research are published in which a huge number of seeming dependent variables are included, and the collective of "significant" differences are then used as a basis from which to draw conclusions. In some ways this problem reverts to the basic formulation of the study, that is, did the investigator really predict specific differences or was the investigation designed to be a "shotgun" model? Whenever the latter is true, the problems concerning the data analysis are very substantial because so many variables are involved.

In reality, the number of dependent variables should be defined by the sample size, and they should be clearly articulated prior to data collection in light of the issues or hypotheses that have been developed as the basis for the study. Post hoc analyses of other variables is appropriate and for many studies will be very important. But, post hoc analyses do not concern true dependent variables. They simply represent additional comparisons of data that have been made, which may or may not shed new or additional light on the overall results of a study. Thus, the method of analyzing the data for the selected dependent variables might be quite different than the methods used to address additional variables in a post hoc analysis.

THE SELECTION OF CONTROL GROUPS

One of the most important aspects of almost any piece of research is the appropriateness of the control group(s) used. Unfortunately, many investigators devote most of their effort to making sure that the target or experimental group is properly formed and afford far less concern with the issue of controls. In the classic independent variable design, subjects are simply randomized from the same pool or population into experimental and control groups, but that type of design is less common in Rorschach research. More often, researchers identify groups based on classification variables, such as diagnostic groupings, and this can lead to enormous problems.

Any useful control group that is not randomly selected from the same population as the experimental group must be selected with careful consideration for numerous variables, most of which will be demographic. By definition, a control group will not be significantly different from the experimental or target group for most basic features such as age range, sex, educational level, marital status, geographic location, and so forth. When patient groups are used as controls, it is very important to insure that the basic psychiatric demography of the target and control groups are not significantly different, such as inpatient, outpatient, first admission, prior treatment, and so on. In addition, control subjects will be administered the test during the same approximate time frame as the experimental subjects, and optimally, will be tested by the same group of examiners. So-called control groups that are not selected by some fairly stringent parameters concerning basic demography are not really control groups and realistically cannot be included in analyses of the data. Altogether too often, good research designs have been markedly comprised because the investigator failed to develop an adequate control group.

There are instances in which data may be presented more meaningfully if control or comparison groups are not used. This is often appropriate when data become available for an apparently homogeneous group of subjects, and the information about the group contributes to a better understanding of the characteristics of the subjects in the group. For instance, suppose that a group of terminally ill subjects living in a hospice become available for study. The data from such a group might shed some light on whether there are common psychological features among those confronting the prospect of death.

Obviously, it can be argued that any findings of significant homogeneity within the group can be interpreted more precisely if some sort of control group is also used. In that context, control groups with some demographic medical similarity—such as hospice living medical patients who are not terminally ill, or terminally ill patients living in a hospital, or people who have had the same medical condition but have survived—could have some comparative value. Even incarcerated criminals waiting execution might serve as a useful control group, but any of these ideal control groups might not be available. The unavailability of such controls should not detract the investigator, and under no circumstances should the investigator try to form a relatively meaningless control group, such as inpatient depressives, to use as a basis from which to study the target sample. Such comparisons only serve to cloud over the descriptive data concerning the target sample.

All too often, researchers tend to avoid studying and/or reporting data for seemingly homogeneous groups because they cannot generate the variety of adequate control groups that seemed warranted when the traditional guidelines for research are applied, or more often, generate control groups that are inappropriate to the task at hand. Either of these strategies bodes negatively when considered in light of the overall quest for information about people and the study of personality.

APPLICATIONS OF NORMATIVE DATA

One of the most common errors noted in Rorschach research occurs when investigators attempt to use normative data as some control or reference sample. Unfortunately, the notion of using normative data as some sort of comparison sample is not unusual among unwitting graduate students who are facing the many pressures to complete their work. It is true that there are considerable normative and reference samples published concerning the Rorschach. For example, "normative" data regarding the Comprehensive System includes 700 nonpatient adults and 1,390 nonpatient children between the ages of 5 to 16. The adult nonpatient sample has been divided by gender and includes groups from varying racial, educational, and socioeconomic backgrounds.

In theory, the combined nonpatient adult and children groups are of sufficient size to be, for all practical purposes, a mirror of the population distribution and they probably do provide an empirical basis for the normative approach to the test. However, they are not very useful as control samples. For instance, the adult nonpatient sample is rather young with approximately 72% being from 18 to 35 years of age. Accordingly, the normative data may be less appropriate for older groups. In fact, because the normative data have been deliberately stratified and randomly selected from somewhat larger samples, the dispersion or variance of scores for any single variable is likely to differ significantly from any target or experimental group selected for a study.

For example, a group of anorexic women collected from a private hospital may be younger, have higher socioeconomic status, be from a specific geographic area or subculture, or have different recent experiences (including hospitalization) than the nonpatient normative group.

Another issue that argues against using nonpatient normative data as a form of statistical control is the size of the target group in relation to the normative group. The large N's in the normative data lend some power to the many statistical comparisons, which, in turn, increases the likelihood that clinically insignificant differences will become statistically significant. For instance, if one were to collect data for 60 anorexics and compare them to the large ($N =$

700) nonpatient sample, a difference of .04 on *Afr*, .02 on *X+%*, or .2 on *m* would be significant in a two-tailed *t* test at *p* < .05. Such differences are of dubious clinical or practical significance and clutter research reports.

In fact, a host of statistical issues come into play when one compares target samples to normative groups. Quite often, investigators work with relatively small target samples of between 20 to 40 subjects so that the numbers differ enormously between groups. Unequal *N*'s increase the threat of Type I error because of violations of assumptions. Nonparametric analysis can be appropriate for some comparisons, but one would need access to the raw normative data to calculate many of them or to test assumptions if parametric methods are to be applied. Without access to the raw normative data, one can neither identify outliers nor transform individual scores. Consequently, issues of normality, skew, and outliers cannot be addressed and significant increases in error rates will be likely to occur. Similarly, many variables have much larger standard deviations among outpatients than among nonpatients. In fact, 46 of the 111 outpatient standard deviations reported by Exner (1993) exceed the nonpatient value by 50% or more. The reverse is not true for a single variable, that is, no nonpatient standard deviation exceeds the corresponding value in the outpatient reference sample. The schizophrenic or depressive samples reveal the same pattern. In *t* tests or analysis of variance (ANOVA), these greater variances, coupled with small sample sizes relative to a comparison, will yield a combination of large variance–small sample size or small variance–large sample size. Either substantially increases the likelihood of Type I errors.

To illustrate this problem, assume that a researcher finds that 20 anorexics produce a distribution of 20 scores for *m* that, except for one observation, mirrors the nonpatient normative distribution for *m*: 4 records with no *m*, 9 with 1 *m*, 5 with 2, and 1 with 3, and 1 extreme outlier with 9. If one were to calculate a *t* test comparing this sample with the nonpatient normative sample, it would be significant at *p* < .05, two-tailed. This finding occurs because of the data for one subject, the outlier. The same level of significance would be obtained if two of the 0 scores were replaced with 4's, so that there were 3 scores with no *m*, 2 with 4, no records with 8, and the same number of 2's and 3's.

The previous considerations may lead one to decide to dispense altogether with using normative data in making comparisons. Although such a decision may be wise in most instances, there are exceptions. For example, if an adult target sample is reasonably large, probably at least 100 subjects, published nonpatient normative data or published reference group data might serve an appropriate use in a direct statistical comparison provided that only a modest number of variables are included in the analysis.

One of the most appropriate applications of the published normative and reference data involves the use of frequency data. The tables published regarding the Comprehensive System include information regarding the number of subjects giving a particular score and the range of scores for the group. A separate table also is included for each group that provides numerous categorical frequencies such as how many subjects in the sample gave no *T*, or how many are introversive, how many have values of 4 on the Schizophrenia Index (SCZI), and so on. These proportional data can, at times, be used in a nonparametric model to study similarities and differences between a target sample and the published sample. The cautions concerning this approach should be obvious. The target sample must be large enough to insure that proportions will not be markedly influenced by the data for two or three subjects. Typically, the target sample should include more than 30 subjects and preferably more than 40 subjects. In addition, the results should be approached cautiously, probably by using conservative alpha levels such as .01 or even less than .01 in some instances. Although this approach has less power than if the data were compared in a parametric model, positive results will be quite important. Stated differently, this approach may increase the possibilities of a Type II error (accepting the Null hypothesis when it is not true), but because of this, positive findings become more definitive.

One of the most appropriate uses of normative or reference data is textual rather than statistical. The insightful investigator often will find it more appropriate to point to obvious similarities or differences between the data for a target group and the published data. For instance, if the mean *X*–% for a target group is .35 and includes a range of from .20 to .55, statistical manipulations are not really required to argue that these findings are quite different from typical nonpatient data, or that they are quite similar to the published data concerning schizophrenics.

Unfortunately, some investigators feel compelled by training or tradition to a routine of including inferential statistics in their review of the data when, in fact, descriptive statistics will serve the same purpose at least as well, if not better. For instance, if a Rorschach sample for 25 9-year-old subjects includes 22 records in which there are no texture responses and 20 records in which the frequency of passive movement answers exceeds active movement answers by more than one, statistical comparisons between the target group and published normative data for nonpatient nines adds essentially no new information. A textual description of these findings will clearly suffice and probably make any report concerning the fact that the groups are quite different for these two variables clearer and less cluttered.

METHODS OF DATA COLLECTION

One of the most important, but often neglected, issues in Rorschach research concerns the actual collection of the data. The problem of experimenter bias has long been a standard topic in texts about research methodology.

The potential for confounding the data through an unwitting bias seems especially likely in Rorschach research, especially when a single examiner is used to collect all of the protocols. The magnitude of the problem increases considerably when the research design focuses on the collection of data to test specific hypotheses.

The side-by-side seating arrangements recommended for use in the Comprehensive System were not selected casually. In fact, with each of the several methods of testing—face to face, side by side, or with the examiner sitting behind the subject—some of the findings suggested that the latter might be preferable if the objective of minimizing inadvertent nonverbal influences were given priority. The side-by-side methodology was selected because it reduced the apparent discomfort of subjects when they could not see an examiner and because it made the mechanical procedures of recording and inquiring much easier. Therefore, some trade-off occurred. It was very clear that side-by-side seating reduced the possibilities of inadvertent examiner influence considerably when compared with face-to-face testing. Nonetheless, the potential for nonverbal influence remains and of course, the potential for inadvertent verbal reinforcement prior to the test, and during the inquiry, remains as a major hazard. In other words, the possibility of experimenter bias continues to exist.

Thus, in most instances, the principle investigator for a research project involving specific hypotheses should not collect any of the records. Instead, the data collection should be left to others who are naive to the nature of the project. Even when there are no specific hypotheses, the principal investigators should restrict their participation in administering the test to no more than one third of the records that will constitute the final sample(s). The importance of using multiple examiners cannot be overemphasized. Ideally, when hypotheses have been put forth, all of the examiners will be naive to the nature of the study and, probably, any one examiner should not test more than 10% to 20% of the subjects. If an investigation includes more than one group, subjects should be randomly assigned to examiners so that each examiner will test some subjects from each group.

For example, in a hypothesis-testing design that includes three groups of 15 subjects each, it would be appropriate to use five naive examiners with each testing 9 subjects and no more than 4 subjects from any one group. Obviously, there are instances in which the number of qualified, available examiners is limited and some compromise with the optimal is necessary, but any compromise that is devised must be weighed carefully when drawing conclusions from whatever findings has evolved.

When no hypothesis testing is involved, the compromise can be more liberal, but the issue of bias cannot be disregarded. If an optimal number of examiners is not available (one for each 10% to 20% of the subjects), then it might be necessary to use as few as three examiners, with each testing approximately one third of the subjects. However, when any single examiner contributes more than one fourth of the total sample it will be necessary to review the data for the protocols collected by that person to insure that the general distribution of scores, and especially R, is not different than the distribution of scores for the protocols collected by other examiners.

ISSUES OF INTERSCORER AGREEMENT

Interscorer agreement or reliability has been a major issue in Rorschach methodology throughout the history of the technique. Many early studies simply ignored this problem and poor interscorer agreement is probably one of several factors associated with the often inconsistent findings of earlier studies. An acute awareness of this problem has been a major factor in selecting criteria for codes in the development of the Comprehensive System. For any scoring category to be included in the system, an interscorer agreement of 85% or better for 15 to 25 scorers across 10 to 20 Rorschach protocols in which the target category occurred with some frequency has been applied. Despite the development of a system that can be scored reliably, some researchers have continued to ignore this important concern or to deal with it in inadequate ways.

Some researchers have reported acceptable levels of interscorer reliability but failed to present the specific procedures by which the reliabilities were obtained. A value of .85 or .90 clearly has a different meaning if it represents a percent of agreement among scorers versus the value of a correlation coefficient. Some investigators have failed to report interscorer reliability, whereas others have attempted to reconcile disagreements in scoring through "consensus" among coders. This latter procedure begs the question of interscorer reliability.

The test should always be scored by the examiner who administers it, but it is always important to challenge the integrity of the scoring or coding for records used in research. This does not mean that the examiner and a second person who has also scored the record should sit down, discuss their differences, and reach some consensus. That procedure has nothing to do with interscorer reliability. It is a naive tactic that assumes scoring criteria cannot be applied uniformly. Hopefully, scoring criteria are applied uniformly by anyone qualified to administer the test. To be sure, there will be some differences in scoring across examiners. Some are legitimate differences of opinion created because the verbiage in a response is not sufficiently precise to be certain whether or not a criterion is met. Others are simply errors, usually of neglect. Nevertheless, the number of differences should be small across any group of qualified examiners.

Some researchers have evaluated levels of agreement by calculating a form of interscorer reliability. Typically this involves the use of the Spearman–Brown formula to the total scores for each variable (number of *M*'s, *T*'s, etc.) to derive correlation coefficients. This is probably not the best approach to use with Rorschach data because the range of scores is overly narrow for many variables. Instead, a simpler calculation of a *percentage* of interscorer agreement seems more definitive and understandable.

Ordinarily, it is not necessary to have all responses for every protocol scored a second time to evaluate interscorer agreement. Usually, a randomly selected 25% to 35% of the records or responses should suffice if several examiners have been used, but that proportion should be larger if the number of examiners is small.

The calculation of interscorer agreement can be done in either of two ways. The most practical approach is to calculate the percentage of concurrence by segments of the scoring or coding. This means that each score will be broken into eight segments and a cumulative tally of agreements and disagreements will be recorded for all responses considered. The eight segments are: (a) location score (includes the Location and Developmental Quality codes), (b) Determinant(s) (whether a Single Determinant or a Blend), (c) Form Quality, (d) Pairs, (e) Contents (can be taken as a single segment or subdivided into main and secondary contents), (f) Popular, (g) *Z* Score, and (h) Special Scores (can be taken as a single segment or subdivided into critical and noncritical).

When this procedure is used, the expected percentage of agreement will vary to some extent by segments. Typically, the percentage of agreement for Location, Pairs, *Z* Score, and Popular should approach 100%. The percentage of agreement for Form Quality and Contents may be somewhat lower but well over 85%. The percentages of agreement for Determinants and Special Scores are likely to be lowest but should not fall below 80%.

Obviously, there are several variations of this procedure that can be used. For example, in most cases when one scorer codes *FC* and a second codes *CF* the difference will be tallied as a disagreement, but if the study has nothing to do with the weighted sum of color, or the *FC:CF+C* ratio, an investigator might decide to tally an agreement because the presence of color was noted.

A much more stringent approach to evaluating scorer concurrence should be applied to research designs in which the integrity of the total score is critical to the research objective. Generally, this occurs only in studies in which sequencing effects are important. In this method, randomly selected responses from numerous protocols, usually approximating no fewer than 20% of the total responses involved, will be coded by several scorers. The results are then tallied, using a straightforward "yes" or "no" procedure. In this instance, the "yes" category is used when the entire score (Location, Determinants, Form Quality, Pairs, Contents, Popular, *Z* Score, and Special Scores) are identical and the "no" category is used when the entire score is not identical with that of other scorers. Experience demonstrates that this very demanding criterion for calculating the percentage of agreement will, in the best of circumstances, yield agreement levels between 70% and 75%. The flaw with this tactic concerns those judgments that are recorded in the "no" category. One scorer might record a coding for a response that is almost completely different than that of a second scorer, whereas another person might agree with the second scorer except for one secondary content category. Nonetheless, both would be considered as disagreements and recorded in the "no" category.

Another approach may hold some promise for assessing interscorer agreement is the use of the kappa coefficient (Cohen, 1960), which was developed to account for agreements that occur by chance, such as when scorers or raters are forced to make a decision from a limited number of categories. An example of such a forced choice occurs when scoring Location, Developmental Quality, or Form Quality. Each is required, and the scorer must select from one of four categories available. Cohen (1968) also developed a weighted version of coefficient *kappa* that permits a differential weighing of the different types of disagreements among raters. The weighted *kappa* appears to be especially applicable to Rorschach studies in which the type or degree of disagreement among scorers may be important. For example, consider two scorers coding the element of Form Quality. If one codes a response as *Fo* and the other assigns a coding of *F+* it would be tallied as a disagreement in a simple running tally of agreements and disagreements. Likewise, a scoring of *Fo* by one scorer and a coding of *F−* by another would also be scored a disagreement. However, the latter disagreement is clearly more serious, with potentially ominous interpretative implications.

The use of weighted kappa allows the researcher to differentially weight these disagreements to reflect the nature of the severity of disagreement. Thus, weighted *kappa* provides a more accurate, stringent, and robust estimate of the interscorer agreement. Light (1971) presented a method whereby the calculation of coefficient kappa can be extended to measure agreement in studies that employ more than two raters. Although this statistic is a more demanding test of interscorer agreement than a simple percentage agreement tally, it can provide a more accurate and meaningful estimate of the true reliability of Rorschach coding among scorers. In some studies, especially those involving the development of criteria for new scoring categories, this approach will yield a more precise understanding of the nature of scorer disagreements when they occur.

CONCLUSIONS

The world of scientific investigation is not simple and although most researchers strive for design perfection, almost every study that comes to fruition and is published can be criticized in retrospect. Some of this criticism may address subtle flaws that have clouded the design, some may focus on methods of data analysis, and others may cast doubt on conclusions drawn. Sometimes more subtle imperfections become obvious as the data are analyzed, but more often they are detected only after the total "package" is complete. Hopefully, a careful review of features outlined here will eliminate any major design problems before an investigator commits to the data collection and also should minimize the potential number of more subtle defects that may exist in the study. Rorschach research is not easy, but it can be done, and it can be done quite well by the investigator who takes care at each step when formulating the methodology.

REFERENCES

Cohen, J. (1960). A coefficient of agreement for nominal scales. *Educational and Psychological Measurement, 20*, 37–46.
Cohen, J. (1968). Weighted kappa: Nominal scale agreement with provision for scaled disagreement or partial credit. *Psychological Bulletin, 70*, 213–220.
Exner, J. E. (1993). *The Rorschach: A comprehensive system: Vol. 1. Basic foundations* (3rd ed.). New York: Wiley.
Light, R. J. (1971). Measures of response agreement for qualitative data: Some generalizations and alternatives. *Psychological Bulletin, 76*, 365–377.

CHAPTER EIGHT

Issues of Probability
and Rorschach Research

Howard Mcguire & John E. Exner, Jr.

Generally, investigators abhor negative findings. Thus, it is not uncommon for researchers to attempt any of a variety of data manipulations to find some support for the contentions underlying their study. The breadth of available statistical methods makes it possible to generate support for almost any conclusion if one is willing to disregard some of the fundamental issues concerning probability. Usually, this disregard occurs in either of two ways. One is to bend or ignore assumptions of the statistical method selected. The second is to afford an unrealistic weight to certain alpha levels selected when comparisons of data sets are made. Either can lead to faulty or misleading conclusions.

Probability is a key element in determining the statistical and psychological "significance" of findings. Probability enters the research picture through comparison of some obtained statistic with one of the standard probability curves to determine the significance or statistically determined frequency of occurrence of that statistic, such as calculating a correlation coefficient between two measures. The coefficient's statistical probability of occurrence is assessed by comparing it with standard critical values in a precalculated table to determine if it is significant. On the basis of that obtained probability and some general decision theory guidelines about alpha levels, power, degrees of freedom, and characteristics of the data analyzed, a decision is made to interpret or ignore the association between the two measures.

In accepting this standardized process of statistical models and their respective assumptions uncritically, investigators surrender some autonomy in return for apparent ease in assessing the importance, or lack thereof, of findings. The exchange involved in using rote standardized statistical test

159

procedures or paradigms may not always be worth the cost. This is especially so when dealing with the small N's, not-so-normal score distributions, or sometimes highly categorical scores of Rorschach data. Rorschach data do not always fit neatly into the usually expected or statistically justifiable assumptions generally seen in psychological research.

A major problem with Rorschach data is that the underlying distributions for certain variables or ratios are not as normal as might be desired. Often, the ranges of scores may be too constrained or restricted. R is limited on both ends of its distribution, and for various reasons the apparent continuous distributions of scores between these limitations is bounded, and therefore not completely continuous. Scores for some scales, although seemingly looking like continuous data, are in reality more categorical in their impact on interpretation or their distribution. For instance, the difference between an $X+\%$ of .75 and .79 is not the same as the difference between .79 and .83. $X+\%$ is a ratio of two finite numbers. Because there is a limited small set of values for both the numerator and the denominator, there is also a fairly limited set of values the ratio can take. Thus, whereas the ratio looks like a continuous variable, it is not. If $X+\%$ was expressed as a fraction, it would be easier to keep this quality in mind, but it would be vastly more difficult to make ordinal comparisons. For example, which is more interpretively important, an $X+\%$ of 15/24ths or an $X+\%$ of 9/19ths?

Most determinant scores have markedly bent distributions and some, such as Vista, have very lopsided population distributions—that is, the majority of protocols do not even yield one. A failure to appreciate the special nature of many Rorschach scores sets up a misapplication of probability-based statistical decision making. Possibly a brief review of standard probability theory can be useful in developing an understanding of the special or extra considerations often required when making statistical decisions in light of the special limits and concerns raised by features of some Rorschach data.

PROBABILITY AND DECISION THEORY

Probability and *decision theory* are terms often regarded as being forbidding, dry, and remote from everyday usage. However, most people are more comfortable with the phenomena these labels describe than any of the terms, theories, or formulas used to describe the phenomena themselves. The following example illustrates probability in action and how that action might be interpreted in terms of specific decisions.

Suppose you and a friend go to lunch on Monday and select choices from the menu that cost about the same. Assume you agree to add a little adventure by tossing a coin to see who pays the bill. You flip a coin, it comes up tails, and you lose. The next day you and your friend decide to flip again for lunch. It is tails and you lose again. Likewise, Wednesday comes and you flip again. It's tails and again you lose. On Thursday do you still want to toss for lunch? Are you now wondering about the coin or how it's being tossed to create your "bad luck"? What will be your decision now faced with this run of losses and the possibility of a future loss? This is decision theory for real.

As a person familiar with the probability significance level of $p < .05$ in making such decisions, you presumably still want to flip for lunch again on Thursday, believing that chance is still at work. But when you toss again, you lose still again, for the fourth straight time. Do those earlier suspicions concerning your friend or the coin resurface even stronger? Now comes Friday. Do you still want to flip again, or are you now of the belief that things are not happening the way they should be? Do you flip again, quit the game, or start checking the coin, or evaluating the morality of your friend (two options that might be called "alternative hypotheses")?

As a person knowledgeable about probability, you really should toss the coin one more time. The actual probability of four straight losses is only .0625, not yet less than the generally accepted level of .05 for significance. The senior author proposed this example to a group of researchers, and most stated that they would "feel something was going on" after four such losses and indicated they probably would have declined any further tossing (some said they even would have quit after three such losses). However, being a person who wishes to be certain of your conclusion before accusing your friend of chicanery, you decide to flip for the fifth time. You lose again. Do you now feel comfortable accusing your friend of wrongdoing in that you have obtained results somewhat less than the $p < .05$ level? Or would you withhold any accusation until reassured by data equating with a $p < .01$ level of certainty? The probability of six straight tails is still only .015625 (not yet at the $p < .01$ level) and the probability of seven straight tails is only .0078125. Would you be willing to go to lunch and lose two more times to reach this higher level of $p < .01$ certainty, or being more generous, would you want to reach a $p < .001$ certainty before issuing forth charges of fraud against a friend? Would you be willing to suffer 10 straight losses?

This is the same dilemma a researcher faces in deciding what alpha level to accept in the face of unreliable instruments or results that contradict someone else's findings. However, in the luncheon illustration, the decision to carry on for 10 losses takes on a different psychological reality than saying that you will accept correlations significant at only the .01 alpha level. Taken in the luncheon context, probability and decision making are no longer quite so remote and dry. In this example, everyday experience conflicts with that accepted as standard practice in psychological research. Those less involved in research on a routine basis may feel more akin to those who prefer to quit after three losses, harboring certain suspicions. To extend this situation, charging a friend with fraud on a game of chance would require strong conviction and thereby raise any required probability stakes considerably. Indeed, the stakes may require alphas far beyond normal research practice because of the perceived cost of a wrong decision.

DEFINITIONS OF PROBABILITY

Some of the confusion about probability arises from the semantic expressions or translations of probability terms. Even simple probability expressions like "two to one" can mislead. If someone said the odds of an event's occurrence was "2 to 1," would the probability of that occurrence be $p = .66$ (two thirds) or $p = .50$ ("fifty-fifty")? The correct response is $p = .66$, or two out of three total possibilities, not one chance in two.

The use of the term *probability* creates some expectations. If it is observed that 5 of 100 people attending a parents' meeting at a school are male, it could be stated that 5% of the group are male, and it is obvious that the probability of being male in this group would be $p = .05$. However, using the phrase "$p(\text{male}) = .05$" raises an issue of doubt or uncertainty not present in the statement of "5% male." We know we are going to find five males with "5%" in the group and the "5%" is perceived to relate only to this group. On the other hand, the phrase "$p(\text{male}) = .05$" takes on a meaning that transcends the description of this parent's group. Yet, in this case, percent and probability have the same mathematical implications.

How should probability be defined? There appear to be three broad classes of probability definitions, provided that one skips over a number of fundamental issues that give rise to a larger number of basic definitions. Those interested in studying this complex issue in detail are advised to review writings concerning various probability theories, such as the Fisherian, Bayesian, or Neymann–Pearson–Wald theoretic positions, and attendant "decision-theoretic" models.

The first of the three broad classes of definition of probability, and probably the closest to what people assume about probability theory, can be categorized under a general rubric entitled the "equally-likely outcomes" definitions. In this style, probability is seen as a ratio of two terms: the numerator being the number of desirable outcomes and denominator the total number of possible outcomes. What is important here is the defining of "outcome." Each outcome must be equally likely to occur. For instance, a die has six faces, only one of which can be up on any roll, with six results equally likely for an honest die. Therefore, the probability of getting a "SIX" on a roll is one to six, or $p = 1/6$. A theoretical necessity is that the sum of probabilities of all such equally likely outcomes must equal 1.00. Thus, the probability of not getting a "SIX" is calculated by subtracting the probability of getting a "SIX" from the total probability, 1.00: $p(\text{SIX}) = 1.00 - 1/6 = 5/6$.

This sort of probability is very dependent on being able to set up the theoretically exclusive and equally likely outcomes at the onset. Often, this is not easy to do when there is a suspicion or observation that prior occurrences can affect following occurrences. If a basketball player makes a basket, the next shot may be affected by that prior success. Thus, each shot's outcome may not be equally likely but some function of prior successes or failures, and this form of probability definition becomes less useful in some instances.

The second class of probability definitions is based on relative frequencies. In a series of trials, occurrences, or tests, a certain event or outcome occurs a few times (say "k"). The relative frequency of k is k divided by the number of trials: k/N. As N grows larger, more trials are accumulated where k could occur and as a result, more confidence exists that the k/N ratio is sounder and more likely to represent the "true" ratio of k in a population of trials or cases. It is important to remember that this ratio provides an estimate that is more empirical in nature of an event's probability than the other classes of definitions: for example, if, after rolling a die 10,000 times, it is noted that the relative frequency of SIX is actually .17 instead of the theoretically expected .166666 as defined by the equally-likely definitions. We would have to accept the p(SIX) = .17 because N is large in this case, but the result is counter to expectation (i.e., $p = 1/6$ or $p = .1666$). As a result, we start examining the die for unevenness or bias in tossing or something that would interfere with obtaining the expected value of p(SIX) = .1666. In this instance, there is a conflict between the equally-likely definition of probability and the more empirically based definition using relative frequencies.

The newest class of probability definitions, and oldest in usage, might best be called "subjective definitions." In its oldest incarnation, subjective probabilities are established by persons to describe their own expectations based on their own experience. Assertion or expressions, such as "I think the NFL is twice as likely to win the Superbowl as the AFL next year," characterize this more informal definition. These statements capture almost as much of the person's personality as real statistical information. As such, this kind of probability is not easily applied to formal statistical analyses, but is becoming a more important aspect of decision-making theorizing (Wright, 1984).

A more statistically rigorous version of this type of probability, called Bayesian probability, is making its way into conceptions. Bayesian probability starts with the idea that there is some prior idea of an event's past probability that must be accounted for in determining that event's current probability estimate. Indeed, some statisticians (Efron, 1986) have argued that all researchers should be Bayesian in their probability thinking because experiments are seldom conducted without some predetermined expectation of significant probability outcomes.

None of these classes of definitions is without difficulties sometimes. The most important thing to bear in mind that the value described by being a "probability" is not a single fixed value, but will vary with the definition of the term.

PROBABILITY, VARIATION, AND DISTRIBUTION

Probability can be loosely thought of as the relative frequency of a specific event to totality of all such events. Totality of all such events is usually construed as being a distribution of variation. There are three sets of distributions involved in probability inferences. The first is the raw data distribution (sample distribution of raw data). This consists of the actual scores for a variable. A classic version of the raw data distribution is the frequency curve constructed from the compiled numbers of times each score value was observed (i.e., how many people with that same score). These values are empirical as they represent real observed data and the distributions can be either discrete or continuous. Marital status or number of siblings are discrete distributions, whereas IQ scores or test completion times are taken as continuous sample distributions.

The second set is the population distribution. The major distinction is in the scope of the population. Usually an investigator has only a sample of the total parent population from which observations have been collected and the goal is to conjecture about the parent population as a whole. Although some parent populations may be limited in actual size, most involve numbers too large to study in entirety, thus it becomes necessary to use some theoretical approximation or assumption regarding the appearance of the parent group distribution.

Usually, estimates about the parent population are derived from the characteristics of a sample and some probabilistic expectations are drawn concerning the characteristics of the larger population. The use of probability to make an approximation about the parent population from the sample is a form of probabilistic inference. As an inference, it must always be examined to see if it is warranted. Inferences from small samples are not as convincing as inferences from large samples. Often, prior research provides information to help judge the current sample's suitability for population inference. For instance, if an adult sample of 100 Rorschach protocols contains 80 subjects who have values for M responses that fall between 9 and 15, and the remaining 20 subjects have values between 5 and 8, prior knowledge about the distribution of M warns that the sample is not highly representative of M scores in the general population.

The third distribution is the sampling distribution. This distribution consists of values from test descriptive statistics such as the frequency of means of multiple samples of 10 people each on variable X. How many groups of 10 people, taken as a sample, have a mean value for M of 9 on the Rorschach? It could also be a distribution of correlation coefficients ($r$xy) that reveal how many times a specific $r$xy of .45 was obtained for groups of 50 subjects each from which values for variables X and Y were obtained.

It is from these sorts of distributions that general recommendations about the advisability of running too many statistics like t's and $r$xy's have evolved. For instance, out of every hundred $r$xy's, at least 5% will occur simply by chance. Obviously, context becomes important. Running one correlation and obtaining significance is much more valuable than running 10 correlations and obtaining 1 that is significant.

Sampling distributions of test statistics can be generated from various probability formulations. Selected values of these outcomes, usually corresponding to probability levels such as .05, .01, and .005, appear in various tables for reference purposes. It is the theoretical versions of these sampling distributions that help to provide the critical comparison values used to evaluate specific sample differences.

Efron (1979) described a different approach to the doing of statistics made possible by the capacities of modern high speed computers. This new approach is labeled "bootstrapping" after the approach of using the computer to re-sample the original sample thousands of times to create a parent population based only on the original data. The following illustrates one way in which this approach might function in place of standard hypothesis testing. Imagine two sets of data from two groups of 10 subjects each. The statistical question is: Are the means for the two groups significantly different? Efron suggested that the computer be used to create a vast distribution of scores by repeating each score thousands of times, thus thousands of sets of 10 scores are drawn from this bootstrapped population. The computer is then used to calculate thousands of sample mean differences by subtracting one randomly drawn sample from the next thousands of times. This permits the creation of a sampling distribution of the differences of those bootstrapped samples. An investigator has only to look if the frequency of the difference is sufficiently low to warrant concluding whether or not a significant difference between the original two groups' sets of 10 scores each does exist (Simon & Bruce, 1991).

Efron's approach could replace much of what has to happen in standard hypothesis-testing probability inference. The data from a single study generates all of the possible population values by the bootstrapping method. Thus, the data from two small samples generate a population of thousands of values, all reflecting the original two samples' data. Significance would then be ascertained by comparing the original mean difference with an exact frequency from the obtained means difference sampling distribution of the bootstrapped population, stating the percentage of the time data equivalent to the original difference occurred. The bootstrap methodology is not for all statistical problems, and not many computational analogs to other statistical tests are yet available, but bootstrapping appears to be a good approach in general (Stine, 1989). The bootstrap methodology vastly reduces the population inferences derived from some model of probability.

In traditional practice, some appeal is usually made to the presumed normality of the unobservable and unobtainable population. With the bootstrap technique, that population may not be so unobservable and unobtainable. In standard practice, an investigator must determine what is an appropriate model for a population's distribution. Usually the *normal distribution*, which is the standard statistical default, is selected. Most psychological data is generated through methods that help to insure normality. Therefore, this assumption concerning normality is not often wrong, although it is to be presumed that exceptions will occur. Standard practice helps provide a more-or-less automatic statistical approximator of the missing population through the utilization of various standard guiding probability functions. There are a variety of probabilistic functions that can govern expectations about what data should look like in distributions. These include the normal, the binomial (also, the negative binomial), the poisson, the multinomial, the hypergeometric, the incomplete gamma, and incomplete beta—to name a few of the better known in psychology (Hays, 1973; Lindeman et al., 1980).

Historically, the normal probability density function and its related bell-shaped curve appears to take precedence in most thinking about probabilistic inference. There are many good statistical reasons for this. One of the most important reasons is that many sampling distributions appear to head for normality as the number of observations greatly increases regardless of the test statistic's appearance for small numbers of observations. Perhaps as important is the fact that much of psychological data looks "normal" in distributional appearance. Fair sized distributions of IQ scores look normal and they should because those constructing the tests have gone to great lengths to obtain normality in score distributions. Many self-report personality tests give similar results. At times, it appears as if normality in score distribution has become a desirable goal in and of itself when a test has been designed.

Normality has a number of beneficial features on which much of test theory depends. The concept of bias and random errors that cancel out in true test score theories depend on the bilateral symmetry of the normal. The three measures of central tendency—the mean, median, and mode—are equivalent in the normal distribution. The equivalence of the area under the normal curve bounded by any two lines drawn from scalar points to probability is of extreme importance for hypothesis testing. The area between a vertical line drawn up to the center of the curve and a line drawn up from the +1 *SD* scalar point is .3413.

The standard deviation scalar size (how big a standard deviation is) can be geometrically determined from the point on the normal curve where a tangent line to that normal curve reverses slope. In other words, a line dropped vertically from the curve at the point where the normal curve changes from a concave surface to a convex surface, as we move away from the mean, gives us a solid basis for determining a standard deviation. In part for this reason, psychologists have had to deal with z's of ±1.96 bounding the 95% region and ±2.56 bounding the 99% region instead of easier numbers like ±1.50 or ±2.00 for the 95% region. These qualities and others of the normal distribution have accounted in part for the large role of the normal in providing a basis for the current stage of hypothesis testing.

One way to avoid the problem of assuming normality is to calculate exact probability, but the effort involved in calculating exact probabilities for a set of test score distributions is massively tedious and thereby limits a researcher's options. Utilization of theoretical probability distributions such as the normal serves to reduce this effort. In effect, by assuming that obtained samples of data have been drawn from a larger population with the characteristics of one of the theoretical distributions, an investigator can make use of fairly standard statistical inferences. The most notable is the equivalence of the size of the area under a probability curve, marked off by a test score's difference from a central tendency value such as the mean, to the probability of obtaining that test score. This is an inference!

One assumes that if very large numbers of scores, which usually are difficult to obtain, were available, those scores would aggregate in a frequency polygon that would yield a distribution looking just like that generated by the probability model, the normal curve. This assumption or inference saves us much time in actually getting the kind of data needed for obtaining relative frequencies to empirically answer questions such as, how many adults in 100 will have an $X+\%$ greater than 94%? The most exact way to obtain the answer is to test 100 adults and count, or the answer can be inferred from a smaller sample. Prior knowledge permits the assumption that a sample will have a mean $X+\%$ of .79 and standard deviation of .08 if 100 subjects were actually tested. Given that prior knowledge, the ".94 cutoff" in relation to the normal distribution is 2 SD distribution points, which yields an area of .0228 beyond the cutoff point. Thus, it can be inferred that 2.28 people would have an $X+\%$ greater than 94%.

The ".28" is indicative of the difficulty of using probability models instead of real world numbers. In an actual sample of 100, two, three, or four people might have $X+\%$'s higher than 94% but not "2.28." The divergence between reality and inference usually is regarded as being worth it to most investigators. It permits much easier decision making about the outcome of an experiment.

There are a wide variety of probability based test statistic distributions used as models for making significance decisions. Some of these various test statistic distributions are very familiar, such as z, chi, F, t, and r. These all reflect a strong and easily seen relationship to the normal distribution. The binomial (and the negative binominal or Pascal distribution) is offered in most statistics texts to illustrate how, as the number of binary events (usually coin tosses) increases, the frequency of outcomes begins to resemble the normal. Most statistics texts also devote space to concepts such as the Central Limit Theorem, the law of large numbers, and the Tchebyeff inequality to convince the reader that as N increases toward infinity, differences between these various probability distributions (and a host of others) tends to merge into the normal. Only in the very small N cases or small frequency cases do these actually diverge, drastically for chi-square and F and not so drastically for t.

The very robustness of t, and other statistical tests, rests upon this phenomenon. Even with very skewed original raw data, the sampling distribution of differences of means drawn from a skewed population of raw scores is constrained to be normal or nearly normal. However, if the original raw data distribution curve resembles a pronounced "J-shape," "U-shape," or some other blatantly non-normal-looking distribution, as is often the case with many Rorschach variables, it is likely that a sampling distribution of differences of pairs of means will not be normal or near enough to normal for testing purposes. For these situations, researchers may see the means of their samples correlating with the sample standard deviations, which is something that should not happen with normal sample distributions.

When unusual (not neatly normal looking) raw distributions occur, some decisions must be made concerning how to proceed with the statistical analyses. If the researcher has reason to believe or infer the true nature of the underlying population is normal and just the sample looks somewhat non-normal, the researcher may be able proceed with standard parametric analysis with either suitable adjustments in the power analysis, raw score transformations that help promote normality or linearity, cautious interpretation of outcome, and the like. If the researcher has reason to believe or infer that the underlying parent population is not normal, the researcher still has some viable options if used cautiously. There are some raw score transformations that may be useful in this situation. A variety of authors have noted various sorts of score transformations that can help modify data to make the resultant transformed data more tractable to more common statistical decision-making processes (Bock, 1975; Green & Carroll, 1978; Nunnally, 1967; Tabachnick & Fidell, 1989), but there are some Rorschach data for which transformations will only serve to obscure the fact that non-normality exists.

The choice of which distribution to use (or which statistic to use) is important in all research, but especially in Rorschach research. Use of normality-based statistics assumes the data for a variable to be normal regardless of the data in the sample. The objective of the analysis is to evaluate the null hypothesis and in reality, there are four elements that contribute to the adequacy of the analysis.

FOUR FACTORS OF POWER ANALYSIS
AND PROBABILITY

The adequate use of any statistical test rests on a combination of statistical decisions, all of which relate the issues of power and probability. There are four basic factors in the analysis of power. Power, in this context, refers to more than the simple suitability of the statistical test procedure, that is, power analysis is more than just the determination of power and Type II errors.

The first factor is the decision about level of significance. What alpha level should be selected, $p < .05$ or $p < .01$, and so on. What size risk of a Type I error (that is, rejecting the null when it is actually true) seems acceptable?

The second factor is sample size. How many subjects must be included to address the issue competently and fairly?

The third factor is power. Power at this level is more specific and refers to what levels of risk or probability of Type II errors are acceptable? At this level of definition, power is written as $(1 - \beta)$ where β is the probability of a Type II error (that is, keeping the null when it is actually false).

The fourth factor is "effect size." How big and what kind of an experimental difference will be required or expected in the data? This last factor is related to what kind of statistical test will be used to do the statistical analysis. It would be rare indeed, using a t test, to get an exact means difference of zero in a study as the usual null hypothesis states. Thus, the question is really what magnitude of difference is large enough to be convincing that something other than chance is operating in the data, or what specific difference is large enough to conclude that a rejection of the null hypothesis is warranted?

These four factors are interdependent. One cannot be modified without affecting the others. Also, once any three are established, the fourth is determined by those three. A value for one cannot be selected without limiting the values possible for the other three factors. Adopt a conservative significance level such as .01, making it harder to reject the null hypothesis, and power will be lower. Raise power to avoid a Type II error, and either you have to raise the acceptable level of significance, such as to .05, or increase the N, or be prepared to look for large sample differences or some combination of these last three. Make choices for three of these factors and the fourth is automatically determined. But this interdependence is all that is automatically determined.

Welkowitz, Ewen, and Cohen (1982) pointed out that these relationships, especially power determinations, have been slighted in most statistics books with a potential result that researchers do not routinely examine or report these aspects of their research. A lack of awareness about these issues often leads to decisions that cause the power level to be too low. The consequence of this oversight may be prematurely foreclosing potentially valuable lines of research.

Many investigators simply follow standard research advice in dealing with these issues, that is, increasing N and/or being conservative in selecting levels of significance. Unfortunately, although these recommendations are easiest to understand, they do not necessarily guarantee good experiments or designs. Huck and Sandler (1984) presented a very thoughtful demonstration of two studies on the same topic, one with 20 subjects and one with 62 subjects. Both yield t's of approximately 2.1, which are significant at $p < .05$. Huck and Sandler asked the question: Which study is more noteworthy? If one does not stop and think carefully about the interplay between the four factors, one is naively tempted to choose the study based on 62 subjects, because of the larger N. But this would be an erroneous selection because a larger effect size (in this case, a larger mean difference for the two samples) is necessary to achieve the same significance level for 20 subjects as for 62 subjects. In reality, the 20 subject study really was demonstrating a very sizable experimental difference. Obviously, good experimental outcomes are not dependent only on large N's. This principle can be important for Rorschach studies where N's are small and cannot be increased at will.

Consider a situation in which a researcher believes that a significant association exists between R and the Afr in a specific population and wants to test that hypothesis with a Pearson product-moment correlation on the scores for the two variables. Unfortunately, only 22 subjects (typical of limited sample sizes of some clinical studies) are available. The researcher decides to examine power (δ) at a preselected significance level of .05. Using a simplified power formula (Howell, 1987) for $r$xy in this case:

$$\delta = r\text{xy} \sqrt{N} - 1$$

A table of significance for $r$xy shows a value of .423 for $\alpha = .05$, $df = 20$, and two-tailed test. Substituting in these numbers into the simplified formula, a value for δ of 1.939 is noted. Looking this value up in power table for $\alpha = .05$, we find a power coefficient of .50.

Generally speaking, a power coefficient around .20 is considered too low, and a coefficient of .80 is considered the highest needed (Cohen, 1988; Kraemer & Thieman, 1987). Less than .20 requires remedial action or very cautious interpretation. Higher than .80 is usually expensive and a potential waste of subjects. In the example, the power coefficient is in the midrange. If researchers really wanted a higher power test, they could estimate how many additional subjects would be required if $\alpha = .05$ is used by applying rxy. In the power table for δ equal to power of .80, a value of 2.80 is required. Substituting these numbers into the power formula and solving for N, the result indicates that the investigator would need 45 subjects to get that higher level of power. Conversely, if the investigator increased the significance level to $\alpha = .01$ and kept the sample size at 22, power drops to .28, very near a level not many would accept. Yet, many times wary researchers, anxious to correct for perceived potential instability in scores, attempt to be cautious by raising α value without realizing that they are making another collateral statistical probability decision, that is, to accept very low power and greatly risk losing a true finding! This may be acceptable to some researchers, but they should be aware that this exchange has occurred.

Recent statistical texts are beginning to include integrated coverage of the power analysis issues with their presentations of various tests to accompany older blanket statements about a test being conservative (i.e., post hoc's like the Scheffè) or liberal (i.e., planned comparisons and the like). Cohen's (1988) extensive volume has extensively documented the various forms and issues of power analysis. Others discuss more specific concerns, such as Kraemer and Thieman (1987), which discusses power analysis from the very focused point of asking how many subjects are needed in a given design. There has been some perception that small N studies and strategies suffer by comparison to larger classically designated good experiments with N's in the thirties and higher. Robinson and Foster (1979) noted this problem and offered a number of sound and proven research strategies designed to deal with small N's in psychology. Davidson and Costello (1969) took it further and detailed a series of strategies focused on the ultimate small N study, the $N = 1$ investigation.

Rorschach investigators should not be deceived, however, into the notion that small sample research is somehow preferable. That is not the case, but there are instances in which small samples are either convenient or the only samples available. Numerous authorities regarding experimental design tend to abhor small sample research. Bausell (1986), for instance, recommended that designs should use as large an N as economically possible whatever the other aspects of the power determination. Bausell relied on other statistical inferences to determine the strength of association and thus stepped outside the interdependencies of the four factors of power analysis. However, it could be argued that the very large differences to reject the null for low N's at the $\alpha = .05$ are equated in terms of their impact on out statistical decision making to the smaller differences for large N's by the very equivalence of the $\alpha = .05$ concept. In that we meet the statistical requirements for significant difference, with either a larger difference from small N's or smaller difference from larger N's, it is difficult to comphrehend the greater lack of willingness to accept the small-N result so often seen. Power analysis does not assign more import to sample size than to the other three factors, yet many researchers do. In reality, it is a question of choice of design philosophy and willingness to accept probability inferences and assumptions. The more sophisticated the design, the more a researcher will be able to accept the results of a small sample study.

THE USE OR NONUSE OF NONPARAMETRIC STATISTICS

Nonparametric statistics are called *distribution free statistics* because these make no or few assumptions about any distributional characteristics or variance of the population distribution from which our study's specific sample was drawn. No particular distribution is assumed, only that the obtained sample's distribution reflects the underlying population distribution whatever form that distribution takes. Some of these statistics do use parameters in the strict mathematical sense of that word, however, those parameters are seldom concerned with means and variances as in the Normal based parametrics. The most often used version of central tendency is the median and the most frequent form of variation is rank orderings. Over the years, a number of analogs to more familiar parametric statistics have been developed (Siegel & Castellan, 1988). For example, a nonparametric Friedman two-way analysis of variance for ranks resembles the familiar two-way ANOVA. The sign test is similar to the t test in that a researcher could use the sign test to examine differences in two experimentally paired groups to see if the two groups are different on some variable. Spearman's rho is usually thought of as a very familiar nonparametric version of rxy for ranked data.

Indeed, the presentation of the convergence between rho and rxy is even closer these days. Owing to potential difficulties with ties in the classic formula for calculating rho, a newer procedure has been recommended that involves ranking the data and using the Pearson product-moment correlation (rxy) procedure to calculate the correlation between the two ranked versions of the raw scores for the variables. However, the obtained coefficient is reported as a rho and uses rho tables to assess the significance of the newly labeled rho coefficient. The difference between these two procedures is small when few tied ranks exist and the ties are limited to two or three score values. As the number of ties increases and the ties incorporate three or more scores in each tie, the old rho calculation formula suffers. This example of increasing homogenization of calculational procedures points out that the parametric and nonparametric statistics differ less in form than in some of their assumptions for inference and what types of data would be best suited for each given those inference assumptions. Indeed, Nunnally (1967) contended that rho is simply not a nonparametric but a shortcut version of a product-moment correlation used on ranked data and noted the equivalence of the two calculational methods. Yet, most researchers still think of rho as a nonparametric version of correlation.

There are numerous Rorschach situations in which the data, or prior information, indicate a non-normal parent population and, as such, do not satisfy the requirements for doing the more familiar parametric statistics. The level of measurement of the data simply may not support parametric analysis. Obviously, most demographic data such as marital status is a nominal or categorical scale with no ordinality apparent between categories of married, widowed, single, or divorced. Likewise, some Rorschach scores have the same or similar lack of ordinality, and parametric analyses do not handle this kind of information scale at all well. Very small sample sizes are not good parametric candidates either unless the parent population is known very precisely, which usually is not the case.

Some nonparametrics can combine data from different populations easily. Although parametrics can do this as well, they do not do it as easily and require all sorts of adjustments in inference. It can be argued that some kinds of data are fundamentally rank data. The ordinality of such data is not in question, because which group has the higher frequency is clear, but it is impossible to tell how much higher. In instances such as this, the data may be subjected to a parametric analysis, but the result usually will give an exaggerated idea about the true meaning of the data. Nonparametrics often are more desirable for Rorschach data because they provide a relative ease of interpretation of statistical outcome because they have made fewer demands on the data.

Siegal and Castellan (1988) contended that most of the unfavorable perceptions of nonparametrics arise from a lack of systematic exposition, dispersion of presentations, and lack of convenience in finding suitable tables. A quick examination of most basic statistics books will support some of their contentions. Nonparametric statistics are usually discussed near the end of the book and only those nonparametrics with easily understood analogies to parametric statistics are included (such as Spearman's rho and/or a Median test).

There is also a concern about the relative power and conservativeness of the two types of statistics. When the data support the use of parametric statistics, then that is what should be used. To not do so runs a risk of missing some significance in the data. Stated differently, the parametric test can assign the same level of significance with fewer subjects than the nonparametric equivalent. The real question is to determine which is more appropriate. The small N advantage of the nonparametric is a case in point. Investigators may be so strongly committed to a parametric model that, rather than use a nonparametric test with small N's, they either keep sampling in hopes of getting larger N's or drop the line of inquiry. This is unfortunate because a slightly altered version of the hypothesis could be tested non-parametrically using the smaller sample.

Some researchers tend to perceive nonparametrics as being less scientific or less exacting than the more organized and familiar parametrics. This just is not true! Indeed, in some cases, nonparametric statistics use a direct calculation of probability that is a more exact finding than the estimates obtained by using an approximate probability model. Fisher's exact test for 2 × 2 tables provides a good example. Siegal and Castellan (1988) demonstrated the application of the Fisher's exact test on the following 2 × 2 table:

	Group		
	I	*II*	
Yes	4	1	5
No	1	6	7
Total	5	7	12

Given this data set, Siegal and Castellan obtained an exact calculation of the probability of obtaining this data configuration or one even more extremely imbalanced in the present direction as being $p = .04545$. Clearly, this probability is in the significant range and was not derived by looking for a p value in a table. If a 2 × 2 contingency chi-square had been calculated for these data, using the standard calculational form,

$$\chi^2 = \frac{N(\mid AD - BC \mid - N/2)^2}{(A + B)(C + D)(A + C)(B + D)}$$

the resulting chi-square = 2.831, and with $df = 1$, the probability, derived from a table for this result is .0925! Obviously, there is a price to pay for the use of probability models like the chi-square distribution (or the normal as well) to estimate outcomes rather than exactly calculate a probability.

These two comparisons of the same data set are rather drastic and in most suitable cases the two outcome probabilities would not differ quite this much. However, the possibility of calculating an exact probability rather than resorting to probability assumptions should not be taken lightly. In fact, new advances in computational ability make the researcher's choice to do exact calculations much easier than has been the case (Agresti, Mehta, & Patel, 1990). These faster computation schema should create less dependence on the computationally simplifying and potentially poorly estimating probability outcomes of standard probability modeling in hypothesis testing. It may even be possible in the future that investigators will not have to worry about normality or bias in some cases, and simply proceed to the calculation of a probability directly for the sample, thereby skipping the problems in inferring characteristics of the population so as to select a statistical model for testing obtained sample differences.

WHAT IS "NULL" ABOUT THE NULL HYPOTHESIS?

Central to the understanding of standard decision theory is the concept of the "Null hypothesis." It is usually written as: H0: $\mu1 - \mu2 = 0$ with its first alternative (the experimental hypothesis) written: H1: $\mu1 - \mu2 = 0$ (very similar but with one major difference). Usually, it is characterized as being the hypothesis of chance expectations *or* of no differences. The *or* in that sentence can be misleading. Chance expectation is not exactly the same as zero difference expectation. The naive assumption that a chance expectation is the same as a zero difference can prove to be very misleading in many statistical applications. Older statistics texts tended to be much more explicit in forcing the reader into an awareness of the implications of this nonequivalence for establishing the appropriate null hypothesis than is often the case in the contemporary literature (Wert, Neidt, & Ahman, 1954).

For instance, the mean $X-\%$ for a group of nonpatients would not be expected to be the same as the mean $X-\%$ for a group of institutionalized patients. In reality, a "chance expectation" difference between the two groups, based on prior results, might be as much as a 20 percentage point difference. Thus, it would be less misleading to state the null hypothesis in the following formula, in which k is some expected value derived from prior research:

$$H0:\ \mu1 - \mu2 - k = 0$$

This may seem unimportant, but there are studies in which the issue of chance expectation can be quite important when formulating a correct statement of the null. Failure to exercise caution about what is the appropriate null hypothesis can result in the testing for a means difference of zero (simple substraction of the group means) rather than the more appropriate correction for the known difference (k), such as in the $X-\%$ example, which is 20 points.

For example, consider the plight of investigators who have access to two groups of inpatients who have received two different forms of treatment. Ideally, the investigators should have initiated their project at the onset of treatment, using a pre–post design in which each of the groups would serve as its own control. But assume that this was not possible, but now the subjects are available for study as is a group of nonpatients that can be used for comparison. The nonpatient group yields a mean $X-\%$ of .79, treated

Group 1 has a mean X–% of .78, and the treated Group 2 has an X–% of .60. A comparison of each of the treated groups with the nonpatient group using a standard null formula (no difference exists) indicates that Group 2 differs substantially from the nonpatient group but Group 1 does not. Can the researcher argue that the Group 1 subjects have improved? That would be a faulty argument unless the correction element of k is included in the null hypothesis. If it is, the researcher can clearly argue that Group 1 is significantly different from the expected while Group 2 is not.

THE NEED FOR BETTER LABELS
IN "SIGNIFICANCE" ASSESSMENT

The meaning of the term *significance*, as implied by the use of the finding "$p < .05$" is not what some have implied in their writings concerning research findings. It might be most appropriate to think of statistical significance as signifying repeatability. A highly significant finding is more likely to be seen again. A correlation initially significant at the $p < .001$ level will be much more likely to be seen as significant than one at the $p < .05$ level. A study yielding a $p < .001$ correlation, occurring within a limited confidence interval range, may appear in another study as only significant at the $p < .01$, but it is still valuable to include in one's theorizing. It might also appear as significant at the $p < .0001$ level in a third study.

Regardless of the p values, each of the three studies is a replication of the others. Conversely, a correlation of $p < .05$ in one study may appear in a second study as only $p < .10$, thus, in general usage, it may not be worthy of inclusion in our theorizing any longer. Clearly, more faith can be vested in the premise that findings at more conservative probability levels will be replicated more often in future research, but the most commonly used levels tend to limit or possibly even distort conclusions that are drawn by researchers.

Typically, most research reports focus only on one of three possible levels ($p < .05$, .01, or .001), although on occasion either of two other levels are reported ($p < .02$, or .005). In any of these instances, the investigators have looked up a desired critical value, relevant to their findings, and compared to determine which, if any, of the three to five significance levels best describes the finding. Unfortunately, reports of "less than" a given level can be misleading. For instance, two correlations might be reported as being significant at less than $p < .05$ when in fact exact probabilities calculations yield $p = .049$ and $p = .012$. Is it appropriate to contend that these two findings are of equal value?

When probability tables were the only option there was little choice, but contemporary researchers should not consider themselves bound by or limited to < .05 or < .01 because exact probabilities can be generated by modern computer technology. Viewed from a different perspective, it may be appropriate to question whether a $p = .0561$ is less worthy of consideration than a $p = .0492$. Traditionally, one is reported and the other not, which may not be in the best interest of science. Research in psychology in general, and Rorschach research in particular, seems to have become overly committed to Fisher's $p < .05$ as a numerical determinant or limiter of significance. Thus, findings associated with slightly higher probabilities of .051 to .075 seem unlikely to reach print even though the findings might be important.

CONCLUSIONS

Several general issues have been discussed regarding common practices in the use of probability-based statistical decision theory. These should not be regarded as criticisms of the theory and its corollaries *per se*, but of the way they have come to be ritualized, especially in Rorschach research. There is an obvious assumption that pervades much Rorschach research: The standardized use of the normal and its approximator test statistic distributions are always the best design evaluators. This assumption seems predicated on the usual statistically fostered expectation that as N increases the expected distribution of scores will go normal and thus reliance on the statistical qualities of the normal probability function is presumed to create a greater legitimacy for thinking normal is best.

In many Rorschach studies, the data do not fit easily into the standard paradigms of normality. This may be by virtue of small N's, or by reason of the selection of dependent variables with few values (such as T, Vista, m, Y, Pure C) that are discrete and noncontinuous, or deceptively appearing scores that imply continuity such as $X+\%$ (where only narrow range of ratios occur in reality even though the variable looks like a .00 to .99 scale).

The Rorschach researcher must make knowledgeable statistical choices if the standard paradigms are be used appropriately rather than simply accept the conventions set forth by others. There is no substitute for *direct inspection* (eyeballing) of a data set before any final decision concerning the statistical manipulation of the data is implemented.

In turn, investigators should make every effort to interpret findings intelligently. The use of $p < .05$ or < .01 are rather needlessly imprecise in light of contemporary methods for calculating exact probability estimates for virtually all outcomes. Unfortunately, the tendency to restrict the concept of "significance" to these probability values often requires an exchange if power determinations are miminized, slighted, or ignored. As a consequence, many research paradigms are formed by the unwary research that have unrealistic premade choices and predetermined risks. Valuable information may go unreported because of a perceived lack of significance, or the misapplication of probability concepts can lead to claims of significance when in fact none really exists.

Finally, there appears to be an orientation that favors the large N solutions regarding what statistical values to assign and risks to take in creating an experimental design. This orientation tends to falsely hinder a researcher faced with a small N design limitation, or even preclude the undertaking of research because of a perception of insufficient statistical rigor. Clinical studies in particular may suffer from this form of prejudice.

Probability concepts and decision theory are valuable tools in research when applied intelligently, which, in effect, means they are used appropriately to understand findings rather than dictums that direct designs and outcomes.

REFERENCES

Agresti, A., Mehta, C. R., & Patel, N. R. (1990). Exact inference for contingency tables with ordered categories. *JASA, 85,* 453–458.

Bausell, R. B. (1986). *A practical guide to conducting empirical research.* New York: Harper & Row.

Bock, R. D. (1975). *Multivariate statistics methods in behavioral research.* New York: McGraw-Hill.

Cohen, J. (1988). *Statistical power analysis for the behavioral sciences.* Hillsdale, NJ: Lawrence Erlbaum Associates.

Davidson, P. O., & Costell, C. G. (1969). *N = 1: Experimental studies of single cases.* New York: Van Nostrand Reinhold.

Efron, B. (1979). Computers and the theory of statistics: Thinking the unthinkable. *Siam Review, 21,* 460–480.

Efron, B. (1986). Why isn't everyone a Bayesian? *The American Statistician, 40,* 1–11.

Green, P. E., & Carroll, J. D. (1978). *Analysing multivariate data.* Hinsdale, IL: Dryden Press.

Hays, W. L. (1973). *Statistics for the social sciences* (2nd ed.). New York: Holt, Rinehart & Winston.

Howell, D. C. (1987). *Fundamental statistics for the behavioral sciences.* Boston: Duxbury Press.

Huck, S. W., & Sandler, H. M. (1984). *Statistical illusions: Problems.* New York: Harper & Row.

Kraemer, H. C., & Thieman, S. (1987). *How many subjects?* Newbury Park, CA: Sage.

Lindeman, R. H., Merenda, P. F., & Gold, R. Z. (1980). *Introduction to bivariate and multivariate analysis.* Glenview, IL: Scott, Foresman.

Nunnally, J. C. (1967). *Psychometric theory.* New York: McGraw-Hill.

Robinson, P. W., & Foster, D. F. (1979). *Experimental psychology: A small-N approach.* New York: Harper & Row.

Siegel, S., & Castellan, N. J. (1988). *Nonparametric statistics for the behavioral sciences* (2nd ed.). New York: McGraw-Hill.

Simon, J. L., & Bruce, P. (1991). Resampling: A tool for everyday statistical work. *Chance, 4,* 22–32.

Stine, R. (1989). An introduction to bootstrap methods. *Sociological Methods and Research, 18,* 243–291.

Tabachnick, B. G., & Fidell, L. S. (1989). *Using multivariate statistics* (2nd ed.). New York: Harper & Row.

Welkowitz, J., Ewen, R. B., & Cohen, J. (1982). *Introductory statistics for the behavioral sciences* (3rd ed.). New York: Academic Press.

Wert, J. E., Neidt, C. O., & Ahman, J. S. (1954). *Statistical methods in educational and psychological research*. New York: Appleton-Century-Crofts.

Wright, G. (1984). *Behaviorial decision theory*. Beverly Hills: Sage.

CHAPTER NINE

Statistical Power
in Rorschach Research

Marvin W. Acklin & Claude J. McDowell II

The Rorschach test has long remained the center of controversy, despite its widespread popularity in clinical settings (Lubin, Larsen, & Matarazzo, 1984). Nowhere is this more evident than in the long, often acrimonious, series of reviews of the test published in the *Mental Measurements Yearbook* (*MMYB*; cf. Jensen, 1965). One long-standing controversy concerns whether the Rorschach is actually a "test" at all or whether it is more appropriately thought of as a clinical "technique" (Eron, 1965; Rabin, 1972; Zubin, Eron, & Schumer, 1965). In the fourth *MMYB*, Sargent, a supporter of the test, stated that "the Rorschach test is a clinical technique, not a psychometric method" (Sargent, 1953, p. 218). As a test, the Rorschach has been assailed by psychometrically minded psychologists as failing to meet many, if not most, of the standard criteria of test construction, including indices of internal consistency, interrater reliability, and validity (Dana, 1965; Jensen, 1965; McArthur, 1972). Further, as early as 1949, Cronbach expressed concerns about the quality of Rorschach research. In a quote used by Eysenck in a scathing *MMYB* review of the Rorschach (Eysenck, 1959), Cronbach declared that "perhaps ninety percent of the conclusions so far published as a result of statistical studies are unsubstantiated—not necessarily false—but based on unsound analysis" (Cronbach, 1949, p. 425).

Cronbach continued, "One cannot attack the test merely because most Rorschach hypotheses are still in the pre-research stage" (p. 426). The critics of the test, alternately, wonder that "years of negative research have not cooled the ardor of the Rorschach supporter" (Knutson, 1972, p. 440). The very nature of the Rorschach; the divergent systems of administration, scoring, and research; the nature of Rorschach scores and the shapes of score distributions obtained; and the type of statistics commonly used (typically distribution free or nonparametric) seem to favor the views of the Rorschach's critics.

Various studies have attempted to answer these criticisms. A steady stream of articles has addressed reliability and validity issues. Most of these efforts relate to Exner's Comprehensive System (1974, 1978, 1986, 1991, 1993; Exner & Weiner, 1982, 1994). His approach to the Rorschach, developed since the late 1960s, has led to a general standardization of the test. It is generally assumed, though it has never been empirically demonstrated, that the Comprehensive System with its emphasis on standardization, increased reliability, and systematic efforts at validation has placed the Rorschach on a solid foundation as a psychometric instrument.

Recently, the test has been subjected to several metanalyses. Parker (1983) found that studies guided by theory, prior research, or both, tended to support the Rorschach but found little support for the Rorschach among studies in which experimental hypotheses lacked a theoretical or empirical rationale. Other studies have found that conceptual, theory-based studies show greater support for the Rorschach than do undirected studies (Atkinson, 1986; Atkinson, Quarrington, Alp, & Cyr, 1986). Further, the power of the statistics used (that is, the tests' probability of detecting an effect when one is actually present) was shown to influence the magnitude of observed differences (Parker, 1983).

Metanalytic studies have compared the Rorschach with the Minnesota Multiphasic Personality Inventory (MMPI), which is "considered the standard of psychological assessment" (Kendall & Norton-Ford, 1982, p. 310) and the Wechsler Adult Intelligence Scale (WAIS) (Atkinson, 1986; Parker, Hansen, & Hunsley, 1988). These studies have found broadly comparable and, concerning the Rorschach, respectable psychometric properties. One study concluded that the Rorschach and MMPI "have acceptable and roughly equivalent psychometric properties when used in appropriate circumstances" (Parker et al., 1988, p. 372). Finally, consistent with earlier studies, the statistics used to report the results were found to influence the magnitude of the findings.

Might one then conclude that the standardization of the test and recent, favorable metanalyses have made the Rorschach "psychometrically respectable" and, consequently, that all is well with Rorschach research? In reality, although some findings tend to support the assumption that the Comprehensive System for the Rorschach has resulted in a psychometrically respectable test, more data are required before that conclusion can be regarded as unequivocal. In the quest to demonstrate the empirical soundness of the Rorschach, another more serious methodological issue has emerged. It is an issue that has serious implications for not only Rorschach research, but for the whole behavioral science research enterprise. It is the issue of statistical power.

A brief digression is necessary to introduce the concept of statistical power in psychological research. The mainstay of psychological research—hypothesis testing, statistical inference, and dichotomous significance-testing decisions, including the sanctified .05 level of significance—are the legacy of the preeminent statistician R. A. Fisher.[1] In Fisher's scheme, the "Null hypothesis" (the hypothesis of no effect; designated as H0) is accepted or rejected on the basis of statistical inference. Concern with obtaining statistical significance has long been a central focus in U.S. behavioral science (Bakan, 1966; Rosnow & Rosenthal, 1989). Starting as early as 1942, there has been consistent criticism of the employment of significance tests as ultimate objectives in experimental research (Chase & Tucker, 1976; Meehl, 1978). These criticisms have had little impact on research in general or in the training of students. Critics have encouraged researchers to examine the magnitude of relationships between variables, not merely the probability of their occurrence. Rosenthal and Rosnow put the matter succinctly: it is important to realize that what the effect size tells us is very different from the *p* level. A result that is statistically significant is not necessarily practically significant as judged by the magnitude of the effect. Consequently, highly significant *p* values should not be interpreted as automatically reflecting large effects (Rosnow & Rosenthal, 1989).

Contrary to the beliefs of many students in psychology (and an alarming number of academic psychologists), the level of statistical significance (*p* values) obtained says nothing about the magnitude or importance of group differences nor about the probability of the truth of the Null hypothesis. Rather, it informs the researcher of the probability of obtaining results assuming that the Null hypothesis is true. Kish addressed the relationship between significance and effect size when he wrote that the function of statistical tests is merely to answer the following: Is the variation great enough for us to place some confidence in the result; or, contrarily, may the latter be merely a happenstance of the specific sample on which the test was made? This question is interesting, but it is surely secondary, auxiliary, to the main question: Does the result show a relationship of substantive interest because of its nature and magnitude (Kish, 1959, p. 336)?

In Fisher's scheme, hypothesis testing is asymmetrical. There is no alternate or research hypothesis (traditionally designated as H1). Positing the alternate hypothesis to the Null hypothesis, an approach advocated by critics of Fisher (Neyman & Pearson, 1928, 1933), gradually made its way into research practice and teaching, creating a sort of hybrid approach to statistical inference. Cohen (1990) stated a proposition fundamental to the Neyman

---

[1] The reader is referred to the excellent discussions of the role of statistical inference in psychological research in Bakan (1966), Chase and Tucker (1976), Cohen (1990), and Sedlmeier and Gigerenzer (1989).

and Pearson approach: "The rejection of the null hypothesis when it is true was an error of the first kind [a Type I error] controlled by the alpha criterion, but the failure to reject it when the alternate hypothesis was true was also an error, an error of the second kind [a Type II error] which could be controlled to occur at a rate beta" (p. 130).

An alpha of .05 corresponds to a .95 probability of a correct statistical conclusion when the Null hypothesis is true (1-alpha). In this sort of decision calculus, a decision can and must be made about the relative seriousness of Type I or Type II errors. Traditional applied statistics has focused almost exclusively on controlling Type I errors (the probability of rejecting a true null hypothesis) with a focus of the level on significance (p values) and has entirely neglected Type II errors (the probability of accepting a false Null hypothesis) and the power of tests. In general, it has been assumed that Type I errors are much more serious than Type II errors (Cohen, 1962; McNemar, 1960).

Assuming the magnitude of the effect size (either predicted in the planning of a study or calculated after a study), and the setting of alpha and beta, one can determine the necessary sample size to meet acceptable conditions for hypothesis acceptance or rejection. One is then in a position to determine the probability of correctly rejecting a false Null hypothesis or accepting a true alternate hypothesis: the power of the test. In short, the power of a study is the probability of detecting a difference when one is really there.

The power of a statistical test is a function of the effect size (a standardized measure of the magnitude of the differences between means or the amount of variance accounted for), error variance, alpha criterion, sample size, and data analysis (the inherent power of the statistical tests to detect differences). Nonparametric tests, or those that rank order or categorize information from dependent variable scores, have less inherent power than do parametric tests, or those that use scores representing degrees of the variable along a continuum. Further, directional tests have greater statistical power than have nondirectional tests (Lipsey, 1990, p. 36). The combination of all of these factors determines "design sensitivity" ("the ability to detect a real contrast or difference between experimental conditions on some characteristic of interest"; Lipsey, 1990). Design sensitivity is also affected by other factors, including use of alpha adjusted procedures (Sedlmeier & Gigerenzer, 1989), nonparametric statistics, violations of independence, false assumptions concerning equality of variances, and false assumptions about measurement scales and the shape of distributions. Cohen (1988) somewhat arbitrarily set desirable power at .80, that is, a study has acceptable power when it can detect an effect 8 times out of 10 when the effect is actually present. He suggested that beta = .20 as a reasonable value for general use, or more specifically, he suggested that .80 as a desirable minimum for statistical power, that is, 1 − beta. The neglect of power has serious implications for the overall conduct and "health" of psychological research, for underpowered studies may not be sensitive enough to detect the differences that they purport to investigate.

Cohen (1962) introduced the concept of power to the psychological literature. He surveyed the 1960 volume of *Journal of Abnormal and Social Psychology* and concluded that, on average, research studies had about 1 chance in 5 or 6 (.18) for detecting small effects (expressed in standard deviation units or proportion of predicted variance accounted for), less than 1 in 2 chances (48%) of detecting medium effects, and acceptable chances (about 8 out of 10) of detecting large effects (83%). Cohen (1962) expressed his concerns about this state of affairs: "The consequences of this state of affairs are fairly obvious. If many investigators are running high risks of failing to detect substantial population effects, much research is resulting in spuriously negative results" (p. 153).

These concerns focus on published research, reflecting the widespread editorial bias against publishing nonsignificant results (Bakan, 1966). According to Cohen, "If anything, published studies are more powerful than those which do not reach publication, certainly not less powerful" (Cohen, 1962, p. 152). Unsubmitted and unpublished "file drawer" studies (Rosenthal, 1979), representing perhaps thousands of investigations and whole lines of research, may have been undertaken and abandoned due to the neglect of design sensitivity. Cohen posited that a generation of researchers could be profitably employed in repeating interesting studies that originally used inadequate sample sizes. Unfortunately, those most needing replication are those least likely to have appeared in print (Cohen, 1962, p. 153). Thus behavioral research as a whole may stand on shaky methodological foundations.

Cohen's findings and warnings have had little or no effect on subsequent psychological research (Rossi, 1990; Sedlmeier & Gigerenzer, 1989). Twenty-five power surveys conducted since 1962 have tended to replicate Cohen's findings (Rossi, 1990). These studies have been conducted in several disciplines—including communications, speech pathology, occupational therapy, management, and educational, social, abnormal, and applied psychology. Rossi (1990) pointed out that "the average statistical power for all twenty-five power surveys (including Cohen's) was .26 for small effects, .64 for medium effects and .85 for large effects and was based on 40,000 statistical tests published in over 1,500 journal articles" (p. 64). With respect to Rossi's findings, the average power for detecting small effects in the research domain was .26; that is, if a small effect were in fact present, the typical test would yield statistical significance only 26% of the time and yield null (nonsignificant) results 74% of the time. In these studies the findings are clear that power to detect small and medium differences is unacceptably low.

The implications of this state of affairs for psychological research are not to be minimized. These include the proliferation of Type I errors, spurious overacceptance of the Null hypothesis, the oft-observed failure of replication studies, and difficulties in interpreting negative findings. Research areas that are controversial—the Rorschach is a prime example—because of equivocal findings may be the victims of "artifactual controversy" (Rossi, 1982). Rossi noted that dependence on statistical tests to establish the existence of an effect may lead to artifactual controversy if the average power of the research designed to detect the effect is only about one half (Rossi, 1982). When average power for a research domain is around .50 (essentially a coin toss), a mixed pattern of significant and nonsignificant findings is likely.

In preparing this chapter, the Rorschach literature published between 1975 and 1990 was reviewed. This time span constitutes the years encompassing the advent and emergence of the Comprehensive System. The study focuses on all of the Rorschach research published in the *Journal of Personality Assessment* (formerly the *Rorschach Research Exchange* and the *Journal of Projective Techniques*), a major outlet for U.S. Rorschach research. The objective of this review was to evaluate average power of studies conducted with the goal of determining to what extent the controversy about the Rorschach's performance as a research tool may be based on "artifactual controversy," that is, on the failure of research designs to detect actual differences. A second interest was to determine the extent to which the Comprehensive System, with its standardization of administration and scoring, has presumably rectified the situation.

All articles published in the *Journal of Personality Assessment* between 1975 and 1990 (Vols. 39–55) were examined and those not reporting statistics were eliminated from the study. Additionally, a number of studies were eliminated because of their inapplicability for power analysis (e.g., canonical and factor analysis, reviews, case studies, and commentaries) or because insufficient information for calculation of an effect size was not reported.

Similar to previous power surveys, a distinction was made between major and peripheral statistical tests. Major tests dealt directly with Rorschach variables whereas peripheral tests did not. Peripheral tests that were excluded from the survey included, for example, all of the correlation coefficients of a factor analysis, cluster analysis, and multidimensional scaling; interrater, internal consistency, and temporal consistency reliability coefficients; tests of statistical assumptions; and statistical tests not bearing directly upon Rorschach variables. Power was determined for the following tests: t tests, Pearson r, partial correlations, chi-square tests, F test in the analysis of variance and covariance. In contrast to other power surveys, but following Cohen (1962), power analyses were calculated for nonparametric techniques, because these are overrepresented in the Rorschach research literature. In these cases, power was determined for the analogous parametric test, for example, the t test for means was substituted for the Mann–Whitney U test and for the Wilcoxon matched pairs signed ranks test, F test for the Kruskal–Wallis H test and for the Friedman test, and Pearson r for Spearman rho.

According to Cohen, the effect of this substitution is a slight overestimation of power based on the usual assumption that the conditions required by parametric tests obtained. Power and effect size coefficients were calculated using the recently published computer program (Borenstein & Cohen, 1988). In cases where the computer program was not helpful, power tables from Cohen (1988) and Lipsey (1990) were used.

A total of 212 studies were examined. Of the total, 109 articles were excluded because they were either inapplicable to power analysis (e.g., case reports or literature reviews) or failed to provide enough information (e.g., means, standard deviations, sample sizes, degrees of freedom, and critical values) to calculate effect sizes. Studies were initially examined as a whole group and those with Comprehensive System methodologies were examined separately.

The customary procedure in power surveys is to identify the order of the magnitude of effect sizes considered small, medium, and large in the domain of interest (see Cohen, 1988), then determine the average power of the studies actually in that domain for detecting such effects (Lipsey, 1990, p. 21). Following Cohen (1962), power was determined by averaging across the statistical tests reported in the article so that each article contributed equally to the overall power assessment. Power estimates were based on Cohen's later revisions for small, medium, and large effect sizes (Cohen, 1988). Mean power of the major tests was determined at the three levels of effect sizes for each study. Mean power values were then distributed and their central tendency and variability determined. An alpha criterion of .05 was assumed as was a nondirectional (two-tailed) test.

The results indicate that studies in which small effects were found had less than one in six chances of detecting significant results (Mean = .153, SD = .118). Studies with medium effect sizes had a slightly better than one chance out of two for detecting significant differences (Mean = .571, SD = .235). Finally, studies with large effect sizes met Cohen's criteria for acceptable power (Mean = .85, SD = .176). The power coefficients indicate that Rorschach research is not very different than behavioral science research in general with respect to the power issue.

The studies that used the Comprehensive System methodology yielded findings indicating low power to detect differences in designs with small effect sizes, slightly better than one chance in six of detecting significance (Mean = .182, SD = .163), slightly more than 6 out of 10 chances in detecting medium effects (Mean = .629, SD = .217), and acceptable levels of power with large effect sizes (Mean = .895, SD = .149).

Rorschach research using approaches other than the Comprehensive System yielded power coefficients for studies with small effect sizes that were significantly underpowered, with about one chance in seven of detecting significant differences (Mean = .135, SD = .080), slightly more than one in two of detecting medium size effects (Mean = .54, SD = .239), and acceptable power for large effect sizes (Mean = .826, SD = .186).

Although there is some variation, it appears that, overall, Rorschach research has approximately the same power (.153, .571, and .850, respectively) as research performed in other disciplines of behavioral science (.26, .64, and .85; Rossi, 1990).

In order to determine whether Rorschach research conducted according to the Comprehensive System yielded higher power, two-tailed t tests of the mean power estimates between Comprehensive System and non-Comprehensive System research were conducted. Visual analysis reveals that non-Comprehensive System research with power coefficients of .135, .540, and .826 were smaller than Comprehensive System research with coefficients of .182, .629, and .895, respectively, for small, medium, and large effect sizes. The differences for small effect sizes were not statistically significant, t (44) = 1.62, p = .11. Differences between Comprehensive System and non-Comprehensive System research for medium effect sizes were statistically significant, $t(78) = 1.92$, p = .05. Differences for large effects sizes were statistically significant as well, t (86) = 2.05, p = .04.

Given the critical reviews of the Rorschach as a research tool, it is something of a surprise to discover that Rorschach research yields findings similar to those observed in other areas of behavioral science. As the data reveal, research in which there is a small effect size has no better than a 18% chance of attaining statistical significance, even assuming that the effect size is actually present. Medium effect sizes have about one to two chances out of three of significance. Large effect sizes have much better chances of detecting significant findings. However, as discussed previously, most research yields effect sizes in the low to medium range. Further, it appears that impact of studies based on the Comprehensive System have indeed yielded significant increases in the power of Rorschach research, at least for studies having medium and large effect sizes. This is apparently the first empirical assessment of the notion that the standardization of the test according to the Comprehensive System improves the quality of Rorschach research.

Clearly, these findings have significance for the health of Rorschach research and likely reflect the "artifactual controversy" that has plagued the field. When medium effect sizes are obtained and power is at or near .50, a pattern of findings emerge that are inconsistent. To the academic researcher, whose focus on the Rorschach is primarily through the lens of design methodology and statistics, the Rorschach fails to achieve the degree of respectability commonly expected in a test. These findings confirm the reason for the uncomplimentary views found, for example, in the *Mental Measurements Yearbooks*.

What are the reasons for the poor showing? Undoubtedly, sample sizes are a primary culprit. Small sample sizes (30 subjects or less) seem to be the norm in Rorschach research, especially in studies in which power was low. However, there are several other features of Rorschach research, in ways similar to and dissimilar from other behavioral science research, that have to be taken into account. The first factor is error variance and its attenuating impact on power. Until the advent of the Comprehensive System for the Rorschach, reliability for certain test variables was quite low. Exner has continued to be concerned about the actual quality of interrater reliability for Rorschach determinants in applied clinical research, despite the respectable coefficients obtained in laboratory work. This concern is reflected in the editorial policy at the *Journal of Personality Assessment* in which interrater reliability data must be included in articles submitted for review. Stringent attention to reducing error variance may help, including for example, the use of kappa statistics for interrater reliability over percentage of agreement. Second, researchers should eschew whenever possible the use of nonparametric statistics, including the power sapping practice of dichotomizing variables (Cohen, 1973). As Zubin and Eron were commenting in the late 1950s and 1960s, content scaling, rather than determinants, tend to yield the most respectable findings. Increasing sample size, reducing error, and relying as much as possible on parametric statistics may go far to increase power and design sensitivity in Rorschach research.

Another disturbing discovery of the current investigation was the number of studies that had to be eliminated because of the poor reporting of findings. Our situation was quite similar to that observed by Katzer and Sodt (1973), who pointed out that "the most frustrating aspect of this study was our inability to quickly understand the statistical procedures employed in each journal article. Usually, this was due to missing information" (p. 261). This laxity on the part of investigators and editors strikes at the very heart of scientific inquiry, with its operational point of view and focus on the provision of sufficient evidence to allow independence of interpretation and replication. In the current era of metanalysis, test statistics (including alpha levels, means, standard deviations, sample sizes, even in tests that are nonsignificant, and preferably, effect sizes) are crucial parameters for reporting.

It is unlikely that change will be forthcoming in this area without vigorous editorial enforcement. However, the quest for greater power does not end here. In effect, concern with power and design sensitivity reflects the quest for more thoughtful research. To this extent, this review of many published works stands in a long tradition of Rorschach research critiques.

Two caveats are in order. The findings most likely are overestimates of statistical power because parametric tests were substituted for the large number of nonparametric tests. Second, this survey of the literature is not comprehensive. Not included were studies published outside of the *Journal of Personality Assessment* (including, for example, the *Journal of Clinical Psychology, Journal of Consulting and Clinical Psychology, Journal of Abnor-*

mal Psychology, and other journals), which may have different publication criteria. Nevertheless, the neglect of power seems to be endemic in behavioral science research in general. Consequently, it is unlikely that statistical power in these studies will be significantly greater than what has been observed here. As knowledge and concern over statistical power becomes more pervasive (Goldstein, 1989), it is likely that the technology for assessing power, both predictively and postdictively, will become more accessible and implemented.

Obviously, several recommendations appear to be indicated. First, investigators should, based on theory and previous research, estimate the probable effect size of the study, ascertain the power of the design, and thereby determine whether the study can actually detect what is being studied. This involves asking if the effect size is likely to be small, medium, or large. If effect size cannot be ascertained in an a priori fashion, then small or medium effect size predictions should be the basis on which the sensitivity of the study is determined. Second, effect size should be viewed not as something to be discovered independent of the methods of investigation, but rather inherent in the well-planned study and to be enhanced by sensitive design methodology. Good theory, as numerous commentators have pointed out, is indispensable. Finally, consideration of the relative importance of Type I versus Type II errors should be considered, as well as a relaxation of alpha, though it is unlikely that the alpha equals .05 convention will change.

Possibly, the use of two illustrative examples may be helpful to those planning Rorschach research. They demonstrate the value of statistical power analysis in Rorschach research in planning and designing studies, in determining sample sizes necessary to detect estimated effects, and in retrospective analysis of research, especially in cases of nonsignificant findings. The power analyses are drawn from Cohen (1988):

Example 1.   Dr. J. wishes to examine the relationship between a commonly used objective personality instrument, the MMPI, and selected Rorschach variables in adolescent psychiatric inpatients. He is particularly interested in validity studies of Rorschach indices related to depression (DEPI) and self-esteem $(3r+(2)/R)$ and counterpart MMPI scales (Scales 2 and 0). Based on reviews of previous research, he hypothesizes that the relationships between the Rorschach indices and MMPI scales should be moderate, that is, he expects two-tailed Pearson product-moment correlations in the range of .30, a medium effect size. Assuming a nondirectional test, a significance criterion of .05, and power set at Cohen's .80 criterion, he would like to know how big his sample would have to be to actually detect the relationship he is interested in.

Turning to Table 3.4.1 in Cohen's handbook, he determines that he will need a sample size of at least 85 in order to detect a medium effect size. He subsequently undertakes the study and increases his sample size for good measure (N = 200). After analyzing his data, he discovers zero-order correlations (r = .11 and r = .09, respectively) on his depression and self-esteem comparisons. He recomputes his power coefficients to determine the probability of falsely rejecting the alternate hypothesis. Utilizing Table 3.4.2 in Cohen he determines that he would need 194 subjects to detect a small effect size (r = .20), 85 subjects to detect a medium effect size (r = .30), and 46 subjects to detect a large effect size (r = .40). He concludes that his sample size was indeed large enough to validly test his hypotheses and concludes that there is actually no relationship between the scales and indices.

Example 2. Ms. Z., a doctoral candidate in clinical psychology, did her dissertation project replicating a study of selected Rorschach variables that discriminate sexually abused latency-age girls from carefully matched nonsexually abused controls. She had 20 subjects per cell randomly assigned from a treatment program. Her data analyses consisted of t tests of means. Despite careful attention to matters of sampling and design—including matching, accurate scoring and acceptable interrater reliability, and care to make sure that her data met statistical assumptions—none of her hypotheses achieved statistical significance. Disappointed and at a loss to interpret her results, she consulted with Dr. A., who suggested a retrospective power analysis of her study to get a better understanding of her findings.

For her t tests, assuming a medium effect size (about one third of a standard deviation, a respectable association between Rorschach variables and the grouping variable), a two-tailed test, and a significance criterion of .05, she consulted Table 2.3.5 of Cohen's handbook and determined that power for her study was only .15 (beta = .85). This indicates that given her sample size and a medium effect size, she would detect significant findings only 15% of the time. Even assuming a strong relationship between her variables (a large effect size of .50, about a half-standard deviation), her power would still be only .45 (beta = .55), slightly less than a coin toss. In other words, even if her hypotheses were actually true, her study would detect them only 45% of the time! Clearly her study is underpowered and she is in no position to make any conclusive remarks about the relationship between the hypothesized Rorschach variables and child sexual abuse.

In many ways, we have come no further than the uncomfortable, but familiar, position of Cronbach in 1949, who stated that criticisms of the test were premature. The developments in Rorschach research stimulated by the Comprehensive System are an improvement and a reason for psychometric optimism. It remains to current and future generations of Rorschach researchers to improve upon the past and design and carry out Rorschach research that clearly brings out the best that test has to offer.

ACKNOWLEDGMENTS

Portions of this chapter appear in Acklin, M. W., McDowell, C., & Orndoff, S. (1992). Statistical power and the Rorschach: 1975–1991. *Journal of Personality Assessment, 59*, 366–379.

REFERENCES

Atkinson, L. (1986). The comparative validities of the Rorschach and MMPI: A meta-analysis. *Canadian Psychology, 27*(3), 238–247.

Atkinson, L., Quarrington, B., Alp, I. E., & Cyr, J. J. (1986). Rorschach validity: An empirical approach to the literature. *Journal of Clinical Psychology, 42*(2), 360–362.

Bakan, D. (1966). The test of significance in psychological research. *Psychological Bulletin, 66*(6), 423–437.

Chase, L. J., & Tucker, R. K. (1976). Statistical power: Derivation, development, and data-analytic implications. *Psychological Record, 26*, 473–486.

Borenstein, M., & Cohen, J. (1988). *Statistical power analysis: A computer program.* Hillsdale, NJ: Lawrence Erlbaum Associates.

Cohen, J. (1962). The statistical power of abnormal-social psychological research: A review. *Journal of Abnormal and Social Psychology, 65*(3), 145–153.

Cohen, J. (1973). The cost of dichotomizing. *Applied Psychological Measurement, 7*, 249–253.

Cohen, J. (1988). *Statistical power analysis for the behavioral sciences.* Hillsdale, NJ: Lawrence Erlbaum Associates.

Cohen, J. (1990). Things I have learned (so far). *American Psychologist, 45*(12), 1304–1312.

Cronbach, L. J. (1949). Statistical methods applied to Rorschach scores: A review. *Psychological Bulletin, 46*, 393–429.

Dana, R. (1965). The Rorschach. In O. Buros (Ed.), *The sixth mental measurements yearbook* (pp. 492–495). Highland Park, NJ: Gryphon Press.

Eron, L. (1965). The Rorschach. In O. Buros (Ed.), *The sixth mental measurements yearbook* (pp. 495–501). Highland Park, NJ: Gryphon Press.

Exner, J. E. (1974). *The Rorschach: A comprehensive system.* (Vol. 1). New York: Wiley.

Exner, J. E. (1978). *The Rorschach: A comprehensive system: Vol. 2. Current research and advanced interpretation.* New York: Wiley.

Exner, J. E. (1986). *The Rorschach: A comprehensive system: Vol. 1. Basic foundations* (2nd ed.). New York: Wiley.

Exner, J. E. (1991). *The Rorschach: A comprehensive system: Vol. 2. Interpretation* (2nd ed.). New York: Wiley.

Exner, J. E. (1993). *The Rorschach: A comprehensive system: Vol. 1. Basic foundations* (3rd ed.). New York: Wiley.

Exner, J. E., & Weiner, I. B. (1982). *The Rorschach: A comprehensive system: Vol. 3. Assessment of children and adolescents.* New York: Wiley.

Exner, J. E., & Weiner, I. B. (1994). *The Rorschach: A comprehensive system: Vol. 3. Assessment of children and adolescents* (2nd ed.). New York: Wiley.

Eysenck, H. J. (1959). The Rorschach. In O. Buros (Ed.), *The fifth mental measurements yearbook* (pp. 276–278). Highland Park, NJ: Gryphon Press.

Goldstein, R. (1989). Power and sample size via MS/PC-DOS computers. *American Statistician, 43*, 253–260.

Jensen, A. (1965). The Rorschach. In O. Buros (Ed.), *The sixth mental measurements yearbook* (pp. 501–509). Highland Park, NJ: Gryphon Press.

Katzer, J., & Sodt, J. (1973). An analysis of the use of statistical testing in communication research. *Journal of Communication, 23*, 251–265.

Kendall, P. C., & Norton-Ford, J. D. (1982). *Clinical psychology.* New York: Wiley.

Kish, L. (1959). Some statistical problems in research design. *American Sociological Review, 24*, 328–338.

Knutson, J. (1972). The Rorschach. In O. Buros (Ed.), *The seventh mental measurements yearbook* (pp. 435–440). Highland Park, NJ: Gryphon Press.

Lipsey, M. W. (1990). *Design sensitivity: Statistical power for experimental research.* Newbury Park, CA: Sage.

Lubin, B., Larsen, R. M., & Matarazzo, J. D. (1984). Patterns of psychological test usage in the United States: 1935–1982. *American Psychologist, 39*, 451–454.

McArthur, C. (1972). The Rorschach. In O. Buros (Ed.), *The seventh mental measurements yearbook* (pp. 440–443). Highland Park, NJ: Gryphon Press.

McNemar, Q. (1960). At random: Sense and nonsense. *American Psychologist, 15*, 295–300.

Meehl, P. E. (1978). Theoretical risks and tabular asterisks: Sir Karl, Sir Ronald, and the slow progress of soft psychology. *Journal of Consulting and Clinical Psychology, 46*, 806–834.

Neyman, J., & Pearson, E. (1928). On the use and interpretation of certain test criteria for the purposes of statistical inference. *Biometrika, 20A*, 175–240, 263–294.

Neyman, J., & Pearson, E. (1933). On the problem of the most efficient tests of statistical hypotheses. *Transactions of the Royal Society of London, Series A, 231*, 289–331.

Parker, K. (1983). A meta-analysis of the reliability and validity of the Rorschach. *Journal of Personality Assessment, 47*(3), 227–231.

Parker, K. C., Hanson, R. K., & Hunsley, J. (1988). MMPI, Rorschach, and WAIS: A meta-analytic comparison of reliability, stability, and validity. *Psychological Bulletin, 103*(3), 367–373.

Rabin, A. (1972). The Rorschach. In O. Buros (Ed.), *The seventh mental measurements yearbook* (pp. 443–445). Highland Park, NJ: Gryphon Press.

Rosenthal, R. (1979). The "file drawer problem" and tolerance for null results. *Psychological Bulletin, 86*, 638–641.

Rosnow, R., & Rosenthal, R. (1989). Statistical procedures and the justification of knowledge in psychological science. *American Psychologist, 44*(10), 1276–1284.

Rossi, J. (1982, April). *Meta-analysis, power analysis, and artifactual controversy: The case of spontaneous recovery of verbal associations.* Paper presented to the Eastern Psychological Association, Baltimore, MD.

Rossi, J. (1990). Statistical power of psychological research: What have we gained in 20 years? *Journal of Consulting and Clinical Psychology, 58*(5), 646–656.

Sargent, H. (1953). The Rorschach. In *The fourth mental measurements yearbook* (pp. 213–218). Highland Park, NJ: Gryphon Press.

Sedlmeier, P., & Gigerenzer, G. (1989). Do studies of statistical power have an effect on the power of studies? *Journal of Consulting and Clinical Psychology, 105*(2), 309–316.

Zubin, J., Eron, L. D., & Schumer, F. (1965). *An experimental approach to projective techniques.* New York: Wiley.

CHAPTER TEN

Basic Considerations Regarding Data Analysis

Donald J. Viglione

Rorschach researchers are confronted with a substantial challenge when deciding on the tactics to be used to analyze their data. This chapter attempts to address this challenge and its complexities. The special problem of Rorschach variable distribution is considered as well as general issues relevant to data analysis. The intricate issues of deciding on parametric or nonparametric statistics are explored, followed by considerations of the interplay between Type I and Type II errors and strength of effects. Finally, the issue of response productivity is addressed. Hopefully, these discussions will provide a framework for researchers to make informed decisions about Rorschach data analysis tactics.

Generally, investigators abhor negative findings. Thus, it is not uncommon for researchers to attempt any of a variety of data manipulations to find some support for the contentions underlying their study. Unfortunately, the breadth of available statistical methods makes it possible to generate support for almost any conclusion if the researcher is willing to bend or ignore the assumptions of the method selected, or is willing to conduct innumerable analyses.

Usually, the first series of data analyses are *preplanned*. They relate to the hypotheses that were formulated when the study was designed. Ideally, researchers selecting the preplanned analyses have considered the potential distributions of scores for the dependent variables and have considered that the distributions and the N's for the samples involved are in accord with the assumptions underlying the statistical method(s) selected. In some studies, however, the best of preplanned intentions can go awry. Anticipated distributions of scores may not occur or actual sample sizes may be less than intended and what was anticipated to be an appropriate approach to data analyses may become inappropriate. Obviously, it is very important for investigators to be acutely aware of the nature of their data. There is no substitute for a direct inspection of a data set when making decisions about analyses.

Even when the data are appropriate for the preplanned analyses, almost every investigator encounters aspects of the total data set that were not anticipated when the design was formulated, and warrant additional analyses. Regardless of the timing or circumstances that exist when a method of analysis is selected, the investigator should make the decision concerning the selection in the context of several critical questions:

1. Is the method of analysis under consideration in accord with the anticipated or real descriptive data?
2. Does the data set have an unusual skew and/or does it include outliers?
3. If parametric statistics are being considered, do the data meet the necessary assumptions?
4. To what extent has the issue of Type I and Type II errors been considered?
5. Does the method selected and the alpha level set provide for sufficient power?
6. Does the question to be addressed require some management of response productivity?
7. Does the question to be addressed require some management of response complexity?

THE DISTRIBUTION OF RORSCHACH SCORES

The complexities that can occur when considering the analysis of Rorschach data have caused many investigators to struggle with a basic methodological problem inherent in the Rorschach research: the nature of the distribution of scores both within and across various populations. As early as 1949, Cronbach discussed the difficulty in applying parametric statistical techniques to Rorschach scores because of the restricted variability of many of the scores. This restricted variability results in scores with high positively skewed distributions (i.e., scores that demonstrate a large floor effect). For example, Exner (1993) presented descriptive statistics for 69 Rorschach scores derived from the data obtained from 700 nonpatient adults. Of these 69 scores, 29 (42%) have a mean value of 2.0 or less and a skew and/or kurtosis value of 2.0 or more. Thus, as is discussed in greater detail later, parametric measures of association, if applied to these scores, will be severely distorted—as would any statistical techniques such as factor analysis that are based on these association estimates.

Hopkins and Weeks (1990) pointed out that little attention has been paid to the issues of skewness and kurtosis in psychological research in general. This is a particular problem in Rorschach research where often many of the variables have markedly non-normal distributions.

As a first step in any analysis of Rorschach data, the distributions of all variables should be examined for departure from normality. Hopkins and Weeks (1990) reviewed six commonly used statistical analysis computer packages and found that most programs provide the ability to calculate measures of skewness and kurtosis and provide at least one omnibus measure of normality. Additionally, all of the programs reviewed provided some method for visually displaying the distribution of any set of scores. Thus, most researchers have the ability to examine the distributions of Rorschach score data prior to applying formal analytic statistical procedures. If through such an analysis one or more variables are found to have markedly non-normal distributions, the investigator is then faced with a dilemma with no one clear resolution.

One method of dealing with non-normality noted earlier, which has frequently appeared in the literature, has been to ignore the non-normality and analyze the data through parametric inferential statistical techniques. Newell and Hancock (1984) showed that ignoring skewness and kurtosis when using parametric inferential techniques "may lead to erroneous inferences concerning such distributions" (p. 320). Specifically, skewness can have a serious effect on significance levels and on the power of one-tailed tests (Glass, Peckham, & Sanders, 1972). Additionally, Hopkins and Weeks (1990) illustrated the serious impact that skewness can have on the accuracy of estimates of Type I errors. With the skewness value set at .90 and alpha set at .05, homogeneity of variance tests actually resulted in Type I error rates that exceeded .10. It is true that large, relatively equal size samples selected by strict criteria can alleviate much of this problem but, unfortunately, much Rorschach research does not involve such samples.

Other alternatives, which recognize the problems associated with skewed and kurtotic distributions, have been tried with limited success. Some researches have analyzed percentage or proportion scores, a method that is much too simplistic and prone to lead to major distortions in the data (Exner, 1992). Other researchers have attempted to utilize some type of statistical control such as covariate analysis, partial correlation techniques, or analysis of residual scores.

Whereas it is possible to use some of these methods with nonlinear data, it is important in these cases to specify the relationship between the variate and covariate (J. Cohen & P. Cohen, 1975). Such specification is difficult, if not impossible, in Rorschach studies where many of the variables will have distributions that are markedly different from one another. The use of such procedures will likely produce erroneous results because of the lack of appropriate specification and the resulting linear regression on variables in which the relationships are actually quite complex and nonlinear (Pedhazur, 1982). Such approaches also rely on additive models that assume equal distance between values, a condition not present in non-normal distributions such as are found for many Rorschach variables. The equal distance assumption may also produce erroneous results when other techniques are used, such as logarithmic transformations or some type of scaled score transformation (Exner, 1992).

Although there is no easy solution to some of these problems, astute researchers will always begin their search for the best solution by an examination of the nature of the distributions of the variable under investigation. If a distribution is found to be reasonably normal, parametric approaches to data analysis may be appropriate. Even in such cases, however, the interpretation of results must be addressed cautiously because of the relatively restricted range of many Rorschach variables. If, on the other hand, the distributions of any variable under investigation is markedly non-normal, the use of parametric procedures is probably almost always inappropriate. In these instances, the investigator should rely on one of the many non-parametric statistical methods whose assumptions are not so seriously violated by non-normality.

The goal of the researcher should be to use the most robust statistical technique for the analysis of any particular variable based on the nature of the distribution of that variable. One result of such an approach is the likely possibility that more than one type of statistical technique will be used in any given study. Thus, some variables may be analyzed parametrically while nonparametric statistics may be used for other variables.

Finally, investigators should use caution when interpreting the statistical results. For example, levels or Type I error rates should be set stringently. There is nothing sacred about the .05 level of significance. In many instances it is logical to set the alpha level at .01 or even .001, particularly when there are a large number of variables and subjects under investigation in a particular study. In effect, the practical significance of the findings should be afforded some priority in relation to the statistical significance. Various estimates of strength of association, such as the intraclass correlation coefficient, omega squared r^2, and R^2, can be calculated in parametric studies and provide important information over and above that given by statistical significance levels.

Statistical procedures based in Bayesian decision theory also show promise for providing adequate solutions to the difficulties encountered when attempting to analyze Rorschach data. Although these procedures have a long history, they have not been used frequently in the psychological sciences. Bayesian procedures combine information obtained from a sample (the prior distribution) with information that the investigator already possesses about the phenomena under study (the posterior distribution). This posterior distribution may have been obtained from a previous sample or samples or may be based on the general findings of previous research investigations. Thus, Bayesian procedures are not bound to evaluating the information collected from only one sample, but use as much information as the investigator has available regardless of the source. As Hayes and Winkler (1971) noted, Bayesian statistics represent extensions of our common classical or sampling-theory statistical methods.

The Bayesian approach is particularly useful in examining conditional probabilities, that is, the probability of a certain event occurring given the occurrence of another event or condition. An example of a common question involving the conditional probabilities of Rorschach data is: "What are the odds that this group (or client) belongs to the depressive (or schizophrenic or normal) population given an $M-$ value of 3?" This question can be evaluated by using information already known about the frequency of $M-$ responses in the comparison population (Exner, 1993) and by applying Bayes theorem to the sample (prior distribution) and population (posterior distribution) information. Note that the differing skews of the distribution of $M-$ responses in the various comparative populations is used in the Bayesian approach when determining the probabilities. Bayesian techniques are not limited to questions of classification or diagnosis. Bayesian regression techniques have also been developed (Pilz, 1991). Thus, the Bayesian approach appears to represent an alternative analytic strategy that is not as severely affected by extreme skew as are the more traditional sampling-theory approaches. In addition, by using more information than that obtained from the sample under study, the generalizability and validity of knowledge about the Rorschach is enhanced.

SELECTING APPROPRIATE STATISTICAL METHODS

In the large majority of psychological research, parametric statistics are used to analyze data. These come in the form of the familiar t test, analysis of variance, analysis of covariance, correlation and regression, and various multivariable versions of these tests. Most often, investigators consider these tests to be a family of techniques in that they are all related to one another in calculation and conceptualization.

The term *parametric* derives from the notion that the statistics are calculated on various parameters of the samples that are presumed to be related to the underlying populations from which the sample is drawn. These parameters include the mean, standard deviation, and variance. Unfortunately, in order to rely on these parameters, the various samples included within a given study and their data distributions must meet certain requirements, that is, the statistical assumptions of the technique. Siegel and Castellan (1988) pointed out that these requirements are assumed rather than demonstrated, and thus the term *assumptions.*

The accuracy by which parametric statistics reflect the truth of any given research finding is associated with the degree to which the assumptions for the given statistical test are met. Until the past 10 or 15 years, the majority of parametric tests were considered to be robust to violations of assumptions. In other words, such violations were thought not to effect Type I (rejecting the Null hypothesis when it is true) and Type II (accepting the Null hypothesis when an alternative is true) errors substantially. It has only been in the last 15 or 20 years, with the widespread use of computers and the calculation of many simulation studies known as Monte Carlo studies, that a greater awareness has evolved concerning the effects of specific violations of assumptions on error rates. Overall, these findings are rather mixed. Some specific patterns of minor or even moderate violations do not undermine the accuracy of the parametric statistics. On the other hand, certain violations have been demonstrated to be more problematic, and less truthful, than what was formerly understood.

An alternative to parametric statistics are the nonparametric statistics, which are also known as distribution free. These statistics do not rely on such a restrictive underlying model and restrictive assumptions as do parametric statistics. Over the long term, however, they typically have not been favored by researchers, mostly because they have less power than parametric statistics when assumptions are met. However, if minor or moderate violations of assumptions do exist, the Monte Carlo simulations studies suggest that many nonparametric statistics may be superior. Nonetheless, researchers often refrain from employing nonparametric statistics even when they are indicated and often distort the designs of their studies so as to avoid employing them. In doing so, one may reduce the meaningfulness and importance of results.

Cronbach (1949) and Exner (1991) argued strongly in favor of nonparametric statistics for many Rorschach analyses, but their cautions are often ignored. Consequently, much Rorschach research has relied on parametric statistical analysis. Comparisons of normative data and clinical samples have routinely employed *t* tests, analysis of variance (ANOVA) and analysis of covariance (ANCOVA) methods, and Pearson product-moment correlation has been used to measure associations between variables. Unfortunately, if one were to compare Rorschach variables to variables used in traditional experimental psychological research, one would find that Rorschach variables are more likely to violate important assumptions. Thus, many of the results that we rely on for interpretation may be in error.

SUBSTANTIVE CRITERIA FOR SELECTING PARAMETRIC
VERSUS NONPARAMETRIC METHODS

There are two main questions that should be posed concerning the best method of Rorschach data analysis. First, are parametric statistics appropriate and, second, what are the costs and benefits of selecting a particular type of statistical analysis? These questions are not always answered easily. It is true that Monte Carlo simulation studies do provide some general guidelines. However, these studies use simulated rather than real data, and each distribution selected for investigation in Monte Carlo studies differs, as does each Rorschach variable distribution. It is not easy to match a given Rorschach distribution in a simulation study. Furthermore, differences in the number of cells, number of subjects, type and degree, and coexistence of various assumption violations make the matter more complicated.

Investigators usually rely on two general criteria to select between parametric and nonparametric tests (Harwell, 1988; Siegel & Castellan, 1988). They are *substantive* and *statistical*. Siegel and Castellan linked parametric statistics to interval and ratio scales. They contended that parametric statistics are appropriate only with scales that have at least equal intervals between consecutive scale points, in other words, that there is the same distance between 3 and 4 as there is between 7 and 8. Others have countered this proposition. Most notably, Lord (1953) asserted that "numbers don't know where they came from, they behave the same way," even if they were to come from football jerseys.

Although the issue remains controversial (Mechl, 1978), in practice most researchers minimize the importance of the type of measurement scale when selecting a type of statistic. For example, deviation IQ actually only meets the standards of an ordinal scale. It is essentially based on a rank ordering. Nonetheless, parametric statistics are routinely employed because the data are transformed into a normal curve. Basically, treating IQ data as interval data has worked in that it is meaningful and important results have been obtained. Accordingly, researchers have tended to use a more technical, pragmatic attitude toward the selection of statistics, basically adopting the position that if it works, use it. Siegel and Castellan's argument has few adherents and most investigators consider it very restrictive.

On the other hand, Harwell (1988) emphasized a point that deserves more consideration. To summarize his argument, considerations about scales of measurement are crucial to interpretation. If rank order data are used, it may be appropriate to use parametric analysis, but it is inappropriate to apply numerical precision to differences between groups. In other words, one may assert that one group may be higher on a given scale, but to attribute a specific significance to the fact that one group is four points higher than the other assumes an interval scale and this leads to misinterpretation. Basically, Harwell applied Siegel's logic to the interpretation of statistical analysis rather than to their selection.

Fortunately, the substantive criteria, or scale of measurement, is less of a problem for Rorschach data than for objective psychological test data and for personality research in general. Rorschach variables quantify actual behaviors, and because of this they are true ratio scales with meaningful zero points. For example, the number of inanimate movement responses (m) are accounts of actual behaviors, four is twice as many as two and no m truly means zero. The same is true for form quality minus scores that quantify the actual number of perceptual distortions, and for $X+\%$ and other ratios and percentages. In other words, although Rorschach variables are typically not continuous, they are on a ratio scale like height or weight so that height or weight of zero is meaningful and the distance between 6 and 8 inches is the same between 24 and 26 inches. With such scales all mathematical operations are theoretically possible. These characteristics are truly a strength of Rorschach data and reflect its behavioral basis. This aspect of Rorschach data, that the data derived from the Rorschach are actual accounts of specific behaviors or responses, is rarely appreciated—much like the number of lever pulls by a rat in a Skinner box. Thus, from a behavioral point of view, many Rorschach variables can be considered to be a form of behavioral sampling.

Cronbach (1949) presented an alternative point of view and argued that Rorschach variable scales are typically not equal interval. He pointed out that the interpretive difference between, for example, a W of 6 points below the mean is clinically as extreme as a W that is 15 points above the mean. Accordingly, he asserted that the units are not psychologically equivalent and recommended using the median as the best estimate of central tendency and a chi-square analysis or normalizing scores around the median with parametric analysis. His argument gives emphasis to the skew inherent in the distributions for many Rorschach variables and the problem that some have true zero points, often with Poisson distributions like small response counts.

When studied from a measurement point of view, the Cronbach argument implies that the units represent differences in location responses rather than differences in some underlying traits that the W response supposedly measures. However, in fact, the equal interval is of one W, not one unit of perceptual ambition. If these one-unit differences for W do not correspond to units of perceptual ambition, then these variables are related in a curvilinear fashion. One could contend that mathematically they are equal interval units, but interpretively they might not be. Following that logic, the data could be analyzed statistically as ratio data; however, a risk is created that the conclusions drawn might neglect the interpretive realities when ascribing meaning to the data.

These features, in and of themselves, do not necessitate nonparametric statistics. The possibility of curvilinear or discontinuous relationships, as

Exner (1991) posited with his interpretive cutoffs, can be explored by examining raw data. Once evidence of interpretive relationships has been established, nonparametric statistics probably should be utilized. They would be used because hypotheses consistent with these nonlinear relationships are best addressed through nonparametric analysis, not because data are unequal interval. Thus, once the relationships between Rorschach variables and underlying traits are understood, chi-square or rank statistics may emerge as the preferable modes of analysis, as Cronbach concluded. Furthermore, such nonlinear relationships, like all findings, are subject to shrinkage, and warrant replication.

Sometimes researchers become concerned that Rorschach data are not continuous as would be height or weight, or other types of normally distributed information. This limitation, in and of itself, does not pose a major liability to analysis. It is the presumed theoretical distribution that needs to be continuous. In other words, we assume the theoretical m distribution is continuous in that the measure (the scoring of them) is imperfect. Therefore, the score of 2 m is an imperfect measure of some score that is relatively close to 2 but that 2.5 m theoretically may be possible. On the other hand, a limited range of values along a discontinuous scale increases the relative amount of error variance to effect variance, in turn decreasing power and necessitating larger samples.

Accordingly, these substantive criteria about measurement scales in Rorschach research are typically not an issue when Rorschach variables are used as independent variables or as predictors in regression-based techniques. However, the concerns about interpretation according to type of scale may very well be important when Rorschach data are used as dependent variables. For example, if judges were to rank order individuals in terms of social skill and correlate these ranks with the isolation index (ISOLATE), one would be limited to interpretations about who is more or less socially adept and could not make statements about the amount of social skills accounted for by ISOLATE.

STATISTICAL CRITERIA FOR SELECTING PARAMETRIC AND NONPARAMETIC METHODS

The second issue in deciding between parametric versus nonparametric routines are statistical criteria. Although the distributions of the variables selected may be quite important in selecting the type of statistical analysis, the characteristics of the published normative samples may not always be the critical factor. In other words, it is incorrect to assert that any research addressing m requires nonparametric techniques or that research addressing the $X+\%$ necessitates parametric techniques. In other words, it is not appropriate to make rigid distinctions between those Rorschach variables that are appropriate or inappropriate for parametric analysis. Rather, a given variable such as m or $X+\%$ may be appropriate for parametric analysis in one study and inappropriate in another. This determination is specific to individual studies and depends on the particular distributions derived in that study. The selection is based on an educated guess about expected error rates, the probability of Type I or Type II error.

Essentially, the issue is whether the violations of assumptions adversely affect the true or underlying alpha and power; that is, do they increase Type I or Type II errors unacceptably? Certain combinations of violations, for example, double the .05 nominal alpha rate so that the true p level is .10. Similarly, distortions of power occur. Accordingly, the selection of parametric versus nonparametric statistics is based on an assessment of the effects of the assumption violations on true or actual error rates. This question can also be posed in the following way: Do the assumption violations distort the inferential statistics (t, F) or the strength of effect measures (r, omega squared)?

No study perfectly achieves all of the assumptions of parametric tests. Nonetheless, parametric statistics typically are not adversely affected by such imperfect parameters. Parametric routines are rightfully considered to be robust to many of these distortions. The problem for researchers is to some-how feel confident that they know to what degree a given application is robust in regard to what degree and type of assumption violations. When stretching assumptions, it is as if even competent, ethical investigators cannot quite tell when they are telling the truth with statistics. The ANOVA is probably a good example of this issue because it has been the focus of most of the work addressing assumptions and error rates.

ANOVA Assumptions

Beyond the consideration of scale of measurement, ANOVA assumptions are independence of observations, normality, and homogeneity of variance. Independence of observations, technically known as independence of error components (Keppel, 1991), is fundamental to all research and can be con-sidered to be a design issue, rather than solely a statistical one. Observations of one subject must not be related to other observations in the same or other groups. If, for example, one subject discusses a study with a second subject and biases the second subject's data, observations are no longer independent and this assumption has been violated. Basically, independence of observations ensures random or unbiased assignment of subjects to treat-ment or static groups. An example of a confound would be if one tested all depressed subjects in the morning but all controls in the afternoon; in this case observations would no longer be randomly selected and inde-pendent and the data could be contaminated. Obviously, this example illustrates how the first ANOVA assumption reduces to a critically important design issue rather than a statistical issue.

Within Rorschach research, the most common violation of this independence assumption occurs when the Rorschach both influences the independent variable (e.g., diagnosis) and functions as a dependent variable. Similar concerns can be offered when the Rorschach is used to validate itself. In other words, studies that seek to investigate the Egocentricity index ($3r+(2)/R$), by correlating it with other Rorschach variables, cannot rule out hidden dependencies between the Rorschach variables as confounds. Two examples of problems within otherwise rather strong studies are those by Blatt and his co-workers. Blatt and Ritzler (1974) divided subjects on the basis of thought disorder special scores and then used Rorschach human responses as a dependent variable. Blatt, Tuber, and Auerbach (1990) correlated two Rorschach scales of object relations. These "intra-Rorschach" findings are quite ambiguous because, in each study, there is a marked possibility that the supposedly "separate" scores were generated from the same responses.

The independence of observation assumption also applies for most nonparametric tests. A grave violation of the independence of observation assumption occurs when responses of a given type are compared across two samples. For example, a researcher may count 59 reflections ($Fr+rF$) among 460 responses from 30 subjects. The researcher then uses a chi-square to compare 22 reflections among 429 responses from another sample of 30 subjects. This technique violates the independence of observation assumption in chi-square and invalidates the test. As Cronbach (1949) noted, the proper way to conduct this test is to compare the number of subjects giving more than some designated number of $Fr+rF$; that is, how many in each group gave reflection answers rather than comparing 59 to 22 reflection answers?

The second ANOVA assumption is that of normality. In other words, the population distributions from which the groups are randomly selected are assumed to be normal. In actuality, few sample distributions are actually normal (Mecceri, 1989), and it is quite difficult to classify real distributions systematically. According to Harwell (1988), most of the tests of normality are themselves subject to Type I and Type II errors, so there is no substitute for inspecting data plots. The accumulated evidence and wisdom on violations of normality, in the absence of other assumption violations, indicate that it is not a major problem for ANOVA or its cousin, the t test (Glass et al., 1972). This is particularly true for Type I error but less is known about Type II error.

Furthermore, equal and large cell sample sizes (N's), go a long way to correct for normality violations. Similar distributions, even if non-normal, across groups also appear to reduce errors. Equal N's as small as 15 can relieve most concerns about Type I error, except when massive violations of normality or violations of other assumptions occur. Even in larger studies, one might still be concerned when p values are significant but close to the nominal or cutoff level. On the other hand, studies with small N's will have little power so that they cannot routinely be recommended.

Other, related statistical tests generate errors under conditions of non-normality and heterogeneity of variance. Post hoc, multiple comparison methods have been shown to have excessive Type I error rates (Petrinovich & Hardyck, 1969). In particular, Duncan, Newman–Keuls, and t-test derived statistics have shown quite high rates, whereas more acceptable error rates are evident for Tukey and Scheffe. All have elevated Type II error rates. F and t tests are often generated to test the significance of correlation and regressions coefficients. There is reason to believe that the type of non-normal distributions might cause large distortions in error rates of these statistics (Edgell & Noon, 1984).

The management of non-normality cannot be addressed regarding ANOVA without discussing the assumption of homogeneity of variance. Indeed, problems with heterogeneity of variance are likely to occur when non-normality is also posing a problem in a Rorschach study. In that light, heterogeneity of variance may be a more precise way of identifying threats to Type I and Type II error. Basically, the assumption of homogeneity of variance is that the within cell variances are equal for all cells. Researchers are becoming much more concerned about violations of this assumption. For example, Keppel (1991) devoted seven pages to this topic in his third edition but only one page and a footnote in his second edition (1982). This previous lack of concern reflected the point of view that ANOVA was robust to this violation. Tests available to test for heterogeneity of variance are unfortunately error prone when data are non-normal and consequently are too often of little usefulness.

Keppel (1991) recommended that when the ratio of the greatest cell variance to the smallest (*Fmax*) exceeds 3, one must become concerned with heterogeneity and error rates. Again, equal and large N's substantially reduce problems with heterogeneity. The actual effects of heterogeneity differ in a complex way according to the distribution of the cell means and the correspondence between the amount of variance and N's. The general finding is that Type I error may be much lower than nominal levels when larger variances (relative to other cells) are matched with greater N's. In these situations, Type II error is greater so that one is less likely to uncover a real difference. The danger of Type I error is greatly enhanced when the larger variances are paired with smaller N's, so that one risks the danger of reporting false-positive results.

A review of published Rorschach research reveals that very few, if any, authors address the homogeneity assumption. Frequently, authors do address the issue of normality and some modify their statistical analysis appropriately. Unfortunately, much Rorschach research violates the homogeneity of variance assumptions. This occurs because so many of the Rorschach variables are skewed with many zero values. Returning to the example of *m*, approximately 24% of nonpatients have no *m* and about 31% of nonpatients have scores of 2, 3, or 4. If an investigator were able to apply a stress of enough strength, one might increase the number of subjects with *m*'s of 2, 3, 4 considerably. In doing so, one would substantially increase the variance of the experimental group and probably violate the homogeneity of variance assumption.

The effect of these distortions on Type I and Type II errors varies from study to study. The complexity of the interaction of various factors typically makes the effect unknown. As is often the case with behavioral count data, positive results are likely to result in heterogeneity of variance with J-shaped distributions.

Figure 10.1 presents this issue schematically. Parametric statistics assume that two distributions that are being compared will both be normal with similar dispersions. If a statistical significance exists, such distributions, according to parametric assumptions, will simply be displaced to the left or right but will retain their shape. Rorschach variable distributions, especially determinants, variables with low frequencies, and those associated with psychopathology, often change their shape rather than being neatly displaced. More often than not, the distribution "leans" to the right—it increases

Approximate Normal Distribution Meeting
Parametric Assumptions -- (Retains Shape)

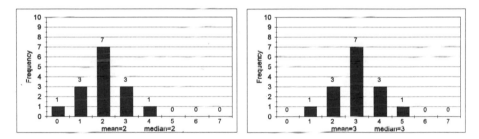

Skewed Rorschach Distributions With
Assumption Violations -- (Lean to Right)

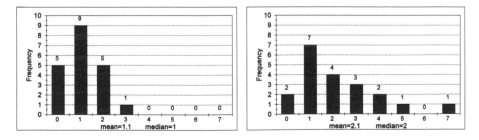

FIG. 10.1. Hypothetical between-group differences.

numbers of subjects having values in the tail of the distribution with greater values. Consequently, differences are significant too often with parametric statistics and nonsignificant with rank order, nonparametric statistics. This type of change occurs when a subgroup of the target population reacted in the predicted way. As a result, the findings may have practical significance in terms of marked reactions of some subjects under certain conditions.

Skew and Outliers

The previous discussion prompts a more in-depth exploration of skew and outliers. Problems with heterogeneity of variance (and non-normality by extension) are much more likely to occur as a result of skewed data and outliers. Routinely, data plots should be examined to uncover outliers. The problem with outliers is that they overwhelm other data points in their effect on parametric statistics. Indeed, authorities concerning statistics (e.g., Harwell, 1988; Siegel & Castellan, 1988) cite the fact that the mean is not robust to skew and outliers. One can conceptualize the effect of an outlier as the square of the distance of that outlier from the mean, once the mean has been adjusted to include that outlier. As a result, extreme data points greatly distort sample parameters.

The m and stress hypothesis described earlier is one that may produce outliers. In a model using increased stress, descriptive and summary statistics that assume a normal distribution and homogeneity of variance are prone to distortion and error. In a multivariate analysis, considerations about outliers led Stevens (1986) to assert that "it is very important to be able to identify such outliers and then decide what to do about them. Why? Because we want the results of our statistical analysis to reflect most of the data, and not to be highly influenced by just 1 or 2 errant data points" (p. 10).

In Rorschach research, there may be studies in the literature where the achievement of statistically significant results occurs simply because of the outlier scores of one or two individuals, yet some investigators will blithely assume that the statistical significance encompasses all of the subjects. Also outliers can greatly influence measures of strength of effects, and planned and unplanned comparisons.

Examples of the powerful effect of outliers are easy to come across or to invent. Recently, a student of one of the authors found that the elimination of one outlier among a sample of 61 resulted in a change from a skew of .8 to −.2. An invented example would be a test–retest correlation of m. Assume, for instance, that a baseline test yields data that mirrors the non-patient normative sample. At retest, 19 subjects gave the identical number of m, but 1 subject increased from 0 m to 8 m. The correlation between these two samples is a mere .18, despite 19 subjects having identical scores! Such an example suggests that temporal consistency reliability data be scrutinized very carefully for outliers.

RORSCHACH VARIABLES AND PARAMETRIC ANALYSIS

Exner (1991) presented detailed descriptive data on 111 variables and comparisons to various cutoffs for 35 variables. These data are the best available because they are the only reasonably large sample data published. Despite the comprehensive descriptive statistics published, it is often difficult to visualize the actual shape of the distributions that correspond to the various parameters. Possibly this is best illustrated by the shapes of Rorschach distributions for two representative important distributions, m and $X+\%$. They are pictured in Figs. 10.2 and 10.3.

Which Rorschach variables are prone to generate outliers and heterogeneity of variance problems? The J-shaped distributions with high percentage of true 0's, few values, and substantial skew (1 or more) are most likely to present these problems. Likewise, Poisson-shaped distributions, distributions in which the mean approximates the standard deviation, are such candidates. A review of the literature suggests that the variables that most often pose problems with adults are individual determinants, various form quality and developmental quality subtypes, refined variables with small distributions (e.g., $W+$, $M-$, Col-Sh blends), individual special scores, and content categories. Many of the individual response scores (Coonerty, 1986; Hirshberg, 1989) also are typically inappropriate for parametric analysis. Those scored on continuum and averaged (Blatt, Brenneis, Schimek, & Glick, 1976; Urist, 1977) are more often appropriate. One group of variables that is particularly troublesome are the actuarial indices. These include Schizophrenia Index

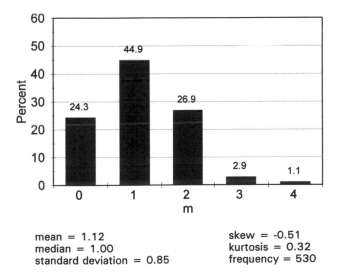

mean = 1.12
median = 1.00
standard deviation = 0.85

skew = -0.51
kurtosis = 0.32
frequency = 530

FIG. 10.2. Distribution of m in nonpatients ($N = 700$).

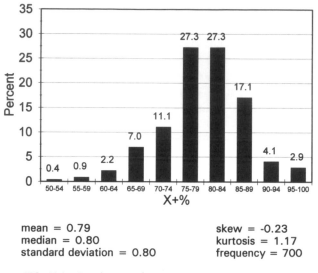

mean = 0.79   skew = -0.23
median = 0.80   kurtosis = 1.17
standard deviation = 0.80   frequency = 700

FIG. 10.3. Distribution of $X+\%$ in nonpatients (N = 700).

(SCZI), Depression Index (DEPI), Coping Deficit Index (CDI), Hypervigilance Index (HVI), Intellectualization Index, Suicide-Constellation and others. The sums (for example, EA) and percentages ($X-\%$) produce these
problems less frequently. However, one should point out that one critical
variable (*Lambda*) is highly skewed in adult nonpatients. Using the number
of pure F responses divided by R probably might cure heterogeneity problems in this instance. This suggested transformation brings up the issue of
how R should be handled in analysis, a topic addressed later in this chapter.
A more comforting note is that under certain conditions all of these variables
can produce arrays that, although non-normal, do not increase error rates
and can be suitable for parametric analysis.

A more systematic presentation of these issues is presented in Table 10.1.
Skew, frequency data, and other descriptive data from Exner's (1991) normative and patient data were used to classify variables as to estimated suitability
for parametric statistics. These data were used to establish criteria based on
the likelihood that non-normality and skew would result in violations of
statistical assumptions and distort inferential decision making and strength
of effect estimates. Few variables are typically suitable for parametric analysis.
This is particularly true if one were to include pathological samples. More
variables are typically suitable when subjects are nonpatients. Many of these
that are suitable are percentages of R, such as described earlier. Many individual determinants and almost all other variables with few values greater
than zero, or those with very restricted ranges, are typically unsuitable for
parametric analysis. R is often skewed so that it may distort results when
used as a covariate or when partialed from correlations. Conversely, some

TABLE 10.1
Rorschach Variables: Predictions of Suitability for
Parametric Analyses Without Transformations

Generally suitable:	W, DQ+, FQo, MQo, 3r+(2)/R, es, a, p, Zf, Blends, Afr, Popular, X+%, F+%, X−%, Xu%
Sometimes suitable:	D*, DQo, FQ−, M*, FM*, FC+CF+C+Cn*, WsumC, SumSh, F*, (2)*, EA*, D-Score, AdjD,Mᵃ*,MP*, Zd*, H*, A*, Isolate*, All H Content*, SumSpSc*, WSUM6*, COP*
Generally unsuitable:	R*, Dd, S, DQv/+, FQ+, FQnone, MQ+, Mqu, MQ−, MQnone, S−, m, FC, CF, C, Cn, Sum C', Sum T, Sum V, Sum Y, Fr+rF, Fd, Lambda, Col-Sh Blds, S−%, (H), Hd, (Hd), Hx, (A), Ad, (Ad), An, Art, Ay, Bl, Bt*, Cg*, Cl, Ex, Fi, Fd, Ge, Hb, Ls, Na, Sc, Sx, Sx, Idio, DV, INCOM, DR, FABCOM, DV2, INC2 FAB2, ALOG, CONTAM, Sum6 Sp Sc2, AB, AG, CFB, CP, MOR, PER, PSV

Note. These predictions based on skew, kurtosis, number of variable values, and percentage of real zero values. Samples used are Comprehensive System adult nonpatient, nonpatient 8-year-olds, and schizophrenic, depressive, outpatient, and character disorder reference samples (Exner, 1991).

*May be suitable with nonpatient samples.

variables with limited distributions unexpectedly meet the criteria for use in a parametric model, such as *MQo, a,* and *p* because of reasonable skew and kurtosis.

RATIO AND DIFFERENCE SCORES

As Cronbach (1949) pointed out, ratio and difference scores present additional statistical problems. Such scores include *EB, EA, es, eb, Lambda, Afr, FC:CF+C, W:M, W:D.* Ratios of scores with contents, determinants, or any scores with a true zero point and no negative values are by definitions skewed and often produce outliers. When the denominator is greater than the numerator scores range from 0 to 1, but when the denominator is less than the numerator scores range from 1 to infinity. Thus, in most cases, the value of the ratio is more highly correlated with the denominator then the numerator. These considerations have led people to calculate difference scores by subtracting the right side from left in the previous ratios. However, such a tactic is often inappropriate because the difference score will covary more with the component that has the larger variance. It is often preferable to normalize both components first either by translating to a *z* score or by using the median and stretching the range above or below the mean to produce a symmetrical distribution. Afterward, one subtracts one component score from another. This method ensures that approximately half of the variance in the difference score derives from each variable. Perry and Viglione (1991) adopted this technique in calculating the Human Experience

Variable based on the difference of z scores between the Poor and Good human scores.

Cronbach (1949) and Exner (1991) offered a different recommendation. They suggested using cutoff scores to summarize important interpretive ranges in the ratio and calculating chi-squares where necessary. More validation work by independent researchers would help to establish this technique. It becomes an empirical question of how much variance is lost when one reduces raw score data to a few discrete ranges.

DEALING WITH RORSCHACH DEPENDENT VARIABLES

In ANOVA studies how should one progress through this confusing thicket of potential distortion of results and threats of Type I and Type II error? First, one should examine data plots of aggregated and individual cell data to identify potential problems with normality, skew, heterogeneity of variance, and outliers. If any irregularities exist, then one should make sure that N's are approximately equal (not more than 1.5 times larger from largest to smallest) and that all N's are sufficient, probably 20 or more per cell. Equal N's reduce the effects of irregularities and sufficient sample sizes allow one to regain power that would otherwise be lost.

As noted earlier, examination of the data is essential to identify outliers. There are a number of ways to handle outliers. One approach is to analyze the data with and without them. The ideal situation would occur when results, without the outliers, support the hypothesis and the outliers are also in the hypothesized direction.

Data can sometimes be transformed. For example, consider a square root transformation that may correct for outliers. In this circumstance, rank order or other nonparametric statistics can be used. It is generally unwise and uneconomical to eliminate outlier data altogether if the outliers are not due to measurement errors. Sometimes, outlier scores can be changed logically to a score that is handled more easily statistically. For example, an m of 8 from a group whose next highest is a score of 3 may be changed to 4. Such seemingly arbitrary modifications are justifiable when the interpretation of the modified data point would not change, that is, an m of 4 and an m of 8 are essentially the same interpretively. It is important to note, however, that changing a score can be inappropriate if the data matrix also includes a variable that could be altered substantially by the change. For instance, although an m of 4 and an m of 8 are interpreted essentially the same, an m of 8 will have a much greater effect on the es and the D score than an m of 4.

Exner (1991) extended the notion of interpretive cutoffs to many variables. In his normatively based interpretive routines, he often asserted that a difference of one on a given variable is meaningful at one point in a side but not at another. For example, he distinguished between 0 and 1 reflections ($Fr+rF$), but not between 2 and 3, and between 0, 1, and 2 texture responses (T), but not between 2 and 3. Accordingly, it would make sense to categorize data accordingly, such as 0, 1, or more than 1 $Fr+rF$, or 0, 1, and 2 or more T. One would then calculate chi-squares or Fisher exact test (Siegel & Castellan, 1988). Such a procedure may be necessary when data irregularities are incurable as will often be the case for many determinants, content scores, and other indices with very few values (especially with skews). In these circumstances, chi-square or exact tests probably are most appropriate. It is also important to keep in mind that small expected frequencies (below 5) result in reduced power so that one might first try cutoffs that keep cell counts reasonably high (Cronbach, 1949). In future research, especially talented researchers might be able to adapt techniques described by Gangestad and Snyder (1985) in attempting to identify discrete classes or cutoffs.

Rank order nonparametric alternatives should be routinely adopted or data transformed when the data are grossly skewed (skew of 2 or more), when distribution shapes differ among cells, or when N's are unequal or insufficient in number. Most of the studies and recommendations in statistics texts prefer the Welch test, although it appears that the Brown–Forsythe test may be superior under some conditions and other rank-order tests are often used (Brown & Forsythe, 1974; Siegel & Castellan, 1988; Tomarken & Serlin, 1986).

Transformations of data introduce complexities in interpretation because the quantitative meaning of the resultant scale is often unclear. Nonetheless, it has been demonstrated that transformations do regain some of the power lost from data irregularities (Levine & Dunlap, 1982). Others have discouraged the use of nonparametric statistics in such situations claiming a loss of power. However, the study of this issue suggests that adopting a nonparametric approach results in a loss of power only when assumptions are "well-satisfied." Thus, power is already lost when data violates assumptions and adopting the best nonparametric routine, Welch's in most cases, does not further reduce power (Keppel, 1991; Tomarken & Serlin, 1986).

Keppel (1991) suggested that heterogeneity can either be identified by an $FMax$ greater than 3 or the Brown–Forsythe F test (pp. 101–108). If sample sizes are sufficient and relatively equal, and $FMax$ is 3 or 4, one might only use a more conservative alpha level ($p < .025$) Of course, this procedure lowers power so that more subjects might help. Contrasts or partial ANOVA's involving cells with equivalent variance may be undertaken at higher unadjusted p levels. When $Fmax$ exceeds 4 and the pattern of data and cell sizes pose other problems, then nonparametric statistics or transformations are essential. More conservative methods should be undertaken with single degree of freedom comparisons because heterogeneous variances pose more serious problems in single degree of freedom comparisons

(Keppel, 1991). One should consider conservative alpha levels and non-parametric statistics more readily in this case. Basically, one needs to identify which comparisons incorporate the heterogeneity.

These basic assumptions of independence of observations, normality and homogeneity of error variances also hold for other ANOVA procedures and pose similar threats. All of the threats outlined here for the between-groups ANOVA would constitute the minimal level of danger to other types of ANOVA. However, other procedures such as within-subjects ANOVA, and analysis of covariance have their own idiosyncratic threats to Type I and Type II errors.

Repeated measure or within-subjects designs hold much promise in Rorschach research in minimizing error variance, increasing effect size and, thus, increasing power. Haller and Exner (1985) demonstrated the efficiency of such an approach by using a Rorschach test–retest, experimental design. Although the precise carryover effects of multiple administrations of the Rorschach are not well known, they appear to be rather small. Multiple administrations allow relatively unambiguous interpretation of within-subjects designs.

Assumptions for within-subjects designs are more numerous and in particular include a variety of homogeneity assumptions about the various data matrices. Typically, these assumptions are violated and corrections of the F test are introduced to compensate for them. However, these threats only occur in studies with more than two levels in the repeated measures. In studies where Rorschach variables are dependent measures, it would seem inadvisable to administer the test more than twice because of carryover effects or feasibility problems. Accordingly, within-subjects designs with only two levels on the repeated measure pose no extra risks for violation of assumptions and conform to the ANOVA considerations noted earlier.

The assumptions underlying analysis of covariance are more restrictive then other forms of ANOVA. On the other hand, less is known about the consequences of violations of these assumptions. The additional assumptions for ANCOVA stipulate that the relationships between the covariate and dependent variables are linear, the slopes of these derived regressions are equal between groups (homogeneity of regression coefficients), and independence of the covariate from independent variables. ANCOVA also incorporates the assumptions of ANOVA. Unlike the ANOVA, recent ANCOVA evidence (Harwell & Serlin, 1988) suggests that larger and equal cell N's (30) may not overcome Type II error problems with distinctly non-normal distributions. If the relationship between the covariate and dependent variable is not linear, then the correlation between them is likely to be small and the use of the covariate ineffective. This may be the case with Rorschach research when R is used as a covariate because R has been shown to have curvilinear relationships with many variables.

The power advantage of the F test that exists when assumptions are met is lost with heterogeneity of regression. Under those conditions, treatment-by-blocks designs are recommended as well as various nonparametric alternatives (Harwell & Serlin, 1988). Indeed, under most conditions that result in substantial power loss in the parametric ANOVA, some nonparametric tests retain a considerable power advantage.

TYPE I AND TYPE II ERRORS
AND STRENGTH OF EFFECTS

Inferential statistics are tools to make decisions about descriptions of reality. They allow us, with some certainty, to conclude that one statement or another is a more likely descriptor of the true state of affairs. Typically, investigators seek support for statements asserting that one variable differs from another, or that one variable is associated with another. The basic assumption in data analyses is that the statement is not true. The investigator begins with the familiar Null hypothesis that no difference exists or that the variables in question are not related.

The Null hypothesis is challenged by the use of appropriate inferential statistic, which yields a probability value. If all the assumptions in parametric tests (or the minimal assumptions of some nonparametric tests) are met and if the Null hypothesis is assumed to be true, it can then be asserted that, at some probability level, the final result is unlikely. In other words, if the derived probability of an analysis is $p = .04$, it means that the likelihood of achieving the result is 4 in 100, if all the assumptions are true. It is also important to remember that the actual probability level of .04 is not the probability that the Null hypothesis is true (Meehl, 1990; Oakes, 1986).

Typically, researchers use an alpha level of .05 to establish the confidence limits—the range of expected scores on the test statistic given the null. In the previous example, the calculated test statistic lies outside the confidence limits. This is an unlikely result, and something is probably amiss, most likely the assumptions. The one assumption that is least defensible in the example is the Null hypothesis. Given that the results are highly unlikely in the context of the Null hypothesis, it can be inferred that an alternative hypothesis is a better descriptor. Thus, the null is rejected and an alternative hypothesis is accepted.

In this logical process of analyzing data, there is a risk of making a number of errors. First, the Null hypothesis may have been true all along and the results somehow mistaken. Therefore, it is possible to err and accept the alternative hypothesis when it is not true. This is the familiar Type I error, defined by the selected alpha level, which in most research is usually .05 or .01. The alpha level provides a probability base against which results are judged. Thus, if all the statistical assumptions are true, there are 5 chances in 100 (for .05) or 1 chance in 100 (for .01) of presenting statistically significant results *when the null is true.*

The second type of error is of the opposite sort, namely, accepting the null rather than the alternative hypothesis when, in fact, the alternative is the true state of affairs. In this case, the analysis has failed to present statistically significant results even though the hypothesis is actually true. This type of error, Type II error, is usually represented by term *beta.* Historically, Type II errors have been of less concern so that most studies are oriented to handling Type I. Recently, it has received more attention (Cohen 1962, 1977, 1990), but the general finding is despite this attention that studies lack sufficient protection from Type II error (Rossi, 1990; Meehl, 1990; Rosnow & Rosenthal, 1989; Sedlmeier & Girgerenzer, 1989). The degree to which a study is prone to Type II error (1 – beta) is generally called *power* but also sensitivity or efficiency. Power estimates how sensitive a study is to detecting differences or associations between variables when they actually exist.

There is another obvious source of error in inferential statistics. When significant results are obtained, they are used to support the contention that the assumption of the Null hypothesis (no differences exist) is unsubstantiated. However, the true state of affairs may be that the assumptions of a given parametric test are false. This predicament represents the rarely detected but possibly frequent violation of statistical assumptions. As noted earlier, Rorschach variable distributions are likely to be skewed and contain outliers. Thus, such errors pose considerable dangers to Rorschach research and can distort if not invalidate results.

The Type I Error

As noted earlier, a Type I error occurs when we reject the Null hypothesis and present significant results when it is actually true. It is very important to recognize that the alpha level, .05 for example, is a conditional probability: If the Null hypothesis is true, the probability of presenting false-positive results is .05. On the other hand, Oakes (1986) and Meehl (1990) suggested that the actual proportion of false-positive results in the literature is much higher than 5%.

The most concise studies may involve a single significance test, for example one *t* test or one test of significance corresponding to an *r.* However, this is not often the case in most research, especially Rorschach research. Studies using Rorschach variables as dependent variables often abound in the number of significance tests. For example, Hirshberg (1989) calculated 82, and Lipgar and Wahler (1991) calculated 67. When multiple tests are calculated, the probability of a Type I error is greatly increased. Although the probability of a given test being significant by chance is still equal to the selected alpha level, multiple significance tests greatly increase the probability that one or more Type I errors will occur in the study as a whole.

This notion of the probability of one or more errors in an entire study is the experimentwise error rate. Often it is not addressed or controlled in Rorschach research. Rorschach studies with 60 tests of significance at an alpha level of .05 theoretically would average about 3 (60 × .05) Type I errors. The experimentwise probability of one Type I error in such a study is about .95 (1-(1-alpha)# tests). In this example, if investigators obtained 4 or 5 significant results, they could not be sure whether the results as a whole are actually improbable given the Null hypothesis. With 7 significant results in an analysis using an alpha of $p<.05$, the researcher might be in a quandary about which of the seven were truly Type I errors and which were true. Because of the large number of Rorschach variables, researchers continue to succumb to the temptation of calculating numerous statistical tests despite Cronbach's (1949) cautions about this problem many years ago.

As an example, Hirshberg's (1989) study of eating disordered subjects suffers from poor control over Type I error rates. In 29 comparisons among eating disordered groups, results approaching conventionally accepted significance levels were obtained for two variables. These significance levels were $p = .08$ and $p = .095$. Accordingly, one would expect at least 2 to 3 significant results by chance, so that the results are unremarkable. To his credit, Hirshberg minimized these findings, but only after spending these pages statistically analyzing these error patterns. Nonetheless, there is no mention of Type I error in this study, an omission that seriously compromises its interpretability.

To reduce the danger of cluttering the literature with false results, various techniques have been developed to control Type I errors. These techniques are described in most contemporary statistics texts. Typically, they involve specifying some overall, acceptable experimentwise error rate and then adjusting the individual alpha levels in accord with this overall rate. Often, reviewers of research suggest quite conservative experimentwise error rates, for example, .20. In Rorschach research with many variables, such a requirement would establish very conservative alpha levels, probably .005 or less. Although this may be appropriate, the typical research study could have unacceptably limited power. In other words, it would be prone to Type II errors. The alternative is to have a very large number of subjects. The first alternative is poor science and the second is, at best, difficult. This conundrum has prompted Weiner, in his chapter in this volume, to emphasize the thoughtful selection of variables, and Cohen (1990) to recommend large N's and few dependent variables. The point is that studies with many significance tests (many DV's and IV's) and few subjects defy interpretation, be they ANOVA or regression based.

Explicit and Implicit Significance Tests

What has been described thus far applies mainly to planned or a priori comparisons. In basic statistics and design courses students learn to discriminate between planned and unplanned or post hoc comparisons. The central distinction is that planned comparisons are hypothesized before the study begins, whereas unplanned comparisons are initiated after inspecting results. Thus, the number of planned comparisons is essentially known beforehand, whereas the unplanned comparisons can be numerous and uncontrolled. If planned analyses included testing all correlation matrices or all comparisons between cell means for significant findings, it is possible that only Type I error findings might evolve and be reported as significant.

Accordingly, with unplanned comparisons, there are stringent controls on Type I errors. Various statistics (e.g., Scheffe, Newman-Keuls) have been developed that vary in their level of conservatism. A review of Rorschach research reveals that such routines are relatively uncommon and that the distinction between planned and unplanned comparisons is not always evident. Obviously, this confusion highlights the design issue of selecting variables thoughtfully.

Any discussion of planned versus unplanned comparisons also must include comment regarding the difference between explicit and implicit Type I errors. At times, research reports contain idiosyncratic but significant correlations or partial ANOVA's identifying differences between subgroups on an individual variable. On occasion, it is not clear why this variable was selected. It may be that some significant findings were selected post hoc, so that the numerous other "unproductive" variables are not listed (Cohen, 1990; Cronbach, 1949). In such instances the implicit experimentwise error rates are very high and include many nonreported insignificant findings. Thus, it is difficult to ascertain whether the reported significant finding has occurred by chance. There are other subtle ways of increasing implicit Type I error rates. This occurs when the statistical hypotheses are selected after inspecting the data but are presented as being a priori.

There are two Rorschach research models in which hidden significance tests have unduly increased implicit Type I error. The first is in static group studies with diagnostic groups and composite variables are used as dependent variables. Composite variables are those scales consisting of multiple subcomponents, such as Exner's actuarial indices, Urist's (1977) Mutuality of Autonomy Scales, Coonerty's (1986) separation–individuation scale, Perry and Viglione's (1991) Ego Impairment Index, and so on. Researchers are prone to draw attention to the statistical significance of a single or few Rorschach subcomponent variables, while ignoring or not presenting other tests with other subcomponents that were undoubtedly calculated. Some authors then overgeneralize from this rather idiosyncratic and possibly random findings and present them as convincing support of the validity of the index or the underlying theory.

An example of incorrect generalization occurs in a study by Kleinman and Russ (1988) regarding the relationship between adaptive regression and anxiety. They interpreted their results as supportive of the notion that adaptive regression binds anxiety and is related to tolerance for psychological stress. They used Holt's (1977) Adaptive Regression score (AR), which consists of scores for Defensive Demand (DD) and Defensive Effectiveness (DE), however, DE and AR are correlated at .97, that is, they are virtually identical! To their credit, Kleinman and Russ presented these subcomponent correlations, but they neglected offering the most parsimonious interpretation of their findings, namely, that tolerance for psychological stress is related to whatever DE measures. In fact, DE is largely based on form quality. Thus, the more accurate interpretation of their findings seems to be that perceptual accuracy is inversely related to anxiety in their population rather than the overgeneralization that the results can be attributed to adaptive regression.

A second more haphazard situation that increases implicit experimentwise error occurs when authors report intercorrelations of Rorschach variables, or correlations with non-Rorschach variables that were not included among the planned comparisons. Often such correlations are presented as "after thoughts" or at least late in results sections. One has no way of knowing how many correlations were calculated or examined to uncover the "significant" result. Accordingly, it is impossible to determine whether the correlation is a chance finding.

These hidden hunt-and-peck excursions raise other design issues. For instance, demonstrating convergent validity between Rorschach variables may be of limited importance when divergent validity is not considered. In other words, one cannot begin to rule out a third variable as the cause of the correlation between *SumY* and *WSumC*, for example. This same issue underlies Weiner's (1977) call for independent validity criteria. Basically, any finding relating one Rorschach variable to another is subject to confound and is not very informative about validity. It may, however, be useful to identify unusual patterns of Structural Summary data (Exner, Viglione, & Gillespie, 1984) whose interpretive validity can later be independently verified. At times, some authors erroneously interpret confounded correlations. For example, if one were to ascribe some significance to the correlation between *EA* and *SumC*, one would be ignoring the fact that *EA* subsumes *SumC*.

The Type II Error

A Type II error is the likelihood of rejecting the alternative hypothesis, when in fact the alternative hypothesis is true. In other words, if a study is repeated many times with independent samples from two different populations, the proportion of nonsignificant findings is the Type II error or *beta*. Its inverse, power (1 − beta), is the likelihood that the study would correctly reveal what we are trying to demonstrate (the alternative hypothesis).

More than 30 years ago, Cohen (1962) demonstrated that the typical study lacks power and, indeed, has less than 50% chance of uncovering significant differences if in fact they do exist. Rosnow and Rosenthal (1989) compared this practice to trying to read fine print and to errors of blindness and concluded that investigators work in a dimly lit room or are partially sighted. It was expected that researchers would feel duly admonished by Cohen's exhortations and that studies with greater power would appear. The recent empirical reviews of Rossi (1990) and Sedlmeier and Girgerenzer (1989) indicate that studies still lack power and are subject to false-negative errors. In fact, there is some evidence that because of controlling Type I error through adjusting alpha, power may be lower (Sedlmeier & Girgerenzer, 1989). It may even be more worrisome that few authors through the middle 1980s mentioned power. Such references in the Rorschach literature are virtually nonexistent.

Power depends on a number of factors: alpha, sample size, population effect size, and the type of inferential statistic. As is intuitively obvious, power is greater with smaller alpha levels, larger sample sizes, and greater effect sizes. Tables and graphs to calculate power are available in various statistical tests (Keppel, 1991; Myers, 1972) and in Cohen's (1977) work on this subject. Cohen identified adequate power as .80, but it is clear that only a minority of studies approach this level. As Cohen (1990) noted, the power to conduct the typical dissertation experiment involving a two-tailed, simple *t*-test comparison of two independent samples of 30 subjects each with an expected medium size effect and an alpha level of .05 is .47. Because of the complexity involved in conducting Rorschach research, sample sizes are often quite modest so that most well-controlled, experimental Rorschach research has modest power. Other investigations that evolve from the use of Rorschach's that are routinely collected as part of a battery for all patients at an institution or for all patients with a certain diagnosis or features, often have much larger *N*'s. However, these studies are typically poorly controlled so that increased error variances limit effect sizes and reduce power.

MAGNITUDE OF EFFECT

The issue of power brings to the fore a central problem in recent psychological research in general and Rorschach research in particular, namely, the failure to address magnitude of effect. Magnitude of effect or effect size measures, also called strength of effect, are estimates of the association between two variables (or more than two in multivariate procedures). It has been only recently that editors and statisticians (see Keppel, 1991) are recommending that magnitude of effect measures routinely be included with research reports. The simple Pearson r is an example of such a measure. *Omega* squared and *epsilon* squared are examples of such measures for ANOVA. Another is d (Cohen, 1977), which is the standardized difference between two means, in other words the difference between two group means divided by the standard deviation. All of these measures can be reduced to the amount of variance or difference in the dependent variable accounted for by the independent variable(s). Accordingly, one can increase the effect size and power by increasing the differences associated with the groups in ANOVA or predictor variables in regression, or by reducing the amount of error variance. Unlike F, chi-square, and other test statistics whose distributions differ as a function of the degrees of freedom, magnitude of effect estimators are theoretically free of the original context of their respective research sources. In other words, F, unlike these measures, varies as a function of the number of subjects and groups.

One of the most important features about the magnitude of effect is that the effect size permits a comparison of results across studies in a way that is impossible with significance tests with differing N's. The cumulative effect of studies with different N's, different Type I and Type II error rates, different designs, controls, and intervening variables is that the complex of research results in a given field is confusing if not outright contradictory (Meehl, 1990).

A simple way to appreciate this confusion is to consider the contradictory and often inexplicable findings associated with gender. Many gender comparisons are made after the fact, so that Type I and Type II errors are poorly controlled. As result, many mistaken results are presented in the literature. Examining effect sizes allows some resolution of these differences in that the same effect size may be statistically significant in a large study but insignificant in a small study or in a study with a small alpha criterion. The same magnitude of effect may produce statistically significant findings in a larger study. The point is, to understand a given research result, one must appreciate the interrelationships among Type I error, power, N, and effect size.

Cohen (1977) set the precedent for identifying small, medium, and large effects. Small effects are conventionally set as $r = .1$ and $d = .2$, medium as $r = .3$ and $d = .5$, and large as $r = .5$ and $d = .8$. Translated to Rorschach variables in a mixed outpatient sample (Exner, 1991), and ignoring the problem of non-normality, these effect sizes would correspond to a difference of .24, .62, and 1.00 on m and .03, .07, and .11 on $X+\%$. Despite the availability of such calculations, there is considerable disagreement concerning the notion of small, medium, and large effects. Rorschach researchers are at somewhat of an advantage in this respect as they usually work with a ratio scale number that can be understood because of experience with the test. Rorschach investigators can rely on what makes an interpretive difference to establish what is probably a large, or not very large, effect in a research study. Furthermore, presentation of results of group differences is rather simple in that Rorschachers easily understand cell means and standard deviations. As Cohen (1990) suggested, one may be more readily able to assimilate the significance of a Rorschach correlational finding if it is presented in a nonstandardized regression equation.

Strength of effect considerations aid in determining how important a given finding may be, that is, help to determine whether a significant finding is indeed meaningful. Despite this fact, some authors who support the use of magnitude of effect estimators in research reports (Keppel, 1991; Strube, 1988; Strube, Gardner, & Hartmann, 1986; see O'Grady, 1982, for an excellent review) warn against the dangers of using it in an automatic, unexamined manner. Basically, the same magnitude of effect may have very different implications in different research contexts or designs. Interpretation of effect sizes must occur in context. Thus, routinely dismissing a small effect size as unimportant is ill-advised because small effects may have considerable importance is some contexts, especially theoretical issues. In addition, the standard error of the sampling distributions of strength of effect statistics does vary as a function of N (Murray & Dosser, 1987). Consistent with this notion, Butcher and Tellegen (1978) recommended that reports of r should be accompanied by confidence intervals. Also, magnitude of effect estimators are distorted by assumption violations and particularly by outliers. Accordingly, they are limited by the reliability of the measures and the effectiveness of experimental manipulations.

Consideration of magnitude of effect estimators raises the issue of presentation of results in studies. Cohen (1990) emphasized a simple, but unfortunately too often forgotten point, that graphic presentation of data may be more informative then abstract statistics. In Rorschach research it seems appropriate to be more satisfied with small effects in experimental research where differences in dependent variables are used to test a theory. On the other hand, small effects must be translated very cautiously if they are to be extended to clinical interpretation. Optimally, interpretive strategies and guidelines should evolve from very large group studies.

The practice of balancing Type I and Type II error in regard to supporting or rejecting the Null hypothesis raises a crucial point in planning studies. The most reasonable approach in balancing Type I and Type II error is a cost–benefit analysis. Concern should be afforded to errors that should be avoided. Stated differently, which errors are most costly? In a proposed design, what are the probabilities of Type I and Type II errors? These questions, rather the arbitrary alpha level of point .05, should guide the investigator. Obviously, the investigator must consider the interrelationships of Type I error, power, sample size, and expected effect size when designing a study. Power analysis can be calculated before the study is undertaken rather than only after the fact. It is important to estimate a strength of effect that one would consider meaningful before undertaking a study. In doing so, the researcher is protected from wasting a lot of time and energy in a study with low power that is likely to produce ambiguous results at best.

Using the Rorschach as a dependent measure brings up a special problem in that multiple DV's are the common, but they inflate the experimentwise error rate. Rather than using the ultra-conservative alpha-adjustment procedures that reduce power to unacceptably low levels, the investigator can set the experimentwise error rate at a level that may generate few random, positive findings. If the resultant findings are considerably more numerous than would be expected by chance, then they can be interpreted. The only problem is trying to distinguish between which are the true and which are the false-positive findings.

Another way of increasing power, which is too often ignored in Rorschach research, is controlling extraneous variance. One of the best ways to increase the effect size is to reduce error variance. Too often, variables such as who examined the subjects, who scored the records, subject demographic variables, procedural issues such as sequence of tests, and other variables that are controlled in experimental research are left uncontrolled in the static group Rorschach research. Exner's (1991) findings regarding differences for many variables in relation to EB styles and Lambda may also prove fruitful. Controlling these variables and utilizing blocking variables where appropriate may reduce error variance, increase effect size, and increase power with little extra effort to the researcher.

The multiple limitations of Rorschach variable distributions and the likelihood of increasing error because of stretching statistical assumptions tends to limit the power of Rorschach research. It is difficult to believe that satisfactory power could be obtained with cell sizes less than 30, or a regression sample of less than 50, but such a statement is probably an oversimplification. Certainly, studies with smaller cell sizes should not be discouraged but should considered to be preliminary. Knowing the effect size of significant and non-significant findings and power of these smaller studies goes far in determining their worth, giving clear directions for future research, and enabling later reviewers to incorporate the complex of findings in a particular area.

CONCLUSIONS

The Rorschach test presents researchers with a multitude of complex methodological and statistical issues. The topics and areas discussed in the chapter were selected based on recurring problems encountered by researchers and documented in the literature. They do not represent an exhaustive survey of the challenging issues encountered in Rorschach research. The approaches and methods presented are intended to facilitate Rorschach research and to improve the quality of the Rorschach knowledge base. Although some of the suggested alternatives appear complex and foreboding, they are offered in the hope of stimulating research studies into the Rorschach and, thereby, increasing our understanding of human cognitive-perceptual functioning and its vicissitudes.

REFERENCES

Blatt, S. J., Brenneis, C. B., Schimek, J. G., & Glick, M. (1976). Normal development and psychopathological impairment of the concept of the object on the Rorschach. *Journal of Abnormal Psychology, 85,* 364–373.

Blatt, S. J., & Ritzler, B. (1974). Thought disorder and boundary disturbance in psychosis. *Journal of Consulting and Clinical Psychology, 42,* 370–381.

Blatt, S. J., Tuber, S. B., & Auerbach, J. S. (1990) Representation of interpersonal interactions on the Rorschach and level of psychopathology. *Journal of Personality Assessment, 54,* 711–728.

Brown, M. B., & Forsythe, A. B. (1974). Small sample behavior of some statistics which test the equality of several means. *Technometrics, 16,* 129–132.

Butcher, J., & Tellegen, A. (1978). Common methodological problems in MMPI research. *Journal of Consulting and Clinical Psychology, 46,* 620–628.

Cohen, J. (1962). The statistical power of abnormal-social psychological research: A review. *Journal of Abnormal and Social Psychology, 65,* 145–153.

Cohen, J. (1977). *Statistical power analysis for the behavioral sciences.* New York: Academic Press.

Cohen, J. (1990). Things I have learned so far. *American Psychologist, 45,* 1304–1312.

Cohen, J., & Cohen, P. (1975). *Applied multiple regression/correlation analysis for the behavioral sciences.* Hillsdale, NJ: Lawrence Erlbaum Associates.

Coonerty, S. (1986). An exploration of separation–individuation themes in the borderline personality. *Journal of Personality Assessment, 50,* 501–511.

Cronbach, L. J. (1949). Statistical methods applied to Rorschach scores: A review. *Psychological Bulletin, 46,* 393–429.

Edgell, S. E., & Noon, S. M. (1984). Effect of violation of normality on the *t*-test of the correlation coefficient. *Psychological Bulletin, 95,* 576–583.

Exner, J. E., Jr. (1991). *The Rorschach: A comprehensive system: Vol. 2. Interpretation* (2nd ed.). New York: Wiley.

Exner, J. E., Jr. (1992). R in Rorschach research—A ghost revisited. *Journal of Personality Assessment, 58,* 245–251.

Exner, J. E., Jr. (1993). *The Rorschach: A comprehensive system: Vol. 1. Basic foundations* (3rd ed.). New York: Wiley.

Exner, J. E., Jr., Viglione, D. J., & Gillespie, R. (1984). Relationships between Rorschach variables as relevant to the interpretation of structural data. *Journal of Personality Assessment, 48,* 65–69.

Gangestad, S., & Snyder, M. (1985). To carve nature at its joints: On the existence of discrete classes in personality. *Psychological Review, 92,* 317–349.

Glass, G. V., Peckham, R. D., & Sanders, J. R. (1972). Consequences of failure to meet assumptions underlying the fixed effects analysis of variance and covariance. *Review of Educational Research, 42,* 237–288.

Haller N., & Exner, J. E., Jr. (1985). The reliability of Rorschach variables for inpatients presenting symptoms of depression and/or helplessness. *Journal of Personality Assessment, 49,* 516–521.

Harwell, M. R. (1988). Choosing between parametric and non-parametric tests. *Journal of Counseling and Development, 67,* 35–38.

Harwell, M. R., & Serlin, R. C. (1988). An empirical study of a proposed test of nonparametric analysis of covariance. *Psychological Bulletin, 104,* 268–291.

Hayes, W. L., & Winkler, R. L. (1971). *Statistics: Probability, inference, and decision.* New York: Holt, Rinehart & Winston.

Hirshberg, L. (1989). Rorschach images of symbiosis and separation in eating disordered and in borderline and non-borderline subjects. *Psychoanalytic Psychology, 6,* 475–493.

Holt, R. R. (1977). A method for assessing primary process manifestation and their control in Rorschach responses. In Rickers-Ovsiankina, M. (Ed.), *Rorschach psychology* (2nd ed., pp. 421–454). Huntington, NY: Krieger.

Hopkins, K. D., & Weeks, D. L. (1990). Tests for normality and measures of skewness and kurtosis: Their place in research reporting. *Educational and Psychological Measurement, 50,* 717–729.

Keppel, G. (1982). *Design and analysis: A researcher's handbook* (2nd ed.). Englewood Cliffs, NJ: Prentice-Hall.

Keppel, G. (1991). *Design and analysis: A researcher's handbook* (2nd ed.). Englewood Cliffs, NJ: Prentice-Hall.

Kleinman, M. J., & Russ, S. W. (1988) Primary process thinking and anxiety in children. *Journal of Personality Assessment, 52,* 254–262.

Levine, D. W., & Dunlap, W. P. (1982). Power of the F test with skewed data: Should one transform or not. *Psychological Bulletin, 92,* 272–280.

Lipgar, R. M., & Wahler, C. A. (1991). A Rorschach investigation of mothers of behaviorally disturbed boys. *Journal of Personality Assessment, 56,* 106–117.

Lord, F. M. (1953). On the statistical treatment of football numbers. *American Psychologist, 8,* 750–751.

Mecceri, T. (1989). The unicorn, the normal curve, and other improbable creatures. *Psychological Bulletin, 105,* 156–166.

Meehl, P. E. (1978). Theoretical risks and tabular asterisks: Sir Karl, Sir Ronald, and the slow progress of soft psychology. *Journal of Consulting and Clinical Psychology, 46,* 806–834.

Meehl, P. E. (1990). Why summaries of research on psychological theories are often uninterpretable. *Psychological Reports, 66,* 195–244.

Murray, L. W., & Dosser, D. A., Jr. (1987). How significant is a significant difference. Problems with the measurement of magnitude of effect. *Journal of Counseling Psychology, 34,* 68–72.

Myers, J. (1972). *Fundamental of experimental design.* Boston: Allyn & Bacon.

Newell, K. M., & Hancock, P. A. (1984). Forgotten moments: A note on skewness and kurtosis as influential factors in inferences extrapolated from response distributions. *Journal of Motor Behavior, 16,* 320–335.

Oakes, M. (1986). *Statistical inference: A commentary for the social and behavioral sciences.* Chichester, England: Wiley.

O'Grady, K. (1982). Measures of explained variance: Cautions and limitations. *Psychological Bulletin, 92,* 766–777.

Pedhazur, E. J. (1982). *Multiple regression in behavioral research* (2nd ed.). New York: CBS College Publishing.

Perry, W., & Viglione, D. J. (1991). The Rorschach Ego Impairment Index as a predictor of outcome in melancholic depressed patients treated with tricyclic antidepressants. *Journal of Personality Assessment, 56,* 487–501.

Petrinovich, L. F., & Hardyck, C. D. (1969). Error rates for multiple comparison methods: Some evidence concerning the frequency of erroneous conclusions. *Psychological Bulletin, 71,* 43–54.

Pilz, J. (1991). *Bayesian estimation and experimental design in linear regression models* (2nd ed.). New York: Wiley.

Rossi, J. S. (1990). Statistical power of psychological research: What have we gained in 20 years? *Journal of Consulting and Clinical Psychology, 58,* 646–656.

Rosnow, R. L., & Rosenthal, R. (1989). Statistical procedures and the justification of knowledge in psychological science. *American Psychologist, 44,* 1276–1284.

Sedlmeier, P., & Girgerenzer, G. (1989). Do studies of statistical power have an effect on the power of studies. *Psychological Bulletin, 105,* 309–316.

Siegel, S., & Castellan, N. J., Jr. (1988). *Nonparametric statistics for the behavioral sciences* (2nd ed.). New York: McGraw-Hill.

Stevens, J. (1986). *Applied multivariate statistics for the social sciences.* Hillsdale, NJ: Lawrence Erlbaum Associates.

Strube, M. J. (1988). Some comments on the use of magnitude-of-effect estimates. *Journal of Counseling Psychology, 35,* 342–345.

Strube, M. J., Gardner, W., & Hartmann, D. P. (1986). Limitations, liabilities, and obstacles in reviews of the literature: The current status of meta-analysis. *Clinical Psychology Review, 5,* 63–78.

Tomarken, A. J., & Serlin, R. C. (1986). Comparison of ANOVA alternatives under variance heterogeneity and specific noncentrality structures. *Psychological Bulletin, 99,* 90–99.

Urist, J. (1977). The Rorschach test and the assessment of object relations. *Journal of Personality Assessment, 57,* 120–129.

Weiner, I. B. (1977). Approaches to Rorschach validation. In M. A. Rickers-Ovsiankina (Ed.), *Rorschach psychology* (2nd ed., pp. 575–608). Huntington, NY: Krieger.

CHAPTER ELEVEN

Some Special Issues
in Data Analysis

Howard Mcguire, Bill N. Kinder,
Glenn Curtiss, & Donald J. Viglione

Sometimes, Rorschach researchers are faced with seemingly knotty decisions concerning the most appropriate methods of analyzing, interpreting, or reporting findings. Every investigator should strive to get the most out of any data set and to generate conclusions about the data that will be useful to others. At times, however, researchers tend to neglect the dilemma with which they are confronted when selecting an appropriate method of data analysis: *The data are!* This seemingly incomplete statement does, in fact, state a basic axiom in research. The objective and procedures of analysis are to reduce the broad data set into a framework from which conclusions can be drawn. Unfortunately, any reduction of the basic data set, statistical or otherwise, means that some of the data will be less than fully represented. This reduction or simplification of the data set has a price, that is, a loss of fidelity concerning the original data.

There is another research axiom that conflicts with the "data are" proposition: *Data are not information!* It implies that an investigator cannot leave the data set as it is, but must frame it in some context that will help to understand it. The second axiom tends to conflict with the first. This conflict poses quite a challenge for the researchers in that they are prompted to reduce the data set in a way that does as little damage to the original data as possible, yet reframes it in some understandable context. There is no single, always appropriate, never-fail way to do this reduction of information. Researchers, especially those dealing with Rorschach data, must be acutely aware that their choices concerning data reduction (analysis) must be made in light of two issues: How much damage can be done in the data reduction without grossly distorting the true nature of the data set? And, how much distortion of the data set is acceptable while affording a true test of the hypotheses that have been formulated? What might be acceptable with regard to one issue might be unacceptable with regard to the other.

Rorschach data consist of a wide variety of standard (Normal) and non-standard data sets. That fact is no surprise to anyone who has been involved with Rorschach research, but sometimes, those who are aware of the unusual forms that Rorschach data may take neglect the fact that there are a wide variety of ways to present their data. For some data sets a straightforward parametric approach may be most appropriate, whereas other data sets seem best addressed by a nonparametric method. In other instances, the simple presentation of descriptive statistics may reflect the data best. Under optimal conditions preplanned analyses suffice, but there are many instances in which the best preplanning is insufficient.

Examination of the basic data distribution is very important and should not be dismissed casually. In some instances, seemingly logically selected statistical approaches may not reveal potential problems concerning the application. For example, a distribution of scores may be bimodal, such as is often the case for variables such as *M*, *WSumC*, or the *Afr*. Unfortunately, the bimodality is not easily recognized by using simple descriptive statistics such as the mean, median, mode, or measures of skewness or kurtosis. When a bimodal distribution exists, many forms of analysis can lead to distorted outcomes when applied by the unwary researcher. In some small sample Rorschach research, it is possible to find that the mean for a variable may be the least frequent score in a distribution, and all variance estimates based on the mean value will not represent the scores of the subjects appropriately.

There is a basic principle in research that is often ignored, probably moreso in Rorschach research than any other area: *Plot the data first!* That principle may sound simple minded, but in reality it affords some insurance against being deceived by the widely varied nature of scoring distributions that are common among Rorschach variables.

This chapter is designed to caution the Rorschach researcher about some potential blunders that can occur when methods of addressing data are being considered. The sections that follows do not contain hard-fast rules. Rather, they reflect a series of cautions and offer some guidelines that, hopefully, will provoke thoughtful decision making.

USING MULTIPLE APPROACHES TO DATA ANALYSIS

As noted earlier, decisions about handling or interpreting data are not as clear-cut as might be desired. Numerous options concerning methods of analysis may exist. Unfortunately, there are many instances in which an investigator selects only one method and discards other possibilities, usually on the assumption that the method selected will yield results that are most compatible with hypotheses, theories, or biases.

The more astute investigator may wisely choose to use more than one approach, being aware that any of three outcomes are possible: All approaches may yield similar positive findings. All approaches may yield similar negative findings. Findings from one approach may be different than findings from other approaches. When the first two outcomes occur, the results simply strengthen the interpretation of the findings, but when the third outcome (different results) occurs, the problems regarding the interpretation of the results poses an interesting and important challenge. Either set of conflicting findings may reflect a Type I or Type II error. In some instances, findings from one analysis will seem more persuasive but that does not mean that findings from the other analyses should be discarded. Instead, they should be used as a source from which to raise cautions and are especially useful as a basis from which to call for additional studies.

Decisions about how many forms of analyses might be employed concerning a data set are not always straightforward and it is important for investigators to consider as many issues as possible. For example, assume that a researcher has collected Rorschach data for two groups of 35 depressed patients each, one an inpatient group and the second comprised of outpatients. The investigator assumes that the Group 1 subjects (inpatients) are more seriously disabled than Group 2 (outpatients) and hypothesizes that, as a result, Group 1 will give significantly more C' responses and more MOR responses. How should the data be analyzed?

Although C' and MOR answers occur infrequently among nonpatients, they do occur much more often among depressed subjects. Thus, a parametric test, such as t, could be used. Conversely, both C' and MOR are not interpretively meaningful unless they exceed critical cutoff scores, therefore a nonparametric categorical approach might be more appropriate. In addition, depressed subjects are notorious for giving brief records, consequently it may be important to consider the R variable when conducting the analysis. Finally, it may be worthwhile to consider combining the two dependent variables into a single score ($SumC'$+MOR) to account for the possibility that some seriously disabled patients may give substantially more of one but not the other. Under optimal circumstances, an investigator will do all of these analyses, but none should be selected unless there is a research logic indicating that each is potentially worthwhile.

It is also important to emphasize that none of the findings resulting from the variety of approaches to the data will be truly meaningful unless the basic *descriptive statistics* are included in the published results. All too often, investigators seek to present their conclusions rather simplistically by providing only the data of the statistical manipulations and casually omitting the basic descriptive data. This should never be the case!

CATEGORICAL ANALYSES

Sometimes it is best to select the method of data analysis in the context of how the test is interpreted. The example concerning C' and MOR answers is a good illustration. Both usually have low frequencies, even in groups of depressed subjects, and although not stated in the general hypothesis, the pivotal issue is whether the inpatient depressive group includes *more records* in which interpretively critical cutoffs are exceeded for either variable. Thus, whereas a t or F test for the means might be appropriate, a categorical approach for both variables might be much more meaningful.

It could be argued that the logic for this suggestion is obvious because both C' and MOR tend to have lopsided J-curve distributions, but in many studies the same suggestion is logical for variables that usually have a much more normal distribution of scores. Assume for instance, that the results from a manipulation design involving two groups of 40 subjects each show that the mean $X+\%$ for the experimental group is .70 (SD = .15), whereas the mean for the control group is .79 (SD = .12). Most parametric tests applied to such findings will yield p values that are "significant" if traditional p cutoff values are applied, yet are the results sufficiently meaningful to impress those who interpret Rorschach test data routinely? The answer is probably not, because both means fall within the commonly expected average range. However, if the data are categorized in the context of interpretation, the results might be more impressive.

For instance, using the the interpretive context and identifying the frequency of subjects who have $X+\%$'s in the four categories of (a) 80% or higher, (b) 70% to 79%, (c) 60% to 69%, and (d) less than 60% the yield might be:

Category	> 79%	70% 79%	60%–69%	< 60%
Experimental N	1	24	14	6
Control N	6	28	11	0

The means suggest that both groups will have many subjects in the second category (70%–79%), which is true, but an examination of the frequency distributions reveals that it tends to be the outliers with $X+\%$ values greater than 79% in the control group and less than 60% in the experimental group that are creating the appearance of a "significant differences" when, in fact, 39 of the 45 subjects from each group have $X+\%$ scores that fall in Categories b and c. In this case, a nonparametric categorical analysis will not yield "significant" results and the findings are interpretively much more meaningful.

On the other hand, the categorical frequencies in this study might be:

Category	> 79%	70%–79%	60%–69%	< 60%
Experimental N	0	21	18	6
Control N	7	30	8	0

In this illustration, the groups are much more discrete and a categorical analysis will yield significant results that support the findings from the parametric analysis. The interpretation of the differences will include appropriate mention of the outliers in Categories a and d but also emphasize the differences that exist between the groups for Categories b and c.

One of the most important issues related to the use of multiple analyses, and the inclusion of a categorical method is that the composite of findings provides the investigator with a wealth of information from which to draw conclusions and make recommendations. Researchers who fail to take advantage of multiple methods of analysis with Rorschach data risk deceiving themselves and those to whom their findings are presented.

CATEGORICAL CORRELATIONS

As noted earlier, data concerning many Rorschach scores that have normal or near normal distributions are often addressed more meaningfully in a categorical model. This is also often the case when a correlational approach to data is employed. The bulk of contemporary Rorschach research does not include the use of correlations, but some studies are designed in a way that a correlational approach is preferable or even a necessity. For example, it is often important to determine the possible relationship between one Rorschach variable and another. This is especially important when new scores or scales are being formulated. Obviously, correlations are required is most test–retest studies, especially those in which issues of retest reliability or temporal consistency are involved.

Correlations represent an important statistical method, but unfortunately, it is not uncommon in Rorschach research for relationships between Rorschach variables, or between Rorschach variables and non-Rorschach variables to be misinterpreted because of the application and interpretation of standard Pearson product-moment (PPM) correlations. For the most part, the PPM is a very robust statistic and procedure. Its calculational format can even serve as the calculational procedures of other correlational statistics such as Spearman's rho when ties in ranks are excessive (Snodgrass, 1977) or in a point-biserial correlation ($rbis$). However, the efficacy of PPM is predicated on assessing the degree of association of two somewhat normally distributed variables. The robustness of PPM is even strong enough to overcome fair deviations from normally like high skewness or extremes in kurtosis. A prime concern in evaluating the suitablity of using PPM in a straight-forward manner is the underlying dimensional characteristic of continuity of the two variables being studied.

There are two basic considerations regarding the use of the PPM: Are the variables fundamentally continuous or discrete? And, is their underlying parent population continuous or discrete? Gender is a discrete variable. A subject is either in one category or another with no values in between. Conversely, the $X+\%$ or Lambda can be considered to be continuous, both in obtained samples and in underlying dimensionality. These distinctions between discrete and continuous require careful study as they can often affect which of several measures of association of the family of correlations might be most appropriate.

For instance, it is appropriate to use the PPM correlation for *most* Rorschach variables that have been categorized and are being studied with regard to their test–retest reliability. However, the use of the PPM is not appropriate for extremely non-normally distributed variables even though some categorization has occurred. Possibly the best illustration of this type of misapplication of the PPM concerns Vista responses. In most samples, the majority of protocols will have no Vista answers and categorization will involve a simple dichotomization into the "absence of" or "presence of" Vista. Because most protcols will fall into the "absence of" category, the correlation coefficient becomes spuriously elevated and tends to conceal those instances in which Vista may not have occurred in Test 1 but does appear in Test 2. Unfortunately, there is no ready statistical alternative for dealing with variables that have extremely non-normal distributions such as Vista. Probably the best solution to the problem is simply to present the data in a tabular or graphical form so that the reader can easily evaluate obvious conclusions warranted by the data. For some samples, this same procedure may be more useful for variables such as *SumT*, *m*, and *SumY* and most of the content categories.

It also may be misleading to use PPM correlation with continuous ap-pearing ratio score scales for statistical reasons. The efficacy of the PPM correlation in describing an association depends on the nature of the score distributions and the nature of the association being studied. For example, consider two variables such as Animal content and Animal movement, both skewed but in opposite directions, content being skewed to the right, *FM* being skewed to the left. Being markedly skewed can happen rather easily with many Rorshach variables. A PPM correlation on these two oppositely skewed variables would be depressed by the deviation from normality and the lack of similiarity in distribution form. If the two distributions are con-verted to normality, or at least the same shape, by some score transformation the PPM correlation would increase. How much would the increase be? A good estimate would be provided by converting the two variables to ranks or categories and calculating a rho correlation. Thus, for this situation of potential error due to distribution, it is possible to have three correlations. One would be a PPM correlation calculated on just the original raw data, depressed by whatever degree of differentness in the two variables' distributions. The second would be a rho correlation estimating a corrected estimate of the true relationship when score distributions were transformed. The third would be a new PPM correlation on the transformed scores also reflecting a more accurate version of the true relationship given any limits or distortions imposed by the transformation itself.

None of the three are completely correct in and of themselves, and yet, all reflect some truth. Which should be selected as the one for simplifying the statistical reduction into a statement about the relationship? The answer to that question depends on a judgment of the degree of departure from normality of the original two variables.

It seems reasonable to suggest that when dealing with variables that have a known history of such skewness, the extra correlation coefficients (rho and the corrected PPM) should be checked as a matter of course for discrepancy. At the very least, a bivariate plot of the two variables should be instructive and informative. Simply assuming that a PPM correlation on raw scores that are not in a J-shaped distribution is statistically appropiate, and proceeding to interpret the findings as though near-normality exists is not good practice and should be avoided.

There is also the issue of the continuity of the underlying dimensions of the variables. The development of several correlation coefficients and techniques reflects the long-standing concern about the appropriateness of the correct correlational procedure for different scoring distributions. Some of these approaches are illustrated in Table 11.1.

As noted in Table 11.1, if the two variables are both essentially continuous, the standard PPM correlation is the choice. This is usually the first choice

TABLE 11.1
Common Types of Correlations for Combinations of
Dimensionality of Variables Being Associated

| | *Y Variable Dimensionality* | | |
	Continuous	*Artificial Dichotomy*	*True Dichotomy*
X variable dimension			
continuous	$r$xy		
Artificial dichotomy	$r$bis	$r$tet	
		ϕ(Phi)	
		Cramer C	
True dichotomy	$r$pt.bis	ϕbis	ϕ(Phi)

decision, the one most researchers are most familar with and the one most commonly found in research reports. Some Rorschach variables can be treated this way, but the PPM cannot be casually applied to all Rorschach variables.

Difficult Issues Concerning Rorschach Data

Two problems regarding the appropriate selection of a correlational technique often confront Rorschach researchers. First, whereas essentially all variables are continuous, many tend to have very narrow ranges. For instance, in most small or modest size samples, the values for many variables such as Texture (*SumT*), Reflections (*Fr+rF*), Inanimate Movement (*m*), Vista (*SumV*), Food (*Fd*), Personal (PER), and so on, will have ranges as limited as 0 to 1, 0 to 2, or 0 to 3. Second, even though a variable may be continuous (such as Vista, Reflections, or Food), the interpretation is based on a dichotomous principle. Namely, the absence is expected and the presence of one or more is treated interpretively as the same. In other words, interpretively, they are dichotomous. Actuarially, it does not matter whether there two Texture answers, three Texture answers, or 10 Texture answers.

This same issue is evident for many variables with more extended score ranges, such as the *X+%* or the Egocentrity Index. Interpretively, an *X+%* of .70 is no different than an *X+%* of .78, and an Egocentricity Index of .26 is interpreted no differently than an Egocentricity Index of .18. They fall in the same interpretive category. Thus, in many instances, the Rorschach investigator probably should artificially dichotomize, trichomotomize, and so on, the data for some variables when a correlational approach seems essential. When this occurs, the statistical approach will depend mainly on the nature of the variables and the method of categorizing. Correlational techniques, just like all statistics, are tools to be used to obtain the most accurate picture of the data. In some instances, issues such as dichotomizing are handled easily, but in other cases the decisions about "what to do" are more knotty.

True Dichotomous Variables Versus Continuous Variables

When one or more of the variables are fundamentally continuous but are being treated as categorical, it is not appropriate to rely on variants of the PPM correlation. Instead, estimates must be used. Estimates often are not used because of the inability to carry the data further or be treated like PPM or a PPM variant correlation coefficient. Yet, the combinations of artificial categorization (in this case, dichotomizing, trichotomizing, etc.) with continuous variables requires special calculations.

When one variable is truly dichotomous and the other is continuous, the point-biserial correlation can be applied. For example, an investigator may be interested in the relationship between gender and scores for the Egocentricity Index. Although a specialized formula for $r$pt.bis exists and can be found in most any graduate statistics text, it can be thought of as another specialized version of the PPM correlation with a specialized data input. In this case, the truly dichotomous variable (gender) will have only two values, and the continuous variable (Egocentricity Index) will have a variety of values. However, the difference in the distributions of the two variables exacts a toll. It is not possible to have a perfect correlation between a dichotomous and a continuous variable.

Artificially Dichotomous Versus Continuous

When a continuous variable (variable X) is to be correlated with a continuous variable that has been artificially dichotomized (variable Y), the most appropriate method is the biserial r ($rbis$). For example, an investigator may want to correlate the distribution of scores on for the Isolation Index (variable X) with Texture ($SumT$) answers (variable Y) that are collapsed into two catagories based on the simple presence or absence of Texture. In this case, the $r$bis is calculated with the following formula:

$$ r\text{bis} = \frac{MX1 - MX2}{sX} \left(\frac{pq}{b} \right) $$

where: $MX1$ = the Mean of their X scores (the continuous scores) for subjects in first category of Y (the dichotomous scores)
$MX2$ = the Mean of their X scores for subjects in second category of Y (the dichotomous variable)
sX = the standard deviation for all subjects on X (the continuous scores)
p = the proportion of subjects in first category on Y
q is $1 - p$
b is the ordinate of a normal curve corresponding to the proportion, p

To test the Null hypothesis that $r$bis = 0, a z statistic is used:

$$ z = \frac{b \ rbis}{\sqrt{\frac{pq}{N}}} $$

where: N = size of the total sample

A z greater than 1.96, or 2.56, indicates significance. Biserial r is not a statistic that can be extended further. Actually, it is not even a good correlation analog. The range of values of $r$bis can be from plus to minus infinity! Thus, a correlation coefficient greater than 1.00 is possible unless you are certain that the underlying data that have been dichotomized are essentially normally distributed, which, of course, is not a given for much Rorschach data.

True or Artificial Dichotomous Versus True or Artificial Dichotomous

The most common problem facing Rorschach researchers and the issue of correlations is the situation in which distribution continuity, or the lack thereof, gives rise to some confusion about interpretation or lack of precision in statistical inference. Some scores/scales can seem continuous, however, as noted earlier, they are in reality more categorical in their impact on interpretation and in their score distribution. For instance, the $X+\%$ implies that values of 0 to 100 are possible but that is not the case because of R. Each of the integers $.x1$, $.x2$, $.x3$, and $.x4$ (such as .51, .52, .53, and .54) are impossible to derive in a 20 response protocol.

In this context, the PPM is probably not the best approach, but if the scores are regarded as fundamentally categorical, and even though the categorization or dichotomization maybe somewhat abitrary, there are ways to treat them statistically. This issue is possibly most important for those investigating the temporal consistency (reliability) of a variable in a retest study. For example, Exner (1978, 1986, 1993) often reported very substantial retest correlations for Vista in both short-term and long-term retest studies. They usually fall in a range from .90 upward. Do these high correlations really mean that Vista is related to some very stable characteristic? The answer is not necessarily, because the high correlations are created because of a huge number of zero values.

Some statistical purists might argue that if both variables in a correlation matrix are artificially dichotomized, the choice becomes limited to a tetracloric r ($r$tet). Use of $r$tet in this case would be to get an estimate of the PPM for the two variables if they had not been dichotomized. The logic for this sort of operation is hard to fathom in the light of the extreme ardous computation of this statistic (McNemar, 1969). It is for this reason that the tetracloric r remains a rarely used statistic.

The phi coefficient (ϕ) is probably a much better choice than the tetracloric r assuming that both variables have a two-valued (dichotomous) discrete dimensionality. ϕ may not be labeled as a correlation coefficient, but it serves to closely approximate a PPM correlation. Some statisticians will argue about what is a truly dichotomous variable and what is not. A purist will argue that true dichotomy must be restricted to variables for which there is no hint of a continuum. Gender is an example of a truly dichotomous variable in this sense. But empirical findings often can be used to argue that a technically continuous variable such as Vista is really dichotomous.

The phi coefficient is calculated using data coded from a 2 × 2 table in four cells, a, b, c, and d, such as shown here:

		Variable Y	
Category		1	2
Variable X	1	a	b
	2	c	d

The phi coefficient is computed using the cell entries from the 2 × 2 table:

$$\phi = \frac{bc - ad}{\sqrt{(a+b)(c+d)(a+c)(b+d)}}$$

The value for ϕ is evaluated for significance by converting to a chi-square:

$$\text{chi–square} = N(\phi)^2 \text{ with } df = 1$$

Whereas this familar formula may look different from the PPM formula, in reality they can yield the same outcome evaluation. However, it is important to remember that all of the scores appropriate for this ϕ are dichotomous and are coded as 1's and 0's. If the values for two dichotomous variables are transformed into standard scores and a PPM correlation calculated, the same result will occur. However, this equivalence of formulation should not be taken casually as a license to artificially dichotomize scores. The procedure of subdividing a distribution of dubious parametric quality into a median split to get a dichotomy is fraught with problems because it will probably distort some underlying assumptions. For example, using a median split for variables such as FM or $SumC$ makes no sense. Thus, it is important to issue a strong caution concerning the dichotomization procedure. Artificially dichotomizing a variable without regard to its fundamental nature is not appropriate. This process was much more common in the days before the advent of computers and calculation time on the mechanical machines or pen and paper was a significant consideration.

Another potentially worthwhile approach to dichtomized data is the Cramer C Coefficient, which is analogous to the phi (Castellan & Siegal, 1988). It has also been referred to as the Cramer V (Howell, 1992). As phi is applicable only to 2 × 2 tables, Cramer devised a different solution that is not limited only to 2 × 2 formats; the formula is:

$$C = \frac{\sqrt{\chi^2}}{N(L-1)}$$

where: N is the sample size
       L is the smaller or either the number of rows or the number of
       columns
       χ^2 is a standard χ^2 conducted category by category

This statistic has the advantage of not being limited to 2 × 2 formats, although it is the equivalent of ϕ when L is 2. It does offer a more simple interpretive schema than ϕ values that range upward, similar to F values. The C values resemble correlation range values, .00 to 1.00. It is not a correlational statistic but it does resemble the correlational statistic value range. Cramer's C is based on the χ^2. Thus, if a χ^2 is significant, C will also be significant, but like χ^2, it has the same problem with cells that have small expected values. Thus, its suitability is questionable in some cases such as the test–retest situation in which a variables will have a very large number of zero values. Although the C provides only minimal information about the association between dichotomized or trichotomized variables, it may be the only way to obtain an association estimate for certain conditions, such as the trichotomization for a variable such as Texture. Obviously, the C coefficient cannot be used to obtain inferences about the amount of variance accounted for as is done in the typical correlation by squaring the correlation coefficient.

There are other forms where the raw score variable distributions are truly discrete and with more than two categories (polytomies) involved in which multiple categories are created but reflect the underlying distribution. The Contingency Coefficient and Cramer's Phi coefficient are two forms that deal with the same general inquiry as correlation in determining significance of a relation between two variables with multiple categories. The Contingency Coefficient is like $r$pt.bis in that it cannot take on a full range of correlationlike values and its value is dependent on the number of categories involved. Cramer's Phi does not depend on the number of categories and looks more like a correlation coefficient in its range of values.

Whatever statistical choice concerning correlations that an investigator selects, the selection must be based on two principles: the nature of the distribution for the variable(s) to be studied and the use of the tactic that will yield the most accurate picture of the data. If these two rules are applied conscientiously, the results will be the most meaningful.

THE ISSUE OF DIFFERENCES IN R

One issue that has emerged time and again in the history of the Rorschach technique concerns differences among subjects in protocol length or variation in R. This variability complicates the researcher's ability to compare

Rorschach scores among subjects, especially when the scores are frequency of production scores. Specifically, should R be allowed to vary freely, or should some method be devised for controlling R in some fashion? This issue has been raised both in terms of the diagnostic interpretation of individual protocols and in a number of research contexts. Cronbach (1949) suggested controlling for R in research by scoring only a fixed number of responses, artificially equating groups on R in some fashion, or performing some sort of transformation on the scores before statistical analysis. Fisk and Baughman (1953) found the R had a complex and often nonlinear relationship to a number of other Rorschach variables in a study where R varied across a very wide range. Indeed, part of the rationale for development of the Holtzman Inkblot Technique was to hold R constant in all administrations (Holtzman, 1978). Issues relating to R emerged again in the Perry and Kinder (1990) review of the Rorschach malingering literature. These authors suggested that lack of control over R both within and between studies may be responsible to some degree for the conflicting data in this area.

In 1990, a symposium on the effects of varying protocol length on research results was held at the meeting of the Society for Personality Assessment. Lipgar (1992) discussed these issues from a historical perspective and from within the context of the many other complexities of the Rorschach technique. While noting that controlling for R in some fashion would make the resulting data "neater" in a variety of ways, Lipgar concluded that variability in R often yields valuable information and that R should remain free to vary for interpreting individual Rorschach protocols.

Meyer (1992) reached a different conclusion following a review of 17 factor analytic studies of the Rorschach. He found that variation of R accounted for approximately 50% of the explainable variance in raw Rorschach scores across these studies. In addition, Meyer suggested that R seems to have much greater importance than we have given it credit for having, that we should explore exactly what R means in more systematic research, and that we should investigate whether or not an R controlled form of Rorschach administration might be beneficial.

Kinder (1992) argued that R does have interpretive significance in the evaluation of individual Rorschach protocols and that important data might be lost if R were controlled in the clinical use of the Rorschach. He suggested, however, that some method of controlling R in some research situations may result in data that are more clearly interpretable.

Exner (1992) argued that the data and recommendations of Cronbach (1949) and of Fisk and Baughman (1953) are no longer sufficient arguments for controlling for R because current Rorschach methodology does not allow for the wide variation in R that was possible several decades ago. Exner presented data from four different populations showing that whereas R was correlated with selected Rorschach variables at a statistically significant level, the relative magnitude of the relationships was quite small in most all instances. He concluded that, for the most part, R is *not* likely to be relevant in the statistical analysis of most variables. Exner also suggested when an investigator is in doubt concerning the possible effects of R, that the data be analyzed twice, once with no control for R and once controlling R in relation to the critical variables.

Other information and data are available that support Exner's contention that it is not necessary to control for R in most instances. For example, brief Rorschach protocols have been found to be invalid and, therefore, should not be used in data analyses. More standardized instructions have resulted in a much more limited range of R, with approximately two thirds of all protocols containing between 17 and 30 responses (Exner, 1992). Finally, the adult normative data in the Comprehensive System (Exner, 1993) indicate that the mean R is almost identical across several patient groups and a group of nonpatients. Taken as a whole, these data suggest controlling for R is not necessary in most research studies. Exner (1992) and Kinder (1992) made some suggestions regarding specific ways to control for R in those situations where it seems most appropriate. For instance, Exner suggested that the use of percentage or proportion scores, or logarithmic or scaled score transformations are all inappropriate methods of controlling for R, and instead, encourages the use of partialing techniques, at least for parametric variables. Kinder described a method of equating groups for R prior to data analysis, which has been used in one study concerning malingering (Perry & Kinder, 1992).

The Issue of R Versus Response Complexity

Viglione and his associates (Cheyette, 1992; Kates, 1994; Morgan & Viglione, 1992) suggested that the issue of handling R is more complex than has been indicated in the past. They have been exploring response complexity by using some traditional measures of response stereotypy, guardedness, and richness (S. J. Beck, A. G. Beck, Levitt, & Molish, 1961; Exner, 1993; Schafer, 1954). They attempted to measure this construct by using variables such as the number of Blends, the frequencies for $DQ+$, Lambda, PSV, Zf, A%, and the total number of secondary contents in an experimental formula that yields a score they have called *Complexity Composite*.

The underlying hypothesis for this work is that response complexity provides a better base from which to make predictions than does R. For instance, will the SCZI, CDI, or DEPI have a greater "hit" rate if protocol complexity is considered. Some of their results are quite interesting. For example, initial findings suggest that the WSum6 may be more closely associated with schizophrenic thought disorders when Blends, $DQ+$, and secondary content are considered.

DEVELOPING NEW SCORES OR SCALES

Most of the newer Rorschach scores and scales have occurred in the development of the Comprehensive System (1978, 1986, 1991) or from the work of those applying a modern psychoanalytic object relations or a developmental approach (Blatt, Brenneis, Schimek, & Glick, 1976; Urist, 1977), separation–individuation (Coonerty, 1986; Hirshberg, 1989), and primitive defenses (Cooper, Perry, & Arnow, 1988; P. Lerner & H. Lerner, 1980). The yield from the Comprehensive System derives from three areas: (a) content variables, developed to address specific interpretations (MOR, COP); (b) weighted sum indices which to measure various characteristics (Isolation Index, ISO; Weighted Sum of Six Special Scores, WSUM6; Intellectualization Index; Hypervigilance Index, HVI); and (c) diagnostic actuarial indices with cutoffs (Suicide Constellation, S-CON; Schizophrenia Index, SCZI; Depression Index, DEPI; Coping Deficit Index, CDI; HVI). Most of the psychoanalytically oriented investigators have developed complex interactive, multivariable scores/scales based on theories of object relations.

Whereas the multivariable scales in the Comprehensive System rely on a combining of scores for individual variables, the psychoanalytic based scales often rate a single response along one or more dimensions. Other examples of new scores/scales include those of Gacono and Meloy (1988) from their work with antisocial personalities, and Perry and Viglione (1991), who have used a different derivation strategy in developing the Ego Impairment Index (EII). It incorporates both the weighted sum and interactive approach.

Selecting Variables for Multivariable Scales

Thoughtful selection of the variables to be included in a multivariable scale is critically important. Choosing variables to incorporate in a scale, based on both theoretical and empirical concerns, greatly reduces the probability of Type I error. In other words, identifying a subgroup of variables to be tested as potential components to new scales limits the probability of including variables that in fact do not add to the intended discriminations and do not cross-validate (Cronbach, 1949).

Multivariable scales take advantage of random error, and because of this, they are especially likely to weaken in replications. This common problem is called *shrinkage*, the high probability that multivariable solutions will not discriminate well in replication unless static group effects are controlled and original *N*'s are quite large. An example of this is the original S-CON (Exner & Wylie, 1977) in the Comprehensive System, which was developed using a discriminant function analysis for a sample of 59 subjects. The "hit" rate for the original scale was about 80%, but when a cross-validation sample of 101 new subjects was tested in 1984, the hit rate dropped to about 60%.

It was only through the addition of one variable (MOR) and a change in the cutoff values for another variable (Egocentricity Index) that the hit rate was improved in the cross-validation sample to 80%.

In addition to Type I errors, another problem exists that was identified by Meehl (1990) as the "crud factor" (p. 204); that is, practically all variables in psychopathology (and other domains) are correlated with all others at some level. The crud factor is especially problematic in that designs are cross-sectional, or in other words, essentially correlational. In such designs latent effects cannot be easily identified and alternative hypotheses cannot satisfactorily be ruled out. Thus, independent replications and extensions with appropriate contrasts and controls are essential. Furthermore, discriminant validity relative to theoretically unrelated Rorschach variables is essential. Finally, more rigorous tests of the effect size must be demonstrated. It is not enough to uncover statistically significant between-group differences of limited practical import. Rather, appreciable hit rates and strength of effect estimators should be established before a variable is suitable for application to individual cases.

Empirically Derived Scales

Most new scales are initially developed by applying a discriminant function analysis, a regression model, or a factorial model to a discrete and homogenized sample. Subsequently, an actuarial cutoff score is selected. Actuarial cutoff scores are especially susceptible to poor cross-validation, as noted with the original S-CON in the Comprehensive System. A review of the work concerning the Comprehensive System (Exner, 1978, 1986, 1991, 1993) with actuarial cutoff scales is instructive in this context. Exner repeatedly modified variables and cutoff scores in his various scales through rigorous, statistical analyses and replications with large samples. Without such care, one can expect considerable shrinkage, particularly with more complex empirically derived scales.

For example, the risk of error in formulating cutoffs for scales is evident in the developmental history of the SCZI and DEPI. Although both were carefully developed and tested, experience and research led Exner (1991) to recognize that the SCZI was too liberal and the DEPI too conservative. More recent modifications appear to have diminished these earlier problems. More recently, developed scales in the Comprehensive System that have not been subject to independent verification are the CDI and the HVI. Although developed on seemingly representative samples, additional data collected for cross-validation purposes may very well lead to future change in either or both of these scales despite their apparent strengths.

An additional concern is the use of cutoffs in these actuarial scales. In the actuarial scales, a point is assigned if the value of a subcomponent variable is in the problematic direction relative to some cutoff score. Although it is controversial (Cronbach, 1949; Exner, 1991), it can be argued that the use of such a dichotomy is artificial and that valuable information is lost. On the other hand, experience has shown (Exner, 1991, 1993) that most of the interpretive weight of Rorschach variables is often associated with a small range of values. Taking these issues into consideration, Exner typically initiated his construction of these indices with various techniques that assume a linear model (factor analytic, discriminant function, and regression) analysis, to identify suitable, potential, subcomponent variables. Afterward, he searched through distributions to find optimal cutting points. In addition, he empirically identified the algorithm and decision rules that maximize hit rates and minimize false-positive results with appropriate contrast groups. Obviously, to avoid false-positive results, this approach is dependent on the large samples that Exner collected. Because this whole procedure is based on maximizing hit rates, it makes sense to establish cutoffs with the final score. On the other hand, the question is still open to other researchers about whether some weighting of variables, as in the WSUM6, might marginally improve accuracy. To his credit, Exner (1991) interpreted this cutoff score along a continuum of increasingly degree of certainty. These probabilities are in turn based on empirical work.

An example of a different strategy is the method adopted by Perry and Viglione (1991) to construct the EII. To address the variable selection problem, they identified a subgroup of variables with both empirical and theoretical support. By selecting only five, all with substantial previous support, they limited the possibility of basing results on chance error. To reduce shrinkage, the EII was developed on one sample and validated on a second sample. Furthermore, the "crud factor" was minimized by using a predictive rather than cross-sectional design.

Other studies also have used predictive designs, providing sturdier data for their scales (Cooper, Perry, & O'Connell, 1991). Perry, Viglione, and Braff (1992) extended their findings to other groups. Unfortunately, these extensions and the overall sample size are rather limited. A statistical issue with this scale is that it is based on factor analysis so that may be distorted by skew and non-normality. Risking such distortion is unfortunately the alternative to losing potentially valuable information with the nonparametric, cutoff approach used by Exner. If the EII purports to measure psychopathology across different diagnoses, a major validation effort should be undertaken to demonstrate its association with level of disturbance across the range of psychopathology from schizophrenic and psychotic to borderline, neurotic, and optimal functioning. It is only through such replication, and with larger samples than Perry and Viglione utilized, that shrinkage can be satisfactorily addressed and scales validly modified. Accordingly, it would be premature to adopt this scale as a measure of severity of internalized psychopathology across all types of subjects.

Similar reservations can be applied to the Meloy (1988) and Gacono (1988; Gacono, Meloy, & Heaven, 1990) scores, despite their careful empirical work and theoretical considerations. These are individual scores rather than composite ones, so that the danger of shrinkage is lessened. Nonetheless, they are developed from small samples and require replication with larger samples. More importantly, given that they are individual scores, discriminant validity must be established through systematic collection of contrast samples.

The Psychoanalytic Based Scales

During the past 20 years, there have been a number of scales based on psychoanalytic notions of object relations (Blatt et al., 1976; Urist, 1977), symbiosis and separation–individuation (Coonerty, 1986, Hirshberg, 1989), and primitive defense mechanisms (Cooper et al., 1988; P. Lerner & H. Lerner, 1980). More often than not, they score responses along multiple, interactive categories and often apply logically based continua. As a result, significant results in well-designed studies lend support to underlying psychoanalytic theory and the scale itself. They differ from scales with empirical construction strategies in that the parameters of the complex scales are based directly on psychoanalytic principles.

The many studies concerning these scales have lent validity to these principles, particularly with adult borderline subjects. Furthermore, results from these studies have advanced analysis of content themes and also movement, human representational, and interactive responses.

Within this approach, however, there is a basic flaw that varies in its effects on studies. The theoretical basis of these studies, for example object relations or separation–individuation theory, are quite complex and sophisticated ideas. The typical procedure is to apply these complex theories to the Rorschach without full respect for the limitations of the test and Exner's plea that "it's only an inkblot" (1980, p. 562). The test cannot and does not make the fine distinctions that these theories would demand. As Mayman (1977) indicated, the test reveals fragments of visual fantasy rather than full-blown reverie with more complex plot sequences. In this regard, the Rorschach cannot be relied on to reproduce the complexities and subtleties of the theories as we might prefer. In a sense, this tactic resembles the use of the Myers–Briggs scale to carry the full weight of Jung's typology of "a theory waiting for a measure to happen." It is as if theoreticians are treating the Rorschach as a full size truck and trailer carrying the full weight of their theories rather than as it is—a Volkswagen.

This tactic leads to a number of problems in these scales. First, raters are asked to search out and discriminate subtle differences that might occur in real relationships but not in Rorschach representations. In doing so, they emphasize responses that rarely, if ever, occur. Unfortunately, research reports on these scales rarely report adequate descriptive data and it is difficult to know how many responses each variable is based on. One recent article (Gacono, 1988), incorporating a number of these scales, indicates that many of these variables may be based on few responses. Indeed, a number of scales yielded scores of zero for many records.

It may be elegant theoretically to include rare distinctions in these scales, but it does not serve the scientific end of developing a meaningful and effective scale. Furthermore, authors also make the mistake of extending optimistic conclusions to these rare variables. In other words, if one is not careful about the distributions of subcomponent variables, one may conclude that there is support, for example, for intestinal organ responses as a measure of "orally-based boundary disturbances" when there was only one such response in the hypothetical sample.

In making fine distinctions among few responses, one also risks the danger of not sampling adequately so that the final score is unstable. In other words, if one only considers a few responses, say only M responses, in deriving a scale of interpersonal or object relations, one may not sample sufficiently from the possible array of Rorschach representations of human experiences on the test. In failing to sample adequately, an investigator does not allow the opportunity of the idiosyncratic error variances contributing to each response to cancel one another out.

A more defensible, statistical practice is to sample from as many responses as possible to adequately capture the target construct. Such an approach may entail a different understanding of the Rorschach response. Hirshberg (1989) attempted to do so by considering multiple categories and addressing both the nature of the Rorschach image and its elaboration. Urist's (1977) approach also attempts to widen the number of responses considered. If one makes the mistake of accepting an M response as a veridical and complete representation of an internal psychic structure, one may conclude that one response is enough, but that claim may reflect wishful thinking rather than a scientific fact.

If classical item theory is applied to the Rorschach, it is impossible to avoid recognition that each Rorschach response contains both true and error variance. The response is a trace or footprint of multiple psychological processes originating in the internal world and perceptions of the subject. To eliminate error variance one needs to maximize the number of responses so that these theoretically unrelated error variances cancel one another out and the trace appears in its fullest form across a number of responses. In a hypothetical object relations scale, a researcher would include all responses that contain any fragment of human experience and would make broad, reliable distinctions rather than subtle but error prone ones.

Accordingly, the Rorschach may be better suited to addressing broad dimensions rather than fine distinctions as it is called on to do in some scales, based on complex theories. A similar approach has been taken in behavioral psychology, in that when target behaviors are of extremely low frequencies, the response class is widened to obtain more stable samples.

A basic knowledge of the Rorschach and scrutiny of the available descriptive data (e.g. Fritsch & Holstrom, 1990; Gacono, 1990) on the theory-based scales suggests that often their distributions are highly skewed. Some of these scales (e.g., Adaptive Regression Complex; Holt, 1977) rely on multiplications, another technique that is likely to increase skew. Skew violates assumptions in parametric statistics and often distorts correlations and Type I and Type II error rates. The highly skewed values and outliers inordinately effect resultant correlations so that positive findings may derive from a few data points, even if there is no effect for the majority of subjects. Cooper et al.'s (1988) use of nonparametric, Spearman rank-order correlations attempts to correct this error by minimizing the influence of skew. In fact, because many of these scales incorporate many variables, researchers are often induced to conduct many significance tests, thus increasing probability of Type I error beyond acceptable levels, or in other cases failing to compare the total number of significant results to the number of likely false-positive results. Furthermore, the strength of effect for these scales is often very weak and exaggerated in research report discussions.

Overall, the research in this group of scales has basically supported modern psychoanalytic theory. This is most likely due to the thoughtful translation of psychoanalytic theory to reliably scorable Rorschach dimensions. However, to evaluate the usefulness of these scales, it is essential that authors present descriptive data of subcomponents. Magnitude of effects are routinely presented in correlational analyses and are typically modest. And, because of this limitation, these scales are not suitable for the routine evaluation of individual cases. They are, however, more appropriate when used as psychoanalytic research tools.

A RECOMMENDATION FOR PARSIMONY

More consideration of parsimony would be helpful in the development of new scales. On a general level, there are hundreds of Rorschach codes in usage, so that one should have a good reason to add to this array. Accordingly, any new scales that are offered should add something new, something beyond what can be derived from previously available, simpler scores.

A more parsimonious view suggests that it is not appropriate to claim support for a complex theory when a more simple one is sufficient. There are simple ways to address this issue. First, it should be demonstrated through hierarchical regression, partialing, covariance, blocking, or preferably design controls that a new scale predicts more variance than available measures of severity of disturbance, such as $X-\%$, WSUM6, and $M-$.

Subcomponent Validity and Weights

From a statistical point of view, one major technical problem in developing composite scales is the setting of weights for various components. In other words, how do you determine that on a scale of object relations that mutual, positive interaction gets a weighting of 3 points whereas a mere pair only gets 1 point. A common practice is to assign weights logically based on theoretical notions. For instance, Hirshberg (1989) arbitrarily assigned weights of 4 to primitive level and integrity compromised responses and 1 to socialized and integrity retained. Similarly, Blatt et al. (1976) assigned a 1 for no action, 2 for unmotivated action, 3 for reactive action, and 4 for intentional action in the category of content to account for motivation of action in their weighting of increasing integration in object relations. It is important to recognize that these weights are based on rank ordering and are ordinal scales. When they produce positive results, which seems to be the case, they support the underlying theories. However, weights should really be assigned by incorporating empirical considerations. Theoretical considerations are best applied to select variables but not to weigh them.

For omnibus scales, that is, scales that are meant to measure a dimension across all types of individuals or all levels of pathology, the sample used to design the scale must represent the variable at all levels of the human continuum. Otherwise, the scales are subject to considerable shrinkage when applied to new types of samples. Accordingly, large samples are necessary. Linear regression, logistic regression, discriminant function, and factor analyses are probably the best techniques to consider, depending on the objective and assumption violations. It is also important to point out that in these techniques, the individual weighting (beta weights or factor coefficients), if they are recalculated, are rather unstable from study to study, even if the overall amount of variance predicted is relatively stable (Cohen, 1990). Because of violations of normality, curvilinear relationships among variables, and heteroscedasticity, logistic regression may be preferable. Unlike other methods, it has fewer assumptions. To explore this instability or shrinkage, coefficients need to be derived from one sample and replicated on others as Perry (Perry & Viglione, 1991) and Exner (1985, 1991) routinely did in deriving actuarial indices.

The Validity of Subcomponents

The discussion of the selection and distribution of subcomponent variables leads to the issue of how to evaluate the validity of subcomponents. This issue is ignored or only partially presented. Even before addressing the issue of validity, it is necessary to demonstrate adequate interscorer reliability for the decisions that go into identifying responses. Beyond this basic issue of scorer reliability, the validity of individual components should be considered.

Does each subcomponent demonstrate the expected association with the criteria? In some studies one component may account for much of the predictive power, yet some authors will extend it to the composite variables and claim support for an underlying theory. A direct examination of subcomponent versus overall score correlations or contingency tables would go a long way to allay these concerns. Ideally, all subcomponents should contribute unique variance, that is, variance beyond what is provided by other subcomponents. Although such requirements make sense for the statistical issues involved in regression equations, that may not be suitable for most Rorschach variables, mainly because of the small distributions for many variables. Thus, it may be necessary to include redundancies.

Nonetheless, caution should be exercised when selecting final subcomponents of a new scale. Including excessive subcomponents simply to make a scale longer is foolish, but if by including more items the valid of the scale is improved by reducing the amount of error variance relative to true variance, the tactic is appropriate. The decision should be based on sturdy empirical findings.

One major problem in subcomponent analysis is the range of the subcomponent distributions that includes many zero values. Accordingly, significant findings may be based on few responses and from skew and outliers. A second critical issue is to demonstrate that the algorithms incorporated in complex scales are valid. In other words, does the decision to score by a specific criterion increase the association between a proposed scale and the characteristics that it purports to measure. This is an issue that can only be answered with large amounts of data, but ultimately they need to be addressed, and anyone developing a new score or scale must be aware of this necessity.

CONCLUSIONS

Rorschach data often are not easily handled by common statistical procedures. Some investigators tend to ignore this fact and apply whatever statistic is in vogue; others search out the statistic that will yield findings most supportive of a preconceived hypothesis. Neither of these tactics serves the purpose of science, and both tend to cloud the pool of knowledge concerning the Rorschach as it continues to accumulate. It is always important to remember that statistics are tools intended to aid the researcher in understanding a data set and drawing appropriate conclusions about it. Statistical procedures should not be abused or misused, and in some instances the astute researcher may decide that the data may be interpreted most easily without any statistical application.

REFERENCES

Beck, S. J., Beck, A. G., Levitt, E. E., & Molish, H. B. (1961). *Rorschach's test: Basic processes* (3rd ed.). New York: Grune & Stratton.

Blatt, S. J., Brenneis, C. B., Schimek, J. G., & Glick, M. (1976). Normal development and psychopathological impairment of the concept of the object on the Rorschach. *Journal of Abnormal Psychology, 85,* 364–373.

Castellan, N. J., & Siegal, S. (1988). *Nonparametric statistics for the behavioral sciences* (2nd ed.). New York: McGraw-Hill.

Cheyette, L. (1992). *The effects of examiner style on Rorschach test results of children with borderline psychopathology.* Unpublished doctoral dissertation, California School of Professional Psychology, San Diego.

Cohen, J. (1990). Things I have learned so far. *American Psychologist, 45,* 1304–1312.

Coonerty, S. (1986). An exploration of separation–individuation themes in the borderline personality. *Journal of Personality Assessment, 50,* 501–511.

Cooper, S. H., Perry, J. C., & Arnow, D. (1988). An empirical approach to the study of defense mechanisms: Reliability and preliminary validity of the Rorschach Defense Scales. *Journal of Personality Assessment, 52,* 187–203.

Cooper, S. H., Perry, C., & O'Connell, M. (1991). The Rorschach Defense Scales: II. Longitudinal perspectives. *Journal of Personality Assessment, 56,* 191–201.

Cronbach, L. J. (1949). Statistical methods applied to Rorschach scores: A review. *Psychological Bulletin, 46,* 393–429.

Exner, J. E., Jr. (1978). *The Rorschach: A comprehensive system: Vol. 2. Current research and advanced interpretation.* New York: Wiley.

Exner, J. E., Jr. (1980). But it's only an inkblot. *Journal of Personality Assessment, 44,* 562–577.

Exner, J. E., Jr. (1986). *The Rorschach: A comprehensive system: Vol. 1. Basic foundations* (2nd ed.). New York. Wiley.

Exner, J. E., Jr. (1991). *The Rorschach: A Comprehensive System: Vol. 2. Interpretation* (2nd ed.). New York: Wiley.

Exner, J. E., Jr. (1992). *R* in Rorschach research: A ghost revisited. *Journal of Personality Assessment, 58,* 245–251.

Exner, J. E., Jr. (1993). *The Rorschach: A comprehensive system: Vol. 1. Basic foundations* (3rd ed.). New York: Wiley.

Exner, J. E., & Wylie, J. (1977). Some Rorschach data concerning suicide. *Journal of Personality Assessment, 41,* 339–348.

Fisk, D. W., & Baughman, E. E. (1953). Relationship between Rorschach scoring categories and the total number of responses. *Journal of Abnormal and Social Psychology, 48,* 25–32.

Fritsch, R. C., & Holstrom, R. N. (1990). Assessing object representations as a continuous variable: A modification of the Concept of the Object on the Rorschach Scale. *Journal of Personality Assessment, 55,* 319–334.

Gacono, C. B. (1990). An empirical study of object relations and defensive operations in antisocial personality disorder. *Journal of Personality Assessment, 54,* 589–600.

Gacono, C., & Meloy, J. R. (1988). The relationship between cognitive style and defensive process in the psychopath. *Criminal Justice and Behavior, 15,* 472–483.

Gacono, C., Meloy, J. R., & Heaven, T. (1990). A Rorschach investigation of narcissism and hysteria in antisocial personality disorder. *Journal of Personality Assessment, 55,* 270–279.

Hirshberg, L. (1989). Rorschach images of symbiosis and separation in eating disordered and in borderline and non-borderline subjects. *Psychoanalytic Psychology, 6,* 475–493.

Holt, R. R. (1977). A method for assessing primary process manifestation and their control in Rorschach responses. In M. Rickers-Ovsiankina (Ed.), *Rorschach psychology* (2nd ed., pp. 421–454). Huntington, NY: Krieger.

Holtzman, W. H. (1978). Holtzman inkblot technique. In B. B. Wolman (Ed.), *Clinical diagnosis of mental disorders: A handbook* (pp. 237–254). New York: Plenum.

Howell, D. C. (1992). *Statistical methods for psychology* (3rd ed.). Boston: PWS Kent.

Kates, J. (1994). *A validity study of the ego impairment index.* Unpublished doctoral dissertation, California School of Professional Psychology, San Diego.

Kinder, B. N. (1992). The problem of R in clinical settings and in research: Suggestions for the future. *Journal of Personality Assessment, 58,* 252–259.

Lerner, P., & Lerner, H. (1980). Rorschach assessment of primitive defenses in borderline personality structure. In J. Kwarer, H. Lerner, P. Lerner, & A. Sugerman (Eds.), *Borderline phenomena and the Rorschach test* (pp. 257–274). New York: International Universities Press.

Lipgar, R. J. (1992). The problem of R in the Rorschach: Comments in the context of other complexities. *Journal of Personality Assessment, 58,* 223–230.

Mayman, M. (1977). A multidimensional view of the Rorschach movement response. In M. Rickers-Ovsiankina (Ed.), *Rorschach psychology* (2nd ed., pp. 229–250). Huntington, NY: Krieger.

Meehl, P. E. (1990). Why summaries of research on psychological theories are often ininterpretable. *Psychological Reports, 66,* 195–244.

McNemar, Q. (1969). *Psychological statistics* (4th ed.). New York: Wiley.

Meloy, R. (1988). *The psychopathic mind: Origins, dynamics and treatment.* Northvale, NJ: Aronson.

Meyer, G. J. (1992). Response frequency problems in the Rorschach: Clinical and research implications with suggestions for the future. *Journal of Personality Assessment, 58,* 231–244.

Morgan, L., & Viglione, D. J. (1992). Sexual disturbances, Rorschach sexual responses and mediating factors. *Psychological Assessment, 4,* 530–536.

Perry, G. G., & Kinder, B. N. (1990). The susceptibility of the Rorschach to malingering: A critical review. *Journal of Personality Assessment, 54,* 47–57.

Perry, G. G., & Kinder, B. N. (1992). Susceptibility of the Rorschach to malingering: A schizophrenia analog. In C. D. Spielberger & J. Butcher (Eds.), *Advances in personality assessment* (Vol. 9, pp. 127–140). Hillsdale, NJ: Lawrence Erlbaum Associates.

Perry, W., & Viglione, D. J. (1991). The Rorschach Ego Impairment Index as a predictor of outcome in melancholic depressed patients treated with tricyclic antidepressants. *Journal of Personality Assessment, 56,* 487–501.

Perry, W., Viglione, D. J., & Braff, D. L. (1992). The Rorschach Ego Impairment Index and schizophrenia: A validation study. *Journal of Personality Assessment, 4,* 530–536.

Schafer, R. (1954). *Psychoanalytic interpretation in Rorschach testing.* New York: Grune & Stratton.

Snodgrass, J. G. (1977). *The numbers games: Statistics for psychologists.* New York: Oxford University Press.

Urist, J. (1977). The Rorschach test and the assessment of object relations. *Journal of Personality Assessment, 57,* 120–129.

CHAPTER TWELVE

Factor Analysis
With Rorschach Data

Eric A. Zillmer & Jacqueline K. Vuz

Factor analysis is one of the most frequently employed statistical techniques in the quantitative social sciences. It is also one of the least understood. This lack of understanding is due, for the most part, to the manner in which didactic materials on multivariate statistical analysis are presented. Quite often, for example, factor analysis is introduced with a myriad of technical concepts and mathematical formulae. A complete mastery of this specialized methodology, however, is not essential for acquiring a basic understanding of the results obtained from factor analysis. On the other hand, it is essential to understand the conceptual and logical foundations of this procedure. Our intent, therefore, is to present a detailed discussion of factor analysis that will be useful to readers of various ability levels. The mathematics will be kept to a minimum and emphasis will be placed on a fundamental understanding of the underlying principles of factor analysis. Three issues will be stressed: the practical and theoretical applications of factor analysis with Rorschach data, the rationale for choosing factor analysis over other statistical techniques, and situations when it would be inadvisable to apply factor analysis.

The last objective is precautionary in nature. Its purpose is to alert the reader to the potential for misusing factor analysis and similar multivariate statistical techniques in behavioral research. Easy access to high-speed computers and the availability of a number of preprogrammed statistical packages has resulted in a proliferation of factor analysis studies in the scientific literature. Whereas many of these studies have yielded notable results, an alarming percentage have lead to erroneous conclusions. The primary objective of this chapter is to enhance the reader's comprehension of factor analysis and to stimulate interest among Rorschach researchers and clinicians to apply such procedures in their work. By providing a better understanding of the principles and assumptions of factor analysis, it is our goal to inform the reader of the appropriateness and inappropriateness of factor analysis with Rorschach data. When mastered, these procedures have tremendous potential for advancing Rorschach theory and practice.

BASIC CONCEPTS OF FACTOR ANALYSIS

The primary goal of multivariate statistical analysis is to describe numerous individual observations in simpler terms. Thus, by manipulating various bits of data, we are often able to obtain a handful of unified concepts regarding one individual, a group of individuals, or a particular test construct. Factor analysis is a statistical technique that attempts to measure such concepts. Essentially, factor analysis is a variable reduction technique. Its purpose is to simplify the description of behavior by reducing the number of test variables to a few common factors (i.e., dimensions, traits, or constructs). Because these underlying factors are source variables that have been created out of the observed variables they are typically not observable, but are latent or hidden to the researcher. Another way of looking at factor analysis, then, is to recognize that the traits identified through this procedure are simply an expression of the overall correlations amongst the test data. Thus, factor analysis is a statistical technique used to identify a relatively small number of factors that can be utilized to represent relationships among sets of many interrelated variables.

Factor analysis differs from other multivariate techniques in several ways. For example, multiple analysis of variance (MANOVA), multiple regression, or canonical correlation all assess relationships between two sets of variables, such as predictor and outcome variables or independent and dependent variables. In contrast, factor analysis makes no distinction between independent and dependent variables, but rather treats all variables as a dependent set. Factor analysis looks inside a single set of variables by assessing the structure of the variables independent of any relationship they may have to the variables outside this set (Harris, 1985). Factor analysis assumes that the underlying dimensions, or factors, can be used to explain complex phenomena such as those presented in a correlational matrix. The number of simple correlations in the matrix is often quite large, particularly in the case of Rorschach variables. Consequently, an accurate summary of what the pattern of correlations represents would be extremely difficult by visual inspection alone. For example, with 30 variables there are over 400 simple correlations to examine. With such a large set of correlations, a statistical method is needed to determine if a smaller number of underlying constructs might account for the main sources of variation. The appropriate statistical method to reduce this complex set of relationships among many variables to only a few constructs is factor analysis.

Perhaps an example would be helpful in demonstrating how factor analysis can assist in the identification of underlying constructs that are not always directly observable. Because the WAIS–R is the most frequently administered cognitive test used nationally (Zillmer & Ball, 1987), most psychologists are familiar with its psychometric structure. Through the procedure of factor analysis we can successfully reduce the original 11 subtests of the WAIS–R into their basic dimensions. Table 12.1 shows the coefficients used in the final, rotated two-factor solution for 167 subjects (see Zillmer, Fowler, Waechtler, Harris, & Khan, 1992). These coefficients are referred to as factor loadings, because they indicate how much weight is assigned to each factor by each variable. Variables with large coefficients (e.g., > .6 in absolute value) are closely related to the factor. For example, WAIS–R subtests Vocabulary, Comprehension, Information, and Similarities display the largest loadings on Factor 1, and thus, the underlying construct of this factor is primarily determined by those four tests (e.g., a Verbal Comprehension factor). Similarly, Factor 2 is principally composed of all the WAIS–R performance tests and can be defined as a Perceptual Organization factor. This familiar two-factor structure of the WAIS–R is well established for a variety of different populations and has demonstrated its utility in clinical practice and research (e.g., Fowler, Zillmer, & Newman, 1988).

The principal aim of factor analysis is the simplification of data, so its value with the Rorschach can be easily appreciated given that the Compre-

TABLE 12.1
WAIS–R Oblique Two-Factor Pattern Matrix (N = 167)

	Factor 1 Verbal-Comprehension	Factor 2 Perceptual-Organization
Vocabulary	.94	-.15
Comprehension	.86	.00
Information	.78	.01
Similarities	.75	.00
Arithmetic	.50	.30
Digit span	.46	.21
Block design	-.08	.88
Object assembly	-.03	.80
Picture arrangement	.02	.73
Digit symbol	.03	.69
Picture completion	.14	.67
Eigenvalue	5.00	1.46
Percent of variance	45.50	13.30

Note. Factor pattern correlation = .52. From "The effects of unilateral and multifocal lesions on the WAIS–R: A factor analytic study of stroke patients," by Zillmer et al., 1992, *Archives of Clinical Neuropsychology, 7,* pp. 29–40. Copyright 1992 by Elsevier Science Ltd. Reprinted with permission.

hensive System uses over 60 scoring indices. Each Rorschach variable, however, may not measure a unique and/or single psychological construct. In fact, Exner (1986) suggested that "not one of the 26 symbols that are used for coding the nine major determinant categories . . . have exacting correlations with behavior or with personality characteristics, . . . but collectively [they do]" (p. 133). It makes sense, therefore, to find some variable reduction scheme that will indicate how Rorschach variables are related to each other. Indeed, factor analysis provides a model for examining the pattern of Rorschach data by sorting variables into relatively homogeneous and independent clusters that may describe unique and specific dimensions of cognitive or personality functioning. Thus, factor analysis of Rorschach data may lead to the recognition of a number of moderately broad group factors that can assist in the understanding of the overall psychometric structure of the test. Such a clustering of Rorschach variables can lead to the systematic classification of personality traits and contribute toward construct definition of the Rorschach.

The Rorschach technique yields human behavior that is varied and complex. Perhaps it is unrealistic to expect any number of common factors to provide an adequate description of over 60 variables that can be scored and calculated using the Comprehensive System. Nevertheless, for descriptive, as well as for theoretical purposes, we can choose appropriate factor analysis procedures with Rorschach data in a variety of research situations. For example, to the Rorschach researcher who is primarily interested in test theory, factor analysis procedures may illuminate whether certain Rorschach variables (e.g., *FC*, *CF*, and *C*) "hang together" due to the fact that all three codes involve a color determinant; or alternatively, if the primary underlying hypothetical concept of these three symbols is the absence or presence of form dominance. If the former is correct, it would support the hypothesis that all color scores, regardless of form demand, would cluster or "load" on a single "Color" factor. If the latter is true, it follows that the factorial composition of *FC* is different from that of *C* and *CF*. The *FC* scoring category would split off to a factor composed of Rorschach determinants with a primary form demand (*FC*, *F*, *FV*, etc.), and non-form-dominant color responses (*CF*, *C*) would load on a separate factor. There is some general evidence from previous factor studies of the Rorschach that this separation of non-form-dominant determinants from form-dominant scoring categories does occur (Meyer, 1989; Shaffer, Duszynski, & Thomas, 1981; Williams & Lawrence, 1953; Wittenborn, 1950a). Other studies, however, suggest the presence of an emotional expression or color factor (Mason, Cohen, & Exner, 1985; Wishner, 1959).

Rorschach researchers have had a long history of showing interest in studying the more theoretical or latent constructs associated with Rorschach variables that cannot be observed directly such as anxiety, cognitive ideation, stress tolerance, or self-perception. Factor analysis can assist in the theoretical as well as clinical understanding of Rorschach responses, because it facilitates the identification of relationships between unobservable, latent processes and Rorschach scoring categories. Statistical models can be a convenient way of describing the structure underlying a set of observed variables. These models provide a simpler explanation of how the observed and latent variables are related to one another. In fact, factor analysis came into being specifically to provide mathematical models for the explanation of psychological theories of human ability (Harman, 1970). It has been extensively used as a means of construct validation and for the identification of psychological traits. After the factor model has been identified, it can be utilized in describing the factorial composition of a test. Thus, factor modeling provides a technique for bridging the gap between theory and research or between test construction and test validation. Naturally, homogeneity and factorial purity are desirable goals for any personality test, but they are not substitutes for empirical validation (Anastasi, 1988).

EXPLORATORY VERSUS CONFIRMATORY FACTOR ANALYSIS

There are two basic empirical approaches to factor analysis: *exploratory* and *confirmatory.* In both approaches linear combinations of the original variables are derived and a small number of these factors frequently accounts for the majority of the variation or pattern of correlations. Most often, the researcher utilizing factor analysis is interested in ascertaining the minimum number of hypothetical factors that can account for the observed correlational matrix as a means of exploring the observations for possible data reduction, hence exploratory factor analysis. In exploratory factor analysis, the researcher does not know the underlying latent variable structure and attempts to uncover (or explore) the minimal number of factors that underlie the Rorschach data set. In exploratory work, little is assumed ahead of time regarding the underlying latent variable structure and the researcher is satisfied with investigating what happens and how the variables will hang together. The focus of exploratory analysis, therefore, is directed toward uncovering the minimum number of factors that underlie the observed variables. The reader should be cautioned that there is a major drawback to exploratory factor analysis. Because of the relative ease with which factor analysis can be calculated, a conceptual understanding of the research question is not necessary. Thus, many investigators will apply this technique to any available data set, often for purely heuristic purposes, without any prior theoretical considerations or discussion of hypothesis testing concerning the expected factor model. As a consequence, there is a tendency to let the statistics guide the research question rather than vice versa. This inclination can lead the unwary novice to meaningless results.

There is an alternative to exploratory factor analysis in which the researcher proposes a model of how the Rorschach variables in any data set would behave once they are factor analyzed. In confirmatory analysis, the researcher has specific assumptions of the underlying latent variable structure and is prepared to test them on an a priori model. In this approach, the researcher has some knowledge of the underlying latent variable structure and attempts to confirm, rather than explore, the model. This knowledge may be guided by theoretical considerations, empirical research, or both. At such times, the researcher may anticipate the underlying factors of a set of variables and hypothesize which variables belong to which factor or dimension. Confirmatory factor analysis, then, is used to test a specific hypothesis regarding the underlying structure of a test. In confirmatory work, we know beforehand—or we think we know—a great deal about what will go on, and are prepared to state rather strong hypotheses about how the data will act (Kaiser, 1970). Thus, confirmatory factor analysis creates specific expectations concerning the number, as well as the loadings, of factors. Confirmatory factor analysis is very flexible and allows the researcher to test specific and often quite complex hypotheses regarding psychometric properties of test data. The advantages of using confirmatory modeling approaches include a direct test of the adequacy of the model, as well as a comparison of competing models (see Fowler, Zillmer, & Macciocchi, 1990). For example, it would be possible to use confirmatory analysis to test the equivalency of Rorschach data across multiple populations or developmental stages.

In contrast, exploratory analysis is a way to discover, or "look and see." As such, this approach can be controversial because in some areas of psychology (intelligence testing, for example) extensive research on the exploratory models of the WAIS–R have been reported. Whereas some critics (e.g., Tukey, 1962) have proposed that exploratory analysis is akin to a fishing expedition or a reconnaissance mission, Savage (1954) suggested that those interested in exploratory analysis prefer to "look before they leap" rather than to "cross that bridge when they come to it." In fact, exploratory analysis does have the advantage of being open to a wide range of alternative explanations. In confirmatory analysis, there may be too much trust placed on one particular model without exploring what other patterns might exist (Hartwig & Dearing, 1979). It has to be pointed out that factor analytic studies are rarely exclusively confirmatory or exploratory. Most often, a given study falls somewhere along the continuum between the two. Indeed, many researchers (e.g., O'Grady, 1982; Ozer, 1985) would argue that any factor model, whether exploratory or confirmatory, should always be interpreted within a theoretical context.

In practice, the precise factor structure is rarely known a priori. Consequently, an exact fit between the data and the model cannot always be expected. For example, it is possible that a researcher using an exploratory approach anticipates a two-factor solution but may not know exactly which variables will be represented in those two factors. The field of Rorschach factor analysis is still in a "let's look and see" state, one that can be appropriately covered using exploratory work as a means of investigating the underlying factor structure without prior specification of a number of factors or loadings. This approach is appropriate when the investigator has to initially establish that a certain model may actually exist. As a result, Rorschach data has been subjected to exploratory factor analysis because confirmatory modeling assumes substantial knowledge about specific models, which at this point are not available with the Rorschach Comprehensive System. Thus, given the current status of factor analytic modeling with Rorschach data, it seems appropriate to be using primarily exploratory models for describing Rorschach data. Once satisfactory models have been described across a wide range of different populations we can then proceed to test them with confirmatory work. This chapter therefore limits itself to applications that fall within the framework of exploratory factor analysis. The underlying assumption is that the more we know about Rorschach data, the more effectively such data can be used to develop, test, and refine Rorschach theory. Those readers interested in confirmatory approaches to factor analysis should consult Byrne (1989), Jöreskög (1963, 1967), or Jöreskög and Sorbom (1986).

STATISTICAL PACKAGES

The mathematical computations that are necessary for factor analysis are complex and the researcher is more or less dependent on existing computer programs and access to high-speed computers (e.g., PRIME 6540, AT&T 3B15, or IBM 3090 mainframe). The availability of statistical packages that perform factor analysis are more accessible now than ever and users include a wider circle of clinicians, researchers, and students. If one is to successfully learn factor analysis, one must be prepared to spend some time learning how to use at least one factor analysis computer program that will calculate the appropriate statistics. The most widely available statistical packages are BMDP (Biomedical, 1983), SAS (Statistical Analysis System, 1985), and SPSS-X (Statistical Package for the Social Sciences, 1988) all of which perform a wide range of analyses and optional statistics.

The control language for these programs is relatively user-friendly and with some practice, factor analysis can be executed easily. For example, the command FACTOR in SPSS-X accepts input in the form of a correlation matrix, calculates principal components or factor analysis results, and allows for the control of the number of factors extracted, the number of iterations for extraction, and specific rotation parameters. For most factor analysis problems, however, it is not necessary to be familiar with all the methods and variants of the procedure, because most programs offer standard default options that the user may depend on. It is not a prerequisite for the reader, therefore, to understand all the options of factor analysis, but to be aware of the most important variations. As with most research designs, there is no single or best solution to most problems and the final choice may be a matter of personal preference.

One criticism that has been raised against preprogrammed statistical packages is that it is too easy to obtain results in the form of a printout. This can lead to thoughtless results that are presented with an aura of mathematical and statistical sophistication, when realistically the results may be inaccurate and invalid. Indeed, once results from factor analysis have been presented, it is difficult to verify the generalizability of the results to other data sets, based exclusively on the reported factor solution. Because it may require little effort to program these statistical packages and obtain results, it is essential for the reader to consider specific assumptions about the data set collection process before considering factor analysis. Violation of these assumptions may render the obtained factor model meaningless. Thus, the following discussion focuses on when and when not to use factor analysis in Rorschach research so that the results will be generalizable and accurate.

DATA COLLECTION OF RORSCHACH VARIABLES

Initially, as with any other research project, all psychometric data need to be collected carefully, accurately, and ethically, with particular emphasis placed on minimizing selection bias, sampling variability, and measurement errors. The Rorschach technique should be administered and scored employing the specific criteria contained in Exner's Comprehensive System workbook (Exner, 1990). The accuracy of scoring and administration, including the presentation of a free association and inquiry period, determines the overall reliability and validity of any subsequent statistical procedure (i.e., "garbage in, garbage out"). The accuracy of scoring can be greatly enhanced by using interscorer analysis (see Zillmer, Archer, & Castino, 1989). For example, an overall interrater reliability score of greater than 90% is consistent with most reliability data for Rorschach researchers (see, Exner, 1993). Furthermore, the use of a computer-generated structural summary (e.g., Rorschach Interpretation Assistance Program–Version 3, RIAP3; Exner & Tuttle, 1994) will further increase the reliability of structural summary codes as well as the accuracy of scoring, because the entry phase of RIAP3 can serve as a scoring tutorial for the user by scanning for more than 90 possible errors involving the internal logic of the Rorschach score (see Zillmer, 1991).

Protocol Validity

Before computing any statistical procedures, the Rorschach researcher must make a decision to exclude from any analysis protocols that are not meaningful. For example, when the number of responses is very low (i.e., $R <$ 14) the protocol is considered to be of insufficient length as to be regarded interpretatively useful. Conversely, if R exceeds 32 responses, it is likely that the respondent has exhausted most, if not all, W possibilities, and thus, a proportionally higher number of D and Dd answers can be expected. Furthermore, the frequency of P may also be above average (Exner, 1986). High Lambda records (e.g., > 1.0) can reflect a subtle form of rejection or nonparticipation in the task and should be viewed as questionably valid. Thus, when considering Rorschach protocols for any type of research, we strongly suggest excluding unreliable or invalid protocols.

Future research may illuminate the precise relationship of R on the psychometric structure of the Rorschach by comparing the factor structure of Rorschach protocols with low response sets with those with a very high number of responses. Such a project would be very ambitious, because it would require a very large number of Rorschach protocols with different rates of R, but it would assist in clarifying how R changes the psychometric structure of the test. Such research remains on the horizon and for the present the cautious Rorschach researcher should exclude invalid protocols from their data set.

DESCRIPTION OF RORSCHACH DATA—RORFAC

To facilitate an understanding of the principles of factor analysis, and to illustrate the use of existing packaged computer programs, we will apply the process of factor analysis to a Rorschach data set labeled RORFAC. The reader should note that, although we have chosen SPSS-X to analyze this data set, other programs can execute the same statistics and it is not necessary to have access to this particular one. By introducing potential users to the basic steps of performing factor analysis on an actual Rorschach data set, it is our hope that the reader can relate more meaningfully to the process of factor analysis.

Briefly, the subjects for the RORFAC data set were 197 psychiatric inpatients who were consecutively referred over a 2-year period for routine psychological evaluation. From this initial population, 20 records with low response styles ($R < 14$) and 17 records with high Lambda values (> 1.0) were excluded. The population from the remaining 160 records, had a mean age of 37.7 years, 46% were male, 92% were right handed, and 82% were Caucasian. The average years of education was 11.4 and 75% were receiving some form of psychotropic medication at the time of evaluation. Based on *DSM–III–R* criteria, 40% were suffering from schizophrenia, 31% displayed major affective disorders, 7% had disorders of an organic nature, 7% had a history of substance abuse, 6% exhibited personality disorders, and 10% had multiple diagnoses. As part of the psychological evaluation all subjects were given a number of psychological measures including the Rorschach, which was administered and scored according to standard procedures for the Comprehensive System (Exner, 1990).

Appendix A presents descriptive data for a number of Rorschach variables as well as several cognitive and demographic measures. In general, this heterogeneous sample of psychiatric inpatients was of average to low average ability in intellectual functioning (mean FSIQ = 88.7, SD = 14) and produced somewhat lower response sets (mean R = 19.8, SD = 5.7) compared with Exner's norms for inpatient schizophrenics, inpatient depressives, or nonpatient adults.

FACTOR ANALYSIS AND SAMPLE SIZE

In terms of sample size required for obtaining reliable factor analysis results, Gorsuch (1983) and Bentler (1985) suggested an absolute minimum ratio of five individuals per variable, but no less than 100 individuals for any analysis. Using the RORFAC data set as an example, we could enter as many as 32 variables using the Gorsuch rule (i.e., 160 divided by 5). A more conservative approach is recommended by Boomsma (1982), who suggested that one have at least an N of 200 before attempting factor analysis. Other more liberal rule-of-thumb estimations for factor analysis include $N - n - 1/50$, where N is the sample size and n is the number of variables. Let us relate the issue of sample size to the use of factor analysis in Rorschach research. In reviewing the factor analytic literature on the Rorschach, only 8 out of 17 research articles meet the 1·5 variable to subject ratio (e g , Mason et al , 1985; Meyer, 1989; Shaffer et al., 1981). The remaining nine studies had an inappropriate balance between sample size and variable size. For example, Lotsof, Comrey, Bogartz, and Arnsfield (1958) included 33 variables in a factor analysis using only 72 subjects. Stevens (1986) suggested that any factor analysis with N sizes below 100 and low variable to N ratios should be treated with considerable caution, because the results are unlikely to replicate.

As we shall see, many Rorschach variables may be unsuitable, or at the very least are suspect, for inclusion in factor analysis. This is related to the fact that many of the Rorschach variables may not meet the measurement requirements for factor analysis and, as such, should not be included in the analysis (i.e., because of colinearity, low base rates, atypical skewness, or kurtosis, which are discussed in detail later). Even if a complete factor model of all Rorschach variables is not attempted, the use of only 20 variables would necessitate over 100 subjects for a reliable factor structure using Gorsuch's recommendation. Furthermore, the greater the sample size, the better the approximation of the model (particularly for maximum likelihood solutions). Thus, to obtain reliable factors with Rorschach data, large N sizes are needed. Because the Rorschach is relatively labor intensive to administer, score, and interpret, only the most ambitious Rorschach researchers will be able to secure the necessary sample size for Rorschach factor analysis. This may be one reason why a relatively small number of Rorschach factor papers have appeared in the literature. If an adequate sample size cannot be secured, then the Rorschach researcher will need to resort to logical clustering or grouping based exclusively on theoretical and/or substantive grounds. Of course, with adequate sample size an empirical approach is preferable.

Another consideration of why factor analysis and sample size are pertinent to Rorschach research is related to the goal of obtaining a small set of predictor variables from a Rorschach data set. For example, when comparing the assumptions for sample size vis-à-vis factor analysis and multiple regressions it is quickly established that the requirements for sample sizes with regression analysis are more conservative (e.g., a minimum of 10 subjects per predictor variable). Often, however, very few components or common factors (i.e., 5) will account for most of the variance of a given correlational matrix. Thus, one could first perform a factor analysis to reduce the initial number of variables to a few factors, and then use those factors as predictors for multiple regression analysis (see section on additional analysis with factor scores for a more detailed discussion).

Computer Entry

Once an adequate sample size has been secured, the data collected, and invalid Rorschach records eliminated, all variables must be entered into a high-speed mainframe computer for purposes of statistical analysis. This process requires considerable patience, as rechecking of data entry, specifically for lengthy and complex data sets, is necessary. The researcher should verify the accuracy of the data entry process by examining carefully the descriptive statistics for each variable in question, including values of the mean, range, frequency, and standard deviation (see Appendix A). Only when the researcher is completely confident that the data have been collected, scored, and entered correctly should one progress with selecting specific Rorschach variables for inclusion into the factor analysis.

Checking Assumptions for Factor Analysis
with Rorschach Data

As mentioned previously, the application of factor analysis to the study of personality organization provides a theoretical basis for systematically identifying, sorting, and defining different personality constructs or abilities. Although the principle of reducing data into fewer dimensions is a simple one, the complexities associated with factor analysis are related to understanding the underlying conceptual model, the numerous methods and possible options of obtaining factor solutions. Additionally, particularly with Rorschach variables, the fact that the research problem is often more complex than the factor model assumes it to be (Kim & Mueller, 1990a). Researchers should be forewarned that factor analysis with Rorschach variables is a complicated matter. As with all statistical procedures, factor analysis is not without pitfalls. For example, there is a tendency to disregard the assumptions underlying factor analysis and their effect on the factor solution. Thus, it is essential that the Rorschach investigator be prepared to commit themselves to the assumptions about the statistical properties of the data prior to attempting factor analysis.

Once the results have been generated, it is difficult to know whether or not factor analysis was appropriate for the data set. Indeed, the obtained results from factor analysis cannot be used to substantiate the validity of the assumptions! The most that can be achieved via exploratory factor analysis is the conclusion that the structure of the observed data is not inconsistent with a particular factor model. Thus, the burden of proof is on the researcher to demonstrate that the underlying structure is actually factorial. It should be re-emphasized that a complete understanding of the statistical and computational problems of factor analysis is not necessary and will not be reviewed here. The user may let the computer do much of the work. It is, however, essential for the reader to gain a thorough grasp of the conceptual foundation of this procedure. This is important in order to use this technique appropriately and creatively.

How does one apply factor analysis and have any assurance that the findings can be interpreted meaningfully? The ultimate validity of any given factor structure results from imposing several basic assumptions regarding the data. These principles must be adhered to by the data analyst if any uncertainties of the interpretability of the model are to be minimized. In this section, we place particular emphasis on addressing the nonspecialist who is interested in using this approach with Rorschach data. Statistical assumptions and practical problems underlying factor analysis—including issues of variable distribution, linearity, colinearity, base rates, and the use of Rorschach summary measures—are reviewed.

Variable Distribution

The general goal in factor analysis is to discover one or more underlying factors that are responsible for the correlational matrix. As such, the correlational matrix serves as the primary data input for factor analysis. Assumptions about the variables submitted for factor analysis are, therefore, related specifically to the statistical concepts that underlie and govern correlational analysis. One such assumption is that variables be normally distributed (i.e., in the form of a Gaussian distribution). By variable, we mean a concept that "varies" and has at least two values. Because correlational analysis requires the variables to be more or less linearly related to each other, factor analysis requires, although there is some disagreement about this issue, that the variables included in the matrix be measured at least at the interval level (i.e., a scale that does not have an absolute zero point, but whose intervals are equal). Thus, when using ordinal data (which assigns values according to ordinal numbers, first, second, third, etc.) or nominal data (a simple system of classifications) the underlying factors of the matrix are not well defined. In fact, there is no factor analysis method that typically incorporates the use of ordinal or nominal variables.

Two additional statistical concepts of importance are mean and variance. The mean describes the central tendency of a variable. Variance is defined as the degree of variability, scatter, or distribution. If a variable is normally distributed, these two statistics are sufficient to characterize the whole probability distribution of the variable. For example, IQ scores have a standard mean of 100 and a standard deviation of 15. If a variable is not normally distributed, it may be skewed (SK) if it is not symmetric, but has more cases (i.e., more of a tail) toward one end of the distribution than the other. Or it may display high values of kurtosis (KU), which indicates that the distribution deviates from normality, because it has either a heavier tail or is peaked (i.e., positive values of KU) or has a lighter tail (i.e., negative values of KU). Values of skewness and kurtosis for variables from normal distribution will fluctuate around zero.

The majority of Rorschach variables are not normally distributed and may not be suitable for inclusion in factor analysis. Examination of Exner's norms for nonpatient adults (1990, pp. 158–159) shows that variables *R*, *D*, *DQ+*, *FM*, and *Zd*, are relatively normally distributed, but many other variables such as *SumY* and *Dd* show high values of SK and KU. Exner identified those Rorschach codes in the normative sample that are not normally distributed by placing standard deviations in brackets and suggested that the use of those variables for any kind of parametric statistic is questionable. Examples of data set RORFAC (Appendix A) clearly demonstrate that the kurtosis and skewness is elevated for many variables and that those variables are most likely not normally distributed. One way to examine the range and degree of SK and KU is to plot a frequency table (i.e., a histogram) that allows for a visual representation of the distribution of any Rorschach variable. SPSS-X offers an optional command that allows the data analyst to specify the interval width as well as to superimpose a normal curve on the histogram for purposes of comparison. Figure 12.1 plots a histogram for RORFAC variables *WSum6*, *FV*, and *P*. Note that *WSum6* in Fig. 12.1a is positively skewed and has an increased peak or kurtosis. Variable *FV* in Fig. 12.1b almost assumes a dichotomous distribution (i.e., either zero or one),

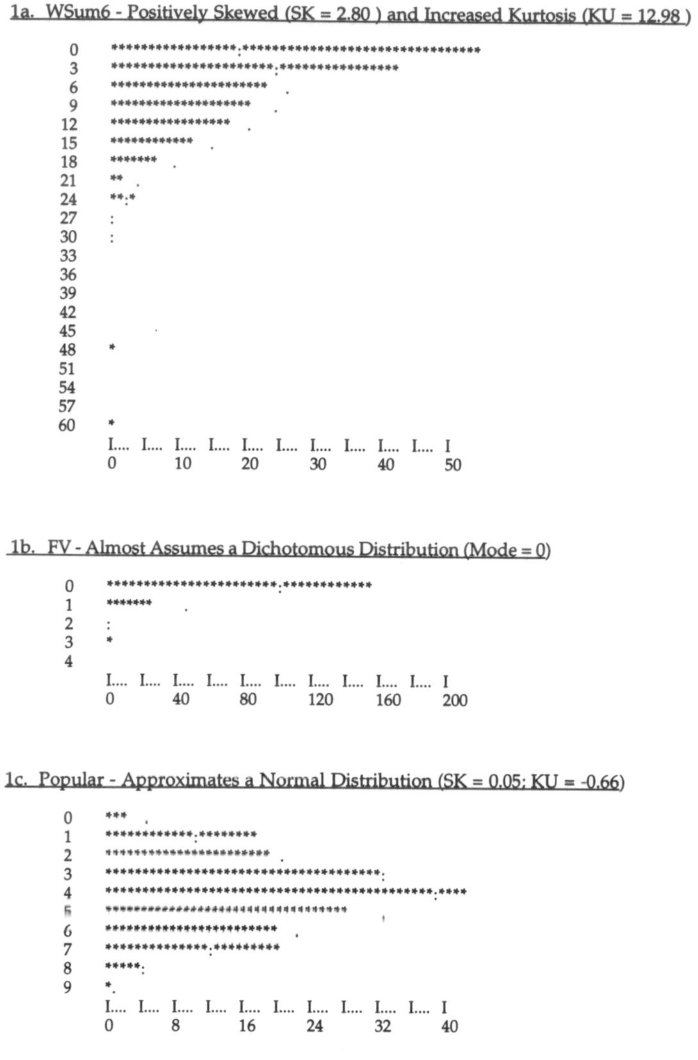

1a. WSum6 - Positively Skewed (SK = 2.80) and Increased Kurtosis (KU = 12.98)

```
 0   *******************.**************************************
 3   ***********************.*****************
 6   **************************
 9   ***********************  .
12   ******************  .
15   *************
18   *******  .
21   **  .
24   **.*
27   :
30   :
33
36
39
42
45
48   *
51
54
57
60   *
     I.... I.... I.... I.... I.... I.... I.... I.... I.... I.... I
     0          10        20        30        40        50
```

1b. FV - Almost Assumes a Dichotomous Distribution (Mode = 0)

```
 0   **************************.**************
 1   *******  .
 2   :
 3   *
 4
     I.... I.... I.... I.... I.... I.... I.... I.... I.... I.... I
     0         40        80        120       160       200
```

1c. Popular - Approximates a Normal Distribution (SK = 0.05; KU = -0.66)

```
 0   ***  .
 1   *************.*********
 2   **********************  .
 3   *******************************************.
 4   *****************************************************.****
 5   ******************************************  '
 6   **************************  .
 7   **************.*********
 8   *****.
 9   *.
     I.... I.... I.... I.... I.... I.... I.... I.... I.... I.... I
     0        8        16        24        32        40
```

FIG. 12.1. Histogram.

and finally the values for *P* in Fig. 12.1c approximate a normal distribution compared with the superimposed normal curve. Prior to conducting factor analysis it should become standard procedure to examine the distribution of Rorschach variables and to evaluate which variables are and are not approximating normal distributions and are suitable for factor analysis.

When Rorschach researchers are confronted with variables that are not normally distributed, they then need to decide whether to include them for factor analysis, to transform them numerically into a new variable, or alternatively, to forgo factor analysis and perform nonparametric statistics. For novices who may not completely understand how a factor solution will be affected by the inclusion of non-normally distributed variables, it is strongly suggested that they exclude those Rorschach variables from factor analysis that clearly violate the normality assumption. For those researchers who have a clear theoretical concept of the resulting factor structure and how a specific non-normal variable would "behave" in a factor model, it is possible to enter such nonstandard variables and still obtain valid results. One way to deal with variables that violate the normality assumption is to calculate the factor analysis with and without the inclusion of suspect variables in order to determine how it affects the adequacy of the factor model. It must be cautioned that when a majority, or a high number, of such nonstandard variables are submitted to factor analysis, unreliable, confusing, and meaningless results may be obtained.

There remains considerable controversy regarding the use of variables for factor analysis that are dichotomous, ordinal, or in any other way not normally distributed. Briefly, the traditional literature on factor analysis suggests that any variable below a ratio or interval scale should not be included in factor analysis procedures, because such a variable would compromise the interpretability of any generated factor solution. For example, if factor analysis methods were to be applied to qualitative data, new equations would have to be derived to fit the data. More modern writings on factor analysis, however, suggest that non-normal variables may be included in factor analysis without effecting the interpretability of the resulting factor model as much as was previously thought. In fact, successful factor analytic studies have generated interpretable factors using exclusively dichotomous data (e.g., on the 566 true–false items of the Minnesota Multiphasic Personality Inventory, MMPI; see Green, 1991). Issues surrounding the inclusion of nonstandard variables or combining dichotomous, non-normal, and normal variables in a factor analysis are complex and the interested reader should consult other sources for further information (e.g., Gorsuch, 1983; Harman, 1970). We do strongly recommend that whereas considerable latitude might be allowed, a variable that is distinctly non-normal should not be included in the analysis.

The conclusion to be drawn from this discussion is that the skilled researcher should carefully examine the data, including the distribution, mean, median, mode, kurtosis, and skewness of variables that are considered for submission to factor analysis. For the novice, it appears inappropriate to consider variables for analysis that are not normally distributed. However, those who attempt to use such variables in factor analysis should do it sparingly and have some basic conceptual ideas about the nature of the factor model, specifically the rationale for the inclusion of nonstandard variables.

In other words, it is important to understand the statistical properties of the data set and to formulate several a priori hypotheses even when using exploratory analysis. One of the reasons, if not the major one, why factor analysis procedures have been used inappropriately, is because the unwary users of factor analysis have subjected their data sets to factor analysis without any consideration of the nature of the variables or any specific theoretical deliberations (i.e., the "let's look and see what happens" approach). Such an approach to factor analysis has only heuristic value, if any. Again, the prudent Rorschach researcher should remain conservative on the issue of including variables that are not normally distributed.

A possible solution to this problem is to consider a numerical transformation of Rorschach variables. This procedure, which is described later in the chapter, results in a new variable that may have better statistical properties than any of the variables of which it is composed.

Problems of Linearity

Because the correlational matrix is the only input procedure for any type of factor analysis, whether exploratory or confirmatory, the cautious researcher should ascertain that the variables to be submitted to factor analysis procedures are linearly related by examining their interrelationship. Of course, as already pointed out, variables that are normally distributed are by definition in a linear relationship to each other. Briefly, a product-moment correlation is a measure of association between two variables and is a general term for describing the linear relationship between variables. A correlation coefficient determines the size or magnitude of the relation between two variables (Ozer, 1985) and permits the prediction of scores on one standardized variable from another. This prediction will be meaningful only if the relationship between the two variables is approximately linear. If the two variables are statistically independent, the magnitude of the correlation is zero; otherwise the magnitude will vary from +1 to −1. Two variables can covary when one variable is caused by the other, when both variables share at least one common cause, or both. Conversely, a correlation only measures the strength of a linear association, not linearity or causality.

As with many parametric statistics, including factor analysis and multiple regressions, it is assumed that there are only linear relationships between the variables; that is, two variables that are normally distributed will fall on a straight line. If the data represents a random sample from a population in which the distribution of variables is normal, then correlational statistics are appropriate and meaningful. If it seems unreasonable to assume that the variables are from normal distributions, one may have to use other statistical procedures that do not require the normality assumptions (e.g., nonparametric procedures). Thus, in using the initial correlational matrix for factor analysis, it has to be recognized that certain assumptions are needed for the acceptance of any factor model. One reason why many researchers misapply factor analysis to a data set is because of their lack of understanding of the basic assumptions of linear combinations of variables. If all variables are standardized (as they surely are not with the Rorschach), it can be assumed that the correlation between two variables sharing one common factor is given by the multiplication of two standardized regression coefficients, or two correlations between the observed variables and the common factor.

In factor analysis, all variables are assumed to be linear functions of underlying factors when the distributions of the variables are normal. However, with respect to linearity, almost no variables in behavioral sciences have a truly linear relationship over their full range. It has been previously suggested that many of the Rorschach variables are not normally distributed and thus may not be in a linear relationship to each other. The researcher may perform an initial "eyeball test" of the curve, bi- or nonlinearity of the the relationship between any two Rorschach variables, by carefully examining the correlational matrix and, if needed, individual correlational plots of any two Rorschach variables. If nonlinearity appears, then at least one of the nonlinear pair is not a linear function of the factors. Using the current RORFAC data set, Fig. 12.2 demonstrates a negative linear relationship between $X+\%$ and $X-\%$ ($r = -.60$) and Fig. 12.3 displays a positive linear relationship between W and Zf ($r = .74$). Within SPSS-X, using the REGRESSION keyword, the PLOT command marks the regression line intercepts with the letter R. For example, Figs. 12.2 and 12.3 include the regression statistics that display the letter R on the vertical axes. When the two R's are connected, as is done here, a regression line is produced. Because factor analysis assumes linear combinations of variables in order to extract the underlying source variables, one should minimize the inclusion of bivariate or other nonlinear relationships in factor analysis.

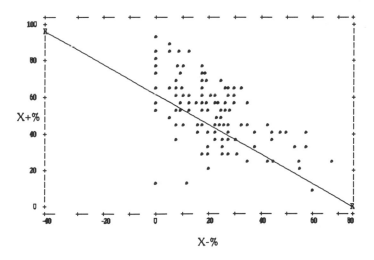

FIG. 12.2. Negative linear relationship between $X+\%$ and $X-\%$ ($r = -.60$).

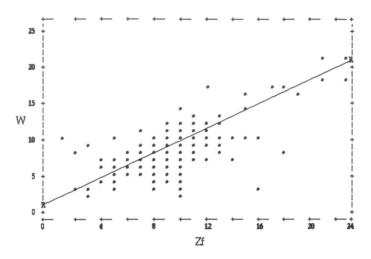

FIG. 12.3. Positive linear relationship between W and Zf ($r = .74$).

Issues of Independence and Colinearity

Another issue pertaining to factor analysis is that of very low or very high interrelationships among the variables. The former refers to a situation where many of the variables submitted to factor analysis are not related to one another and subsequently do not "hang together." In factor analysis, this independence among variables makes it increasingly difficult to extract any common factors, because the variables share little common variance. In an extreme case of independence, the factor analysis would produce as many factors as there are variables because each variable would account for its own unit variance. Colinearity, in contrast, refers to a very high degree of interrelationships among variables in which one can predict with a high degree of accuracy the value of one variable from the other. In data sets with high colinearity it becomes increasingly difficult to extract common factors when all variables hang together and share the same variance. This would result in a one-factor solution in which there is such high colinearity among all variables that no separation into smaller common factors is possible (e.g., Spearman's one-factor concept of g in which all intellectual activities share a single common factor; 1904).

Most psychological tests are, in fact, heavily intercorrelated (e.g., Wechsler Adult Intelligence Scale–Revised, WAIS–R) and in this respect the Rorschach is no different. Although, to add to the previously cited difficulties of factor analysis of Rorschach data, there are instances of independence among certain Rorschach variables as well. Thus, the careful Rorschach researcher needs to examine issues of both independence and colinearity and needs to attempt to minimize both. One rule of thumb is to estimate the interrelationship in a data set by calculating the sum of all correlations in the matrix and dividing that number by the number of correlations. The result is the approximate mean correlation of the matrix. If it is very large (e.g., > .7), the matrix is demonstrating high colinearity because the interrelationship between all variables in the matrix is, on average, very high (i.e., approximate 49% shared variance) and a satisfying factor solution is probably not obtainable.

For example, Table 12.2 shows a correlational matrix for 17 variables from data set RORFAC. The correlation of a variable with itself is always 1.0 and can be found on the diagonal of the matrix (i.e., identity coefficients). In this example, only the lower triangle of the matrix (referred to as off-diagonal elements) is presented, because the upper triangle is a mirror image. The off-diagonal correlation coefficients range, in absolute value, from .001 between $F+\%$ and FC, to .74 between Zf and W. The average intercorrelation is .24 for the 136 correlations and suggests neither strong evidence of general independence or colinearity of the variables in the matrix. The average correlation should only be used as a general guide, because it does not take into account the shared variance of single variables with other variables in the factor solution, which in some cases can be relatively high. For example, every variable in the RORFAC matrix displays some colinearity with at least one other variable.

Base Rates of Rorschach Variables

Base rates refer to the actual frequency count of occurrences of a particular observation in the sample population. Base rates of Rorschach variables can be examined in the frequency column of the descriptive statistics in Exner's workbook (1990) for a variety of different sample groups such as nonpatient adults, children, and psychiatric patients. When base rate values are lower than .25 (i.e., scores obtained by less than 25% of the sample population), it is questionable whether that variable should be included in factor analysis simply because of the variable's low count and its subsequent effect on the distribution of the variable. Although the presence of low base rate scoring categories in a Rorschach record can be very useful for clinical, interpretative purposes and their occurrences are often pathognomonic (e.g., CONTAM), many Rorschach variables would not qualify for factor analysis because of their low base rates (using the 25% cutoff). For nonpatient adults (Exner, 1990) Rorschach variables with very low base rates include, among others: C (7%; i.e., only 51 out of 700 nonpatient adults give at least one pure color response), Cn (< 1%), $SumV$ (20%), $Fr+rF$ (7%), and CONTAM (0%).

However, base rates do change from population to population. For example, the base rate for a Color-Shading-Blend is 36% in the nonpatient adult population, but only 6% in 5-year-old nonpatients (Exner, 1990). Similarly, $SumV$ increases to 56% for inpatient depressive over the base rate of 20% in nonpatient adults. Thus, it must be remembered that low base rates

TABLE 12.2
Correlation Matrix of 17 Rorschach Variables (N = 160)

	FSbd	SbdF	R	W	S	M	FD	FC'	CF'+C	m	Zf	FC	CF+C	P	X+%	F+%	X-%
FSbd	100																
SbdF	26	100															
R	40	45	100														
W	37	43	44	100													
S	41	38	48	33	100												
M	18	23	40	21	20	100											
FD	21	31	24	21	34	25	100										
FC'	23	08	24	26	34	15	07	100									
CF'+C	11	43	30	21	38	08	04	25	100								
m	37	47	42	40	37	35	04	14	32	100							
Zf	45	41	61	74	41	51	25	27	11	47	100						
FC	54	21	43	27	38	28	32	24	21	33	45	100					
CF+C	20	55	35	46	30	29	19	17	47	44	38	10	100				
P	14	02	32	06	-03	25	16	04	-04	09	33	15	-08	100			
X+%	-10	-13	-10	-28	-21	-05	18	-14	-17	-06	-06	-10	-21	51	100		
F+%	-04	-05	-03	-06	-18	-04	02	-16	-11	11	06	00	-18	37	45	100	
X-%	13	01	02	06	17	-12	-07	03	03	-10	-01	-06	02	-42	-60	31	100

Note. Decimals omitted; FSbd = FV + FT + FY; SbdF = VF - V + TF + T + YF + Y; r > .13 = p < .05; r > .19 = p < .001.

are sample specific and should be evaluated within the context of the data set that the researcher is submitting for factor analysis. According to Appendix A, which shows descriptive statistics and base rates of the RORFAC sample, several variables have base rates below .25, including C', TF, T, Y, FV, VF, V, and CP. Consequently, it would be ill advised to include these low base rate variables in factor analysis.

The same assumption about low base rates is true for very high base rates with extremely low variances. For example, although most nonpatient adults receive some form of texture response (i.e., base rate = 89%), there is very little variation in their score (i.e., mode = 1; SD = 0.58; and kurtosis, the degree of flatness or peakness of a frequency curve in the region of the mode, is 5.39; Exner, 1990). This suggests that most nonpatient adults give one texture response of some kind, but that there is very little variation around the mean (range = 0 to 4). Such variables with very high base rates, high values of kurtosis, and extremely low SD's (i.e., little or no variability) are probably not suited for factor analysis because they approximate a dichotomous variable and are not normally distributed.

Rorschach Indices and Summary Measures

Often, the researcher can perform a numerical transformation of those variables that show evidence of either low base rates or a non-normal distribution. One strategy centers around converting such variables into true, nominal group-membership types (e.g., Group 1 is composed of individuals with $SumT < 1$, Group 2 $SumT = 1$, and Group 3 $SumT > 1$). The new nominal variable lends itself to ANOVA, MANOVA, or alternatively nonparametric designs, instead of statistical techniques that require linear analysis (including factor analysis, multiple regression, or canonical analysis). In this way, the nonstandard Rorschach variable can be transformed by giving it a numeric value without necessarily distorting the underlying properties of the variables. The drawback here is that, unless a large amount of data is available, the particular cutoff point established for each variable's set of categories may be arbitrary and could yield extremely small subgroups of subjects having a specific combination of scores on the various measures (e.g., Group 3 $T > 1$).

An alternative solution is to include a summary measure in the factor analysis rather than individual scores, because individual scores may not be distributed normally and/or may have extremely low base rates. This defines a new variable that may or may not have better statistical properties in terms of kurtosis, skewness, and variability than any of its components. For example, $FShade$ (i.e., the total of all shading responses with a primary form demand) may be a more acceptable variable than any of the individual three shading determinants (see Appendix A). Conversely, adding variables that are themselves normally distributed will give rise to new variables that will also be normally distributed. This mathematical concept is known as the normality of sums of normally distributed variables (Bernstein, 1988) and may assist in cutting down the high number of variables present in the Comprehensive System for purposes of factor analysis.

When using summary measures, there are at least two statistical issues that the prudent factor analysis researcher has to examine. First, the summary measure may have different statistical properties than any of the individual variables from which it is composed and needs to be carefully examined for its use in factor analysis (i.e., normal distribution). Second, once a numerical transformation or Rorschach index has been submitted to factor analysis, it would be inappropriate to also submit the individual Rorschach codes of which the specific summary code is composed. The reason for this is that variables caused directly by other variables would artificially increase the colinearity of the correlation matrix. This is related to the factor model assuming that all observed variables are caused by the underlying factors, not each other.

Thus, using theoretical considerations as well as an examination of the statistical distribution of the variables, only the Egocentricity Index or the single codes (2) and $Fr+rF$ should be considered for inclusion in factor analysis, not all of them, which would be considered redundant. In fact, many structural summary indices on the Rorschach are composed of individual Rorschach variables, including the D score, SCZI, $WSum6$, EA, or Col-Shd blends, to name just a few. The inclusion of summary measures in factor analysis should only be considered if they have a better statistical distribution than the variables of which they are composed, in which case the number of variables for factor analysis would be reduced. Summary measures may also be utilized for theoretical reasons if the researcher is interested in the summary measure itself and what factor loading it would assume.

Not surprisingly, this assumption has been often violated in Rorschach factor analysis research. For example, in a number of studies (e.g., Geertsma, 1962; Wishner, 1959) $C+CF$, $C+CF+FC$, and Sum C/R were all entered for purposes of factor analysis. This, obviously artificially increased the colinearity of the correlational matrix (e.g., the reported correlation between $C+CF+FC$ and Sum C/R was, not surprisingly, very high; $r = .95$). Furthermore, these redundant variables would naturally load on the same factor, not related to an unobservable construct, but rather due to the simple fact that the variables are mathematically related to each other.

STEPS IN FACTOR ANALYSIS

The correlation matrix serves as the starting point for factor analysis, so the level of measurement of each Rorschach variable must be such that the correlation coefficient is an acceptable summary statistic. The previous discussion has reviewed a number of assumptions that must be made before Rorschach variables are to be considered for factor analysis. The Rorschach researcher should be absolutely sure, therefore, that the Rorschach records included in the data set are valid, that the Rorschach variables submitted to factor analysis are from a multivariate normal population, that problems with low base rates, redundant variables, and colinearity have been minimized, and that an adequate sample size has been secured. Only when these conditions have been met should the actual statistics for factor analysis be calculated.

Typically, the statistics involved in factor analysis proceed in a planned and systematic fashion. The initial step involves evaluating the suitability of the correlational matrix for factor analysis. Next, the method for factor extraction is determined. This includes calculating the initial factor statistics and subsequently retaining a smaller number of factors that represent the data in a more satisfactory fashion. Often, factor solutions are then *rotated* in order to improve the interpretability and labeling of the factor model. A final, optional step is related to a number of additional analyses that can be performed, after newly derived factor scores have been computed (Norusis, 1988).

At this juncture of the overview, it seems important to remind the reader that the current example of the RORFAC factor model serves only as an exercise. No attempts are made to provide the reader with a comprehensive factor model of the Rorschach test. Rather, the intent is to simplify the model somewhat, by including only 17 Rorschach variables of the RORFAC data set, so that readers with varying ability levels are able to follow the procedural steps involved. Thus, Rorschach variables included in the analysis were not selected because of any specific theoretical considerations. Instead, they were selected because they satisfied the aforementioned statistical assumptions. As a result, the Rorschach factor model has been kept purposely elementary, compared to more complex factor solutions that may be obtained if a larger number of Rorschach variables were chosen. As previously mentioned, the current sample size ($N = 160$) would have allowed a larger number of variables (i.e., > 30) to be submitted for factor analysis.

EXAMINING THE CORRELATIONAL MATRIX
FOR ITS SUITABILITY FOR FACTOR ANALYSIS

Every factor analysis begins with a table of intercorrelations among all variables or set of tests involved in the analysis, known as a correlational matrix (e.g., see Table 8). The purpose of factor analysis is to reduce this correlational matrix to its simplest elements. Every factor analysis ends with a table showing the weight or loading of each variable for each of the final factors (e.g., see Table 12.2).

Because the goal of factor analysis is to obtain a smaller number of common factors that help explain these correlations, the variables must be related to each other for the factor model to be appropriate. For example, when the correlations between the variables are very small, it is unlikely that they share common factors. Conversely, if the matrix as a whole manifests very high intercorrelation (i.e., colinearity), it is difficult for the matrix to converge on separate factors. Table 12.2 shows the correlational matrix for those 17 Rorschach variables that have been selected for the analysis. The reader can appreciate that on a purely inspectional basis it is difficult to comprehend the 136 off-diagonal relationships of all variables to each other. Thus, a more precise statistical technique (i.e., factor analysis) is necessary to define the common factors that account for the obtained correlations. Prior to computing the factor analysis, however, it is good practice to examine the correlational matrix for its suitability for factor analysis (Dzuiban & Shirkey, 1974a, 1974b). Several methods for accomplishing this are reviewed here, all of which are available in SPSS-X.

Bartlett's Test of Sphericity

Researchers, who are contemplating using a factor analysis with a small sample size (N around 100), should utilize Bartlett's sphericity test. This precautionary measure examines the Null hypothesis, which states that the variables in the population correlation matrix are uncorrelated (i.e., all diagonal correlations are 1.0 and all off-diagonal correlations are 0.0). This test takes into account sample size, the number of variables in the analysis, and the determinant of the correlational matrix (Bartlett, 1950; Cooley & Lohnes, 1971; Knapp & Swoyer, 1967). As the value of the test increases (which is based on the chi-square transformation of the determinant of the correlational matrix) and the associated significance level decreases, the likelihood increases that the Null hypothesis can be rejected and the alternative hypothesis accepted (i.e., the population correlation matrix is, in fact, correlated). Alternatively, when the significance level is large (e.g., > .05), the hypothesis that the population correlation matrix is uncorrelated cannot be rejected and one should reconsider the use of the factor model, because it is unlikely that the data share common factors (Norusis, 1988).

Results of the Bartlett's test for three different data sets are displayed in Table 12.3. The values for the test are all within normal limits (i.e., sufficiently large with associated small significance level) to reject the Null hypothesis. This suggests that not one of the three correlational matrices for data sets RORFAC, WAIS–R, or Mini-Mental are uncorrelated, even though the average correlation for the current RORFAC matrix was somewhat low (i.e., $r = .24$).

TABLE 12.3
Suitability of the Correlation Matrix for Factor Analysis

Index	Mini-Mental[*] (N = 110)	WAIS–R[**] (N = 167)	Rorschach (RORFAC) (N = 160)
Average Correlation of Matrix	.44	.44	.24
1. Bartlett's Test of Sphericity	$\chi^2 = 1343.1$ $p < .001$	$\chi^2 = 1050.8$ $p < .0001$	$\chi^2 = 1005.8$ $p < .0001$
2. Kaiser–Meyer–Olkin (KMO) Estimate of Variables' Sampling Adequacy	.92 "marvelous"	.88 "meritorious"	.77 "middling"
3. Number of Off-diagonal Elements > .09 in the Anti-image Covariance Matrix	9.6%	23%	21%

Note. [*]See Zillmer, Fowler, Gutnick, and Becker (1990); [**]see Zillmer et al. (1992).

The Kaiser–Meyer–Olkin Index

This procedure involves the computation of the Kaiser–Meyer–Olkin Measure of Sampling Adequacy (KMO) for the correlational matrix (Kaiser, 1970, 1974). The KMO is an index for comparing the magnitudes of the observed correlation coefficients to the size of the partial correlation coefficients. Partial correlations are the net correlation between two variables in which the influence of one or more additional variables has been eliminated. The index provides an assessment of the appropriateness of the matrix for factor analysis, based on whether the variables in the matrix belong together psychometrically (Dzuiban & Shirkey, 1974a, 1974b).

When the KMO measure is close to 1, the sum of the squared partial correlation coefficients between all pairs is small, compared to the sum of the squared correlation coefficients. The index improves as the number of variables increases, the number of subjects increases, and the overall level of correlation increases. A reasonably large value is required for a valid factor analysis. According to Kaiser (1974), if the KMO index is below .50, then the data set is unacceptable for factor analysis, in the 50s it is miserable, in the 60s mediocre, in the 70s middling, in the 80s meritorious, and above .90 marvelous. These general decision rules can be implemented regarding the overall quality of the correlational matrix for factor analysis and offer an advantage that the other procedures lack. A value any lower than .50 clearly indicates that the matrix should not be factor analyzed, because the correlations between pairs of variables cannot be explained by the other variables. All the KMO indices in Table 12.3 are in an acceptable range.

Examining the Count of the Number of Off-diagonal
Elements in the Anti-image Covariance (AIC) Matrix > .09

The third and final procedure of examining the correlational matrix involves an assessment of the magnitude of the off-diagonal elements in the anti-image covariance matrix (Dzuiban & Shirkey, 1974a, 1974b). This is another indicator of the strength of the relationship among variables. If the variables share common factors, the anti-image correlation (i.e., the negative of the partial correlation coefficient) between pairs of variables should be small or close to zero, because the linear effects of the other variables have been eliminated. By examining the frequency of correlations where an association remains, we can estimate whether or not the approximation for factor analysis is good. When the count of large coefficients greater than .09 (in absolute value) in the AIC matrix is high (i.e., > 30%), the Rorschach researcher should reconsider the use of the factor model, because a substantial number of correlations remain. In our example (see Table 12.3) the number of off-diagonal elements > .09 was slightly elevated (in the borderline range) only for the WAIS–R and RORFAC matrix.

METHODS OF FACTOR EXTRACTION

After the correlational matrix has been determined to be suitable for factor analysis, the next step is to extract the number of factors that can adequately explain the observed correlations of the data. Several methods can be used to obtain estimates of common factors that differ in the criterion used to define *good fit*. We discuss two major alternatives: the Maximum Likelihood (ML) method factor analysis and the Principle Components Analysis (PCA).

Maximum Likelihood (ML) Factor Analysis

The primary goal of factor analysis is to reduce, as accurately as possible, the original intercorrelation matrix into a smaller number of hypothetical variables. The overall objective of ML factor analysis is to find the factor structure that maximizes (in terms of the best fit) the likelihood of the observed correlational matrix, by finding, under any given hypothesis, the underlying population parameters that are expressed in common factors. The maximum likelihood method accomplishes this task by initially establishing a measure of "goodness of fit" from the observed correlational matrix. The factor loadings are then calculated to optimize this measure, that is, to be the one most likely (hence maximum likelihood) to have produced the observed correlational matrix. All correlations are weighted by the inverse of the uniqueness of the variables, and an iterative algorithm is employed in order to estimate the composition of the common factors. Variants of the common factor model are principal axis factoring, the least square procedures, and the alpha method (see Harman, 1970; Kim & Mueller, 1990a, 1990b).

Principal Components Analysis (PCA)

In ML factor analysis, a mathematical model is established in which the factors can only be estimated. In contrast, PCA transforms the original set of correlated variables into new, smaller sets of linear combinations of un-correlated principal components (Stevens, 1986). Unlike the factors derived from ML factor analysis, PCA is closely related to the original variables, with each subject's score on a principal component being a linear combination of the score on the original variable (principal meaning primary).

Principal component analysis is a separate technique from ML factor analysis, because it partitions the variance of the correlational matrix into new principal components. However, both are similar in that they are sound psychometric procedures that allow for data reduction. Principal component analysis partitions the total variance of all original variables by finding the first linear combination of variables that accounts for the maximum variance. Then, the procedure finds a second linear combination that is uncorrelated (i.e., orthogonal) with the first one. This second principal component (PC) accounts for the next largest amount of variance after the variance attributed to the first component has been removed. The third PC is constructed to be uncorrelated with the first two, and accounts for the third largest amount of variance in the system, and so on. Thus, each successive PC accounts for the maximum amount of the variance that is left. The result is that a much smaller number of components summarize the majority of the variance of the original set of variables. That is, typically 60% to 75% of the variance can be explained by five or less principal components.

Interpretation of ML and PCA

The results from ML factor analysis and PCA are interpreted similarly by examining the variables with the highest loadings on each factor or component. Within ML factor analysis, however, the primary aim is directed toward explaining the correlation between the variables via the use of hypothetical constructs. In contrast, PCA does not necessarily equate the existence of a PC with that of a hypothetical construct, because a PC is simply a mathematical function of the observed variables. Thus, PCA is used as a way of achieving economy of representation by examining the first few components in order to account for as much variance of the data as possible. This retention of only the first few major components is also known as a *truncated* PCA and often yields results similar to ML factor analysis.

Advantages and Disadvantages of ML and PCA

There are at least three advantages to using PCA. First, the principal components are orthogonal with each other (Harris, 1985). In this way, PCA provides
for an automatic partitioning of the variables. This may be of benefit to the
Rorschach researcher because the comparisons made between separate
components do not provide redundant information because they are uncorrelated. Second, it has the advantage of hierarchical ordering of the components in terms of the percentage of variance accounted for. In other words,
the results from PCA, unlike those represented by the common factor model,
are designed to account for the highest percentage of the variation among the
variables with as few principal components as possible. Thus, Principal
Component 1 accounts for the largest portion of the variance, with each
successive PC contributing as high a percentage of the total variance as
possible, while remaining uncorrelated with all preceding components (Harris, 1985). The third advantage of using PCA with Rorschach data is related to
the degree of high colinearity that many Rorschach data sets may have. PCA
is less affected by problems of colinearity than ML factor analysis, and as such,
will calculate principal components on data sets when ML factor analysis may
not converge on separate common factors. Of course, if there is evidence of
very high colinearity, one may discuss the wisdom of performing any kind
of data reduction analysis, whether it is PCA or ML, because the identification
of meaningful, separate factors or components is unlikely.

    As with most statistical procedures, the choice between using ML and
PCA depends on the goals of the user. If the main objective of the analysis
is to explain the correlational matrix in terms of a smaller number of factors,
by achieving an imposition of a hypothetical model or an underlying hypothetical structure, then ML factor analysis is preferred. One further advantage
of the ML method is that it provides the user with a large sample significance
test (i.e., the chi-square goodness-of-fit test), which offers a probability value
of whether a given factor model significantly deviates from the observed
data. The Rorschach researcher who is primarily interested in data reduction
should consider PCA. Many researchers use PCA because they expect a clear
and compelling substantive interpretation, that is, the presence of simple
structure (i.e., the factors can be most readily and unambiguously interpreted). If simple structure does not occur, ML factor analysis can then be
considered as the next step.

    One main criticism of PCA is that the resulting principal components may
not be related to a hypothetical construct at all, but may simply display
components with common variance. Thus, the results from PCA may leave the
researcher with relatively few theoretical implications of the model. Conversely, the criticism directed toward ML analysis centers around the issue of
whether a hypothetical or theoretical model realistically exists with a particular
data set.

Having discussed the advantages of both procedures, it should be noted that, more often than not, both methods yield similar results. In fact, most statisticians would consider PCA a variant of ML factor analysis, because both use similar algorithms. In order to demonstrate the different results, if any, we examine both PCA and ML factor analysis solutions for the simplified RORFAC data set.

INITIAL STATISTICS:
THE ISSUE OF COMMUNALITIES

Up to this point, factor analysis has been discussed on a purely descriptive level, that is, as an aid in describing the structure underlying a system of variables, or in explaining the covariance among these variables. We now turn to the actual mathematical procedures involved in factor analysis. Tables 12.4 and 12.5 contain the initial statistics from the SPSS-X printout for the RORFAC data using PCA and ML methods of extraction, respectively. The first two columns in each table provide information about the individual Rorschach variables (i.e., the variable name and the communality of that variable), and the last four columns describe the factors. Although variable names and factors are displayed on the same line, there is no correspondence between the two (in fact, they are separated by an asterisk). Because the algorithms used for PCA and ML factor analysis are comparable, the outputs of the initial statistics are identical for both procedures. The only exception is that all communalities have a value of 1 in the initial statistics for PCA.

TABLE 12.4
Initial Statistics: Principal-Components Analysis ($N = 160$)

Variable	Communality	*	Factor	Eigenvalue	Pct. of Var.	Cum. Pct.
FShade	1.00	*	1	5.03	29.6	29.6
ShadeF	1.00	*	2	2.56	15.1	44.7
R	1.00	*	3	1.39	8.2	52.9
W	1.00	*	4	1.08	6.4	59.3
S	1.00	*	5	.98	5.7	65.0
M	1.00	*	6	.96	5.6	70.6
FD	1.00	*	7	.78	4.6	75.2
FC'	1.00	*	8	.70	4.1	79.4
C'F + C'	1.00	*	9	.64	3.7	83.1
m	1.00	*	10	.54	3.2	86.3
Zf	1.00	*	11	.49	2.9	89.1
FC	1.00	*	12	.43	2.5	91.7
CF + C	1.00	*	13	.42	2.4	94.1
P	1.00	*	14	.34	2.0	96.1
X + %	1.00	*	15	.27	1.6	97.7
F + %	1.00	*	16	.27	1.6	99.3
X − %	1.00	*	17	.12	.7	100.0

TABLE 12.5
Initial Statistics: Maximum Likelihood Factor Analysis ($N = 160$)

Variable	Communality	*	Factor	Eigenvalue	Pct. of Var.	Cum. Pct.
FShade	.45	*	1	5.03	29.6	29.6
ShadeF	.48	*	2	2.57	15.1	44.7
R	.54	*	3	1.39	8.2	52.9
W	.70	*	4	1.08	6.4	59.3
S	.48	*	5	.98	5.7	65.0
M	.41	*	6	.96	5.6	70.6
FD	.24	*	7	.78	4.6	75.2
FC'	.21	*	8	.70	4.1	79.4
C'F + C'	.43	*	9	.64	3.7	83.1
m	.43	*	10	.54	3.2	86.3
Zf	.80	*	11	.49	2.9	89.1
FC	.47	*	12	.43	2.5	91.7
CF + C	.51	*	13	.42	2.4	94.1
P	.52	*	14	.34	2.0	96.1
X + %	.59	*	15	.27	1.6	97.7
F + %	.32	*	16	.27	1.6	99.3
X − %	.48	*	17	.12	.7	100.0

Communalities are very important in factor analysis, because the actual calculation of how communalities are derived defines the different approaches to factor analysis. The communality is the amount of systematic variation for each variable accounted for by the set of factors (in this case the 17 factors that make up the initial statistics). Communalities can range in value from 0 to 1, with 0 indicating that the common factors do not explain any of the variance of that particular variable, and 1 indicating that all the variance of the variable is explained by the common factors. In an orthogonal factor model, the communality is equivalent to the sum of the squared factor loadings. The precise calculation of the values of communalities in the maximum likelihood model, however, are very complex and a detailed discussion of these formulae would be too lengthy for this review. The present discussion only serves the purpose of making the Rorschach researcher aware of high and/or low communalities among Rorschach variables and their effect on extracting common factors. For our purposes, then, the value of communalities is simply the variance of an observed variable accounted for by the common factors.

Factor analysts have been plagued since the beginning of multiple factor approaches by the lack of a priori knowledge of the values of the communalities. If many of the variables have high communalities (e.g., > .7), it would be difficult to define a factor solution, because all variables in the matrix have a strong degree of association (high colinearity), suggesting the likelihood of a one-factor model. Conversely, if communalities are very low (e.g., < .3), then a situation occurs in which very few variables are associated with each other and a suitable approximation of the number of common factors is not possible.

Stevens (1986) proposed that when the number of variables is moderately large (e.g., > 30), and the analysis contains virtually no variables with low communalities (e.g., < .4), then practically any of the available factor procedures will lead to the same interpretation. Differences can occur when the number of variables is fairly small (e.g., < 20) and some communalities are low.

The value of communalities influences how quickly the factor process stops at convergence (i.e., the "coming together" or "merging" of factors). Convergence occurs when the optimal number of common factors have been identified, or alternatively, after a preset number of iterations for the factor extraction has been calculated. In factor analysis, iterations are a computational method in which a succession of approximations, each building on the preceding one, is used to achieve a desired degree of factor simplicity. Particularly when matrices display high colinearity, the process of factor analysis does not need to always converge and will exceed the default value, which in SPSS-X is set at 25 iterations. In such cases, no factor solution can be obtained, because the independence of variables assumption has been violated and the statistical analysis will be terminated because of the correlational matrix being ill-conditioned (SPSS, 1988).

Note that for the initial PCA statistics displayed in Table 12.4, all variables have a communality of 1 because all are assumed to be uncorrelated. Table 12.5 shows that, within the ML model of extraction, the communalities range from .21 for FC', to .80 for Zf, suggesting that FC' has the least variance and Zf the most variance accounted for by the 17 common factors. Only two of the 17 variables have communalities below .3 (i.e., FD and FC') and two have communalities above .7 (i.e., Zf and W). The average communality of .47 indicates neither high colinearity nor complete independence of the variables. Thus, the extraction of common factors should be possible. These communality values will change, however, once the factor solution is simplified by means of retaining a smaller number of factors.

DETERMINING THE NUMBER
OF FACTORS TO BE RETAINED

At this point, there is no need to be concerned with whether the initial factors are meaningful or interpretable. The primary concern is whether a smaller number of factors can account for the covariation among all 17 RORFAC variables. The simple goal here is to decide on the number of common factors that best represents the correlational matrix. To obtain this goal, the researcher must now determine the criterion or set of criteria by which a specific number of common factors can be extracted. Because there are many different components that contribute to the assessment of model fit, there are several procedures that have been proposed for determining the precise number of factors to be retained in any given factor model.

Eigenvalues > 1

The most commonly used procedure for determining the number of initial factors to be extracted is the Eigenvalue > 1 criterion or Kaiser rule (Kaiser, 1960), which states that only factors that account for variances greater than 1 should be retained. Unless otherwise specified, the default criteria for SPSS-X and BMDP are set at the Eigenvalue > 1 criterion. Factors with a variance less than 1 are no better than a single variable. For the RORFAC data set, the Kaiser rule suggests that we should retain the first 4 components or factors (see Tables 12.4 and 12.5). Although the Kaiser rule allows for the identification and subsequent retention of the most important factors, one criticism of this procedure is that it often leads to retaining additional factors with no practical significance (in terms of percent of variance explained). In general, the Eigenvalue criteria is more accurate when the number of variables is small or moderate (10 to 30) and the communalities are high (> .70).

The Scree Test

This is an additional procedure used for both ML and PCA, by which one examines the graph of Eigenvalues (or variances) associated with each factor and attempts to identify the point at which the Eigenvalues begin to level off (Cattell, 1966; Kim & Mueller, 1990b). Typically, the plot shows a distinct break between the steep slope of the large factors and the gradual trailing off of the rest of the factors. This is referred to as factorial litter or scree, a geological term used to describe debris that collects on the lower parts of a rocky slope (Cattell, 1966). Experimental evidence recommends that all Figenvalues in the sharp descent before they level off be retained. A scree plot for the RORFAC data set is illustrated in Fig. 12.4, which suggests that the straightening of the line or the breaking point indicates that no more than three factors should be retained. These three factors account for large or fairly large and distinct amounts of variance (i.e., 29.6% for Factor 1, 15.1% for Factor 2, and 8.2% for Factor 3, for a total variance of 52.9%).

There may be instances in which there are several major breaks in the slope of Eigenvalues, thus the process of scree analysis can be rather subjective given the absence of any unambiguous rules. Furthermore, blind use of this criteria can lead to rejection of factors that may have practical significance, although they may account for a smaller amount of variance. Hakstian, Rogers, and Cattell (1982) suggested that both the Kaiser and scree rules will yield accurate estimates of the true number of factors to be retained when the sample size is large (i.e., $N > 250$), when the mean communality > .60, and when the Q/P ratio is < .30 (were P is the number of variables and Q is the number of factors). In our RORFAC example, N is 160, the

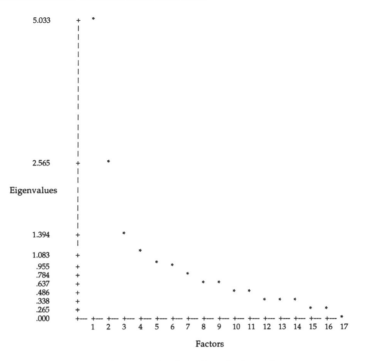

FIG. 12.4. Scree plot for RORFAC Eigenvalues.

mean communality is .47, and the Q/P ratio is .24 for a four-factor solution and .18 for a three-factor model. With smaller communalities and larger Q/P ratios the Kaiser rule is less accurate and the scree rule much less accurate.

Total Percent of Variance Explained

The column labeled *Pct. of Var.* in Tables 12.4 and 12.5 contains the percentage of the total variance attributable to each factor. For example, the linear combination formed by Factor 3 has a variance of 1.39, which is 8.2% of the total variance. The third column *Cum. Pct.* displays the cumulative percentage, which indicates the percentage of variance attributable to that factor and those that precede it in the table. Note that the factors are arranged in descending order of variance explained. Tables 12.4 and 12.5 show that 52.9% of the total variance is explained by the first 3 factors. The remaining 14 factors together account for only 47.1% of the variance. Conversely, the retention of the first 5 factors accounts for 65% of the total variance.

In behavioral science research, we want to generally account for at least 70% variance of the correlational matrix, although in some cases the investigator may not be satisfied unless over 80% of the variance is explained (Stevens, 1986). Naturally, the higher the total variance accounted for, the better the factor model represents the data. The drawback with retaining a high number of factors to ensure a predetermined amount of variance, is that it often increases the number of common factors that are essentially variable specific (i.e., they only load highly on a single variable).

Chi-square Goodness-of-Fit Test

In addition to the previous procedures, the ML method of factor analysis also provides a large sample statistical significance goodness-of-fit test. This global index, which is not available for PCA, reflects how well the model as a whole reproduces the relationship among variables in the form of a chi-square test of significance, by calculating a probability value that the correlational matrix was generated by the proposed model. The p value associated with this test corresponds to the hypothesis of obtaining the observed data if the covariance matrix has the structure of the matrix (i.e., if, in fact, the model were true). This procedure can be of assistance to the researcher, because the specific number of factors is not known in most factor analysis applications and the number of factors is increased until a reasonably good fit is obtained (i.e., until the chi-square variate is no longer significant).

Table 12.6 contains the goodness-of-fit statistics for ML extraction of the RORFAC data set, when different numbers of common factors are retained. As the number of factors increases, the chi-square value decreases and the associated p value increases. Also, the number of iterations, the process when factoring stops and convergence is achieved, increases as more factors are included in the solution. In this example, seven factors should be retained in the ML model to adequately explain the RORFAC data using the chi-square test criterion. In practice, and specifically with large sample sizes, one difficulty with relying exclusively on the chi-square significance test is that, more often than not, the researcher ends up with more common factors than are desirable for a meaningful factor solution. Thus, the goodness-of-fit test may cause rather small discrepancies in fit to be deemed statistically significant, often resulting in a larger number of factors being retained than are really necessary. The researcher may, therefore, reject the test in favor of choosing a more parsimonious factor model with fewer common factors and less goodness-of-fit, but better interpretability.

TABLE 12.6
Goodness-of-fit Statistics for RORFAC Data

Number of Factors	Chi-square Statistic	Iterations Required	Significance (p)
3	192.81	7	.0000
4	124.51	6	.0002
5	96.60	19	.0025
6	75.49	15	.0089
7	50.48	17	.0801

Maximizing the Interpretability of the Factor Model

Using the previous procedures it has been determined that the final factor solution of the RORFAC data set should retain either 4 factors based on the Eigenvalue criteria, 3 factors based on the scree test, 5 factors if we want to explain at least 70% of the total variance, or 7 factors (in the case of ML extraction) based on the chi-square test of significance. The "true" number of common factors for the current model is therefore somewhere between 3 and 7 factors, depending on the criteria used for goodness-of-fit. There is, however, one additional consideration that needs to be addressed before deciding on a specific number of factors and it is related to the issue of factorial simplicity. The reader will recall that the chief aim in factor analysis is to attain scientific parsimony or economy of description of observable behavior (Harman, 1970). This goal should not necessarily be construed to mean that factor analysis attempts to discover all basic dimensions of Rorschach data, but that factor analysis can provide coverage of as many aspects of a given population as possible. Thus, factor analysis should provide a simpler interpretation of the original data set.

One guideline in selecting the number of factors to be retained is to use the previous decision rules as a general rule of thumb and to choose a final factor solution based on statistical simplicity and psychological meaningfulness—that is, to rely on parsimonious models in favor of complex ones. For example, a certain degree of parsimony can be achieved by initially selecting the minimum number of common factors that could produce the observed covariance structure. If a three-factor model explains the observed data as well as a four-factor solution, the researcher should retain the more parsimonious one.

When more complex models are presented, the burden is on the researcher to explain, usually in the form of a theoretical discussion, why a more complex model is better suited than a simpler one. In actual factor analysis where one has to deal with sampling and measurement errors, the choice may never be clear-cut. The final selection of a particular factor model may be a matter of personal preference or of the general interpretability of the factor structure, because the appropriate rotation of the factor axes can change the suitability of different models. In the end, the final factor structure can be open to discussion and often more than one model is presented to the reader (e.g., see Zillmer et al., 1992).

EXAMINING THE FINAL FACTOR MATRIX

In the initial factor extraction phase, the number of common factors needed to adequately describe the data was explored by examining the percentage of total variance accounted for, the Eigenvalues (or plot thereof), the goodness-of-fit statistic (in the case of ML analysis), and the interpretability and overall appropriateness of the factor solution. Regarding the current example, we will initially examine the most parsimonious three-factor solution and will only reject it for a more complex four- or five-factor model, if such a model is more meaningful.

PCA Three-factor Model

The three-factor model for PCA is shown in Table 12.7. In SPSS-X, these tables are labeled as Final Statistics because they show the communalities and factor statistics after the desired number of factors (in this case three) have been extracted. When the factors are estimated using the method of PCA, the factor statistics are the same in the tables labeled *initial* and *final* (compare Tables 12.4 and 12.7). The values of the communalities have changed, however, because the variance of all variables is not explained when only a subset of factors is retained. For the PCA three-factor solution these communalities range from .22 for variable *FD*, to .73 for *X+%*. The average communality is .53 and the first three components account for 52.9% of the total variance.

The PCA three-factor matrix is displayed in Table 12.8, which shows the factor loadings for each component sorted in order from highest to lowest loading. When the estimated factors are uncorrelated with each other, as they are in PCA, the factor loadings are also the correlations between the factors and the variables. Variables with large coefficients (in absolute value)

TABLE 12.7
Final Statistics: Principal-Components Analysis ($N = 160$)

Variable	Communality		Factor	Eigenvalue	Pct. of Var.	Cum. Pct.
FShade	.56	*	1	5.03	29.6	29.6
ShadeF	.64	*	2	2.57	15.1	44.7
R	.59	*	3	1.39	8.2	52.9
W	.50	*				
S	.50	*				
M	.34	*				
FD	.22	*				
FC'	.23	*				
C'F + C'	.50	*				
m	.52	*				
Zf	.72	*				
FC	.53	*				
CF + C	.71	*				
P	.66	*				
X + %	.73	*				
F + %	.44	*				
X - %	.60	*				

TABLE 12.8
Factor Matrix: Principal-Components Analysis ($N = 160$)

	PC 1	PC 2	PC 3
Zf	.80	.22	.18
R	.75	.13	.09
W	.71	−.08	−.00
m	.67	.12	−.24
S	.67	−.20	.13
ShadeF	.66	−.07	−.45
CF + C	.61	−.20	−.54
FShade	.60	.02	.44
FC	.58	.12	.43
M	.51	.28	.03
FD	.43	.18	.04
FC'	.40	−.12	.24
X + %	−.23	.81	−.13
P	.19	.78	.11
X − %	.05	−.72	.28
F + %	−.10	.60	−.09
C'F + C'	.47	−.22	−.48

Note: PC = Principal Component.

are closely related to their principal component. Thus, Principal Component 1 (PC 1) is defined primarily by Rorschach variables *Zf*, *R*, and *W*, which are correlated with the first component .80, .75, and .71, respectively.

ML Three-factor Solution

If a factor extraction method other than PCA is used, there are differences in the factor output. For example, Table 12.9 contains the final statistics for a three-factor solution of the RORFAC data set when the ML algorithm is used. The final three factors extracted explain only 43.6% of the total variance compared to 52.9% for the first three components derived from PCA. The first factor accounts for 21.2% of the total variance as compared to 29.6% for the first principal component. The communalities for the ML three-factor model are also different than those for the PCA output, ranging from .12 for variable *FC'* to .99 for variable *Zf*, with an average communality of .44. The factor matrix for the ML solution is displayed in Table 12.10.

Naming and Interpreting the Factors

Once a factor matrix has been computed, we can proceed with the interpretation and naming of the factors. This commonly involves an examination of the factor structure, that is, the relationships between each of the original variables and each of the three factors. By far the most common procedure

TABLE 12.9
Final Statistics: Maximum Likelihood Factor Analysis ($N = 160$)

Variable	Communality	*	Factor	Eigenvalue	Pct. of Var.	Cum. Pct.
FShade	.25	*	1	3.59695	21.2	21.2
ShadeF	.50	*	2	2.30459	13.6	34.7
R	.49	*	3	1.51610	8.9	43.6
W	.63	*				
S	.38	*				
M	.29	*				
FD	.15	*				
FC'	.12	*				
C'F + C'	.48	*				
m	.43	*				
Zf	.99	*				
FC	.24	*				
CF + C	.46	*				
P	.50	*				
X + %	.76	*				
F + %	.27	*				
X − %	.48	*				

TABLE 12.10
Factor Matrix: Maximum Likelihood Analysis ($N = 160$)

	Factor 1	Factor 2	Factor 3
Zf	.99	.00	.00
W	.75	.26	.04
R	.62	.12	.32
M	.51	−.09	.16
m	.47	.13	.44
FC	.45	.08	.18
FShade	.45	.15	.16
S	.41	.34	.32
FD	.32	−.01	.20
FC'	.27	.18	.12
X + %	−.06	−.84	.22
X − %	−.01	.61	−.32
P	.33	−.60	.16
F + %	.05	−.51	.08
C'F + C'	.11	.35	.59
ShadeF	.41	.27	.51
CF + C	.39	.35	.44

for naming the factors is to single out those variables that have the highest loadings on each factor. Factor loadings or correlations below .25 are chance loadings and, as such, are not considered significant or interpretable (Cliff & Hamburger, 1967). If simple structure has been achieved there should be few, if any, variables with large loadings (> .25) on more than one factor.

When examining the Rorschach variables that have the highest loading on any particular factor we attempt to understand what psychological dimension these variables have in common. For example, it is apparent that Factor 1 and PC 1 (see Tables 12.8 and 12.10) are primarily composed of Rorschach variables *Zf*, *W*, and *R*, which represents a Holistic Response Frequency dimension. Factor 2 and PC 2 can be labeled a Perceptual Accuracy factor, because they are primarily defined by Rorschach scoring categories *X+%*, *X–%*, *P*, and *F+%* (although the order of factor loading differs somewhat for PCA and ML).

Highly positive loadings help to identify one end of the underlying dimension, whereas highly negative loadings (if any) define the opposite end of that same dimension. Thus, the different signs for Factor 2 and PC 2 in Tables 12.8 and 12.10 simply imply that the variables are related to that dimension in opposite directions. For example, *X+%* and *X–%* load on the same construct, but on opposite ends. Factor 3 in the ML three-factor model can be labeled a non-form-dominant Response factor composed of variables *C'F+C'*, sum of all non-form-dominant shading responses, and *CF+C*. PC 3 is defined by only one variable (*C'F+C'*) and cannot be readily interpreted.

Because the process of interpreting factors or components depends on an examination of those measures or items having the highest loadings on each factor, it is obviously subjective in nature and often left open to controversy. This raises the potential problem of naming or labeling in factor analysis and refers to the very persistent, and at times difficult, task of finding substantive interpretations of some set of hypothetical latent variables that have been derived through PCA or ML factor analysis. In our example, the ML three-factor solution is easier to interpret than the PCA model, because each ML factor has at least two variables. The PCA model in Table 12.8 is somewhat difficult to interpret as 12 of the 17 variables load highly on PC 1 and only one variable loads on PC 3. Most researchers would agree that for any factor or principal component to be meaningful, it should be composed of at least two variables. However, the PCA factor solution accounts for almost 10% more than the model derived from ML extraction.

INCREASING THE INTERPRETABILITY
OF THE FACTOR MODEL BY ROTATION

There remain some restrictions for both the PCA and ML solutions, however, which make the interpretation of the current three-factor models difficult. For example, the factors are not clearly defined because many variables have low to moderate size loadings. Also, in some instances, variables load on more than one factor, which makes it difficult to ascertain how the factors differ. Furthermore, most of the 17 Rorschach variables load on Factor 1 or PC 1. One way to adjust the interpretability of the factor model is to adjust the model through a set of operations known as rotations. By rotating the solution, the size of the loadings in the factor model can be changed in order to obtain more readily interpretable results and a more parsimonious model.

Plotting the Reference Axes

The primary goal of rotation is to achieve simple structure to permit the factors to be differentiated from each other more clearly. In our example, the three-factor model is adjusted (rotated) with the goal of providing a more meaningful interpretation of the factor model compared to the unrotated PCA and ML solutions. The method of rotation does not change or improve the degree of fit between the data and the factor structure, but rather serves the purpose of a possible simplification of the factor model. In this sense, rotating the factor structure does not change the final statistics or the communalities; instead, it rearranges the variables and the loadings in the factor matrix. Thus, through the process of rotation, the explained variance for the individual factors is redistributed. Different rotation methods often result in the identification of somewhat different factors. Any simplification of the factor structure that results in more meaningful dimensions is at the heart of exploratory factor analysis. Thus, any available method of rotation that accomplishes this simplification of the factor model is acceptable. Therefore, there is no harm in altering or adjusting the positions of the reference axes in such a way as to make the task of providing substantive interpretations of the hypothetical variables as meaningful as possible.

A customary way of examining factor patterns is to represent factors geometrically in factor space as reference axes. For example, the SPSS-X command PLOT = ROTATION provides a graphic representation of the factor loadings that can aid in the identification of factors. It is difficult to illustrate graphically a three-factor model in two-dimensional space, thus we attempt to simplify this procedure by plotting only two factors, in this case Factors 2 and 3 from the ML method solution. In fact, most factor models yield more than two factors, which complicates the geometrical representation but does not alter the basic procedure described here. For example, in Fig. 12.5, each of the 17 Rorschach variables from Table 12.10 have been plotted against Factors 2 and 3 using the SPSS-X command PLOT = ROTATION (2 3). Rorschach variables representing Factor 2 (i.e., X+%, X−%, P, and F+%) are located closer in proximity to the horizontal axis and Rorschach variables representing Factor 3 (i.e., C′F+C′, ShadeF, CF+C) are closer to the vertical axis.

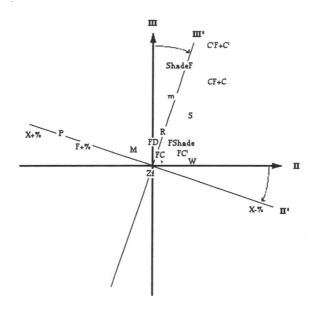

Note. Horizontal Axis II = Factor 2 (Perceptual Acuracy); Vertical Axis III = Factor 3 (Non-Form Dominance).

FIG. 12.5. Two-dimensional factor plot.

All the Rorschach variables are plotted corresponding to their weights given in Table 12.10 for Factors 2 and 3. Thus, variable $X+\%$ is located in factor space by moving .22 of the distance along Axis III (Factor 3) and $-.84$ of the distance along Axis II (Factor 2). If a rotation has achieved a simple structure, clusters of variables should occur near the ends of the axes and at their intersection. Variables at the end of an axis are those that have high loadings on only that factor. Variables that are not near the axes are explained by both factors (e.g., $CF+C$), and variables near the origin (i.e., the cross section) of the plot have small loadings on both factors (i.e., Zf, R, FC, FD, M, FC', $FShade$, W). Most psychologists are at least as interested in describing the axes (or dimensions) themselves as they are in describing the relationship among the variables.

It is important to understand that the position of the axes is not fixed by the data. The factor matrix determines only the position of the Rorschach variables in relation to each other. The same variables can be plotted with the axes in any position until a satisfactory and easily interpretable pattern emerges. As Anastasi (1988) pointed out, this is a "legitimate procedure, somewhat analogous to measuring longitude from Chicago rather than Greenwich" (p. 376). There are several methods of rotation. The first one is to examine the pattern of variables graphically and then *hand rotate* the axes, or define the new axes, in such a way that they satisfy one's criterion of simple and meaningful structure. However, when the pattern is not very clear, or there are many factors to examine, such a graphical rotation is not practical.

The second approach is to rely on some analytic rotation method that is free of subjective judgment, at least after a particular criterion of simplicity is chosen. There are in fact numerous variations, but only two different subtypes to this approach—orthogonal (uncorrelated) and oblique (correlated) rotations—are discussed here. When the axes are maintained at right angles, the rotation is called orthogonal. If the axes are not maintained at right angles, the rotation is called oblique. Again, the goal of the rotation procedure is to achieve the simplest possible factor structure. We discuss orthogonal rotations first.

Orthogonal Rotations

In this rotation procedure, we do not have to rely on the initial rigid reference axes, but can instead draw the axes directly through the cluster of variables to find a factor solution that is closest to the simplest ideal structure. In Fig. 12.5, for example, the reference axes can be rotated orthogonally to position II' and III' to maximize simple structure. Note that if the axes went directly through the data points, a simpler factor pattern matrix would emerge than with the original nonrotated model. After rotation, Rorschach variables $X+\%$, P, $F+\%$, and $X-\%$ fall along or very close to Axis II'. Similarly, Rorschach variable $C'F+C'$, $ShadeF$, $CF+C$, and m cluster closely around Axis III'.

Before attempting orthogonal rotations, the reader must understand that the initial factor loadings are nothing more than the projection of all variables onto the two axes. An orthogonal rotation will set up another reference axis that is perpendicular, but that passes through the majority of the data points (see Fig. 12.5). A variety of algorithms are used for orthogonal rotation to simple structure (which are also referred to as orthogonal transformations or rigid rotations). The most commonly used orthogonal rotation is the Varimax method, which attempts to minimize the number of variables that have high loadings on a factor by simplifying each column of the factor matrix (Kaiser, 1960).

The Varimax method of rotation "cleans up" the factors and will generally make the interpretation of the resulting factor matrix easier. The Quartimax criteria tends to produce final solutions in which there is a general factor with moderate and small loadings on some variables. Here the rotation is completed so that each variable loads on mainly one factor, subsequently making the interpretation of the factor difficult (which is one of the shortcomings of the Quartimax method of rotation). Finally, the Equimax criteria obtains an orthogonal solution that is a compromise between the Varimax method, which simplifies the factors, and the Quartimax criteria, which simplifies the variables. Most existing computer programs for factor analysis have available several rotation commands from which to choose, with Varimax being the default option in SPSS-X and BMDP.

Next we shall consider Table 12.10, which shows the factor matrix for the RORFAC data before rotation, and Table 12.11, which displays the matrix after a Varimax orthogonal rotation procedure. If a simple structure has been achieved, there should be few, if any, variables with large loadings on more than one factor (Norusis, 1988). After rotation, the number of large and small factor loadings should increase, making the interpretation of factors easier. In Table 12.11, Factor 3 is now somewhat better defined as primarily a Non-form-dominant factor because the first three variables $C'F+C'$, *ShadeF*, and *CF+C* load highly with this factor. The second factor is composed of $X+\%$, $X-\%$, *P* and $F+\%$, a Perceptual Accuracy factor. The first factor remains more complex than the other two, as it is associated with a holistic Response Frequency as well as a Form-dominant Response dimension.

Oblique Rotations

In the rotated Varimax solution, the reference axes remain rigid in the sense that they retain the orthogonality of the factors. Even after an orthogonal rotation the resulting factors may still correspond poorly to the researchers' preconceptions of the nature of the latent factors, because realistically, the underlying hypothetical constructs are almost never uncorrelated to each other. If this is the case, allowing for correlations among factors may provide

TABLE 12.11
Factor Matrix: ML Varimax Rotation

	Factor 1	Factor 2	Factor 3
Zf	.99	.08	.06
W	.75	−.17	.18
R	.59	.06	.38
M	.49	.18	.15
FShade	.44	−.04	.23
FC	.44	.03	.23
FD	.30	.11	.20
FC'	.27	−.10	.19
X + %	−.13	.85	−.11
X − %	.06	−.68	−.07
P	.28	.65	−.05
F + %	.02	.51	−.11
C'F + C'	.07	−.10	.68
ShadeF	.37	−.03	.60
CF + C	.36	−.13	.56
m	.43	.08	.48
S	.40	−.16	.45

a better fit to reality. Thus, there are several reasons why rotations that allow for correlation among the factors have come into favor. It is unlikely, for example, that determinants of behavior are uncorrelated. Oblique rotations have therefore often resulted in yielding substantively meaningful factors compared to orthogonal rotations. Although the orthogonal (i.e., uncorrelated) rotation provides a simpler and clearer picture of the relationship of the Rorschach variables to each other, the oblique rotation may fit the data better, because most meaningful categories need not be uncorrelated. This is particularly the case in social sciences where there are rarely traits that are completely uncorrelated to each other. Rather, they are highly correlated yet remain useful in describing distinctively different behaviors. Thus, an oblique rotation can be advantageous in psychology, because it does not arbitrarily impose the restriction that factors be uncorrelated.

When employing an oblique rotation, the researcher will most often use a criterion based on simplifying loadings on the primary factor. As with orthogonal rotation, oblique rotations preserve the communality of the variables. When oblique rotation is used, however, the factor loadings are still partial regression coefficients. But because the factors are correlated, they are no longer equal to the simple factor variable correlations. Therefore, SPSS-X presents separate tables for the factor loadings and factor structure matrices as part of the printout with oblique rotations (in SPSS-X this rotation is referred to as OBLIMIN). In the oblique rotation, the pattern matrix and structure matrix each tells us about different aspects of the relationship between factors and variables for factor solutions of an oblique nature. The pattern matrix reflects the causal weights and the structure matrix reflects the correlations. The great majority of factor analysts would assume as a matter of course that it is the loadings, rather than the factor coefficients, that define a given factor.

Thus, most Rorschach researchers are interested in reducing the relationship between all Rorschach data entered for factor analysis to their source variables and prefer the examination of the pattern matrix displayed in Table 12.12. In this case, the coefficients below .25 have been suppressed in order to highlight the factor loadings and facilitate interpretation of the factors. This format subcommand is available in SPSS-X using FORMAT = BLANK (.25). Note that the loadings are no longer constrained to a range from −1 to +1 (e.g., *Zf* has a loading of 1.10). This should be of little concern to the factor researcher unless the rare situation occurs in which the communality of the variable is also greater than one. Such a solution is known as a "Heywood" case (see Harman, 1970).

A convenient method of examining the success of an oblique rotation is to plot the variables using the factor loadings as coordinates. In Fig. 12.6, the variables are plotted using Factors 2 and 3 after an oblique rotation (i.e., the factors are rotated without imposing the orthogonality condition and

TABLE 12.12
Pattern Matrix: ML Oblique (Oblimin) Rotation

	Factor 1	Factor 2	Factor 3
Zf	1.10		
W	.80		
R	.55		
M	.50		
FShade	.43		
FC	.42		
FD	.28		
FC'	.25		
X + %		−.86	
X − %		.70	
P	.30	−.63	
F + %		−.50	
C'F + C'			.74
ShadeF	.25		.55
CF + C	.25		.50
m	.34		.41
S	.32		.36

Note. Factor loadings < .25 have been omitted.

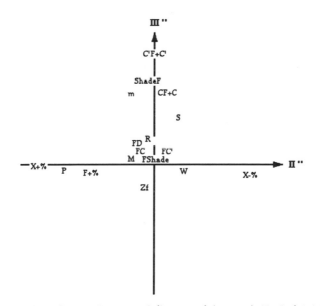

Note. Horizontal Axis II″ = Factor 2 (Perceptual Accuracy); Vertical Axis III″ = Factor 3 (Non-Form Dominance).

FIG. 12.6. Two-dimensional factor plot for ML method after oblique rotation.

295

resulting factors are generally correlated with each other). The coordinates correspond to the factor loadings in Table 12.12 for the oblique rotated solution. If a rotation has achieved simple structure (as is the case here), the clusters of variables should occur near the ends of the axes and at their intersection. Variables near the origin of the plot have small loadings on both factors (in this case, variables that load on Factor 1). Thus, the test clusters are so situated that a better fit can be obtained with oblique axes (compare Fig. 12.5, before rotation, with Fig. 12.6, after oblique rotation). For example, all variables defining Factor 2 fall along or very close to Axis II' and all variables from Factor 3 cluster closely around Axis III'.

In our RORFAC example, the orthogonal rotation has resulted in a somewhat clearer identification and naming of the factors, which was subsequently improved with the oblique rotation, although the interpretation of the factors did not change in either of the two rotation procedures. For comparison purposes, we also present the three-factor pattern matrix for principal component analysis in Table 12.13. Readers can compare for themselves that the oblique rotation for ML and PCA (see Tables 12.12 and 12.13) are very similar. For the most part, the factors are composed of the same variables with similar loadings. The only exception is that Rorschach variable S loads on Factor 1 within the PCA model, but on Factor 3 in the ML solution.

Because the factors in the oblique solution are correlated, we can examine the relationships among the three factors in a factor correlation matrix. Conversely, in the case of an orthogonal rotation, the factor correlation matrix

TABLE 12.13
Pattern Matrix: PCA Oblique Rotation

	PC 1	PC 2	PC 3
FShade	.79		
FC	.78		
Zf	.75		
R	.62		−.26
S	.55		
W	.49		−.35
FC'	.46		
M	.43	.26	
FD	.36		
X + %		.82	
X − %		−.77	
P	.33	.73	
F + %		.65	
CF + C			−.85
ShadeF			−.76
C'F + C'			−.73
m	.30		−.53

Note. Factor loadings < .25 have been omitted.

is an identity matrix; that is, there are 1's on the diagonal and 0's elsewhere. The correlation matrices for the three-factor ML and PCA oblique rotations are displayed in Table 12.14. Note that Factor 1 or PC 1 (Response Frequency/Form Dominance) and Factor 3 or PC 3 (Non-form Dominance) are correlated the highest ($r = .50$ to $.39$ in absolute value). Thus, Factor 1 and Factor 3 share approximately 25%, and PC 1 and PC 2 approximately 15% common variance. This suggests that when values of variables defining Factor 1 or PC 1 increase, variables defining Factor 3 or PC 3 will also increase in value. Correlations between Factors 1 and 2 (or PC 1 and 2), as well as Factors 2 and 3 (or PC 2 and 3) are very small, ranging from .04 to .14 in absolute value. This suggests a relative independence among dimensions of Perceptual Accuracy and Response Frequency/Form Dominance or Non-form Dominance.

Simple Structure Principles

In the past, principles of simple structure have been vaguely defined and were often based on intuitive concepts rather than on any specific criteria. The criteria under consideration here are specifically intended for multiple-factor solutions and are as follows (Harman, 1970):

1. Each row of the factor matrix should have at least one zero loading.
2. If there are n common factors, each column of the factor matrix should have at least n zeros.
3. For every pair of columns of the factor matrix there should be several variables whose entries vanish in one column but not in the other.
4. For every pair of columns of the factor matrix, a large proportion of the variable should have vanishing entries in both columns when there are four or more factors.
5. For every pair of columns of the factor matrix there should be only a small number of variables with nonvanishing entries in both columns.

The psychological basis for this definition was perhaps best summarized by Thurstone (1954): "Just as we take it for granted that individual differences in visual acuity are not involved in pitch discrimination, so we assume that in intellectual tasks some mental or cortical functions are not involved in every task. This is the principle of simple structure" (p. 174).

The foregoing principles may be applied to either an orthogonal or an oblique multiple-factor solution. In general, the rotation of axes in order to arrive at simple structure may be viewed as an attempt to reduce the complexity of the variables. The ultimate objective would be an orthogonal uni-factor model in which each variable would not be related to other variables at all. As noted before, such a factor solution is practically impossible with Rorschach data, and not very likely seen even when factors are permitted to be oblique. Nevertheless, this is the ultimate objective, and it is toward that end that the simple structure principles are proposed for the multiple-factor solution. If the multiple-factor solution satisfies all five criteria listed, then the graphical plot in the plane of each pair of factors will exhibit many points near the two final factors, a large number of points near the origin, and only a small number of points removed from the origin and between the two axes (compare Figs. 12.5 and 12.6). When the two-dimensional diagrams for all combinations of factors satisfy these three characteristics, Thurstone referred to the structure as "compelling" and concluded that the "whole configuration is to be accepted as stable and ready for interpretation" (p. 179).

Comparing Three- and Four-factor Solutions

Thus far, we have focused exclusively on a three-factor solution for both ML and PCA methods of factor extraction. There remain, however, two problems with the current three-factor solution. First, both the PCA and ML method retain only 52.9% and 43.6% of the variance of the original data, respectively (see Tables 12.7 and 12.9). Most factor analysts will attempt to explain a larger proportion of the variance before they are satisfied. Second, the final, oblique-rotated pattern matrices (which are displayed in Tables 12.12 and 12.13) indicate that a number of Rorschach variables still have meaningful loadings on more than one factor (i.e., > .25). For example, it is interesting to note that Rorschach variables *P*, *ShadeF*, *CF+C*, *S*, and *m* load on more than one factor and that the lowest loadings were *FShade*, *FC*, *FD*, and *FC'*, variables that are sometimes associated with a form Dominant Response factor (see Table 12.12).

Thus, the proposed three-factor oblique model is not a perfect fit. A more complex factor model may account for a greater proportion of the variance and also reduce multiple loadings of variables. The reader will recall that the "true" number of factors for the RORFAC data may be anywhere between 3 and 7, depending on the criterion of good fit (e.g., the Eigenvalue > 1 criterion suggested retention of a four-factor model). It is therefore necessary to examine more complex factor models and to explore whether such models would provide a better fit of the data than did the three-factor model we have just discussed. Thus, it is common practice among factor analysts to examine more complex factor solutions and to retain them if they improve the overall interpretability of the data, and to reject them if they do not.

The four-factor pattern matrix (ML oblique rotation) is shown in Table 12.15. When comparing the four-factor model and the ML three-factor model displayed in Table 12.12, not one of the Rorschach variables have dual loadings in the four-factor model (i.e., > .25). Whereas Factors 2 and 3 are similar to the three-factor solution and can be labeled as Perceptual Accuracy

TABLE 12.14
Factor Correlations Matrix for ML Method Oblique Rotation

	Factor		
	1	*2*	*3*
Factor 1	1.00		
Factor 2	−.04 (.03)	1.00	
Factor 3	.50 (−.39)	.14 (.03)	1.00

Note. Correlations for PCA Oblique Rotation are in parentheses.

and Non-form-dominant Response factors, respectively, Factor 1 from the
three-factor solution in Table 12.12 has been split into two new factors. In
the four-factor model, Factor 1 is now composed of *Zf, W,* and *M*, which
define a Holistic Response factor, and Factor 4, which is defined by variables
FC, FShade, S, R, FC', and *FD*, a Form Dominant Response dimension.

Factor pattern correlations are also displayed in Table 12.15 and are very
similar to those reviewed in Table 12.14 for the three-factor solution. Interest-
ingly, the Perceptual Accuracy factor is not related to any of the other three
factors. The ML four-factor model accounts for approximately 50% of the
variance (i.e., over 6% more than the three-factor ML model) and also presents
a somewhat clearer clustering of Rorschach variables. This four-factor model

TABLE 12.15
Four-Factor Pattern Matrix: ML Oblique Rotation

	Factor 1	*Factor 2*	*Factor 3*	*Factor 4*
Zf	.88			
W	.73			
M	.40			
X + %		−.85		
X − %		.71		
P		−.65		
F + %		−.50		
CF + C			.73	
C'F + C'			.66	
ShadeF			.61	
m			.41	
FC				.74
FShade				.64
S				.57
R				.47
FC'				.32
FD				.26

Note. Factor loadings < .25 have been omitted. Factor pattern correlations are: Factors 1
and 2 = −.09, Factors 1 and 3 = .35, Factors 1 and 4 = .51, Factors 2 and 3 = .11, Factors 2 and
4 = .00, and, Factors 3 and 4 = .39.

is, therefore, a closer solution to simple structure and is the one that should be retained. However, some researchers may prefer the previously discussed three-factor solution, or alternatively, may continue to examine even more complex five- or six-factor models (not displayed here, because they failed to improve the overall interpretability of the four-factor model).

The current four-factor example, however, does not offer a complete model of Rorschach scoring categories. There are two reasons for this: First, the purpose of the present example was intended as nothing more than an exercise in factor analysis and not as a detailed investigation of the multi-dimensional factor structure of the Rorschach. Second, a smaller subset of variables was included in the factor analysis in order to simplify the obtained solution. Thus, no information about the factorial composition of Rorschach variables Egocentricity Index, D, or Lambda, among others, were offered. Nevertheless, the current results did suggest that the 17 Rorschach variables from the RORFAC data set have a four-dimensional factor structure and indicate that the Rorschach Comprehensive System provides distinct domains of personality. In this regard, the present findings are comparable to previous work in Rorschach factor analysis.

For example, the dimensions identified in both the three- and four-factor models are familiar ones, and have been reported for the Rorschach test with a variety of clinical samples (e.g., for a review of previous studies using Rorschach factor analysis see, Adcock, 1951; Borgatta & Eschenbach, 1955; Coan, 1956; Consalvi & Canter, 1957; Cox, 1951; Geertsma, 1962; Lotsof, 1953; Lotsof et al., 1958; Mason et al., 1985; Meyer, 1989; Shaffer et al., 1981; Williams & Lawrence, 1953, 1954; Wishner, 1959; Wittenborn, 1950a, 1950b).

ADDITIONAL ANALYSIS WITH FACTOR SCORES

In the previous discussion, different methods of obtaining linear resolution in terms of hypothetical factors of a set of Rorschach variables have been demonstrated. The results have been several different orthogonal and oblique three- and four-factor solutions. A further issue that has not been addressed, is related to the measurement of these factors as observed variables once they have been calculated. Because one of the goals of factor analysis is to reduce a large number of variables to a smaller number of factors, it is often desirable to estimate factor scores for each factor. These factor scores can then be used in subsequent analyses to represent the values of the factors. For example, having determined some underlying dimension of the Rorschach data (e.g., a Perceptual Accuracy factor), the researcher may want to examine the cases in terms of this construct, rather than in terms of each variable separately. Alternatively, the researcher may want to use one or more factors as variables in yet a different study, for example, as variables in a regression analysis. Thus, the discussion in this final segment on factor analysis focuses primarily on the creation of newly derived factors in terms of variables or factor scores.

There are several methods for estimating factor score coefficients. The three procedures available in SPSS-X are the Anderson–Rubin method, the regression method (which is the default procedure), and the Bartlett method. Each of the three methods has different properties and results in different factor scores (see Harman, 1970). All three procedures, however, result in a new set of factor score variables, with a mean of 0, which are based exclusively on the results of factor analysis.

Briefly, the Anderson–Rubin method produces uncorrelated scores with a standard deviation of 1, even when the original factors are estimated to be correlated. The factor scores derived from the regression method have a variance equal to the squared multiple correlation between the estimated factor scores and the true factor values. Regression method factor scores can be correlated even when factors are assumed to be orthogonal. The method for estimating the factor scores proposed by Bartlett is a mathematical variant of the regression method. If PCA extraction is used to determine the loadings of the factors, all three methods will result in the same factor scores, because they are no longer estimated, but are exact. In making a choice among these three methods of estimating factor scores, there is usually a very high degree of correlation among the three scaling methods and the differences are often minimal (Alwin, 1973; Kim & Mueller, 1990b).

In order to calculate the factor scores using any of the aforementioned procedures, one needs only to select an appropriate factor pattern, to specify the number of desired factor scores (in our RORFAC example either three or four), and to assign a name to the new factor score variables. For example, the SPSS-X FACTOR command SAVE REG (4 ROR) will calculate four-factor scores named ROR1, ROR2, ROR3, and ROR4 using the regression method.

Compared to the previous procedures, a simplified estimation of the factor scores is that of adding variables with high factor loadings. Here one may ignore specific variations in the factor loadings and consider only one type of information as relevant, whether or not a variable loads on a specific factor. This factor-based scale is determined by adding all the variables with substantial loadings and ignoring the remaining variables with minor loadings (e.g., < .25). Such a scale is easy to create; however, it is no longer a factor scale, but merely factor based. Although some object to such scale construction, simple weighting can be justified because the relationship between the newly formed scale and the total set of variables does not change substantially. Thus, the simple-weighted, factor-based scales have a legitimate place in research alongside the factor scales (Gorsuch, 1974). For example, it is possible to compute simple-weighted factor scores and then relate them to other indices, including cognitive functioning or diagnosis, in a series of multivariate analysis of variance or regression analysis (e.g., see Fowler et al., 1988).

One additional analysis that can be performed with factor analysis is related to introducing marker variables as part of the factor structure. This involves the selection of previously well-validated variables (e.g., WAIS–R's Vocabulary and Information for the concept of Verbal Comprehension) to examine the contribution of these new variables to the factor structure. For example, the inclusion of previously defined measures of Verbal Comprehension in the RORFAC factor structure may reveal whether a specific relationship pertaining to verbal intelligence and Rorschach variables exists. This, in turn, would allow us to systematically examine how traditional measures of intelligence and those of the Rorschach Comprehensive System hang together psychometrically.

Finally, it is important to reemphasize that anyone using factor analysis must make certain that the purely statistical restrictions for factor analysis have been carefully checked. This is often neglected as it requires labor. If the basic assumptions are met, the powerful statistics described in this chapter will lead to sound conclusions. Factor analysis with Rorschach data is a complex matter. However, it can be mastered with some effort. When used appropriately, this objective procedure for determining the underlying dimensions of observable data can be very stimulating, both theoretically and empirically, and can become a respected branch of multivariate analysis in Rorschach research.

APPENDIX A

Descriptive Statistics for Psychiatric Inpatients (N = 160)

Variable	Mean	SD	Min.	Max.	Baserate (%)	Median	Mode	SK	KU
Age	37.73	15.34	18.00	81.00	100	33.00	25.00	0.81	-0.38
Yrs. Ed.	11.39	3.17	0.00	18.00	98	12.00	12.00	-0.70	1.23
VIQ	90.83	14.12	57.00	125.00	78	90.50	79.00	0.18	0.02
PIQ	87.64	13.75	61.00	125.00	78	85.00	89.00	0.50	0.08
FSIQ	88.67	13.60	55.00	125.00	78	88.50	77.00	0.33	0.36
R	19.75	5.66	14.00	34.00	100	18.00	14.00	0.99	-0.06
W	8.27	3.94	2.00	29.00	100	8.00	7.00	1.66	5.12
D	5.23	4.22	0.00	22.00	94	4.00	2.00	1.25	1.54
Dd	1.67	1.90	0.00	10.00	69	1.00	0.00	1.67	3.41
S	1.54	1.64	0.00	7.00	69	1.00	0.00	1.22	1.07
DQ+	4.23	3.00	0.00	15.00	90	4.00	1.00	0.91	1.30
DQo	8.79	5.27	1.00	30.00	100	8.00	6.00	1.56	2.86
DQv/+	0.30	0.69	0.00	4.00	20	0.00	0.00	2.79	8.60
DQv	1.80	1.87	0.00	9.00	72	1.00	0.00	1.53	2.59
M	2.26	1.90	0.00	9.00	78	2.00	1.00	1.05	0.90
M-	0.41	0.69	0.00	4.00	30	0.00	0.00	2.23	5.97

(Continued)

Variable	Mean	SD	Min.	Max.	Baserate (%)	Median	Mode	SK	KU
FM	2.51	2.07	0.00	10.00	84	2.00	1.00	1.41	2.59
m	1.65	1.65	0.00	8.00	67	1.00	1.00	1.32	1.75
FC	0.94	1.16	0.00	8.00	54	1.00	0.00	2.11	8.13
CF	1.34	1.35	0.00	6.00	64	1.00	0.00	1.15	1.31
C	0.43	0.79	0.00	4.00	27	0.00	0.00	2.09	4.35
CF+C	1.78	1.71	0.00	9.00	75	1.00	1.00	1.36	2.40
SumC	2.71	2.15	0.00	11.00	85	2.00	1.00	1.21	2.01
FC'	0.98	1.15	0.00	5.00	52	1.00	0.00	1.19	1.00
C'F	0.41	0.82	0.00	5.00	25	0.00	0.00	2.58	8.25
C'	0.16	0.47	0.00	3.00	11	0.00	0.00	3.43	12.87
C'F+C'	0.57	1.03	0.00	7.00	34	0.00	0.00	2.78	11.27
SumC'	1.54	1.72	0.00	8.00	59	1.00	0.00	1.23	1.34
FT	0.62	0.99	0.00	7.00	37	0.00	0.00	2.72	11.97
TF	0.17	0.44	0.00	2.00	14	0.00	0.00	2.65	6.59
T	0.03	0.16	0.00	1.00	2	0.00	0.00	6.14	36.18
SumT	0.81	1.15	0.00	7.00	44	0.00	0.00	2.13	6.71
FY	1.29	1.48	0.00	7.00	57	1.00	0.00	1.27	1.26
YF	0.81	1.32	0.00	8.00	40	0.00	0.00	2.67	9.25
Y	0.15	0.43	0.00	2.00	11	0.00	0.00	2.93	8.26
SumY	2.25	2.19	0.00	13.00	76	1.00	1.00	1.79	4.64
FV	0.29	0.65	0.00	4.00	20	0.00	0.00	2.87	9.86
VF	0.17	0.50	0.00	4.00	12	0.00	0.00	4.16	22.93
V	0.01	0.11	0.00	1.00	1	0.00	0.00	8.86	77.45
SumV	0.81	1.15	0.00	7.00	30	0.00	0.00	2.13	6.71
FShade*	2.20	2.28	0.00	12.00	77	2.00	1.00	1.85	4.79
ShadeF**	1.33	1.77	0.00	9.00	60	1.00	0.00	2.13	5.43
FD	0.76	0.97	0.00	4.00	44	0.00	0.00	1.28	1.18
X+%	0.52	0.17	0.00	0.90	99	0.54	0.50	−0.10	−0.39
F+%	0.54	0.27	0.00	0.99	87	0.50	0.50	−0.19	−0.46
X−%	0.21	0.15	0.00	0.69	90	0.19	0.00	0.79	0.60
3r+(2)/R	0.37	0.20	0.00	0.94	95	0.39	0.50	0.17	−0.09
P	4.18	1.96	0.00	9.00	99	4.00	9.00	0.05	−0.66
WSum6	7.24	8.37	0.00	61.00	79	5.00	0.00	2.80	12.98
LAMBDA	0.59	0.49	0.00	2.00	98	0.42	0.38	1.11	0.46
MOR	1.33	1.47	0.00	6.00	62	1.00	0.00	1.27	1.27
PER	1.63	2.00	0.00	9.00	57	1.00	0.00	1.46	1.92
PSV	0.56	1.22	0.00	8.00	32	0.00	0.00	3.26	12.50
AG	0.85	1.35	0.00	8.00	38	0.00	0.00	2.15	5.77
CP	0.04	0.19	0.00	1.00	3	0.00	0.00	4.91	22.44
Zf	9.33	3.94	1.00	26.00	100	9.00	8.00	1.28	3.22
Zd	−0.45	3.90	−9.90	12.00	100	−0.50	0.00	0.18	0.36
D	−1.28	1.64	−5.00	3.00	100	−1.00	0.00	−0.66	0.30
AdjD	−0.55	1.20	−5.00	3.00	100	0.00	0.00	−0.51	2.12
Afr	0.45	0.18	0.05	0.99	100	0.40	0.37	1.42	1.98
H	1.90	1.64	0.00	9.00	77	1.00	1.00	1.16	1.88
Isolate	0.18	0.15	0.00	0.85	83	0.14	0.00	1.22	1.77

*FShade = FY + FT + FV; **ShadeF = YF + Y + TF + T + VF + V.

ACKNOWLEDGMENTS

The authors would like to thank Patrick C. Fowler, Associate Professor and Director of Pediatric Neuropsychology at the University of Virginia Health Sciences Center, for his comments on drafts of this chapter. We also want to acknowledge Gregory J. Meyer, of the University of Alaska in Anchorage, for his assistance with the literature review, and Linda Meisenhelder for her editorial work.

REFERENCES

Adcock, C. J. (1951). A factorial approach to Rorschach interpretation. *Journal of General Psychology, 44*, 261–272.

Alwin, D. F. (1973). The use of factor analysis in the construction of linear composites in social research. *Sociological Methods and Research, 2*, 191–214.

Anastasi, A. (1988). *Psychological testing* (6th ed.). New York: Macmillan.

Bartlett, M. S. (1950). Test of significance in factor analysis. *British Journal of Psychology, 3*, 77–85.

Bentler, P. M. (1985). *Theory and implementation of EQS: A structural equations program.* Los Angeles: BMDP Statistical Software.

Bernstein, I. H. (1988). *Applied multivariate analysis.* New York: Springer-Verlag.

BMDP (1983). *BMDP statistical software.* Berkeley, CA: University of California Press.

Boomsma, A. (1982). The robustness of LISREL against small sample sizes in factor analysis models. In H. Wold & K. Jüreskog (Eds.), *Systems under indirect observations* (pp. 147–173). New York: Elsevier North-Holland.

Borgatta, E. F., & Eschenbach, A. E. (1955). Factor analysis of Rorschach variables and behavioral observation. *Psychological Reports, 1*, 129–136.

Byrne, B. M. (1989). *A primer of LISREL: Basic applications and programming for confirmatory factor analytic models.* New York: Springer-Verlag.

Cattell, R. (1966). A scree test for the number of factors. *Multivariate Behavioral Research, 1*, 245.

Cliff, N., & Hamburger, C. D. (1967). The study of sampling errors in factor analysis by means of artificial experiments. *Psychological Bulletin, 68*, 430–445.

Coan, R. (1956). A factor analysis of Rorschach determinants. *Journal of Projective Techniques, 20*, 280–287.

Consalvi, C., & Canter, A. (1957). Rorschach scores as a function of four factors. *Journal of Consulting Psychology, 21*, 47–51.

Cooley, W. W., & Lohnes, P. R. (1971). *Multivariate data analysis.* New York: Wiley.

Cox, S. M. (1951). A factorial study of the Rorschach responses of normal and maladjusted boys. *Journal of Genetic Psychology, 79*, 95–115.

Dzuiban, C., & Shirkey, E. (1974a). When is a correlation matrix suitable for factor analysis? *Psychological Bulletin, 81*, 358–361.

Dzuiban, C., & Shirkey, E. (1974b). On the psychometric assessment of correlation matrices. *American Education and Research Journal, 11*, 211–216.

Exner, J. E., Jr. (1986). *The Rorschach: A comprehensive system: Vol. 1. Basic foundations* (2nd ed.). New York: Wiley.

Exner, J. E., Jr. (1990). *A Rorschach workbook for the comprehensive system* (3rd ed.). Asheville, NC: Rorschach Workshops.

Exner, J. E., Jr., & Tuttle, K. (1994). *Rorschach Interpretation Assistance Program–Version 3* [Computer program]. Tampa, FL: Psychological Assessment Resources.

Fowler, P. C., Zillmer, E. A., & Newman, A. C. (1988). WAIS factor patterns for neuropsychiatric inpatients. *Journal of Clinical Psychology, 3,* 398–402.

Fowler, P. C., Zillmer, E. A., & Macciocchi, S. N. (1990). Confirmatory factor analytic models of the WAIS–R for neuropsychiatric patients. *Journal of Clinical Psychology, 46*(3), 324–333.

Geertsma, R. H. (1962). Factor analysis of Rorschach scoring categories for a population of normal subjects. *Journal of Consulting Psychology, 26,* 20–25.

Gorsuch, R. L. (1974). *Factor analysis.* Philadelphia: Saunders.

Gorsuch, R. L. (1983). *Factor analysis.* Hillsdale, NJ: Lawrence Erlbaum Associates.

Green, R. L. (1991). *MMPI-2/MMPI: An interpretive manual.* Needham Heights, MA: Allyn & Bacon.

Hakstian, A. R., Rogers, W. D., & Cattell, R. B. (1982). The behavior of numbers factors rules with simulated data. *Multivariate Behavioral Research, 17,* 193–219.

Harman, H. H. (1970). *Modern factor analysis* (2nd ed.). Chicago: University of Chicago Press.

Harris, R. J. (1985). *A primer of multivariate statistics.* Orlando, FL: Academic Press.

Hartwig, F., & Dearing, B. E. (1979). *Exploratory factor analysis.* Newbury Park, CA: Sage.

Jöreskög, K. G. (1963). *Statistical estimation in factor analysis.* Uppsala, Sweden: Almquist & Wiksell.

Jöreskög, K. G. (1967). Some contributions to maximum likelihood factor analysis. *Psychometrika, 34,* 183–202.

Jöreskög, K. G., & Sorbom, D. (1986). *LISREL: Analysis of linear structural relationships by the method of maximum likelihood* (Version VI). Mooresville, IN: Scientific Software, Inc.

Kaiser, H. F. (1960). The application of electronic computers to factor analysis. *Educational and Psychological Measurement, 20,* 141–151.

Kaiser, H. F. (1970). A second generation Little Jiffy. *Psychometrika, 35,* 401–417.

Kaiser, H. F. (1974). An index of factorial simplicity. *Psychometrika, 39,* 31–36.

Kim, J. O., & Mueller, C. W. (1990a). *Introduction to factor analysis: What to do and how to do it.* Newbury Park, CA: Sage.

Kim, J. O., & Mueller, C. W. (1990b). *Factor analysis: Statistical methods and practical issues.* Newbury Park, CA: Sage.

Knapp, T. R., & Swoyer, V. H. (1967). Some empirical results concerning the power of the Barlett's test of significance of a correlation matrix. *American Education Research Journal, 4,* 13–17.

Lotsof, E. F. (1953). Intelligence, verbal fluency, and the Rorschach test. *Journal of Consulting Psychology, 17,* 21–24.

Lotsof, E. F., Comrey, A., Bogartz, W., & Arnsfield, P. (1958). A factor analysis of the WISC and Rorschach. *Journal of Projective Techniques, 22,* 297–301.

Mason, B. J., Cohen, J. B., & Exner, J. E., Jr. (1985). Schizophrenic, depressive, and nonpatient personality organizations described by Rorschach factor structures. *Journal of Personality Assessment, 49,* 295–305.

Meyer, G. J. (1989). *An empirical search for fundamental personality and mood dimensions within the Rorschach test.* Unpublished doctoral dissertation, Loyola University of Chicago.

Norusis, M. J. (1988). *The SPSS guide to data analysis for SPSS-X.* Chicago: SPSS, Inc.

O'Grady, K. (1982). Measures of explained variation: Cautions and limitations. *Psychological Bulletin, 92,* 766–777.

Ozer, D. J. (1985). Correlation and the concept of determination. *Psychological Bulletin, 97,* 342–355.

SAS Institute, Inc. (1985). *SAS user's guide: Statistics.* Cary, NC: SAS Institute, Inc.

Savage, L. J. (1954). *The foundation of statistics.* New York: Wiley.

Shaffer, J. W., Duszynski, K. R., & Thomas, C. B. (1981). Orthogonal dimensions of individual and group forms of the Rorschach. *Journal of Personality Assessment, 45,* 230–239.

Spearman, C. (1904). "General intelligence" objectively determined and measured. *American Journal of Psychology, 15,* 201–293.

SPSS Incorporated (1988). *SPSS-X user's guide* (3rd ed.). Chicago: SPSS, Inc.

Stevens, J. (1986). *Applied multivariate statistics for the social sciences.* Hillsdale, NJ: Lawrence Erlbaum Associates.

Thurstone, L. L. (1954). An analytical method for simple structure. *Psychology, 19,* 173–182.

Tukey, J. W. (1962). The future of data analysis. *Annals of Mathematical Statistics, 33,* 1–67.

Williams, H. I., & Lawrence, J. P. (1953). Further investigation of Rorschach determinants subjected to factor analysis. *Journal of Consulting Psychology, 17,* 261–264.

Williams, H. I., & Lawrence, J. P. (1954). Comparison of the Rorschach and MMPI by means of factor analysis. *Journal of Consulting Psychology, 18,* 193–197.

Wittenborn, J. R. (1950a). A factor analysis of Rorschach scoring categories. *Journal of Consulting Psychology, 14,* 261–267.

Wittenborn, J. R. (1950b). Level of mental health as a factor in the implications of Rorschach scores. *Journal of Consulting Psychology, 14,* 469–472.

Wishner, J. (1959). Factor analyses of Rorschach scoring categories and first response times in normals. *Journal of Consulting Psychology, 23,* 406–413.

Zillmer, E. A., & Ball, J. D. (1987). Psychological and neuropsychological assessment in the medical setting. *Staff and Resident Physician, 33*(7), 602–609.

Zillmer E. A., Archer, R. P., & Castino, B. (1989). The Rorschach records of Nazi war criminals: A reanalysis using current scoring and interpretation practices. *Journal of Personality Assessment, 53*(1), 85–99.

Zillmer, E. A., Fowler, P. C., Gutnick, H. N., & Becker, E. (1990). Comparison of two cognitive bedside screening instruments in nursing home residents: A factor analytic study of the Mini-Mental State Examination and the modified Blessed test. *Journal of Gerontology: Psychological Sciences, 45*(2), 69–74.

Zillmer, E. A. (1991). [Review of Rorschach Interpretation Assistance Program–Version 2]. *Journal of Personality Assessment, 57*(2), 381–383.

Zillmer, E. A., Fowler, P. C., Waechtler, C., Harris, B , & Khan, F. (1992). The utility of the WAIS–R in clinical neuropsychology: A factor analytic study of neural patients. *Archives of Clinical Neuropsychology, 7,* 29–41.

Author Index

Subject Index

A

Adaptive regression score, 64, 219
Affective disturbance, 134
Affective ratio, 10
Affective salience, 134
AFR, *see* Affective ratio
Ambitent response style, 7, 9
American Psychological Association, 4
ANOVA assumptions
  covariance analysis, 214
  independence of observations, 204–205, 214
  normality, 205, 214
    violations, 205–206
  variance homogeneity, 206, 214
Anti-image covariance matrix, 276
Artifactual controversy, 186, 188

B

Biserial *r* correlation, 235
BMDP statistical package, 257
Body-image boundary scoring system, 44
Bootstrapping methodology, 165–166
Borderline disorder study, 81–82, 107–108
Bubble hypothesis, 25–26

C

CDI, *see* Coping deficit index
Central limit theorem, 168
Children
  divorce study, 91
  play study, 64
  sexual abuse, 91
    group comparisons, 27
  social/academic adaptation study, 62–63
Children's depression inventory, 91
Clinical psychology, 73, *see also* Psychology
Color projection, 39
Complexity composite, 240
Comprehensive system
  actuarial cutoff score, 242
  adjusted D score, 132
  agressive movement variable, 135
  critical special scores, 44
  depression index, 74
  development, 241
  D score, 77, 89–90
  information processing, 133
  methodology, 187
  morbid score, 78
  normative data, 63, 151–153
    demographic characteristics, 141
    descriptive statistics, 153
    frequency data, 152–153
    statistical issues, 152

315